CCTV

CCTV

Vlado Damjanovski

Boston Oxford Auckland Johannesburg Melbourne New Delhi

In this book the author has attempted to explain the principles of Closed Circuit Television and teach the techniques of system design, using information, knowledge, and experience which the author believes to be accurate. However, the author makes no warranties, expressed or implied, that the examples, drawings, or any other information in this book are error-free. Therefore, the author assumes no responsibility for any damage resulting from the use of the information contained herein and suggests that independent testing and verification are conducted where needed.

Library of Congress Cataloging-in-Publication Data

Damjanovski, Vlado, 1956-
        CCTV / written and illustrated by Vlado Damjanovski.
                p.   cm.
        Includes bibliographical references and index.
        ISBN 0-7506-7196-3 (alk. paper)
        1.   Closed-circuit television. I. Title.
        TK6680.D36 1999
        621.388—dc21   99-32637
                                            CIP

British Library Cataloguing-in-Publication Data
A catalogue record for this book is available from the British Library.

The publisher offers special discounts on bulk orders of this book.
For information, please contact:
Manager of Special Sales
Butterworth–Heinemann
225 Wildwood Avenue
Woburn, MA 01801–2041
Tel: 781-904-2500
Fax: 781-904-2620

For information on all Butterworth–Heinemann publications available, contact our World Wide Web home page at:
http://www.bh.com

To contact the Vlado Damjanovski, you can e-mail him at: cctv@ozemail.com.au or visit his World Wide Web home page at: http://www.ozemail.com.au/cctv

10 9 8 7 6 5 4 3 2 1

Printed in the United States of America

Contents

Preface...xi

Introduction...xv

1. SI Units of Measurement...1
The basic units...1
Derived units...2
Metric prefixes...4

2. Light and Television...7
A little bit of history...7
Light basics and the human eye...8
Light units...13
Calculating the amount of light falling onto an imaging device...17
Colors in television...21
Color temperatures and light sources...23
Persistency and the motion pictures concept...27

3. Optics in CCTV...31
Refraction...31
Lenses as optical elements...32
Geometrical construction of images ...37
Aspherical lenses...40
Contrast and Modulation Transfer Functions (CTF & MTF)...42
F and T numbers...44
Depth of field...47
Neutral Density (ND) filters...49
Manual, Auto and Motorized Iris lenses...51
Video- and DC-driven auto iris lenses...54
A few words about AI lens electronics...55
Image and lens formats in CCTV...57
Angles of view and how to determine them...59
Fixed focal length lenses...64
Zoom lenses...65
C- & CS-mount and Back-focus...70
Back-focus adjustment...73
Optical accessories in CCTV...77

4. General Characteristics of TV Systems...81

A little bit of history...81
The very basics of television...82
The video signal and its spectrum...90
Color video signal...92
Resolution...95
Instruments commonly used in TV...97
    Oscilloscope...97
    Spectrum analyzer...99
    Vectorscope...99
Television systems around the world...101
HDTV ...105

5. CCTV Cameras...109

General information about cameras...109
Tube cameras...110
CCD Cameras...113
Sensitivity of the CCD chips...117
Types of charge transfer in CCDs...121
Pulses used in CCD for transferring charges...125
CCD chip as a sampler...127
Correlated Double Sampling (CDS)...128
Camera specifications and their meanings ...129
    Sensitivity...130
    Minimum illumination...131
    Camera resolution...133
    Signal/Noise ratio...135
    Dynamic range of a CCD chip...137
Color CCD cameras...139
    White balance...142
CMOS cameras...143
Special low light intensified cameras...145
Camera power supplies and copper conductors...147
V-phase adjustment...151
Camera checklist...152

6. Monitors...155

General about monitors...155
Monitor sizes...158
Monitor adjustments...159

Impedance switch...164
Viewing conditions...165
Gamma...167
LCD monitors...168
Projection monitors...169
Digital micromirror display (DMD) technology ...169
Plasma display monitors...171
Field emission technology displays ...172

7. Video Processing Equipment...175
Analog switching equipment...175
   Video sequential switchers...175
   Synchronization...176
   Video matrix switchers (VMS)...179
Digital switching and/or processing equipment...183
   Quad compressors...183
   Multiplexers (MUX)...185
   Recording time delays...187
   Simplex and duplex multiplexers ...190
   Video Motion Detectors (VMD)...190
   Framestores...193
   Video Printers...194

8. Video Recorders ...197
A little bit of history and the basic concept...197
The early VCR concepts...198
The video home system (VHS) concept...199
Super VHS, Y/C and Comb filtering...202
   Using consumer model VCRs for CCTV purposes...206
Time Lapse VCRs (TL VCRs)...208
Digital video ...212
Digital video recorders (DVR)...214
Digital image size and compression...216
   MPEG-1...217
   MPEG-2 ...218
   JPEG ...219
   Wavelet...221
The playback quality of digitally recorded video signal...224
D-VHS format...225
DV format and the fire wire...225

9. Transmission Media...229

    Coaxial cables...230

        The concept...230

        Noise and electromagnetic interference ...231

        Characteristic impedance...231

        BNC connectors...235

        Coaxial cables and proper BNC termination...236

        Installation techniques...239

        Time domain reflectometer (TDR)...242

    Twisted pair video transmission...242

    Microwave links...244

    RF wireless (open air) video transmission...246

    Infrared wireless (open air) video transmission...247

    Transmission of images over telephone lines...248

        PSTN ...250

        ISDN...251

        Cellular network...252

    Fiber optics...252

        Why fiber?...253

        The concept...254

        Types of optical fibers...256

        Numerical aperture...258

        Light levels in fiber optics...259

        Light sources in fiber optics transmission...260

        Light detectors in fiber optics...263

        Frequencies in fiber optics transmission...264

        Passive components...266

        Fusion splicing...266

        Mechanical splicing...266

        Fiber optics multiplexers...267

    Fiber optics cables...268

    Installation techniques...272

    Fiber-optic link analysis...274

        OTDR...275

10. Auxiliary Equipment in CCTV...279

    Pan and tilt heads...279

    Pan and tilt domes...281

    Preset positioning P/T heads...282

    PTZ Site drivers...283

    Camera housings...286

Lighting in CCTV...289
Infrared lights...290
Ground loop correctors...293
Lightning protection...293
In-line video amplifiers/equalizers...294
Video distribution amplifiers (VDAs)...296

11. CCTV System Design...299
Understanding the customers' requirements...299
Site inspections...303
Designing and quoting a CCTV system...304
Installation considerations...306
Drawings...309
Commissioning...310
Training and manuals...311
Handing over...312
Preventative maintenance...312

12. The CCTV Test Chart...315
Before you start testing...315
Setup procedure...316
What you can test...318

Appendix A: Common Terms Used in CCTV...323
Appendix B: Bibliography...357
**Appendix C: CCTV Manufacturers and Their Major Distributors
Listing...359**
Appendix D: Book Co-sponsors...369
About the Author...380
Index...381

Preface

Closed Circuit Television, or commonly known as **CCTV**, is an interesting area of television technology. It is usually used in surveillance systems, but a lot of components and concepts can be implemented in an industrial production monitoring system, or, equally, in a hospital or university environment. So, even though the majority of readers would be looking at this book as a great help in understanding and designing surveillance systems, my intention was not to limit the topics to this area only.

I've tried to encompass the theory and practice of all components and fundamentals of CCTV. This is a very wide area and involves various disciplines and products from electronics, telecommunications, optics, fiber optics, digital image processing, programming and so on. One can hardly find a book covering all of these areas, as I was repeatedly reminded at the many seminars I conducted over the past number of years throughout Australia.

So, my intention was to put all my knowledge and experience, as well as all the research I had to do on various new trends and products, into one complete book.

I have deliberately simplified things when explaining concepts and principles, but basic logic and technical understanding are still required from the reader.

Having had hands-on experience with various systems and situations, and knowing the difference between the simplicity of theory and the many problems one encounters in practice, I have tried to make life easier for many installers, designers and consultants by adding a lot of helpful hints, suggestions, checklists, tables, system designs and, finally, a specially designed CCTV test chart.

You will find some of the book's contents are available on my web site and will be constantly updated with various listings, tables and information. The web site is under the name of **CCTV Labs** and is now over 3 years on the Internet. My intentions are to have as much useful information on the web as possible, and in addition to the information already mentioned previously I hope to have all the CCTV manufacturers from around the globe included in the links section. This way, by visiting the CCTV Labs web site you will have instant access to almost every CCTV product and manufacturer. Of course I cannot include manufacturers that are not on the Net yet, but if you are reading this and are a manufacturer but cannot see your name in the link page please send me an e-mail and I will include it.

Our current web site address is **http://www.cctvlabs.com**.

Please check regularly for the latest updates and give us your feedback on the contents.

The book is intended for, and will be very helpful to installers, sales people, security managers, consultants, manufacturers and everyone else interested in CCTV, providing they have some basic technical knowledge.

The specially designed CCTV test chart printed on the back cover of the book will help you in various quality testings. This will be very handy for evaluating cameras, monitors and transmission, but also for evaluating the playback quality of a recording system. To find out how to use this test chart, see Chapter 12 **The CCTV Test Chart.**

For the readers that need a bigger and better test chart, CCTV Labs has produced a high resolution, laminated A3 format of the same chart, which can be purchased by filling out the Order Form on the CCTV Labs web site.

This is a third edition, coming out exactly three years after the first one, and is now published by Butterworth-Heinemann.

I am very grateful to all the readers that have purchased the previous two editions and spread the word around the globe about the book's quality. I am proud to hear many have already called it "The CCTV Bible." I will certainly do my best to maintain this compliment, but I also would like to hear critical comments and suggestions from all of you, the old and the new readers.

I would like to thank many readers who have already made numerous suggestions and corrections. I am especially thankful to a young chap called Jason Rigley from Sydney who has even gone to the extent of preparing an entire 8-page report on my book with his remarks and corrections. Please understand that English is my second language and I sometimes still find it a bit more difficult to understand than CCTV.

I owe a special thanks to the publishing company Butterworth-Heinemann and in particular, a few people who have spent countless hours working on the final and fine details of this book. Firstly, Laurel DeWolf, senior acquisitions editor, who first had the opportunity to see the previous edition and trusted in its value, also, Rita Lombard - the assistant editor, Cate Rickard Barr - the design manager, Kathryn Geiger - the senior manufacturing and print coordinator and finally, Susan Prusak - the production editor.

This book has been made possible by the publisher Butterworth-Heinemann in first place, but also by the CCTV manufacturers who have believed in me and co-sponsored this edition.

On a personal basis, I would like to thank my wife, Vesna, and my kids (Aleksandar, Damian and Filip) for the immeasurable sacrifice they've made while I spent countless hours of writing, drawing and photographing instead of being with them.

I owe a special thanks and appreciation to my eldest sons Filip and Damian, for being brave enough and accepting the challenge to edit the book. I decided to have the book initially edited by someone who knows English much better than I do (being my second language) but who is also next to me all the time so as to have all the technical terms and meanings preserved as I understand them. The final and detailed proof reading was done by the production editor Susan Prusak from Butterworth-Heinemann, who enlightened me with so many small, but important corrections and writing rules.

I am also very grateful to my parents and my motherland Macedonia who have enabled me to educate in peace and of course my respectable Television Professor Mr. Ljupcho Panovski from the University "Sv.Kiril i Metodij" in Skopje, who helped me nurture a love for this magical science.

I also appreciate the creative freedom I enjoy in this new homeland of mine called Australia, which has enabled me to widen my CCTV knowledge and, of course, made it possible to produce this work you are holding in your hands.

I encourage and welcome all suggestions and comments.

Thank you for purchasing the book and I hope you enjoy it.

Vlado Damjanovski, B.E. Electronics

     Sydney, April 1999

E-mails: **cctv@ozemail.com.au**

                    damjanovski@ozemail.com.au

Web Page: **http://www.cctvlabs.com**

Introduction

This book has 12 chapters and they are written in a logical order.

Chapter 1, **SI Units of Measurement,** introduces the basics of the units of measurement which I thought are important to mention, even though they are not only a CCTV subject, but rather a technical issue. Many products, terms and concepts exist in the world of CCTV which sooner or later need to be referred to with a correct unit. SI units are suggested by the ISO (the International Standardization Organization), and if we accept these units as universal it will make our understanding of the products and their specifications clearer and more accurate. I have also listed the common metric prefixes as I have found a lot of technicians don't know them. If you are an engineer or have a good technical background, you may find this chapter of no interest, so you can go directly to Chapter 2, Light and Television.

Chapter 2, **Light and Television,** starts with a little bit of history so we can gain a wider perspective of the television revolution. Then we go to the very basics of human vision: light and the human eye. It is necessary to explain the human eye and how it works because television relies greatly on the human eye physiology. It is interesting to compare the similarities between the eye's and the camera's operation.

Optics in CCTV is Chapter 3, which focuses on the first and important product used in CCTV the lens. Apart from the discussion on how lenses work and what their most important features are, there is also a practical explanation of how and what to adjust (ALC and Level) on a lens, how to determine a focal length for a particular angle of view, and very important for CCTV, how back-focusing should be done. Also, C, and CS-mounts are discussed and explained.

Chapter 4, **General characteristics of TV Systems,** is very important, especially for readers without prior knowledge of how television works. I have discussed both major standards PAL and NTSC. I do apologize to readers using the SECAM for not going into details on this standard. I simply could not find sufficient literature to study it, although there are many similarities with PAL, at least in the number of lines and fields per second used. General discussion on resolution is also included, and more importantly the difference between a broadcast signal and CCTV video signal. Near the end of the chapter I have also mentioned the most common instruments used in TV and what they measure. At the end, I have included tables that show the differences between various television system subgroups, as well as a listing of all the countries in the world with their adopted TV system.

Chapter 5, **CCTV Cameras,** is probably the most interesting one. It discusses at length the concepts of CCD cameras, various designs and camera specifications. Here, I have also included a discussion and calculation of power supplies and voltage drops. I consider this a very important practical issue which I have been asked about very often, and although it seems very trivial, a lot of problems and system failures have been caused by improper camera powering (unregulated or overrated power supply, thin wires, high voltage drop). I found it suitable to discuss this issue in the camera section as power supplies form a part of the camera assembly. I have also included, at the end of this chapter, a very practical checklist which you or your installers can use in order to make the CCTV installation trouble free.

Monitors are discussed in Chapter 6, and I have devoted space to both B/W and color monitors. Obviously, my main concentration is on the CRT monitors, as they are the most common in CCTV today. You will find explanations on various important issues associated with monitors, like Gamma, the impedance switch and viewing conditions. At the end of this chapter, I have included a description of some major new developments in the display technology. At the time of the release of the previous edition of this book, many of these technologies were only technocal news, but today some of them have been or are being widely adopted.

In Chapter 7, **Video Processing Equipment,** I have encompassed the "good old" sequential switchers and then the matrix switchers, as representatives of the "analog" processing range, and of course quads, multiplexers, video motion detectors and frame stores as representatives of the "digital" range.

Chapter 8, **Video Recorders,** discusses their very important role in CCTV. The VHS format is explained as it still is the most common type, but I have also included the S-VHS format. Digital video storage, however, is becoming increasingly popular and I found it important to say a few words about it. Interestingly enough, from the time of the previous edition of this book (1996) up until now (1999) there is a whole new range of products appearing on the market which are replacing VCRs. These include the Digital Video Recorders (DVRs) using various compression techniques. Most of these topics where briefly mentioned in the previous edition of the book, but under the section of "Digital Video" and "New Trends in TV and CCTV." They are now included under the **Video Recorders** heading as they are not a novelty any more, but rather just one of the many components we meet in CCTV.

Transmission Media, Chapter 9, is one of the biggest due to the large variety of types of transmission used in CCTV. Clearly the coaxial cable is the most common and widely accepted so I have dedicated most of the space to the coaxial cable concept. Through my practical experience, and I believe a lot of readers will agree, I have found that the majority of problems in the existing or just recently installed CCTV systems are due to bad cable installations and/or terminations. So I have devoted some space on the actual termination techniques. In the rest of the chapter you will find explanations on the other media, like twisted pair, microwave, RF wireless, infrared, telephone lines and, the most important for the near future (at least in my opinion), fiber optics. You will find quite a lot of space devoted to fiber optics, starting with the explanation of the concepts, light sources used in fiber, cables and installation techniques. This technology is not as new as some may think, but rather it has become very affordable and easier to use and thus more common in larger CCTV systems.

Chapter 10, **Auxiliary Equipment in CCTV,** includes discussion on pan and tilt heads, housings, lighting, infrared lights, ground loop correctors, lightning protection, video amplifiers and distribution amplifiers.

The previous ten chapters focus on the equipment side of a CCTV system, so in Chapter 11 I discuss my understanding of how to **design a CCTV system**. This chapter is based purely on practical experience as well as feedback from installers and users. You don't have to accept this as the only way to design a system, but I have certainly found it is very efficient and accurate. In this chapter I have also included the actions taken after the system design is finished and installed. These are: commissioning, training and handing over. Preventative maintenance is often forgotten but it is an important part of a complete CCTV system offer. Even if preventative maintenance is done after the system is finished I think it is important for this to be listed here as part of the complete picture of CCTV.

The CCTV Test Chart, Chapter 12, advises readers on the usage of the video test chart I have designed specially for this book, printed on the back cover. Many people found the **CCTV Test Chart** very useful in the previous edition, so I decided to modify it and enhance it by adding some more useful measurements. Now you can use the test chart to determine not only camera resolution, but also see if you can recognize a person at a certain distance. For the more dedicated CCTV technicians, the same test chart is also available on A3 format, foam framed, and printed on a non-reflective chemical proof paper with durable and stable colors. Also, the full description on how to use the Test Chart, apart from appearing in the book, is also available on our web site.

Appendix A, **Common Terms Used in CCTV,** explains exactly what the heading says. I have tried to include all the terms, acronyms and names one might come across in CCTV and accompanying fields. In the 32 pages I have not only listed them but also explained their meanings as used in CCTV.

In the previous edition of the book I had a chapter called **Some CCTV Systems Examples**. These were sample drawings copyright free, which could also be downloaded from our web site. After three years I found these were not requested as much as I expected, so I decided to leave them out of this edition. Instead, I have decided to offer something else, which I think will be more useful to the readers, and this is a worldwide **listing of all the manufacturers of CCTV equipment,** in Appendix C. Experience from the previous edition shows that this book is read worldwide, and I often find myself surprised by a particular CCTV product made by an unknown manufacturer. I think that you, the reader, whether you are a user, distributor, consultant or installer, deserve to know all the manufacturers, their range of products and their contact details. I will also put all of these details on the CCTV Labs web site with links to all of them. Please note, when I say all, I mean all that I have found in various magazines, exhibition listings and e-mails I have received. Please understand that this would be an ever-changing database and you will have the up-to-date details available on the CCTV Labs web site.

I hope that this book will be very helpful and informative in all your dealings in CCTV.

I also hope that this book will be on your shelves and in your suitcases for a long time to come.

Thanks for buying the book and enjoy the reading.

1. SI Units of Measurement

The basic units

The Laws of Physics are expressions of fundamental relationships between certain physical quantities.

There are many different quantities in physics. In order to simplify measurements, and to comply with the theory of physics, some of them are taken as basic quantities, while all others are derived from those basic ones.

Measurements are made by comparing the magnitude of a quantity with that of a given unit of that quantity.

In physics, which Electronics and Television are a part of, the **International System of Units,** known as **SI** (from the French *Système Internationale*), is used.

The following are **the seven basic units**:

Unit	Symbol	Measures
Meter	[m]	length
Kilogram	[kg]	mass
Second	[s]	time
Ampere	[A]	electric current
Kelvin	[K]	temperature
Candela	[cd]	luminous intensity
Mole	[mol]	amount of substance

These basic units are defined by internationally recognized standards.

The standard for meter, for example, until 1983 was defined as a certain number of wavelengths of a specific radiation in the spectrum of krypton. In October 1983 it was redefined as the distance that light travels in vacuum during a time of 1/299,792,458 second.

The standard of kilogram, for example, is the mass of a particular piece of platinum-iridium alloy cylinder kept at the International Bureau of Weights and Measurements in Sevres, France.

The basic unit of time, the second, was defined in 1967, as a "time required for a Cesium-133 atom to undergo 9,192,631,770 vibrations."

Kelvin degrees have the same scale division as Celsius degrees, only that the starting point of $0°$ K is equivalent to $-273°$ C and this is called the **absolute zero**.

All other units in physics are defined with some combination of the above-mentioned basic units.

For example, an area of a block of land is defined by the equation:

$$P = a \times b$$

where "a" is the width of the block of land, and "b" is the length. If both "a" and "b" are expressed in meters [m], the product P would be expressed in [m^2].

We all know that speed, for example, is defined as [m/s], although we quite often use [km/h]. We can easily convert [km/h] into [m/s] by knowing how many meters there are in a kilometer and how many seconds there are in an hour.

SI units are almost universally accepted in science and industry throughout the world and we should all be aware that measurements like: "inches" for length, "miles per hour" for speed and "pounds or stones" for weight should be used as little as possible. They often cause confusion in people from various professions and various parts of the world. If you use SI units more people will understand you and your product. Also it is easier to compare products from various parts of the world if they use the same units.

Another very important thing to clarify is that every symbol in the SI system has a precise meaning relative to the letter used (capital or small). So, a kilometer is written as [km], not [Km] or [klm]. A megabyte is written as [MB], not [mB]. A nanometer is written as [nm], not [Nm] and so on. As technical people involved in closed circuit television, we should stick to these principles.

Derived units

All other physical processes can be explained and measured using the basic units. We will not go into the details of how they are obtained, nor is it the purpose of this book to do so, but it is important to understand that there is always a fundamental relation between the basic and derived unit.

The following are some of the derived SI units, some of which will be used in this book:

Quantity	Unit	Symbol / Definition
Area	Square meter	m^2
Volume	Cubic meter	m^3
Velocity	Meters per second	m/s
Acceleration	Meters per second per sec.	m/s^2
Frequency	Hertz	$Hz = 1/s$
Density	Kilograms per cubic meter	kg/m^3
Force	Newton	$N = kg \cdot m/s^2$
Pressure	Pascal	$Pa = kg/m \cdot s^2$
Torque	Newton meter	$T = N \cdot m$
Energy, work	Joule	$J = N \cdot m$
Power	Watt	$W = J/s$
Electric charge	Coulomb	$C = A \cdot s$
Electric potential	Volt	$V = \Omega/A$
Electrical resistance	Ohm	$\Omega = V/A$
Electrical capacitance	Farad	$F = C/V$
Conductance	Siemens	$S = A/V$
Magnetic flux	Weber	$Wb = V \cdot s$
Magnetic field intensity	Tesla	$T = Wb/m^2$
Inductance	Henry	$H = Wb/A$
Illumination	Lux	$lx = lm/m^2$
Luminous flux	Lumen	$lm = cd \cdot steradian$
Luminance	Nit	$nt = cd/m^2$

Metric prefixes

When the number of units (i.e.,the value) for a particular measurement is very high or very small, there is a convention for using certain symbols before the basic unit and each has a specific meaning. The following are metric prefixes accepted by the international scientific and industrial community that you may find not only in CCTV but also in other technical areas :

Prefix	Multiple	Symbol
exa-	10^{18}	E
peta-	10^{15}	P
tera-	10^{12}	T
giga-	10^{9}	G
mega-	10^{6}	M
kilo-	10^{3}	k
hecto-	10^{2}	h
deca-	10	D
unity	$10^{0} = 1$	
deci-	10^{-1}	d
centi-	10^{-2}	c
milli-	10^{-3}	m
micro-	10^{-6}	μ
nano-	10^{-9}	n
pico-	10^{-12}	p
femto-	10^{-15}	f
atto-	10^{-18}	a

By using these prefixes, we can say 2 km, referring to 2000 meters. If we say 1.44 MB, we are thinking of 1,440,000 bytes. A nanometer will be 0.000000001 meters. The frequency of 12 GHz would be $12 \cdot 10^{9} = 12,000,000,000$ Hz and so on.

Now that we have laid the basics of a technically correct discussion, i.e., introduced the basic units of measurement, we can start with the fundamentals of all visions, including photography, cinematography and television - **light**.

2. Light and Television

Let there be light.

A little bit of history

Light is one of the basic and greatest natural phenomenon, vital not only for life on this planet, but also very important for the technical advancements and ingenuity of the human mind in the visual communication areas: photography, cinematography, television and the newly introduced multimedia.

Even though it is so "basic" and we **see** it all the time and it is all around us - it is the single biggest stumbling block of science. Physics, from a very simple and straightforward science at the end of 19th century, became very complex and mystical. It forced the scientists in the beginning of this century to introduce the postulates of quantum physics, the "principles of uncertainty of the atoms" and much more. All in order to get a theoretical apparatus that would satisfy a lot of practical experiments, but equally, make sense to the human mind.

This book is not written with the intent of going deeper into each of these theories, but I would rather discuss the aspects which affect the television and video signals.

The major "problem" scientists face when researching light is that it performs twofold: it behaves as though it is of a wave nature (immaterial) – through the effects of refraction and reflection – but it also appears as though it has material nature – through the well-known photo-effect discovered by Heinrich Hertz in the 19th century and explained by Albert Einstein in 1905.

As a result, the latest trends in physics are to accept light as a phenomenon of "dual" nature.

It would be, however, fair at this stage to give credit to at least a few major scientists in the development of physics, and light theorists in particular, without whose work it would have been impossible to come to today's level of technology.

Isaac Newton was one of the first physicists to explain many natural phenomena including light. In the 17th century he explained that light has a particle nature. This was until Christian Huygens, later that century, proposed an explanation of light behavior through the wave theory. Many scientists had deep respect for Newton and didn't change their views until the very beginning of the 19th century when Thomas Young showed the interference behavior of light. August Fresnel also did some very convincing experiments that clearly showed that light has a wave nature.

A very important milestone was the appearance of James Clerk Maxwell on the scientific scene, who in 1873 asserted that light was a form of high-frequency electromagnetic wave.

His theory predicted the speed of light as we know it today: 300,000 km/s. With the experiments of Heinrich Hertz, Maxwell's theory was confirmed. Hertz, however, discovered an effect that is known as the **photo-effect**, where light can eject electrons from a metal whose surface is exposed to light. However, it was difficult to explain the fact that the energy with which the electrons were ejected, was independent of the light intensity, which was in turn contradictory to the wave theory. With the wave theory the explanation would be that more light should add more energy to the ejected electrons.

This stumbling block was satisfactorily explained by Einstein who used the concept of Max Planck's theory of quantum energy of photons, which represent minimum packets of energy carried by the light itself. With this theory, light was given the dual nature, i.e., some of the features of waves combined with some of the features of particles.

This theory so far is the best explanation for the majority of light behavior and that is why in CCTV we apply this "dual approach" theory to light.

In explaining the concepts of lenses used in CCTV we will be using, most of the time, the wave theory of light, but we should always have in mind that there are principles like the CCD chip's operation, for example, based on the light's particle behavior, i.e., light of a material nature. That is why, in this case, we will be using the material approach to light.

Clearly, in practice, light is a mixture of both of the approaches, and we should always have in mind that they do not exclude each other.

Light basics and the human eye

Light is an electromagnetic radiation. The human eye is sensitive to this radiation and to various radiation frequencies the eye picks up as colors. Electromagnetic radiation obviously comes in all frequencies, i.e., wavelengths, as can be seen on the drawing. The visible light occupies only a very little "window" in this range. This window is between 380 nm and 780 nm. We take this, however, to be roughly from 400 nm to 700 nm, for easy remembering.

The 400 nm corresponds to violet and 700 nm to red color. There is a continuous color change from the violet, to blue, green, yellow, orange and red as the wavelength increases. Many experiments and tests have

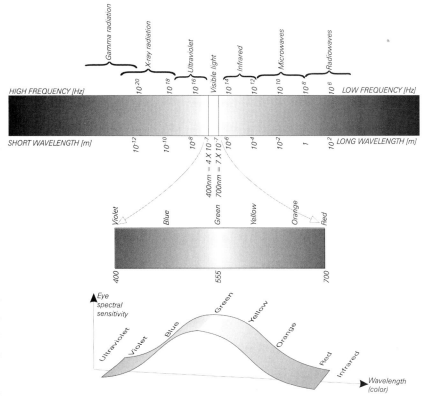

The electromagnetic spectrum and human's eye sensitivity

been done to check the sensitivity of an average human eye and, as it can be seen from the drawing, **not all colors produce the same effect on the eye's retina.**

Green color excites the eye the most. In other words, if we have all the wavelengths of the light with an equal amount of energy, the green will produce the highest "output" on the retina. Frequencies higher than the violet (wavelengths shorter than 400 nm) and lower than the red (wavelengths longer than 700 nm) cannot be detected by the "average" human eye. I emphasize this "average" because human eye sensitivity is a statistical curve. There are people who are "color blind," which means their eye's spectral sensitivity is different (usually narrower) than the one shown. Some "color blind" people can't see red color, some can't see blue. A trained, professional eye of a painter or a photographer may develop very high sensitivity for detecting various frequencies (colors) which might look the same to others. Some may even extend their minimum and maximum detectable frequency limit, i.e., see deeper violet or red colors that are invisible to other individuals.

A very interesting question to ask ourselves is why is the eye's spectral sensitivity maximum in the green color area (at around 555 nm)? This can be associated with the fact that of all the sun's energy that penetrates the Earth's atmosphere, the biggest amount is contained in the wavelengths at around 555 nm.

With millions of years of evolution of life on this planet, we (and most of the animals) have developed vision using wavelengths that are most readily available (at least during the daytime). An obvious alternative are the night vision eye characteristics of animals whose food targets are warm-blooded mammals. Body heat is nothing more than infrared radiation. Typical examples of this are snakes, cats, and owls. Some snakes, for example, apart from the eyes for general vision, also have infrared sensitive pit organs with which a snake can detect temperature change of less than 0.5°C (1°F). Cats, including wild cats such as leopards, pumas and other members of the cat family, are known for their good night-time vision, which would mean that their near infrared response is far better than that of the human eye.

We will concentrate on the human eye, and it is very important to understand the "construction" of it. This will be perhaps of general interest, but we'll also see a lot of conceptual similarities between the eye and the TV camera construction.

This cross section shows that the eye has a lens that focuses the image onto the retina. The retina is actually the "photo sensitive area," which is composed of millions of cells, called **cones** and **rods**. These cells can be

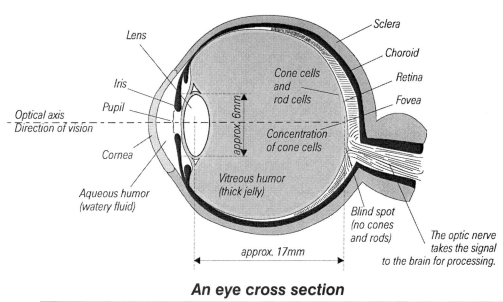

An eye cross section

considered a part of our nervous system. **The cones are sensitive to the medium and bright intensity of light and they actually sense the colors.** **The rod cells are sensitive to lower light levels, and they do not distinguish colors.** We use rod cells to see at night, which means **when it is dark we cannot distinguish colors.**

The number of cones in each eye is approximately 10 million and the number of rods over 100 million. The cones are concentrated around the area where the optical axis passes. This area is colored with a yellowish pigment and is called the **fovea.** The fovea is the central area that our brain processes and although it is a small area, the concentration of cones there is approximately 50,000. The average focal length of an eye (i.e., the distance between the lens and the retina when an infinitely distant object is being viewed) is approximately 17 mm. This focal length gives an undistorted image in a solid angle of approximately 30°. This is also the size of the area most populated with the cone cells. **This is why an angle of about 30° is considered a standard angle of vision.**

The concentration of cones increases towards the center of the optical axis with the peak being at only 10°. Each of these cone cells is connected to the brain via **separate optic nerves, through which electrical pulses are sent to the brain.** The eye, of course, sees a much wider angle, since the retina covers nearly a 90° solid angle and there are cones outside the yellow area as well, but these other cones are connected to each nerve in groups. With this area we don't see as clearly as when we use the single nerve cones and that is why this area is known as the **peripheral vision area.**

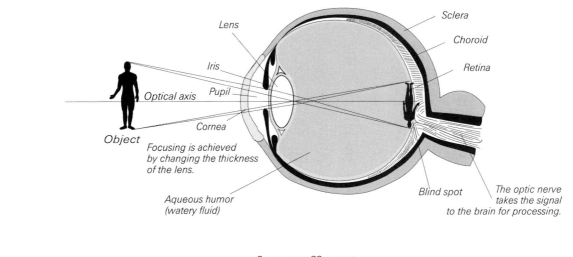

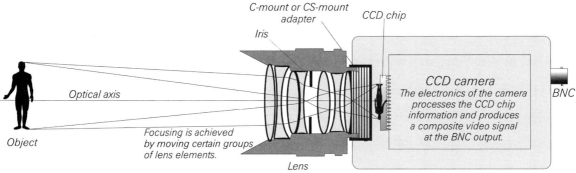

Eye-Camera similarities

The brain's "image processing section" concentrates on 30°, although we see best at around 10°. This processing is further supported with the constant eye movement in all directions, which is equivalent to a pan/tilt head assembly in CCTV.

For an SLR camera the standard angle of view of 30° is achieved with a 50 mm lens, for a 2/3" camera this is a 16 mm lens, for a 1/2" camera a 12 mm lens and for a 1/3" camera an 8 mm lens. In other words, images of any type of camera, taken with their corresponding standard lenses, will be of a very similar size and perspective as when seen through our eyes.

Lenses shorter in focal length give a wider angle of view and are called **wide angle** lenses. Lenses with longer focal length narrow the view and therefore they look as if they are bringing distant objects closer, hence the name **telephoto** ("tele" meaning distant). Another matter of interest associated with CCTV is that by knowing the focal length of the eye and the maximum iris opening of approximately 6 mm, we can find the equivalent "F-number" (discussed later in the book) of the eye:

$$F_{number-eye} = 17/6 = 2.8.$$

With such a fully opened iris we can still see quite well in full moonlight (this is approximately 0.1 lux at the object). Have this number in mind when comparing different cameras' minimum illumination characteristics.

The **focusing that the human eye** does in order to see objects at various distances **is achieved by changing the thickness of the lens**. This is done by the ciliary muscles. If the eye is normal, it should be able to focus from infinity down to a minimum distance of about 20 cm in early childhood, to 25 cm at age 20, to 50 cm at age 40 and to 5 m at age 60. When we look at something very far away, i.e., eye focused on infinity, the ciliary muscles are relaxed and the lens is **thin**.

If the eye cannot focus at infinity that vision defect is called **nearsightedness, or myopia**. Such eyes require glasses to help the "defective" human eye lens focus the image on the retina. These glasses are sometimes called reducing glasses because they have a negative focus (or diopter).

A diopter is the inverse value of the focus of a lens, where the focus is expressed in meters. Reducing glasses have a negative diopter. So, "reducing" glasses with a diopter of − 0.5, for example, have a negative focus of 1/(− 0.5) = − 2 m.

Another defect an eye may have is when it cannot focus on an image that is very close, i.e., the eye's lens cannot be thickened enough for some reason.

This defect is called **farsightedness, or hypermetropia**.

People with hypermetropia need glasses to be able to see close objects sharply. These glasses would need to

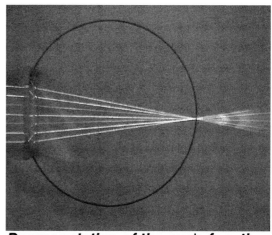

Representation of the eye's function

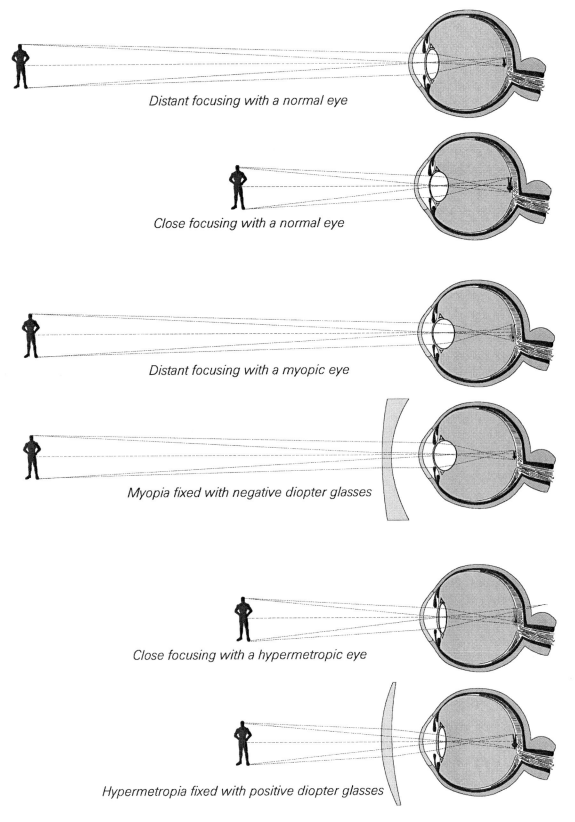

Distant focusing with a normal eye

Close focusing with a normal eye

Distant focusing with a myopic eye

Myopia fixed with negative diopter glasses

Close focusing with a hypermetropic eye

Hypermetropia fixed with positive diopter glasses

Correcting eye deficiencies with glasses

have the opposite characteristics from those in the previous case, i.e., they would have to be magnifying glasses with positive focus and diopter.

Two eyes produce images that, when mixed in our brain, give a stereoscopic impression of the volume of space. If we cover one eye, it is very hard to judge the "three-dimensionality" of the space in front of us.

The distance between the eyes (60-70 mm) ensures our perception of three-dimension up to 10-15 m away. After this distance it is very hard to judge which of two objects is closer. This can be experimented by trying to see two objects in the air at different long distances, for example. If we are looking at, let's say, two distant trees, the brain brings a conclusion on the basis of the soil and perspective in front of us, but the perspective "decision" would not be concluded on the basis of the eye's "stereoscopic mechanism."

It is amazing when you think about the complexity of the eye and the brain's power for "image processing." We do these operations hundreds of times a day without even thinking about it. Not to mention the fact that the images that fall on the retina are upside down, due to the nature of the optical refraction, and we also do not consider the eye movement in all directions when we follow something. All of these things are being deciphered and controlled by the brain.

The "eye/brain" configuration is far superior to any camera that the human mind has, or will ever invent. But, as technical people, we can say that by understanding how the eye "works" and using the ever improving visual technology, both in hardware and software, we are getting better images and more sophisticated information about the world around us and we can view things the human eye can't see or monitor things in places where the human can't be present.

Light units

Light is a physical phenomenon, but is interpreted by psychological processes in our brain. It is, therefore, a bit more complex to measure than other physical processes. Some prerequisites have to be established in order to make objective measurements. One of these is the bandwidth of the light frequencies considered, and this is usually from 400 nm to 700 nm. All of the frequencies contribute to the light energy radiated by the source.

Let's, first of all, make clear the kind of light sources we have.

The basic division is into two major groups:

> - Primary sources (the sun, street lights, tungsten lights, monitor CRTs)

> - Secondary sources (all objects that do not generate light but reflect it)

We do not apply the same type of measurement when measuring the amount of light radiated by a tungsten globe, for example, and the light reflected by an object. It is not the same if we are analyzing light radiated from a source in all directions, or just in a narrow solid angle. These are some of the reasons why we have so many different units of light measurement.

The science that examines all these different aspects is called **photometry** and the units defined are called **photometric units.**

Many different units have been defined by various scientists, depending upon the point of view taken. Because of this, CCTV camera specifications are even harder to understand and describe precisely. But let's try to shed some light on these units and explain what they mean. We will start in a logical order, i.e., the source of the light, travelling through space, falling onto an object and finally as it is reflected from it.

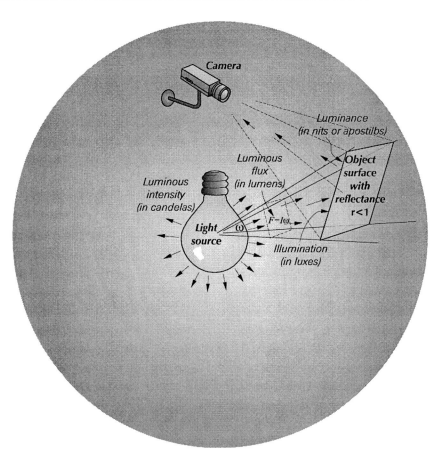

Light units and their meaning

Luminous intensity (*I*) is the illuminating power of a primary light source, radiated in all directions. The unit that measures this kind of light is **candela** [cd]. **One candela is approximately the amount of light energy generated by an ordinary candle.** Since 1948 there has been a more precise definition of a candela as **the luminous intensity of a black body heated up to a temperature at which platinum converges from a liquid to a solid state**.

Luminous flux (*F*) is the luminous intensity, but in a certain solid angle. The unit for luminous flux is, therefore, obtained by dividing the luminous intensity with 4 π (pi) radians (a sphere has 4 π = 12.56 steradian) and is measured in **lumens** [lm]. **One lumen is produced by a luminous intensity of 1 cd in one radian of a solid angle.**

Because the sensation of brightness depends on the human eye sensitivity, the luminous flux depends on the wavelength as well. For example, 1 watt of light power with 555-nm color (green) produces approximately 680 lm, while all other wavelengths, with the same light power, produce proportionally fewer lumens (see the eye spectral sensitivity curve). It is therefore meaningless to express light power in watts, even if, theoretically, light energy like any other energy can be expressed in watts.

Illumination (*E*) is the most commonly used term in CCTV, especially when referring to the camera's minimum illumination characteristics. Illumination is very similar to the luminance except that we are now referring to objects that are secondary sources of light.

Therefore, **the illumination of a surface is the amount of luminous flux on a unit area**.

When luminous flux of 1 lumen falls on an area of 1 m^2 (square meter) it is measured in **lumens per square meter** or **meter-candelas**, but it is better known as **lux** [lx].

This means that if we have a sphere of 1 meter radius, a light source, with luminous intensity of 1 candela inside this sphere, it will produce illumination on the internal surface of 1 lx. Mathematically, this relation can be described as:

$$E = \text{Flux} / \text{Area} = F/A \qquad [\text{lx}] \qquad (1)$$

The flux F is, by definition, equal to luminous intensity times the solid angle, i.e.,

$$F = I \cdot \omega \qquad [\text{lm}] \qquad (2)$$

From the basics of volumetric trigonometry, and assuming a punctual source of light, we can express ω through the area A being lit and its distance from the source d:

$$\omega = A / d^2 \qquad [\text{rad}] \qquad (3)$$

When (2) and (3) are replaced in (1) we get

$$E = I / d^2 \qquad [\text{lx}] \qquad (4)$$

which means that **the illumination falls off with the square of the distance when the perpendicular area is being lit**. If, however, this area is at a certain angle to the incoming light, we can approximate the real area with the projection at an angle θ, as per the diagram shown on Page 36. In that case the formula (4) becomes:

$$E = I \cdot \cos \theta / d^2 \qquad [\text{lx}] \qquad (5)$$

Typical levels of illumination are shown on the drawing below:

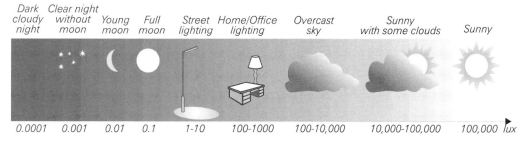

Some typical levels of illumination

Very rarely, in certain small areas and from very strong light sources, levels higher than 100,000 lx can be experienced (in the vicinity of a strong flashlight, for example). To describe such illuminations, higher units called **phots** are sometimes used. **One phot is equal to 10,000 lx.**

In American terminology, where square feet are still widely used instead of the SI units, illumination is expressed in **square-foot candelas**, or better known as **foot-candelas**. Because of the "square meter/square foot" ratio equal to nearly 10 (or more precisely 9.29), it is reasonably easy to convert luxes into foot-candelas and vice versa. Basically, if an illumination is given in foot-candelas, just divide it by 10 and the approximate value in luxes is obtained, and if a value is given in luxes, in order to convert it to foot-candelas, multiply it by 10.

Luminance (*L*) describes the brightness of the surface of either a primary or a secondary source of light. Since brightness embeds subjective connotation, luminance is used as an objective, scientific term. Luminance depends on the luminous intensity of the surface itself, and depends on the angle at which it is being observed. It is therefore measured per unit of projected surface area perpendicular to that direction. There are quite a few units for luminance. The internationally preferred metric unit is **nit. One nit is equal to one candela per square meter of projected surface area** (*I/A*). If, instead of candelas, lumens are used to describe the luminous flux of a source, the luminance would then be expressed in **apostilbs** [asb]. Things get a bit more complicated when we have a surface where the luminous flux radiated, or reflected, in a direction θ to the normal is directly proportional to cos θ. Such a surface will appear equally bright when seen from all directions because both the reflected light and projected surface area follow the same cosine law. This type of surface is called a **lambert** radiator or reflector (depending on whether the surface is a primary or secondary source of light) and is usually described as a **perfectly diffusing surface**. For the purpose of measuring such light luminance in the metric system, a unit called **lambert** was introduced. The equivalent American unit would be the **foot-lambert**.

How much of the illumination is seen by the camera really depends on the intensity of the source itself, but also on the reflectivity of the object being illuminated. Obviously, it is not the same if the object is white as opposed to black. With the same amount of light we can, naturally, see more if the objects are white. This is why we have to introduce another factor when talking about illumination and this is the percentage of object **reflectivity**. The definition of reflectivity could be described with the following simple relation:

$$\rho = \textit{light reflected from surface/light incident on surface} = E/L \ [\%] \tag{6}$$

Realistically, this percentage ranges from a very low 1% for black velvet, 32% for a typical soil surface and up to 93% for bright snow in the field of view. Caucasian human flesh has a reflectivity factor between 19% and 35%.

This is an important factor when stating a camera's minimum illumination since with the same level of illumination and various reflectivity factors, an object may appear more or less bright, indirectly affecting the camera performance.

Calculating the amount of light falling onto an imaging device

In order to fully understand the "light issue," as seen by the camera, we need to know how much light actually falls on the imaging area.

The illumination amount at the CCD chip (or tube's faceplate), E_{CCD}, depends, first and most, on the luminance L of the object, but also on the F-stop of the lens, i.e., the light-gathering ability of the lens. The lower the F-number the more light will get through the lens, as will be explained later in the book. It is also proportional to the **transmittance factor τ of a lens**. Namely, depending on the quality of the glass and its manufacture, as well as the inner walls of the lens mechanics, a certain percentage of the light will be lost in the lens itself.

All of the above factors can be combined into the following relation:

$$E_{CCD} = L \cdot \tau \cdot \pi / (4 \cdot F^2) \qquad [lx] \qquad (7)$$

In the next few lines we will show how this relation is approximated, so that the technical people using these formulas can have a clear understanding of what is being assumed and approximated in order to get to formula (7). However, because these calculations involve slightly more complex mathematics, I suggest that readers with no interest, or without the background, should just directly use relation (7) as it is, knowing that L is the average luminance of the object (in lux), τ is the transmittance of the lens (in percentage), F is the F-number and π is 3.14.

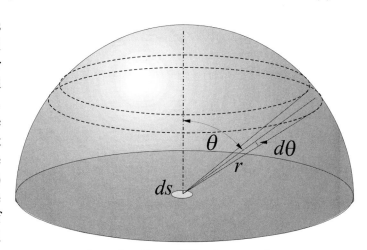

Lambertian diffusing surface

An object viewed by a camera, when lit by a light source, radiates light, more or less, in all directions, depending upon the reflectivity function. In practice, the majority of smooth surface objects can be approximated with a **lambertian perfectly diffusing surface**.

The flux, then, can be regarded as passing through a hemisphere of radius r and center ds. If we now consider the incremental angle $d\theta$ at an angle θ to the normal, the flux occupying the volume of a revolution swept out by the angle $d\theta$ passes through an annular ring on the surface of the sphere, with width $rd\theta$ and circumference $2\pi r \sin\theta$.

This elementary surface area is given by:

$$dA = 2\pi r^2 \sin\theta \, d\theta \qquad (8)$$

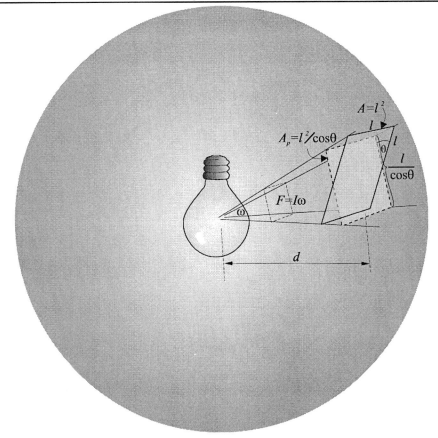

Calculating the light radiation

and hence the solid angle ω that it subtends at the center of the sphere is given by:

$$\omega = dA / r^2 = 2\pi r^2 \sin\theta\, d\theta / r^2 = 2\pi \sin\theta\, d\theta \quad \text{[steradian]} \tag{9}$$

Since for a Lambert surface the luminous intensity (flux per steradian) in a given direction falls as the cosine of the angle to the normal, we have the luminous intensity of the whole surface in the direction of the normal as I, and then at an angle θ it will be given with $I\cos\theta$. The luminous intensity dI of a small area ds will be given by:

$$dI = I \cos\theta\, ds / s \qquad\qquad \text{[lumens/steradian = candelas]} \tag{10}$$

Since I/s is the actual luminance L in the perpendicular direction, the above relation becomes:

$$dI = L \cos\theta\, ds \qquad\qquad \text{[cd]} \tag{11}$$

The elementary flux dF is equal to the elementary intensity dI times the solid angle:

$$dF = L \cos\theta\, ds\, 2\pi \sin\theta\, d\theta \qquad\qquad \text{[lm]} \tag{12}$$

The total light emitted into a cone of an angle θ can be found by integration from 0 to θ:

$$F = \int 2\pi L ds \sin\theta \cos\theta\, d\theta = \pi L\, ds \sin^2\theta \qquad \text{[lm]} \tag{13}$$

If we want to find the total flux radiated in all directions, we have to put 90° for the angle θ so the total flux emitted in all directions will then be:

$$F_t = \pi L\, ds \qquad\qquad\qquad [\text{lm}] \qquad\qquad\qquad (14)$$

Now, if we have to calculate the flux emitted into a solid angle smaller than 90°, as may be the case when a camera is viewing an object, the total flux F_o is given by the formula:

$$F_o = \pi L\, ds_o \sin^2\theta_o \qquad\qquad [\text{lm}] \qquad\qquad\qquad (15)$$

If the lens transmission factor is t, then the flux falling on the CCD (or tube's faceplate) plane is:

$$F_{CCD} = F_o\, \tau = \tau\, \pi L\, ds_o \sin^2\theta_o \qquad [\text{lm}] \qquad\qquad\qquad (16)$$

The illumination of the CCD chip (or tube's faceplate) would be flux divided by the area, i.e.

$$E_{CCD} = \tau\, \pi L\, ds_o \sin^2\theta_0 / ds_{CCD} \qquad [\text{lx}] \qquad\qquad\qquad (17)$$

From the drawings, showing the lambertian diffusing source, $\sin\theta_o$ can be expressed as:

$$\sin\theta_o = d/(2D) \qquad\qquad\qquad\qquad\qquad (18)$$

and then the relation (17) becomes:

$$E_{CCD} = \tau\, \pi d^2 L / (4D^2) \qquad\qquad [\text{lx}] \qquad\qquad\qquad (19)$$

We will use one more formula, the known formula for a lens (which will also be discussed later in the lens chapter):

$$1/p + 1/D = 1/f \qquad\qquad\qquad\qquad\qquad (20)$$

where p is the distance from the lens to the image plane, D is the distance between the object and the lens and, of course, f is the focal length of the lens itself. A so-called magnification factor of a lens is given by the factor m described as the ratio between p and D:

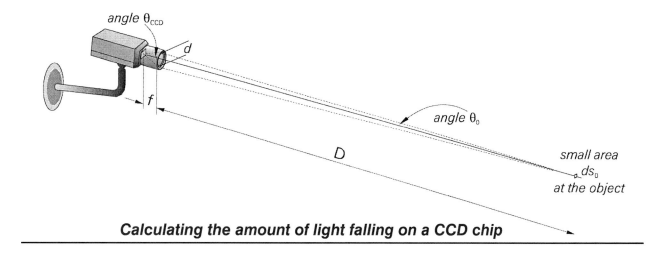

Calculating the amount of light falling on a CCD chip

$$m = p/D \tag{21}$$

Using (20) and (21), D can be expressed as:

$$D = f(m+1) \tag{22}$$

If this D is replaced back into formula (19) we will have:

$$E_{CCD} = \tau \pi L d^2/(4 f^2 (m+1)^2) \tag{23}$$

We know (to be shown later in the lens chapter) a lens's F-number is defined by the ratio of the lens's focal length and the diameter where the light passes through, in our case, this is d:

$$E_{CCD} = \tau \pi L/(4 F^2 (m+1)^2) \tag{24}$$

In practice, D is much larger than d, thus m becomes insignificant, i.e., 0. Then, (24) becomes approximated by:

$$E_{CCD} = \tau \pi L/(4 F^2) \tag{25}$$

This might be a very useful formula if you want to calculate how much light reaches the CCD chip or the tube, by knowing the luminance of an object L (assuming it is reasonably far, as compared to the focal length of the lens) and the F-number on the lens at the moment of measurement. Usually the lens transmittance factor τ ranges between 0.75 and 0.95. For calculation purposes, it is realistic and common to take 0.8.

Let's work out an example. If the light at the object plane is around 300 lx, like in an average office area (this would be E_{object}), the luminance can be found using the reflection coefficient of the surrounding objects, i.e., $L = E_{object} \cdot \rho$. As mentioned earlier, reflection factors vary substantially with various objects, but we won't be far from a real office situation if we assume 50%. If the lens we are using has an iris setting of, say, F-16, the illumination at the CCD plane would be approximately $E_{CCD} = 0.8 \cdot 3.14 \cdot 300 \cdot 0.5 / (4 \cdot 256) = 0.36$ lx. This, combined with the camera's AGC, is a realistic illumination for a CCD chip plane for a full video signal. If, however, the lens iris is set to F-1.4, for example, the illumination of the CCD plane would be approximately 48 lx (using relation (17)). This is a far higher value than the CCD chip needs, and in practice it can only produce a recognizable video if an auto iris lens is used, or if the camera has an electronic (or CCD) iris built-in. If a manual iris lens is used with an F-1.4 and the camera's AGC is set to off, 48 lx at the chip will produce a saturated, or washed-out, white image.

A very basic rule of thumb is that even a lens with the lowest F-number attenuates the light for a factor of 10+. The higher the F-number, the lower the amount of light that reaches the CCD plane. In fact, it is inverse proportional to the square of the F-number.

With the above conclusions we are actually tapping into a very interesting question raised with CCD cameras (especially B/W) : If the object illumination is as at a full sunny day (approximately 100,000 lx), the F-number has to be very high in order to "stop-down" the light as required by the CCD chip. This is in the vicinity of 0.1 ~ 0.3 lx (or close) for a full video. Such an F-number is actually so high that it requires the attenuation of the lens to be in the order of over 1,000,000 times. Using the approximated formula (16), assuming the same values for $\tau = 0.8$, $\rho = 0.5$, and assuming the camera CCD chip requires 0.2 lx for a 1 V_{pp} signal, we will get an F-number of 886.

This is an extraordinarily high number to be achieved by mechanical means (leaves shutter). The precision of the leaves' movement is limited, and, more importantly, an unwanted optical effect called a Fresnel Edge Refraction becomes noticeable with small iris openings. This means, in practice, very high F-stops cannot be achieved by using just mechanical methods. So, special optical neutral density (ND) filters are used to "help" the leaves shutter achieve high F-stops as required by the sensitive CCD chips.

For a B/W CCD chip to produce a fully saturated signal of 1 V_{pp} at the camera's output (with AGC off), the E_{ccd} needs to be around 0.1 lx . Some manufacturers quote lower numbers, usually referring to only a percentage of the video signal.

Colors in television

Colors are a very important and complex issue in CCTV. Although a lot of people still prefer monochrome (B/W) cameras because of their better sensitivity and response to the infrared invisible spectrum, color cameras are becoming more and more widely accepted. Color offers valuable additional information on the objects being monitored. More importantly, the human eye captures color information quicker than the fine details of an object. The drawback is the not so good performance in low light levels. With the ever improving CCD technology, however, the color camera minimum illumination performance has improved dramatically. From 10 lx@F1.4 at the object, of a few years ago, we now have cameras that can see down to 2 lx @F1.4 at the object, or even lower.

Color images on TV are made up of three phosphor mosaics (RGB)

As already discussed, the colors we see are actually various wavelengths of light.

When we see red, for example, it is a wavelength reflected from a red object when white light is shone on it.

Black absorbs almost all wavelengths, while white reflects most of them.

The science of colors is a very complex one, and becomes even more complicated when the natural colors around us are reproduced by the phosphor coating of the CRTs.

The concept of producing colors in TV is by **additive mixing** of three primary color phosphor dots next to each other. These are tiny dots, representing parts of a mask that is on the inside of a monitor's CRT.

The actual color mixing happens when we view the monitor from a normal distance (a couple of meters) and the resultant color of each of the three dots appears in our eyes.

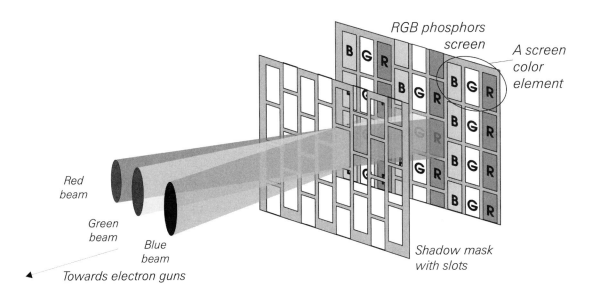

RGB phosphors screen

A screen color element

Red beam

Green beam

Blue beam

Towards electron guns

Shadow mask with slots

The RGB shadow mask

This is opposite to the case in painting and printing technology, where colors are obtained by **subtractive mixing**.

In additive mixing, light is produced by the phosphor coating of a CRT and adding colors makes the resultant color brighter. Therefore, to get white, all three colors need to be present with their corresponding amounts. Resultant colors are obtained by adding and therefore the name *additive.*

With subtractive mixing of colors, when we use paper or acrylic as a secondary source of light (reflected), colors are mixed in our eye after they are reflected from the surface. If we mix (add) all the primary colors we produce darker colors, instead of brighter. The colors are mixed by reflected light, whose color is defined by the pigment, which absorbs (subtracts) the wavelength its surface has.

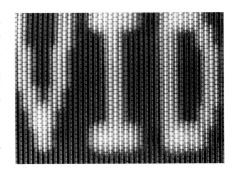

Getting back to television, three colors, as mentioned, are used as primary colors: red, green and blue, usually referred to as RGB.

Television theory and experiments have shown that with these three primary colors **most** of the natural colors can be represented (but not all).

Obviously, there are **three different phosphor coatings** inside the color CRT, each of which radiates its own color when bombarded by the electron beam.

The three primary phosphor coatings have different luminosity properties, which means **equal beam intensity produces unequal brightness**. In order to compensate for these discrepancies of the primary phosphors, every color TV and monitor has a special matrix circuit that multiplies each of the color channels with a different compensating number. This can be shown by the very well-known color TV luminance equation, which is electronically applied to the three primary signals in the CRT:

$$L_{screen} = 0.3R + 0.59G + 0.11B \hspace{4cm} (26)$$

The blue phosphor produces more light than the other two and because of this it has to be multiplied by 0.11 in order to reduce the luminance to be equal to the other two components.

In this book we will not go much deeper into the theory of colors in television, as it requires a book on its own, but it is important for the reader to appreciate the complexity of the issue and accept that all colors as seen on TV are obtained by visual additive mixing of the three primary colors of the CRT phosphor: red, green and blue.

Color temperatures and light sources

Color temperature refers to the temperature to which an imaginary perfectly black body is heated and consequently produces light.

The theory of physics states that **the spectrum of light generated by heating is mostly dependent on the temperature of the body and *not on the material*.** This very important statement has been proven by the physicist Max Planck whose formula explains the relationship between the peak wavelengths radiated and the temperature to which the body is heated:

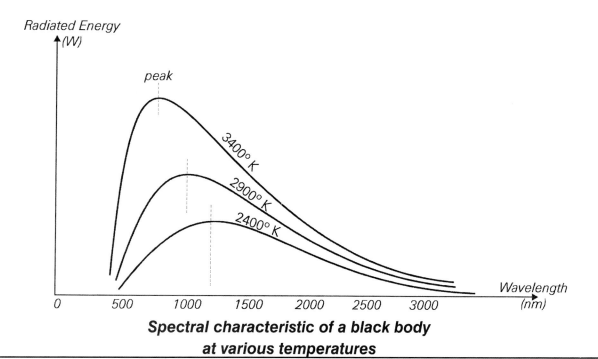

Spectral characteristic of a black body
at various temperatures

$$\lambda_m = 2896/T \tag{27}$$

In the previous relation, λ_m is the wavelength and T is the temperature in Kelvin degrees.

From the diagram on page 23 it can be noted that the peaks for different temperatures are outside of the visible spectrum, i.e., in the infrared region. For tungsten (wolfram) filament light, the working color temperature is around 2800° K, and more than 3/4 of the energy is radiated in the infrared region in the form of heat. Heat is nothing more than infrared light. Higher temperatures for tungsten lights cannot be used because the melting point of wolfram is around 3500° K. Increasing the temperature to more than 2800° K will dramatically shorten the lifetime of the tungsten light. In today's tungsten globes, the air is extracted from inside the bulb in order to minimize the burning of the filament.

Tungsten light is good for B/W cameras, since they are more sensitive to the infrared portion of the spectrum. Color cameras have to be compensated for the yellow/reddish color produced by a 2800° K light source. In photographic cameras, this compensation is done with blue (complementary color) optical filters placed on the lens itself, while electronic cameras do that electronically by changing the primary colors' information by a certain percentage.

The sun, as a natural source of light, has a very high physical body temperature, but the equivalent light color temperature that we get on the earth's surface varies with the time of the day and the weather conditions. This is due to the light reflection and refraction through the atmosphere. As shown on the table of *Color temperatures for various light sources* on page 26, on a clear day, at noon, the color temperature reaches over 20,000° K, while on a cloudy day it drops down to nearly 6000° K. This is the reason why photographics taken at sunset hours appear reddish. The lower the color temperature, the redder the pictures will appear, and the higher it is, the bluer they will appear.

Artificial sources of light have various color temperatures, depending on the source. The previously mentioned formula (27) applies to heat sources only, i.e., sources of light where a metal is heated up to a high temperature. There are, however, gas sources of light, where light generation is of a different nature. Neon lights, or mercury vapor lights, for example, generate light when an electromagnetic field is applied to them. The atoms are excited by an energy sufficient to cause certain atom reactions and energy is released in the form of light. **This light is of a discrete character due to the quantum behavior of the atoms**. The position(s) of the wavelength(s) will depend on the gas used. Some of the glass tubes used with such gases are coated on the inside with a fluorescent powder that might absorb certain primary wavelengths and then regenerate a continuous secondary spectrum of visible light.

Gas sources can also be described by their color temperature, only in this case we use a so-called **correlational color temperature**.

For the purposes of having a reference point and correct color reproduction, standard sources of white light have been defined. There are a few definitions (standards) used in practice. These standard sources of white light are marked as **A, B, C, D$_{6500}$** and **W**.

Source **A** is the most natural standard as it represents a tungsten (wolfram) light globe, filled with some gas to reduce burning of the filament. That is why most of the other later developed standards are based on source A. As mentioned earlier, at a certain temperature, the characteristics of a wolfram light coincide a great deal with the radiation of a black body. This means **the spectrum of source A, at a certain temperature, can be represented by only *one* detail – the temperature, which is equal to the temperature of the black body.** To be precise, the real temperature of the wolfram and the black body at which their spectrums are supposed to be identical is not exactly the same. The black body is hotter by approximately 50° K. The spectrum characteristic of the standard source A is defined as a color temperature of 2854° K, while the real filament temperature is approximately 2800° K. This is, however, an insignificant difference and the theoretical approximation is valid and accepted as a descriptive factor for the color temperature of such sources.

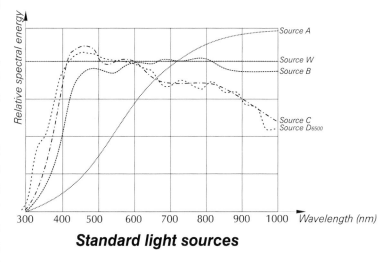

Standard light sources

Standard source **B** radiates white light, similar to direct sunlight at noon. Source B can be obtained by filtering the light from source A through a special light filter.

Similarly, by using another type of light filter, standard light source **C** can be obtained. The characteristics of sources B and C cannot be represented with the color temperature of a black body, as can be seen on the diagram. However, if the color of a black body looks similar to either of the sources B or C, we use the term *correlational color temperature*. So, the correlational temperature of source B is 4880° K, and for source C it is 6740° K.

The **International Committee for Light (CIE)** in 1965 suggested a new standard source of light, which is supposed to represent an average daylight color temperature and is represented as **D** standard.

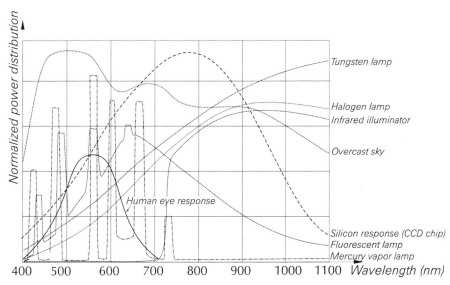

Spectral energy dissipation of various light sources

The recommended correlational color temperature for the standard D is 6500° K, so the standard is marked as D_{6500}. This source of light cannot be obtained by modifying source A, but its spectral characteristic can be approximated with some other physical sources, as is the case with a correct mixture of the three phosphor coatings of the CRT of a color monitor. For us in CCTV, it is important to remember this fact, as D_{6500} is often used as a reference for color monitors.

Last, there is another, fictitious, light source with a uniform

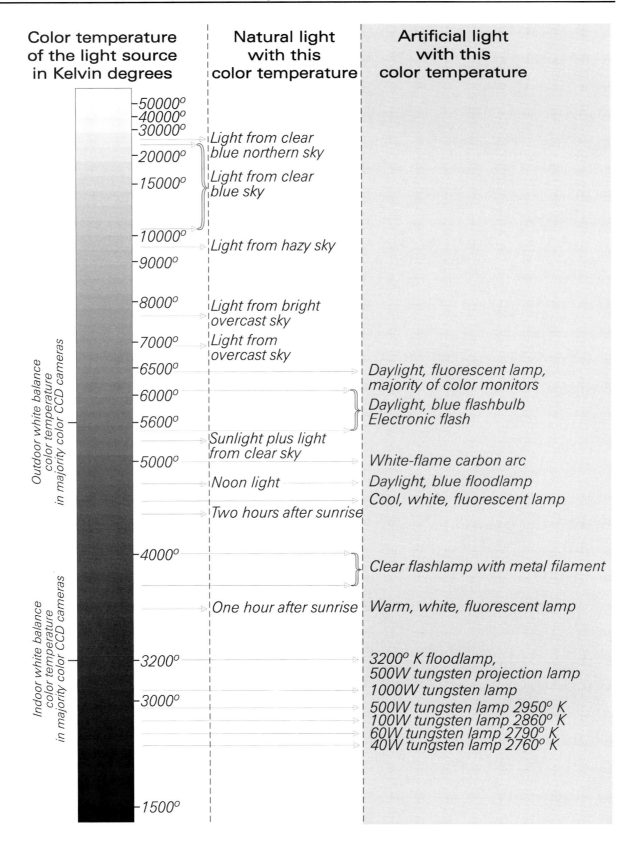

Color temperature of the light source in Kelvin degrees

- −50000°
- −40000°
- −30000°
- −20000°
- −15000°
- −10000°
- −9000°
- −8000°
- −7000°
- −6500°
- −6000°
- −5600°
- −5000°
- −4000°
- −3200°
- −3000°
- −1500°

Outdoor white balance color temperature in majority color CCD cameras

Indoor white balance color temperature in majority color CCD cameras

Natural light with this color temperature

- Light from clear blue northern sky
- Light from clear blue sky
- Light from hazy sky
- Light from bright overcast sky
- Light from overcast sky
- Sunlight plus light from clear sky
- Noon light
- Two hours after sunrise
- One hour after sunrise

Artificial light with this color temperature

- Daylight, fluorescent lamp, majority of color monitors
- Daylight, blue flashbulb Electronic flash
- White-flame carbon arc
- Daylight, blue floodlamp
- Cool, white, fluorescent lamp
- Clear flashlamp with metal filament
- Warm, white, fluorescent lamp
- 3200° K floodlamp, 500W tungsten projection lamp
- 1000W tungsten lamp
- 500W tungsten lamp 2950° K
- 100W tungsten lamp 2860° K
- 60W tungsten lamp 2790° K
- 40W tungsten lamp 2760° K

Color temperatures of various light sources

distribution of radiated energy, which looks like a flat horizontal line. This is only for calculating purposes and the code of this light source is **W**. The human eye adapts to the color temperature differences quite easily, and our brain automatically compensates the color variation due to different light sources. Film emulsions, tubes and camera CCD chips are a bit different. When using a film camera, special films or optical filters have to be used if color temperature needs to be corrected. With TV cameras this is achieved by electronic compensation, which can be either manual or automatic.

Finally, and as already mentioned, don't forget to take into account the color temperature of the monitor screen. The majority of CRTs are 6500° K, but some of them might have higher (9300° K) or even lower (5600° K) temperatures.

Persistency and the motion pictures concept

For us in CCTV, it is very important to know how the human eye works, and as we will see further in the text, we actually use an anomaly of the human eye in order to "cheat" the brain into thinking we see "motion pictures." This anomaly is the **persistency** of the human eye.

Persistency is the most important "eye defect" used in cinematography and television. The eye does not react instantly to the changes of light intensity. There is a delay of more than a few milliseconds during which the brain gets the information about the object we are watching. This delay increases with an increase of the object's illumination.

Not all parts of the retina have equal persistency. The central area around the fovea has longer persistency. Persistency also depends on the spectral characteristics of the light source, i.e., its color and brightness.

The above mentioned is very important for the concept of motion pictures. As can be seen on the graph on page 28, the persistency depends very much on the intensity of the light, or the brightness of the area we are looking at. The brighter the area is, the faster we have to change the pictures if we don't want to notice the flicker.

The first movies from the beginning of this century, cartoons and even the cartoon "flipping books" we used to play with as kids are based on the concept of persistency.

When pictures with a logical consecutiveness are played in front of our eyes at a speed equal to or faster than the persistency of the eye, we will see continuous moving pictures even though the pictures are **still,** individually.

A movie camera records images with a speed of 24 pictures/second. This is usually enough for the film to be projected with a very low light intensity projector, like in the beginning of the cinema revolution. For bigger audiences, bigger and stronger light projectors were needed, as well as brighter screens (as we have today). So it was obvious that the initial 24 pic/s speed needed increasing.

From a photographic point of view, which is very similar to the cinematographic one, it is impractical to increase the frame rate of the movie camera from 24 pic/s to a higher rate because the exposure time of every film frame will have to be shortened. To achieve that, the film either has to be of a higher

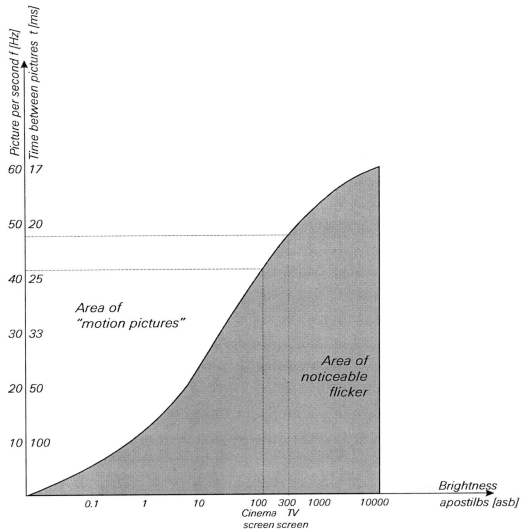

Persistency curve of the human eye

sensitivity, which is reflected in the bigger grain structure of the film, or the iris of the lens needs to be opened more, which results in not-so-good pictures at lower light levels as well as a reduced depth of field.

Neither of these two suggestions was acceptable for the cinematographers, so the solution was found in increasing the projection frequency (not the recording) from 24 to 48 with a simple but clever design. This was achieved with the so-called Maltese Cross shutter, which is a circular blade that is cut in the shape of the Maltese Cross. This rotates in front of the projection light bulb and not only blocks the light when the film moves from one frame to another (so the viewers don't see black lines between each film frame), but it also interrupts the projection while the frame is stationary (for the duration of 1/24 s) and produces two flashes of the same frame. As a result we have a projection, of 48 frames/s, which is flicker-free to the eye. Clearly, there are only 24 **different** pictures recorded each second, but the cross produces 48 of the same, and our brain perceives flickerless continuous moving pictures.

Television uses the same principles of persistency to achieve the illusion of motion. The conceptual difference is in composing the images not by using a light projector through a celluloid film, but with

electronic scanning of a CRT screen. In television, still images are created by scanning, where a picture is formed line by line, in the same manner as when reading a book, from left to right and from top to bottom. These principles shall be explained in more detail later in the book.

It is important for the reader to understand that **television also projects static images which, when displayed fast enough, are seen as "motion pictures."**

In the world today there are three basic television systems that differ in the number of pictures per second, the number of lines each picture is composed of and the method of color encoding. But in all of them the concept of producing motion is the same.

> PAL: 625 scanning lines/50 interlaced pictures per second

> NTSC: 525 scanning lines/60 interlaced pictures per second

> SECAM: 625 scanning lines (used to be 819)/50 interlaced pictures per second

Although different in the number of scanning lines and pictures per second, the general concept is the same from the point of view of composing picture frames field-by-field and line-by-line, scanning them at a fast rate to make use of the persistency concept as in film.

The NTSC's 525-line, 30-frames-per-second system is shared primarily by the United States, Canada, Greenland, Mexico, Cuba, Panama, Japan, the Philippines, Puerto Rico and most of South America. The NTSC standard was first developed for black and white (monochrome) television in 1941. The first color TV broadcast system was implemented in the United States in 1953.

More than half of the countries in the world use one of two 625-line, 25-frame systems: the PAL (Phase Alternating Line) system or the SECAM (Sequential Couleur Avec Memoire or Sequential Color with Memory) system.

The PAL standard was introduced in the early 1960s and implemented in most European countries, Australia, New Zealand, China, India and many countries in Africa and the Middle East. The PAL standard utilizes a wider channel bandwidth than NTSC, which allows for better picture quality. Also, the color encoding in PAL, being designed after the introduction of NTSC, offers more accurate color reproduction and better immunity to noise.

The SECAM standard was introduced in the early 1960s and implemented in France and is used in parts of Europe, including countries in and around the former Soviet Union. SECAM uses the same bandwidth as PAL but transmits the color information sequentially. The extra 100 lines in the SECAM and PAL systems add significant detail and clarity to the video picture, but the 50 fields per second (compared to 60 fields in the NTSC system) means that a slight flicker can sometimes be noticed.

3. Optics in CCTV

Some people take optics quality in CCTV for granted. With the camera resolution development, as well as the miniaturization of CCD chips, we are coming closer to the limits of optical resolution and we need to know a bit more than an average technician. This chapter discusses, again in a simplified way, the most common optical terms, concepts, and products used in CCTV.

Refraction

The very first and basic concept we have to understand is the concept of **refraction and reflection**.

When a light ray travelling through air or a vacuum enters a denser media, like glass or water, it reduces its speed by a factor **n** (always bigger than 1) known as **the index of refraction**. Different media (which are transparent to light) have different indices of refraction. For example, the speed of light in air is 300,000 km/s (almost the same as in vacuum). If a light ray enters glass, for example, which has an index of 1.5, the speed is reduced to 200,000 km/s.

According to the wave theory of light, the reduction of the light speed is reflected in its shortened wavelength. This phenomenon represents the base of the concept of refraction. If a light ray enters the glass perpendicularly, the wavelength of the light ray shortens, but when the ray exits the glass it resumes to normal speed, i.e., returns to the original "air wavelength" and continues its travel in the same direction. If, however, the light ray enters the glass at any angle other than the perpendicular, interesting things happen: the light ray (considered to be of a wave nature in this case) has a front that does not enter the glass media at the same time (because it comes under an angle). The parts of the front that enter the glass first are "slowed down" first. The end result is the refraction of the light ray, i.e., the ray does not continue in the same direction but deflects slightly. This deviation depends upon the density of the media.

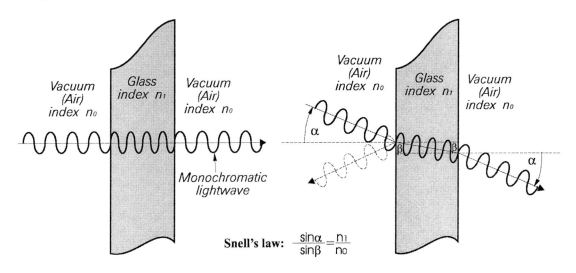

Snell's law: $\dfrac{\sin\alpha}{\sin\beta} = \dfrac{n_1}{n_0}$

Light refraction and Snell's law

The denser the media, i.e., the higher the index of refraction, the greater the inclination of the original direction.

There is a very simple relation between the angles of incidence and refraction and indices of refraction between the two different media. This relation was discovered by the Dutch physicist Willebrord Snell in the early 17th century. By using a very simple calculation we can determine the angles of refraction in various media. As we shall see later on, the same concepts are used when calculating the angles of total reflection and numerical aperture in fiber optics.

Laser light refraction through a prism

The basics of refraction are graphically explained in the diagram on the next page, where it is assumed a monochromatic (single frequency) light ray enters the glass. The bottom drawing also shows that a percentage of the incident light is always reflected back into air (or vacuum); in the case of glass this percentage is very small.

The refraction and reflection theories will be used in the next headings when explaining lens and fiber optics concepts.

Lenses as optical elements

There are two basic types of lenses: **convex** and **concave**.

The first one, convex, has a positive focal length, i.e., the focus is real and we usually call it a magnifying glass, since it appears to magnify the objects.

The second one, concave, has a negative focal length, i.e., the focus is virtual and it appears to reduce the objects.

Every lens has the following important parameters:

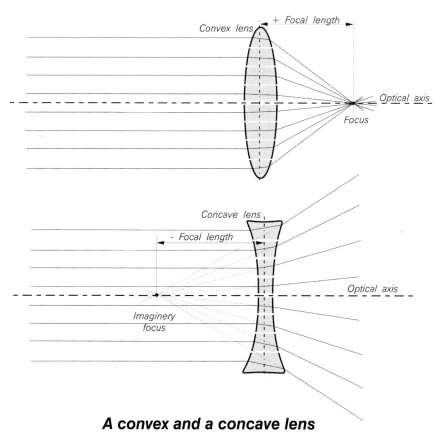

A convex and a concave lens

- Optical plane (a plane passing through the center of the lens)

- Optical axis (an axis perpendicular to the center of the optical plane)

- Focus (a point where rays falling parallel to the optical axis converge)

- Focal length (the distance between the optical plane and the focus, in meters)

- Diopter (an inverse value of the focal length, where the focal length is stated in meters)

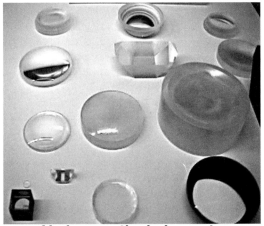

Various optical elements

In respect to the physical size and the type of surface of the lens, there are many different types, such as plano-convex, convex-concave, plano-concave, etc. The name describes the physical appearance of the lens, where plano means one of the two surfaces is a plane.

Different types of lenses have been put together in order to correct various distortions (aberrations) caused by different factors.

As an example of why this is necessary, let's examine a sun ray falling onto a prism.

We all know the rainbow effect produced on the other side of the prism. This happens because the "white" rays coming from the sun are composed of all the wavelengths (i.e., colors) the human eye can see. Because they all enter the glass prism with the index of refraction $n_1 > n_0$, different wavelengths are changed at slightly different "rates" (proportional to their frequency), thus producing the rainbow at the other end of the prism. This is actually a **decomposition of the white light**. The color red has the longest wavelength (lowest frequency); therefore, it is refracted least. The color violet has the shortest wavelength (highest frequency); therefore, it is refracted the most.

A very similar effect is the fabulous rainbow after the rain, which is actually the refraction and reflection of sun rays through the raindrops.

No matter how impressive this effect looks, it is an unwanted effect in a lens design.

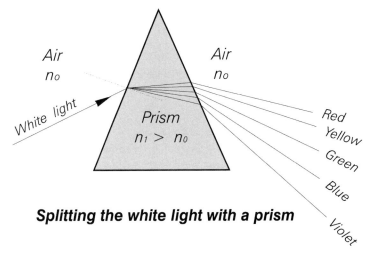

Splitting the white light with a prism

A convex lens can be approximated with many little prisms next to each other, forming a mosaic. It is, then, obvious that the image created by such a lens using daylight (which is actually most common), will be decomposed into the basic colors as is the case with the prism light decomposition.

This means that when white rays fall onto a simple convex lens, **the focal point will vary for different colors.** This is an unwanted effect, called color distortion of a lens, or a **chromatic aberration.**

So, it should be clearly understood that chromatic aberration happens not so much because of the imperfection of the lens manufacture (although this is not excluded), but rather because of the physical process of decomposing white light into the basic wavelengths when the light passes through a single piece of lens.

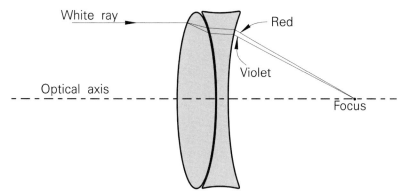

Chromatic aberation correction

Chromatic aberration **can** be minimized by **combining convex and concave** lenses together, where a white ray is first split by the convex lens into a "dispersed rainbow" but is then "put back together" by the concave lens **because of the opposite effect of the concave lens** (relative to the incident angle).

When the two lenses (convex and concave) are chosen carefully (in respect to their thicknesses and focal points), the result is that all the colors come together in the focus and form a single focusing point. This is achieved with a proper selection of the convex-concave pairs, preserving the wanted combined focal length as in the single-piece lens. A special transparent glue is used to join the two lenses.

This is just a very simple example of why numerous optical elements are required to compose a lens of a certain focal length.

There are many other distortions produced by lenses, not just the chromatic aberration, but also geometrical ("pincushion" and "barrel"), spherical, etc. The name suggests the type of distortion it adds to the image. These can also be corrected by adding some more optical elements to the group.

Photo courtesy of Edmund Scientific

Group of lenses with an iris

When designing a lens, optical engineers have to balance between a lens with as many corrections as possible (in order to get a good quality picture), but also as few elements as possible (in order to be economical and technologically acceptable).

One can imagine how many combinations are possible when designing a lens with a particular focal length with half a dozen (or more) different optical elements. Earlier, optical engineers used to work together with mathematicians when designing a lens with a certain focal length and size, and they used to do hundreds and hundreds of calculations and iterations manually. The physical size, the focal length and the absolute and relative positions of every element are all variables. The only way to find such a combination of a known focal length was by painfully long iterations.

Obviously, the wanted result was to get a good quality lens without going overboard with the number of optical elements. Since this was quite a challenging task, manufacturers used to register the particular lens design with their "recipe" of how many lenses, what focal length and at what positions they were placed. That is why in cinematography and photography we may still see the lenses of a certain manufacturer with names like "Planar," "Xenar" etc. These names are actually patented designs of lenses for a particular lens size and focal length.

Typical markings on a CCTV lens

Today, in the computer era, there are many professional programs for computerized optical simulations. Within a few minutes optimum results are obtained, suggesting only as many optical elements as necessary, yet correcting all the visible distortions.

This is why lenses of a certain focal length are available with different costs and sizes, all giving the same viewing angle, but different picture quality.

Lens quality depends on many factors, and one should not take it for granted. This is especially important with zoom lenses, as there are so many variables in their design. Zoom lenses are widely used in most of the bigger CCTV systems, so we should be very careful when choosing them.

There is no simple rule, so the best suggestion, again, is to do some testing and comparisons.

The factors that determine the lens quality can be summarized by the following points:

1. Lens design

    - Number of elements

    - Relative position

    - Aberration correction in the design stage

2. Lens elements manufacture

    - Glass type

    - Technology and type of glass manufacturing (heating, cooling, cleanness)

    - Precision of grinding and polishing (very important)

    - Antireflection coatings of the glass (micrometer layers for minimizing losses)

3. Lens mechanical composition

    - The lens's positional fixing and stability (shock, temperature,...)

    - The lens's moving mechanics (especially zooming, focusing, iris leaves)

    - Internal light reflections (matt black absorption)

    - Gears used for motorized lenses (plastic, metal, precision)

4. Electronics (refers to auto iris and motorized lenses)

    - Auto iris electronics quality (gain, stability, precision)

    - Electric consumption (auto iris – usually low, but some older models may require more than a camera can give since the camera powers the auto iris)

    - Zoom and focus control circuitry (voltages: 6, 9 or 12 volts, three- or four-wire control)

Zoom lens mechanics

Disassembled zoom lens

Geometrical construction of images

Images can be constructed by using simple optical and geometrical rules.

As can be seen on the following drawing, at least two rays are used to create the image of an object.

There are three basic rules to follow:

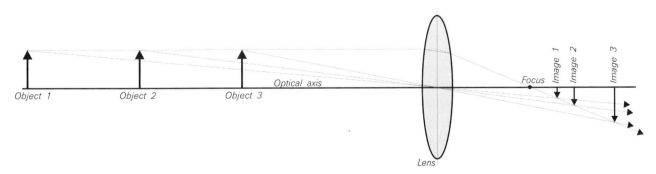

Image projection of different object distances

- Objects taken at various distances touch the optical axis with one end.

- By definition, rays that pass through the center of the lens do not change direction, i.e., in the center, a lens behaves like parallel glass and no refraction occurs.

- By definition, all rays parallel to the optical axis pass through the focus.

There is a very basic lens formula, worth mentioning, which we use when calculating the light falling onto a CCD chip:

$$1/D + 1/d = 1/f \tag{28}$$

where D is the distance from the object to the lens, d is from the lens to the image and f is the focal length of the lens. Note that d refers to a non-infinite distance object image and that's why it is bigger than f, whereas if the object is at an infinite distance, d would be equal to f.

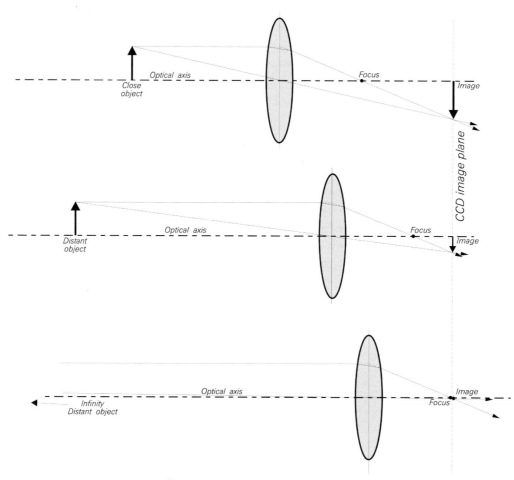

The concepts of focusing

Please note the position of images for various distance objects. **Lens focusing is achieved by changing the distance between the lens and the image plane** (which is where the CCD chip is located). So, *only* **when a lens is focused at an infinitely far object does the image projection coincide with the focus plane**. In all other cases the distance between the lens and the image is bigger than the focal length of the lens.

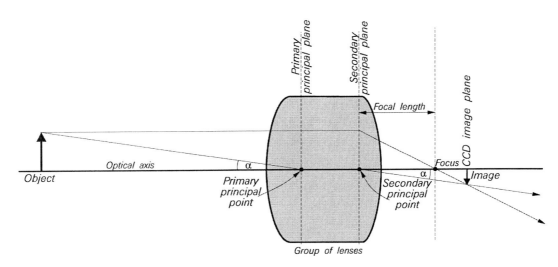

Principal points and planes

It should also be noted that, in practice, a lens is composed (as discussed earlier) of many optical elements. Therefore, they are represented by an equivalent single element lens located at the principal point. The following drawing explains this.

A lens composed of many optical elements (single thin lens) has **two principal points** called **primary** and **secondary principal points**. **For a thin lens, these points coincide and they are located at the center of the lens.**

The planes that pass through these principal points and are perpendicular to the optical axis are called **principal planes**.

The principal planes have the following properties:

> - A ray incident to the primary principal plane (and parallel to the optical axis) will leave the secondary principal plane at the same height, travelling toward the focal point (focus).

> - An incident ray directed toward the primary principal point will leave the secondary principal point at the same angle.

> - The focal length of such a lens is measured from the secondary principal plane to the focus.

Using the above properties, a geometrical image can be constructed in the same manner as it was shown with the single optical element.

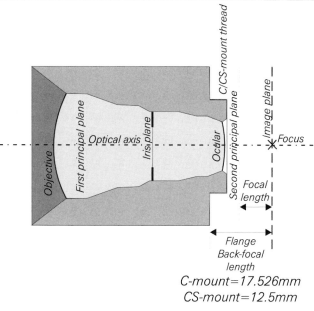

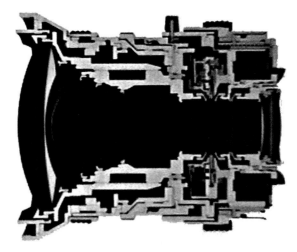

Cross section of a manual iris lens

Cross section of a wide-angle lens called Distagon, by Carl Zeiss, 1989

It is worth noting that the secondary principal point may fall outside the group of lenses. This is the case with very short focal length lenses. The shorter the focal length is, the more optical elements have to be added for correcting various distortions, making the lens more expensive. With the CCD chip reduction (2/3" down to 1/2", then to 1/3" and now to 1/4"), shorter focal length lenses have to be manufactured in order to preserve the same wide angle as the preceding chip sizes. This, in turn, has forced the industry to reduce the C-mount 17.5-mm back-flange distance in order for the optics to get simpler, smaller and cheaper. The new format of back-flange distance is 12.5-mm, and since it is smaller, it is referred to as the CS-mount standard.

Aspherical lenses

As mentioned earlier, spherical aberration is a common distortion that appears in the majority of lenses of a spherical type. Spherical-type lenses are the most common since they are produced by grinding and polishing in the easiest mechanical way, following the spherical laws. This refers to a circular machine polishing with the result being a lens of a spherical appearance. It can be shown that apart from the chromatic aberrations present in a single lens element (the "color decomposition" of white light) there is also aberration that happens because of the spherical profile of the lens. The focus is not a very precise single point.

Theoretically, using the physical laws of refraction, it can be shown (but we won't go into the details) that a bell-shaped lens (that does not follow the spherical law) is the ideal shape for obtaining a single focusing point without spherical distortions. The cross-section profile of such a lens is a curve that slightly deviates from a circular shape, appearing more bell shaped.

The drawing on the next page shows this in an exaggerated form in order to understand it.

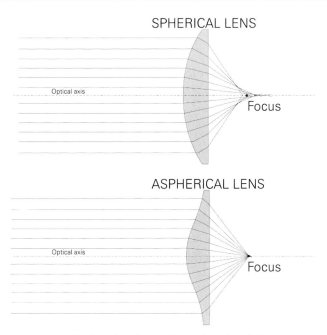

Spherical and aspherical lenses

This type of lens is called an **aspherical lens**.

Understandably, such a shape is hard to produce by regular polishing techniques, but if properly manufactured, it offers quite a few advantages over the conventional spherical lenses, including **higher iris openings** (which is reflected in lower F/stop), **wider angles of view, shorter minimum object distances** and **fewer optical elements** because there are fewer aberrations to correct (thus resulting in lighter and smaller lens designs).

Aspherical auto iris lens

This technology, however, is more expensive due to the aforementioned complex polishing techniques.

Some optical companies have started producing **molded** aspherical lenses, avoiding the critical process of grinding. This process does not offer the same glass quality as the regular one, but it does offer a solution for more economical production of aspherical lenses.

The quality of such lenses is yet to be proven, but they do exist and are available in the CCTV market as well.

Contrast and Modulation Transfer Functions (CTF & MTF)

What we want from a lens is sharp and clear images, free of distortions.

As already mentioned, lenses do have limited resolving power and this is especially important to have in mind when using them in high resolution systems.

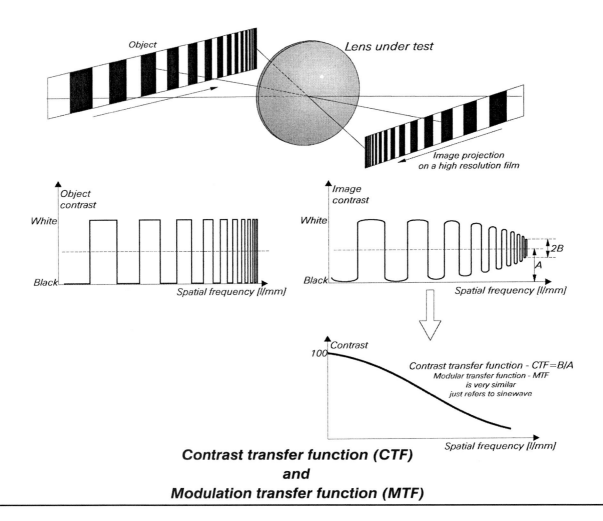

Contrast transfer function (CTF)
and
Modulation transfer function (MTF)

Resolution refers to the lens's ability to reproduce fine details. In order to measure this, a chart that consists of black and white stripes with various density (spatial periods) is used. **This is usually expressed in lines per millimeter** (lines/mm). When counting how many lines/mm a lens can resolve, we count both black and white lines.

A characteristic that shows the "response" of a lens to various densities of lines/mm is called a **Contrast Transfer Function** (CTF).

Theoretically, it is better to know the lens characteristics for a continuous variation of black to white (in the form of a sinewave), and not just for stripes that abruptly change from black to white. This would be especially suitable for TV lenses since the optical signal is converted into an electrical signal with which sinewaves are easier to represent and evaluate. This characteristic is known as a **Modulation Transfer Function** (MTF).

In practice, however, it is much easier to produce a test chart with just black/white stripes rather than the sinewave variation between black and white. CTF is not the same as MTF, but it is much easier to measure and is **precise enough to describe the lens's global characteristics.**

The easiest analogy of MTF to understand would be the spectral response of an audio system. In an audio system we usually describe the output level (voltage or sound pressure) versus the audio frequency. In optics it is similar, where MTF is expressed in contrast values (from 0 to 100%) versus spatial frequency (expressed in lines/mm), as can be seen on the previous page.

Different lenses have different MTF characteristics, depending on the quality of the glass, optical design, and application. For example, a photographic lens will have a better MTF than a CCTV lens. The reason for this is simple: the photographic film structure can register over 120 lines/mm and manufacturers need to produce better lenses in order to minimize picture deterioration when film is blown up to a poster size.

CCD chips have a lower resolution than the film crystal structure. Technically, **there is no need** to go to the "expense" of producing a lens with much higher resolution than a CCD chip. With the miniaturization of CCD chips, however, we are actually coming closer to the film resolution limits, so lenses need to feature better characteristics.

An average 1/2" B/W CCD chip, for example, has approximately 500 pixels (picture elements) in the horizontal direction. When we take into account the physical width of the 1/2" CCD chip (6.4 mm), we'll come to the conclusion that the maximum number of vertical lines (black and white pairs) we can have is (500:6.4):2 = 39 lines/mm. This resolution is easily achieved with most TV lenses, since the optical technology can easily produce over 50 lines/mm. But for a 1/3" B/W CCD chip, with the same density of 500 pixels horizontally, we are actually talking about (500:4.4):2 = 57 lines/mm. This means that a 1/3" CCD camera **demands more** from the lens resolution than a 1/2" one.

Different lenses have different MTF characteristics and sometimes it may be necessary to decide which one to use on the basis of these characteristics.

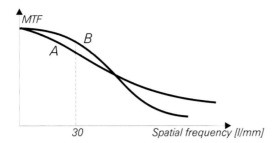

MTF curves of two different lenses

The diagram above shows such an example. We can evaluate this in the following way. The lens A has its MTF extending into the high spatial frequency range, which means it can resolve finer details than lens B. Lens B, however, has better response in the lower frequencies. If we need a lens for a high resolution output, like film, for example, lens A would be a better choice, but for CCTV purposes, where a CCD chip cannot see more than 50 lines/mm, we are better off with lens B since we will have better contrast with it.

F and T numbers

In addition to the MTF and CTF characteristics of a lens, the **F-number** (or more commonly known as **F-stop**) is also a very important parameter.

The F-number indicates the brightness of an image formed by a lens. This is usually written (engraved) on the lens itself as F/1.4, for example, or sometimes in another form, such as 1:1.4. The F-number depends on the **focal length** of the lens and the **effective diameter** of the area through which the light

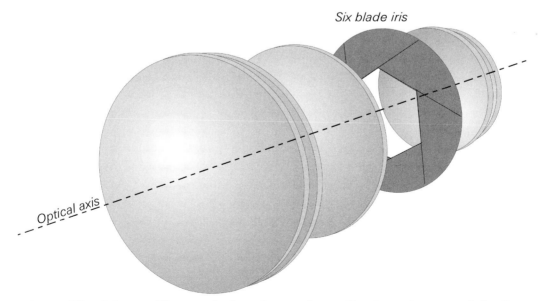

The iris position and size depends on the lens type and design

rays pass. This area can be controlled by a mechanical leaves assembly, which we usually refer to as the *iris*.

It is important to note that the **effective diameter** of a lens is not the actual lens diameter, but rather the **diameter of the image of the iris as seen from in front of the lens.** The first lens diameter is usually called the **entrance pupil.** There is also an **exit pupil**, as shown on the diagram. The actual iris

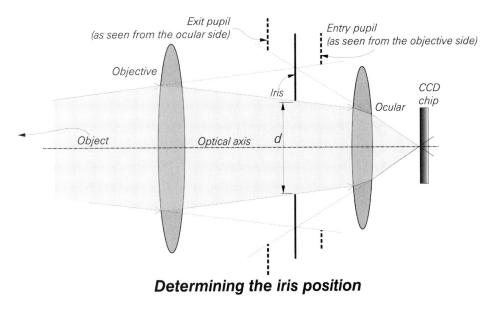

Determining the iris position

diaphragm is positioned in between these two pupils, which also happens to be between the two principal points.

The lower the F-number the bigger the iris opening is, and that means more light is transmitted through the lens. The lowest number for a particular lens is the number engraved (or written) on the lens itself, representing the **light gathering ability** of that lens.

Often, the lower F-stop lenses are called **faster lenses**. The reason for this is that, in the early days of photography, by increasing the amount of light (lower F-stop), the film exposure time needed to be shortened, thus allowing pictures with fast action to be taken without losing any sharpness because of camera movement.

If a 16-mm lens has a minimum F-stop of 1.4, for example, it is usually written as 16 mm/1.4, or sometimes as 16 mm 1:1.4. The maximum effective iris opening is equivalent to a circle with a diameter of 16/1.4 = 11.43 mm.– equivalent because the iris leaves would usually make a triangle, a square, a pentagon or a hexagon opening.

In order to understand the consecutiveness of the F-numbers we will have to do some simple calculations.

Starting with the above example of a 16 mm /1.4 lens, let's find the area when the iris is fully open (i.e., at F/1.4):

$$A_{1.4} = (d/2)^2 \cdot \pi = (11.43/2)^2 \cdot \pi = 32.66 \cdot 3.14 = 102.5 \text{ mm}^2 \qquad (29)$$

Let's have this area halved, i.e., take 51.25 mm² as a new area, and let's calculate what the iris opening is:

$$A_x = (x/2)^2 \cdot \pi \Rightarrow x = 2 \cdot \sqrt{A_x / \pi} = 8 \text{ mm} \tag{30}$$

Now, the F-stop with an 8-mm iris opening would be 16/8 = 2, i.e., F/2.

Here we have F/2 representing an area that is exactly half of the F/1.4. If we proceed with the same logic we would get the following familiar numbers:

2.8; 4; 5.6; 8; 11; 16; 22; 32; etc.

All of these numbers are common to all types of lenses, and what they mean is that

Photo courtesy of Edmund Scientific
Group of lenses with an iris

every next higher F-number transmits half the amount of light of the previous F-number.

Now it should be much clearer why a 16 mm/1.0 lens makes the same camera look more sensitive than, for example, when a 16 mm/1.4 lens is used.

For zoom lenses, the F-numbers quoted refer to the iris opening at the shortest focal length of the zoom lens. This is obviously the best light gathering number of every lens. The F-number of the same zoom lens at a longer focal length setting (tele) is always smaller than at the shorter end. But it is wrong to assume a linear function of the F-stop versus the focal length. Namely, if an 8-80 mm/1.4 lens is in question, it makes an 8/1.4 = 5.7 mm effective iris opening, while with the same iris at 80 mm we should have an F-stop of 80/5.7 = 14. This simply isn't the case because it depends on the zoom lens construction. The iris plane may vary in relation to the moving parts of the zooming components, obeying a **nonlinear law**. In most cases we have much better values for the F-stop at the higher focal length than indicated, but they are still worse than at the lower focal length.

It is fair to say that every piece of glass, no matter how good it is, introduces some light loss. These losses might be a very small percentage of the total light energy, but they should be considered if accurate lens characteristics need to be taken into account. An indication of the level of light transmission a lens has is shown by the **transmittance factor**, which is always less than 100%.

This is why many professionals prefer to use T-numbers instead of F-numbers.

The definition of a T-number takes the F-stop and the lens transmittance into account:

$$\text{T-number} = 10 \cdot \text{F-number/SQRT(Transmittance)} \tag{31}$$

where SQRT means square root. Since the transmittance of a lens is, as mentioned, always less than 100% (usually 95 to 99%), it is obvious that the T-number will be a bit higher than the F-number.

For example, if a 16 mm/1.4 lens has a transmittance of 96%, the T-number will be equal to 1.43.

Depth of field

When a lens is focused on an object, theoretically, the whole plane passing through the object and perpendicular to the optical axis should be in focus.

Practically, objects slightly in front of and behind the object in focus will also appear sharp. This "extra" depth of sharpness is called **depth of field**.

A wide depth of field might be an undesired feature, like in photography, for example, when we want an object we are taking a picture of to be isolated from the foreground and the background. This is very characteristic when taking portrait shots with a telephoto lens, where the depth of field is very narrow.

In CCTV, however, we often want the opposite effect. We want to have as many objects in focus as possible, no matter where the real focusing plane is.

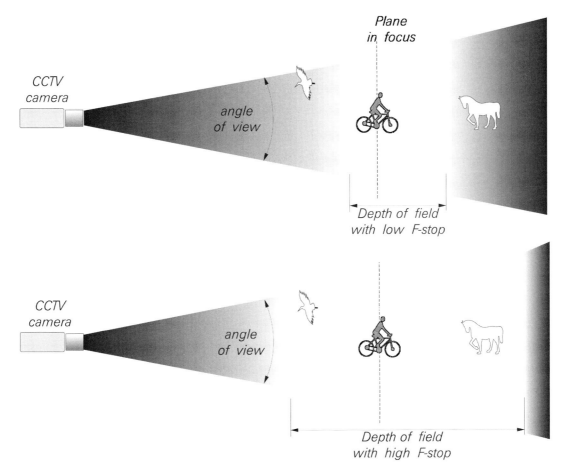

Depth of field with various F-stops

The depth of field depends on the focal length of the lens, the F-stop, and the format size of the lens (2/3", 1/2", etc.). A general rule is **the shorter the focal length, the wider the depth of field; the higher the F-stop the wider the depth of field and the smaller the lens format, the wider the depth of field.**

The depth of field effect is explained by the so-called **permissible circles of confusion**.

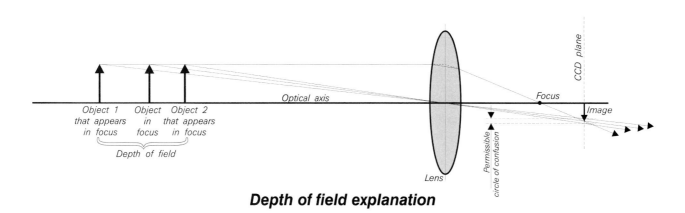

Depth of field explanation

The permissible circle of confusion is a projected circle of the depth of field area. If the smallest picture element (pixel) of the CCD chip is equal to or bigger than the permissible circle of confusion, then it is obvious that we cannot see details smaller than that circle. In other words, all objects and their details that appear within the circle will look equally sharp, since that is the actual size of the pixels. From this it is clear that the size of the permissible circles of confusion for a CCTV camera is determined by the pixel size of the CCD chip, in other words, the chip resolution.

It may now be understood why some short focal length lenses in CCTV, like 2.6 or 3.5 mm, **do not have a focusing ring** at all but only an iris adjustment. This is because even with the lowest F-stop for that lens (be it 1.4 or 1.8) the depth of field is so wide that it actually shows sharp images from a couple of centimeters in front of the lens up to infinity. There is literally no need for focusing.

Photos courtesy of Canon

**Photos with a low F-stop and a high F-stop
(lens focused on the central object)**

As shall be explained later in the book, the depth of field is an effect of which we should be very aware, especially when adjusting the so-called back-focus. If the back-focus is not adjusted properly and a camera is installed at daylight (that is, when the auto iris of the lens closes the iris as much as possible, due to excessive light), the depth of field will produce sharpness even in areas that are not really in focus.

Practical experience shows that depth of field applied in this way (when the back-focus isn't done correctly) is the biggest source of frustration for a 24-hour operating system. The reason is obvious: at night, when the iris opens due to a low light level (providing the AI functions properly), the depth of field narrows down and shows the images out of focus even if they were in focus during the day. When an operator complains to the installer or service people, not knowing the cause of such a problem, he or she usually gets the service to visit during the daytime. Obviously, the problem will not be there then, thanks to a wide depth of field that reappears "inexplicably" at nighttime.

The moral of the above is that the back-focus adjustment (discussed later in the book) should be done when the iris is fully opened. The easiest way to have the iris opened is when low light levels reach it, either at the end of the day (or at night), or by artificially reducing the daylight with external neutral density filters (usually placed in front of the lens objective). All this is in order to reduce the depth of field and consequently make back-focus adjustment easier and more accurate.

Quite often, when B/W cameras with infrared lights are used, another effect is present. Due to the extremely long wavelength of the infrared light (compared to normal light), and the lesser angle of refraction, we get the focused image plane slightly behind the CCD chip. Refer to the **prism light decomposition** section for further explanation of this phenomenon. If an image is sharp at day, then at nighttime objects of the same distance will be out of focus. This might be a quite noticeable and unwanted effect. In order to minimize it, it needs a lens designed with a special compensation for infra-red viewing (some manufacturers have special glass lenses for this purpose). However, a more practical and common solution would be to have the camera back-focused at night with an infrared light on, in which case the depth of field is minimal but the objects are in focus. At day, the depth of field will increase the sharpness to a wider area, compensating for the difference between the infrared and the normal light focus.

Neutral Density (ND) filters

Earlier, when F-stops were discussed, we mentioned some F-numbers – 1.4, 2, 2.8, 4, 5.6, 8, 11, 16, 22, 32, and so on. This list continues – 44, 64, 88, 128, etc. The higher the F-number is the smaller the iris opening is, we said.

For photographic or movie film, F/32 is considered quite a high number. The sensitivity of the film emulsion is such that even on the sunniest days, this F-stop, combined with the available shutter speed, is enough to compensate for the excessive light.

Film sensitivity is measured in ISO units, and the most common film we use for everyday purposes has a 100 ISO units' sensitivity.

CCD chips are much more sensitive than a 100 ISO film. Especially the B/W cips. Starting from known light levels, the F-stop and shutter speed of a photographic camera, the typical electronic exposure time of a TV camera (1/50 second for CCIR) and the iris setting, we can calculate that a B/W CCD chip's sensitivity is somewhere close to the 100,000 ISO units mark. This is quite a high sensitivity.

Translated into everyday language, this means that CCD chips are so sensitive that the low light level situation is not really a problem (although you would have a lot of customers asking you "How sensitive is your camera?"), but rather the strong light.

Since television cameras use one exposure speed only, 1/50 second in CCIR and SECAM, and 1/60 in NTSC (not considering the CCD-iris cameras), we can only manipulate the F-stop to reduce the amount of light.

An average B/W CCD chip requires 0.1 lx at the chip to produce a full video signal. A bright sunny day at the beach, or on the snow, produces more than 100,000 lx at the object. To reduce this to 0.1 lx, very high F-stops, in the order of up to F/1200, need to be used. Using the basic definition for F-stop, for an average 16 mm/1.4 lens, we'll get F/1200 to be an effective iris opening of 16/1200 = 0.013 mm.

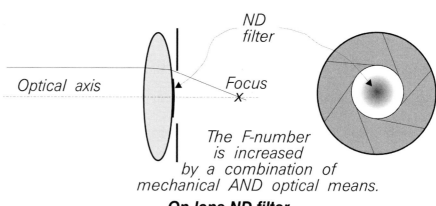

On-lens ND filter

Mechanically, this is impossible to produce due to the very small size and precision required, but also because with such a small iris we would introduce new problems such as edge diffraction of light (known as the Fresnel effect), which will affect the picture quality.

The solution was found in the use of **internal neutral density ND filters**.

These are very thin films of circular, neutral color coatings, positioned in the middle of the lens, close to the iris plane. The filters get less transparent towards the middle of the concentric circles. The F-stop is thus achieved by a combination of the mechanical iris (leaves) and the optical ND filter (optical attenuation). This is a very simple and efficient way of battling strong light. The filters are called neutral because they attenuate all wavelengths (colors) evenly, therefore not changing the color composition of the image.

It should be noted that the optical precision of such thin films is very important in order to preserve the lens's MTF characteristics as the F-stop increases. Theoretically, the resolving power of any lens is best in the middle of the mechanical iris setting, and it reduces as the F-stop goes lower or higher (this is different to the depth of field effect), but the ND filters may reduce it even further. Whether this will be obvious or not depends on the quality of the lens in general.

ND film filters in an auto iris lens

Apart from the internal ND filters, there are also **external ND filters,** which are not so sophisticated. These are just precise semitransparent pieces of glass, or optical filters if you like, that attenuate the light × number of times. This may be 10, 100 or 1000 times. Two or three of these can be combined, so, for example, 10 with 1000 times will result in an ND filter with 10,000 times attenuation.

Sometimes, and probably more correctly, the attenuation of the external ND filters is expressed in F-stops. Knowing that every next F-stop will divide the light gathering ability by 2 (50% of the previous number) we can establish the following logic: 100 times ND filter is divided by 100, which is halfway between 2^6 and 2^7 ($2^6 = 64$, $2^7 = 128$). This means 100 times attenuation is approximately 6.5 F-stops. One thousand times attenuation is close to 2^{10}, which means approximately 10 F-stops.

These types of ND filters are very handy, as already explained, for minimizing the depth of field for the purposes of back-focus adjustments or AI level adjustments during the daytime.

Manual, Auto and Motorized Iris lenses

Manual iris (MI) lenses adjusts the iris manually, i.e., by hand. These lenses are very common in areas with constant light, such as shopping centers, underground car parks, libraries, etc. Basically, these are areas where natural light does not interfere noticeably with the ambient, and therefore we have almost constant artificial light. Eventual small variations are compensated by the camera's automatic gain control (AGC).

With the introduction of the CCD-iris cameras, though, fixed iris lenses are used in light varying areas as well, since the CCD electronic iris adjusts the exposure time, compensating for the light variations.

There are two major factors that decide at what F-stop (iris) a manual iris lens should be set for optimum performance:

- Light intensity

- Depth of field.

They contradict each other and that is why MI settings are always a compromise. When using it in very low light level situations, or when using not so sensitive cameras, the general tendency would be to open the iris (low F-number) as much as possible. Obviously, in such cases the depth of field, as well as the MTF, as explained previously, would be minimal. We should not forget that apart from the depth, the lens resolution at the lowest F-stop is usually the poorest. A compromise is often the best solution (if the camera's minimum illumination characteristic allows for it), and the lens is set to one or two F-stops higher than the lowest, e.g., F-2, F-2.8.

Manual iris fixed focal length lenses

Auto iris (AI) lenses have electronic circuitry that processes the video signal coming out of the camera and decides, on the basis of the video signal level, whether the iris should open or close.

Auto iris works as automatic electronic-optical feedback. If the video signal is low the electronics tells the iris to open and if it is too high it tells it to close.

In order to do this, the AI lens **takes power from the camera** (usually 9 V DC), **as well as the video signal** and references the electronics of the lens and the camera with a third common wire (called zero, negative or common). Quite often, you'd find lenses with shielding as well. This is to protect the video signal wire from strong external electromagnetic interference. Usually, this wire does not have to be connected to the camera body, because the connection is already made with the lens's metal ring when fitted on the camera. By keeping the AI cable as short as possible the amount of unwanted interference induced in the video signal is minimal. This goes hand in hand with the ever decreasing

A typical video-driven auto iris lens wiring

camera size. Be aware though, of plastic C/CS-mount adaptors that will not common the lens case with the camera's body.

Photo courtesy of Cosmicar (Asahi Precision Co.Ltd.)

Auto iris fixed focal length lenses

Following are some color codes for the AI wires that are widely accepted in the industry:

- Black is usually used for common,

- Red for power (derived from the camera), and

- White for video.

Some manufacturers, in order to lower manufacturing costs, have started using two wire AI cables (red-power and white-video) with a shielding used as the common wire.

Often, lenses with four wire cables can be found, where the fourth wire is usually green. In most cases this is an unused wire, but in some lenses it offers remote control of the iris, usually known as **motorized iris** (MRI) control. When such control is wanted, the iris opens and closes as instructed by the voltage from a site driver (controlled by an operator), much in the same way as zoom and focus are controlled.

The latter type of lens is the preferred one in systems with CCD-iris cameras. The reason for this is that CCD-iris and auto iris do not work well together. If the two of them are enabled, the electronic iris usually works faster, and by the time the mechanical auto iris responds to the light fluctuations, the electronic iris has already reduced the shutter exposure, forcing the auto iris to open more. The end result is a widely opened iris and a very short electronic exposure. This gives a 1 V_{pp} output signal as is expected, but the **depth of field is minimal and vertical smearing is more noticeable**, because of the very short exposure of the CCD chip.

Because of this, when auto iris lenses are used, it is suggested the CCD-iris be switched off. The electronic iris is, however, quicker and more reliable since there are no moving parts (only electronics), although it **does not control the depth of field.**

So, to gain the benefits of both, motorized iris lenses are now recommended with CCD-iris cameras. This can obviously be done only if a site driver with an iris control is used. In such systems, operators can adjust the iris according to the light level situation and required depth of field, but only when drastic light changes occur.

The current consumption of the AI circuitry is usually below 30 mA and it doesn't represent any noticeable load on the camera power supply. Be aware though, as mentioned earlier, older lenses (especially bigger zoom lenses) may demand more current drive, in which case (if a camera output current is not sufficient), a separate 9 V DC power supply has to be used for the auto iris electronics inside the lens.

Video- and DC-driven auto iris lenses

The division of lenses gets a bit more confusing in respect to the processing circuitry when auto iris lenses are in question. Namely, apart from the "normal" AI lenses we have in the majority of cases, where the electronics are built inside the lens itself and which we call **video-driven AI** lenses (since they require a video signal from the camera), we can also find so-called **DC-driven AI** lenses. These lenses are similar to the video-driven ones, only that **the processing electronics are not inside the lens but rather inside the camera.** The lens, in that case, has only the motor and the iris mechanism. Clearly, when DC-driven lenses are used, the camera has to be designed to have such an output. Instead of having power, video and common wires, we will have power, DC level and common connection. Often, these type of lenses are called Galvanometric auto iris lenses.

A DC-driven lens cannot be used on a camera that hasn't got that type of connector, and vice versa. If a camera has a DC auto iris connector, you would usually find level and ALC adjustments (explained in the following paragraphs) on the camera itself, instead of their being on the lens.

AI lenses, both fixed and zoom, have two potentiometers for adjusting the response and type of operation: **level** and **ALC**. This also applies to DC-driven lenses, only in that case, as mentioned above, the settings are on the camera itself.

Level adjusts the iris opening on the basis of the average level of the signal. The level is also known as sensitivity adjustment because of its appearance on the monitor screen as brightness variation of the object. When the level potentiometer is adjusted, daily and nightly iris operation should be checked. If the working point is shifted too high, the picture may look OK at day, but very dark at night. The opposite is also true: if the working point is shifted too low, it may be acceptable at night but too bright at daylight. To make sure that this doesn't happen, the best

ALC and Level pots

adjustment is achieved in the late afternoon with a little help from a torch. First, make sure the picture is as good at low light as it can be, i.e., iris fully opened. Then, shine the torch at the lens and see if the iris closes sufficiently to see the torch filament only.

If tests cannot be conducted in the late afternoon, the alternative would be to use some external ND filters. These filters can be selected to attenuate the daylight to the level equivalent to a low light level situation, which is usually a couple of luxes. Then, instead of using a torch, all it requires is to remove the ND filters and see whether and how the iris reacts.

ALC stands for automatic light compensation. **The ALC is a photometric adjustment of the iris and it should be thought of as "automatic backlight compensation."** The ALC part of the auto iris circuit decides on which portion of the video signal level the auto iris should react. ALC adjusts the video reference point for the iris operation depending on the picture contrast. In most cases, when the signal is "rich" with details from the darkest to the brightest (0 to 0.7 V), the reference level is in the middle. If very bright spots appear in the picture, they will participate in the calculation of the reference point and will force the auto iris to close to produce a video signal with "full dynamic" range. The visual appearance then will be a high contrast picture. So, very bright objects (like sun reflections, bright lights, windows and similar) will force the iris to close, making the dark objects even darker, sometimes too dark to distinguish any details. In situations like these we may change the ALC setting from the factory default to the extreme position to make the iris disregard the bright areas and open more than usual. This allows for the objects in shadow to be more distinguishable.

This adjustment is equivalent to the backlight compensation found in many camcorders. The backlight compensation is used, as the name suggests, to fight against the backlight. The idea is to tell the lens electronics to disregard the very bright areas of the image and open the iris more in order to see details of the darker objects in the foreground.

This is very useful when positioning the camera in hallways, for example, looking through glass doors and against a bright background. If a person walks in the hallway he or she would be a silhouette. When the ALC is adjusted, the iris can be forced to open by one or two F-stops more, thus brightening the face of the person. Similarly, the ALC can be adjusted to do the opposite job, i.e., close the iris more than it should in order to see details of the very bright background, like through the hallway door.

The ALC setting has two ends marked as Peak and Average. The first example above would correspond to Peak setting, while the second to the Average setting. Factory defaults are usually in the middle of these two positions. Please note that, in order to see the effects of the ALC adjustments, a very high-contrast scene is needed.

A few words about AI lens electronics

As the optics quality of a lens cannot be taken for granted, neither should the electronics of an auto iris lens. Different circuit designs offer different quality and precision of operation. This, combined with the mechanical construction of the iris shutter, determines whether a lens is good, average or bad. The responsiveness of the iris to abrupt light changes is not instant and ranges anywhere from half a second to two seconds. This needs to be taken into account when adjusting level and/or ALC settings on a

A disassembled fixed auto iris lens

lens. The delay depends on the feedback, i.e., the electronic and mechanical combination. The electronics have automatic gain control (AGC), but how effectively this combination works depends also on the camera's electronics, including the AGC.

The combination of the two could be such that they may produce oscillation in the auto iris operation, which is usually called "ringing" or "hunting." The ringing appears as a pulsating picture, depending on the camera viewing direction and light conditions. It is especially common when looking against strong light. To minimize it, usually, level adjustment is sufficient, and sometimes ALC or both. There are unfortunate camera/lens combinations, however, where ringing cannot be eliminated. The solution is usually found in replacing the lens with that of another brand. Some newer auto iris lenses come with an additional potentiometer for adjusting the level of the lens's AGC.

As mentioned earlier, the auto iris lens cable is usually protected with a shielding that is often not connected to the auto iris. The shielding's purpose is to protect the video signal wire from picking up noise. In order for it to be effective, it is sufficient for one end of the shielding to be connected to the common of the signal electronics, which happens to be done through the lens body (the C- or CS-mount ring) and the camera C-mount thread. With camera miniaturization, the cables are getting shorter, further minimizing the risk of unwanted external noise interfering with the operation.

Finally, let's remember that the AI current consumption is very low, usually below 30 mA.

A fixed auto iris lens

Image and lens formats in CCTV

A lens sees objects with the same angle of vision in all directions, i.e., the angle of vision has a conical shape. Therefore, the image area projected by a lens has a circular shape, but the camera's sensitive area (CCD chip in our case) is a rectangle **within** the imaging circle.

In today's television, this rectangle is with the **aspect ratio of 4:3**, i.e., the standard is 4 units in width by 3 units in height. As mentioned at the beginning of the book, this aspect was adopted for the film format in the early days of television.

The all-new high-definition television (HDTV) system, which is already accepted with its basic standard, has an aspect ratio of 16:9. This is with the idea of having better movie presentations.

The "imaging rectangles" are within the image circles, which have all (or at least the majority) of the aberrations corrected.

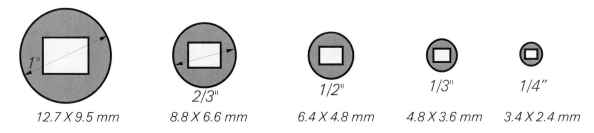

1"	2/3"	1/2"	1/3"	1/4"
12.7 X 9.5 mm	8.8 X 6.6 mm	6.4 X 4.8 mm	4.8 X 3.6 mm	3.4 X 2.4 mm

Actual sizes of the image area in CCD chips

There is no point in making a lens that produces a much bigger image circle than is required. Therefore, the lenses are made to suit the image format, no less and no more. There are exceptions, like when lenses made for other purposes, photography, for example, are used on a CCTV camera with a special C-mount adaptor.

Today in CCTV, we have quite a few different chip sizes: 2/3", 1/2", 1/3" and 1/4". High-definition cameras and some special application cameras may have 1" or even larger chip sizes. In order to understand this variety, we should know a little bit of the history of TV.

The very first TV cameras used imaging tubes of a certain diameter, and were referred to as 1" Vidicon or perhaps 2/3" Newvicon cameras. **These dimensions referred to the actual diameter of the imaging tube.** The imaging area is a rectangle with a 4:3 aspect ratio, and this rectangle has a diagonal that is **smaller** than the actual tube diameter mainly because of the tube photo-sensitive area (called **target**). When the electron beam scans the imaging area, it does not go to the edges of the tube. Therefore, a 2/3" tube camera has an imaging area, scanned by the electron beam, of approximately 8.8 × 6.6 mm. This area gives a diagonal length of approximately 11 mm. **This is not equal to 2/3", which, converted into millimeters, is 17 mm.** So, don't think that the CCD chip measurements are as with TV screens, where CRT size is expressed with its diagonal.

When we say 2/3" CCD chip, we are really referring to a device that has an imaging area equal to what a 2/3" tube would have.

When the first CCTV CCD cameras were made, the common tube size was 2/3". The image area of such tubes, as mentioned previously, was 8.8 × 6.6 mm, so the CCD chips designed in those days were of the same imaging area size and they were called 2/3" chips. The idea was to use the same lenses as tube cameras did.

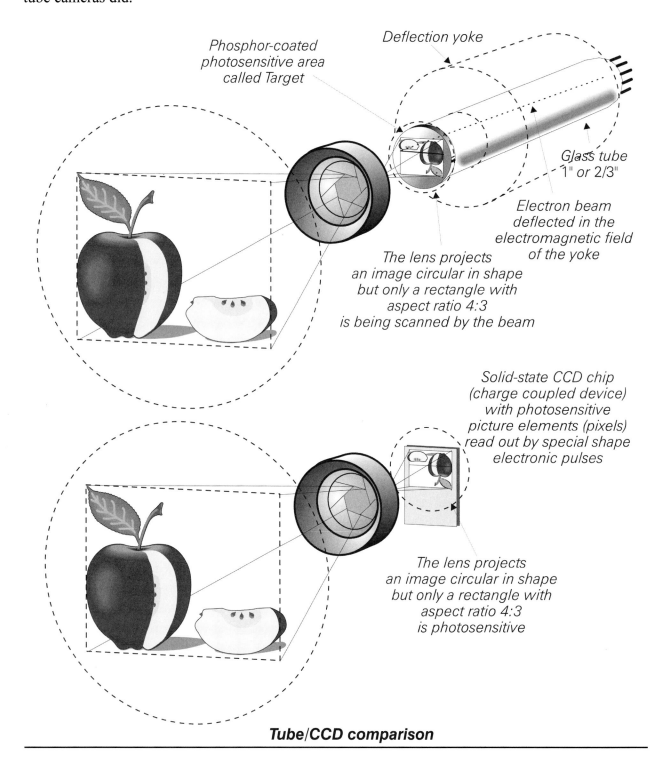

Phosphor-coated photosensitive area called Target

Deflection yoke

Glass tube 1" or 2/3"

Electron beam deflected in the electromagnetic field of the yoke

The lens projects an image circular in shape but only a rectangle with aspect ratio 4:3 is being scanned by the beam

Solid-state CCD chip (charge coupled device) with photosensitive picture elements (pixels) read out by special shape electronic pulses

The lens projects an image circular in shape but only a rectangle with aspect ratio 4:3 is photosensitive

Tube/CCD comparison

With the evolution of technology, CCDs were getting smaller, and the new chip size called 1/2" measured an imaging area of only 6.4 × 4.8 mm. The compatibility with the 2/3" lenses was preserved (using the same C-mount), but of course, the angle of view changed, i.e., it got smaller compared to when the same type of lens was used on a 2/3" camera.

So, new lenses were designed for the 1/2" chips, which did not project as big an image as with 2/3" chips. In other words, due to this reduction of the imaging area, lenses were designed to have the desired focal length but with a smaller imaging circle projected, i.e., a circle with a diameter sufficient to cover a 1/2" chip, but not necessarily 2/3". These new type of lenses are called 1/2" lenses. They still have the C-mount ring, but they are smaller, and consequently cheaper, than their 2/3" counterparts.

The same development is now happening with 1/3" chips, where 1/3" lenses are made to produce an image circle sufficient in diameter to cover only the 1/3" chips.

An obvious problem that will occur if a 1/3" lens is used on a 1/2" chip is that the image corners will be cut off (imagine a rectangle and a circle with a smaller diameter drawn inside).

The same applies when a 1/2" lens is used on a 2/3" chip. There is no problem, however, if a bigger lens is used on a smaller chip. Since a lens of a bigger format will project an image circle much larger than the actual chip size, there will be no corners cut off or any other deformation.

It should be taken into consideration, though, that the reduction in the imaging pickup area may result in a relative resolution reduction, since a smaller area is used (see the discussion on MTF and CTF). In addition, the excessive light around the chip (when a larger format lens is used) may get reflected inside the lens and CCD block, so if there are surfaces that are insufficiently neutralized with a black matt finish, the usable image will be affected.

Angles of view and how to determine them

Different focal length lenses give different angles of view.

We quite often use the horizontal angle of view as a reference since the vertical can be found from it, knowing that the video signal aspect ratio is 4:3 and the same applies to the horizontal vs. vertical angle of view.

There are some very basic rules to follow when analyzing the angles of view:

- The shorter the focal length, the wider the angle of view is.

- The longer the focal length, the narrower the angle of view is.

- The smaller the CCD chip, the narrower the angle of view (with the same lens) is.

- The vertical angle of view can be easily determined if the horizontal is known.

As mentioned earlier, **approximately 30° is considered a standard angle of view for whatever size the image format is**. Just to refresh our memory, 30° is taken as standard because it corresponds to our perspective impression and what the human eye sees as normal.

The following are image formats with their corresponding standard lenses for a 30° horizontal angle of view:

$$1" \quad = 25 \text{ mm}$$

$$2/3" = 16 \text{ mm}$$

$$1/2" = 12 \text{ mm}$$

$$1/3" = 8 \text{ mm}$$

$$1/4" = 6 \text{ mm}$$

In CCTV, the widest angle of view that manufacturers offer is approximately 94°, which is achieved with 4.8 mm for a 2/3" CCD camera, 3.5 mm for a 1/2" and 2.8 mm for a 1/3".

There are some unique "fish-eye" lenses offering almost a 180° angle of view, but these are very specialized and show only a circular (thus the name "fish-eye") image on the screen (within the CCD chip image area).

Lenses do come in discrete values, i.e., one cannot order any value one wants, like 5.8 mm or 14 mm, for example. So it is useful to know the most common focal length lenses:

2.6 mm, 3.5 mm, 4.8 mm, 6 mm, 8 mm, 12 mm, 16 mm, 25 mm, 50 mm and 75 mm.

You may find some manufacturers have 3.7 mm instead of 3.5 mm, or 5.6 mm instead of 6 mm, but the values are very close and there is practically no difference in the angle of view.

The above values have horizontal angles of view that differ, more or less, in steps of 10°-15° from one to the next. These are quite sufficient to cover all practical situations, but should you really require a special focal length that is not listed above, inquire at your supplier as some manufacturers do have manually variable-focus lenses (both MI and AI) where the focal length can be varied from 6-12 mm or perhaps from 8-16 mm. The optical quality of such lenses, though, is not as good as that of fixed lenses, due to the limited precision and simplicity of the moving mechanics. But again, the quality in most cases goes with the price.

What focal length lens for a particular application? This is probably the most commonly asked question when designing a CCTV system. There are many techniques used to determine the angles of coverage, and which one you are going to use is entirely up to you, as long as the result is what your customer will be happy with.

Here is a listing of all practical methods. These are:

- Viewfinder calculator. This is usually a circular shaped calculator, supplied by the lens manufacturers (ask your supplier for one), where, in order to find the lens, three things need to be known: the CCD chip size, the distance between the camera and the object and the width of the object. By adjusting these few things the calculator should give you the focal length in mm. There are also ruler-shaped calculators with the same concept.

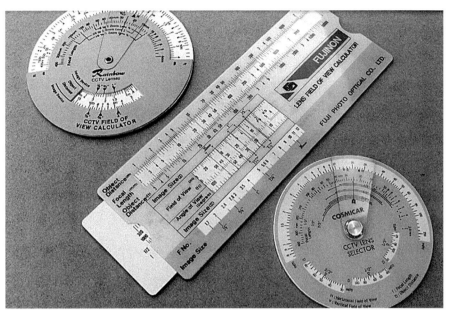

Various lens calculators

- Optical viewfinder. This is a device that looks like a zoom lens, but it's used not on a camera but by eye. When you are on site, you can manually zoom in and out and set the view to what your customer requires. A scale indicator on the viewfinder shows the focal length of the lens that will give you the same view on the particular type of camera (2/3", 1/2" or 1/3"). In order to see the same view that the camera would see, you have to position yourself close to where the camera would be installed. One little drawback with this instrument is that you cannot see the very wide angles, i.e., most of the optical viewfinders only show focal lengths down to 6 mm.

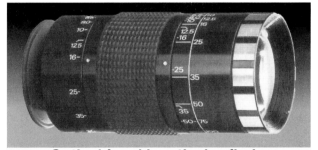

Optical focal length viewfinder

- Camcorder with a zoom lens. This is quite a simple and practical method, especially these days when we have such a huge choice of camcorders with built-in zoom lenses. We need to know the chip size in the camcorder in order to refer to the same size CCTV camera, or substitute it accordingly. Obviously, it is good to have a camcorder with a wide range of zooming, but more importantly the lens should have an indicator of each focal length at its corresponding position. When we go on site, we have the added advantage of showing our customer what the options are, and we can record and document what he or she chooses.

- **Using a simple formula**.   This seems the most complicated way of determining angles of view, but it is actually the simplest. This formula uses the similarity of triangles, as shown in the figure below. It is easy to understand and therefore it can be easily produced whenever necessary. The only thing you need to memorize are the CCD chip widths of the most commonly used cameras: 6.4 mm for 1/2", 4.8 mm for 1/3" and 3.4 mm for a 1/4" chip.

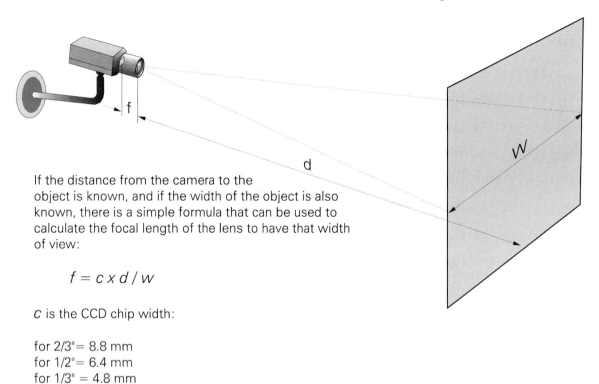

If the distance from the camera to the object is known, and if the width of the object is also known, there is a simple formula that can be used to calculate the focal length of the lens to have that width of view:

$$f = c \times d / w$$

c is the CCD chip width:

for 2/3" = 8.8 mm
for 1/2" = 6.4 mm
for 1/3" = 4.8 mm
for 1/4" = 3.2 mm

A simple "lens-find" formula worth remembering

This formula gives you the focal length of the lens directly into millimeters.

$$f = c_{CCD} \cdot d/w_{object} \tag{32}$$

where f is the lens focal length we are looking for (in mm), c_{CCD} is the CCD chip width (in mm), d is the distance from the camera to the object (in meters) and w_{object} is the width of the object we wish to view (in meters).

The same formula can be used if we want to find what focal length lens we need, to see a certain object's height, in which case instead of w_{CCD} and w_{object} we will be working with h_{CCD} and h_{object}, where h stands for height.

- **Using a more complicated formula**. This formula gives the resulting angle of view in **degrees**. It is based on elementary trigonometry and requires a scientific calculator or trigonometric tables.

$$\alpha = 2 \cdot arctan \, (w_{object}/2d) \tag{33}$$

where α is the angle of view (in degrees), **arctan** is an inverse **tangent** trigonometric function (you need a scientific calculator for this), which is sometimes written as **tan^{-1}**, w_{object} is the object width (in meters) and d is the distance to the object the camera is looking at.

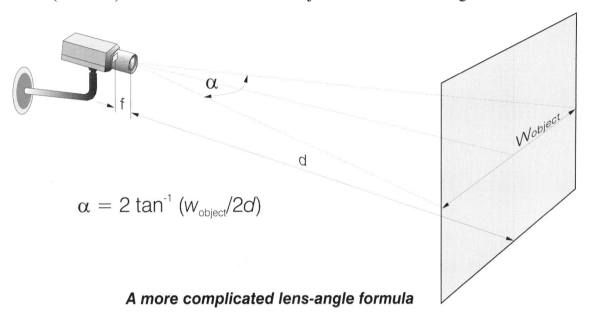

$$\alpha = 2\tan^{-1}(w_{object}/2d)$$

A more complicated lens-angle formula

- **Using a table and/or graph.** Easy to use, but always requires a table or graph to be handy.

Approximate horizontal angles of view with various CCD chip sizes (in degrees)				
Focal length	2/3"	1/2"	1/3"	1/4"
2.0mm	-	-	-	82
2.8mm	-	-	86	57
4.0mm	-	77	67	47
4.8mm	83	67	57	40
6.0mm	70	56	48	32
8.0mm	56	44	36	25
12mm	39	30	25	17
16mm	30	23	17	13
25mm	18	15	12	8
50mm	10	7	6	4

This table gives only the horizontal angle of view for a given lens, as this is most commonly required. Vertical angles are easily found by applying the aspect ratio rule, i.e., divide the horizontal angle by 4 and then multiply it by 3.

In all of the above methods, we have to take into account monitor overscanning as well. In other words, most monitors don't show 100% of what the camera sees. Usually, 10% of the picture is hidden by the overscanning by the monitors. The viewfinder calculator may allow for this 10%.

Some professional monitors offer the underscanning feature. If you get hold of such a monitor, you can use it to determine the amount of overscanning by the normal monitor. This is very important to know when performing camera resolution tests, as will be described later.

Fixed focal length lenses

There are two basic types of lenses (in respect to focal length) used in CCTV: **fixed focal length** and **variable focal length** (often called **zoom**) lenses.

Fixed focal length lenses, as the name suggests, are designed with a fixed focal length, i.e., giving only one angle of view. Such lenses are usually designed to have minimum aberrations and maximum resolution, so there are not many moving optical parts, except the focusing group.

The quality of a lens depends on many factors, of which the most important are the materials used (the type of glass, mechanical assembly, gears, etc.), the processing technology and the design itself.

When manufacturers produce a certain type of lens, they have in mind its application and use. The lens quality aimed for is dictated by the practical and market requirements. As mentioned previously, when MTF&CTF were discussed, there is no need to go to the technical limits of precision and quality (and consequently increase the cost) if that cannot be seen by the imaging device (CCD chips in this case). This, however, doesn't mean that there is no difference among different makes and models of the same focal length. Usually, the price goes hand in hand with the quality.

A manual iris and an auto iris lens

More than two decades ago, when 1" tube cameras were used, 25-mm lenses offered a normal angle of view (approximately 30° horizontal angle).

With the evolution of the formats, i.e., with their reduction, the focal length for the normal angle of view was reduced too. The mounting thread, however, for compatibility purposes, remained the same.

With the C-mount format this thread was defined as **1"-32UN-2A**, which means it is **1" in diameter with 32 threads/inch**. When the new and smaller CS format was introduced, the same thread was again kept for compatibility, although the back-flange distance was changed. This will be explained later in this chapter.

In respect to the iris there are two major groups of fixed focal length lenses: manual iris (MI) and automatic iris lenses (AI), and these were described under the previous heading.

C-mount thread

Finally, let's mention the Vari-Focal group of lenses. These lenses should be classified as fixed focal length lenses, since once they are manually set to certain angle of view (focal length) they have to be re-focused, unlike zoom lenses, which once focused, stay in focus if the angle of view is changed.

Zoom lenses

In the very early days of television, when a cameraman needed a different focal length lens, he would use a specially designed barrel, fitted with a number of fixed lenses that rotated in front of the camera. Different focal lengths were selected from this group of fixed lenses.

This concept, although practical compared to manually changing the lenses, lacked continuity of length selection, and more importantly, optical blanking was unavoidable when a selection was being made.

That is why optical engineers had to come up with a design for a continuous focal length variation mechanism, which got the popular name **zoom**. The zoom lens concept lies in the simultaneous

Photo courtesy of Cosmicar (Asahi Precision Co.Ltd.)
Zoom lenses

movement of a few group's of lenses. The movement path is obviously along the optical axis but with an optically precise and **nonlinear correlation**. This makes not only the optical, but also the mechanical design very complicated and sensitive. It has, however, been accomplished and as we all know today, zoom lenses are very popular and practical in both CCTV and broadcast television.

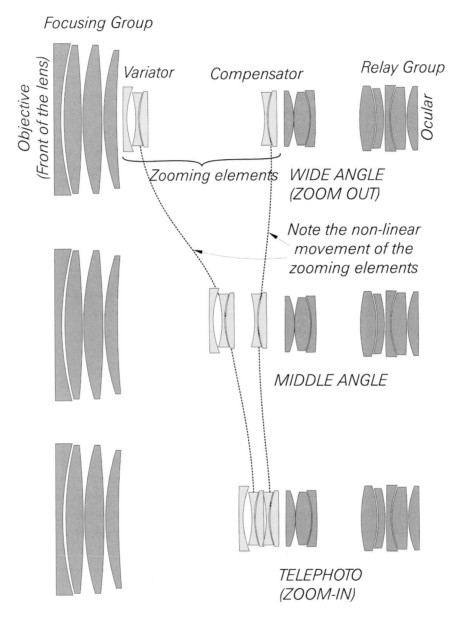

**Zoom lenses have a complex but very precise movement
of their optical elements**

With a special **barrel cam mechanism**, usually two groups of lenses (one called **variator** and the other **compensator**) are moved in relation to each other so that the zooming effect is achieved **while preserving the focus** at an object. As you can imagine, the mechanical precision and durability of the moving parts are especially important for a successful zooming function.

For many perfectionists in photography, zoom lenses will never be as good as fixed ones. In the absolute sense of the word this is very true, because the moving parts of a zoom lens must always have some tolerance in its mechanical manufacture, which introduces more aberrations than what a fixed lens design has. Hence, the absolute optical quality of a certain focal length setting in a zoom lens can never be as good as a well-designed fixed lens of the same focal length.

For CCTV applications, however, where the CCD chip resolution is nowhere near a film structure, compromises are possible with good results. Continuous variation of angles of views, without the need to physically swap lenses, is extremely useful and practical. This is especially the case where cameras are mounted in fixed locations (like on a pole or on top of a building) and resolution requirements are not as high as with film cameras.

It should not be assumed, however, that in their evolution zoom lenses will not come very close to the optical quality of the fixed ones.

Zoom lenses are usually represented by their **zoom ratio**. This is the ratio of the focal length at the telephoto end of the zoom and the focal length at the wide angle end. Usually, the telephoto angle is narrower than the standard angle of vision, and the wide angle is wider than the standard angle of vision. Since the telephoto end always has a longer focal length than the wide angle, the ratio is a number larger than one.

The most popular zoom lenses used in CCTV are:

-6×: Six times, with 6-36 mm, 8-48 mm, 8.5-51 mm and 12.5-75 mm being the most common.

-10×: Ten times, with 6-60 mm, 8-80 mm, 10-100 mm, 11-110 mm and 16-160 mm as the most common examples.

-15×: Fifteen times, with 6-90 mm, 8-120 mm.

Other ratios are available, such as 20×, or even 44× and 55×, but they are much more expensive and, therefore, not so common.

Zoom lenses are also characterized by their F-stop (or T-number). The F-stop, in zoom lenses (as already mentioned when F-numbers were discussed), refers to the shortest focal length. For example, for a 8-80 mm /1.8 lens the F/1.8 refers to the 8 mm. The F-stop is not constant throughout the zoom range. It usually stays the same with the increase of focal length only until a certain focal length is reached, after which a so-called **F-drop** occurs. The focal length at which this F-drop occurs depends on the lens construction. The general rule, however, is the smaller the entrance lens is the higher the likelihood of an F-drop. This is one of the main reasons why lenses with bigger zoom have to have bigger front lens elements (called **objective**), where the intention is to have a minimal F-drop.

Zoom lenses, like fixed ones, come with manual iris, automatic iris or motorized iris. Even though AI was explained in the previous section with fixed lenses, and because there is an additional and common subgroup with motorized iris, we'll go through this again.

A manual iris zoom lens would have an iris ring which is set manually by the installer, or by the user. This is a very rare type of lens in CCTV and it is used in special situations, like when doing demonstrations or camera testing.

An automatic iris zoom lens, or often called auto iris (AI), is the most common type of zoom lens. These lenses have an electronic circuit inside, which acts as an electronic-optical feedback. It is usually connected to the back of the camera where it gets its power supply (9 V DC) and its video signal. The lens's electronics then analyze the video signal level and act accordingly: if the signal exceeds the video level of

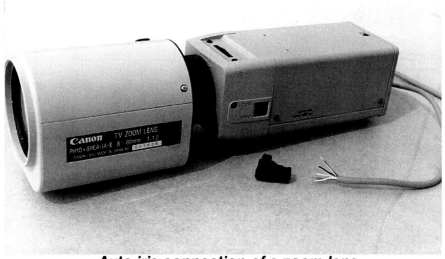

Auto iris connection of a zoom lens

0.7 V, the lens closes the iris until a 0.7 V signal is obtained from the camera AI terminal. If, however, the signal is very low, the iris opens in order to let more light in and consequently increases the video level.

Two adjustments are available for this type of lens (like with fixed lenses): **level** and **ALC**.

Level, as the name indicates, adjusts the reference level of the video signal that is used by the electronics of the lens in order to open or close the iris. This affects the brightness of the video signal. If it is not adjusted properly, i.e., adequately sensitive for daylight and low-light situations, a big discrepancy between the day and night video signals will occur. Obviously, the camera sensitivity has to be taken into account when adjusting the iris level for low light level situations.

ALC adjustment refers to the automatic light compensation of the iris. This is in fact very similar to the back light compensation (BLC) found in many camcorders (as we have already explained in the fixed lenses section). This light compensation is usually applied when looking at scenes with very high contrast. The idea behind BLC operation is to open the iris more (even if there is a lot of light in the background) **so as to see details of the objects in the foreground.** A typical example would

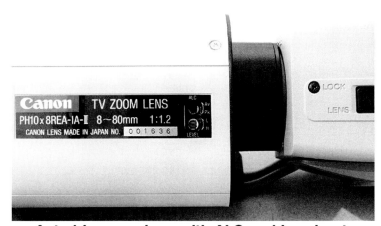

Auto iris zoom lens with ALC and Level pots

be when a camera is looking through a hallway (with a lot of light in the background) trying to see the face of a person coming towards the camera. With a normal lens setting the face of the person would appear very dark because the background light would cause the iris to close. A proper ALC setting could compensate for such difficult lighting conditions. The bright background in the example above will become white, but the foreground will show details. The ALC setting actually adjusts the reference level relative to the video signal average and peak values. This is why the marks on the ALC of a lens show Peak and Average.

One thing to remember is that, when adjusting the ALC, a very high contrast scene needs to be viewed by the camera. If the opposite (low contrast scene) is seen, no visible change of the video signal will occur. So, by tweaking the ALC pot in a scene with normal contrast, a misalignment may occur that will be visible only when the picture light changes.

All of the above mentioned refers to the majority of AI lenses, which are driven, as described, by the video signal picked up from the AI connector at the back of the camera. Because of this, and because there is another subgroup of AI zoom lenses that are not driven by the video signal taken from the camera, we also call this AI type **video-driven AI**.

The other subgroup of the AI group of lenses are the **DC-driven AI** zoom lenses.

The DC-driven AI lenses do not have all the electronics for video processing, only the motor that opens and closes the iris. **The whole processing, in DC-driven auto iris lenses, is done by the camera's AI electronic section.** The output from such a section is a DC voltage that opens and closes the iris leaves according to the video level taken from the inside of the camera. Cameras that have DC AI output, also have the Level and ALC adjustments, but in this case on the camera body and not on the lens.

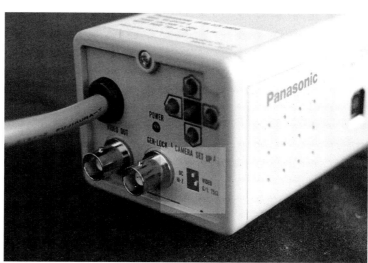

Some cameras can "drive" both types of AI lenses

It should be clearly noted that video-driven AI zoom lenses cannot be used with cameras that provide DC AI output, nor can DC AI be used with a video AI output camera. Some cameras can drive both these types of AI designs, in which case a switch or separate terminals are available for the two different outputs. Pay attention to this fact, as it can create problems which initially seem impossible to solve. In other words, make sure that both the camera and the lens are of the same type of AI operation.

The advantage of video-driven AI zoom lenses is that they will work with the majority of cameras. The advantage of DC-driven AI zoom lenses is that they are cheaper and are unlikely to have the "hunting" effect as the camera processes the gain. The disadvantage is that not all cameras have a DC-driven AI output. To date, video-driven AI lenses are more common.

Motorized iris lenses belong to the third lens subgroup, if selection on the basis of the iris function is made. This is an iris mechanism that can be controlled remotely and set by the operator according to the light conditions. This type of zoom lens has become increasingly popular in the last few years, especially with the development of CCD-iris cameras.

In order to open or close the iris, instead of an AI circuit driving the iris leaves, a DC voltage, produced by the PTZ site driver, controls the amount of opening or closing. PTZ site drivers will be explained later in the book, but to put it very simply they are boxes with electronics that are capable of receiving encoded digital data for the movement of the Pan/Tilt head as well as the zoom lens functions, and converting it into voltage that actually drives the PTZ assembly. In the case of motorized iris lenses, the PTZ site driver has to have an output to drive the iris as well.

With the CCD-iris camera it is better to have this type of lens iris control than an automatic one. Namely, the CCD-iris (electronic function of the CCD chip) is a faster and more reliable light controlling section of the camera but it **does not substitute the depth of field** effect produced by the high F-stops of an optical iris. **Optical and electronic irises, cannot function properly if working simultaneously**. The video camera usually balances with a low F-stop (high iris opening), which results in a very narrow depth of field, and a high electronic shutter speed, which produces a less efficient charge transfer, i.e., high smear. This is especially obvious when such a camera/lens combination comes across a high- contrast scene. To avoid a low-quality picture, and yet use the benefits of a fast and reliable CCD-iris function, and even more, have depth of field, motorized iris lenses are the solution. It will obviously require an operator's intervention, but that does not have to happen until the picture demands it, since the CCD-iris will be functioning constantly to compensate for the abrupt light variations.

When ordering zoom lenses, you are expected to specify whether you want a motorized iris lens; otherwise, the manufacturer may supply you with a standard video-driven AI zoom lens as they are the most common.

And finally, let's mention the **vari-focal** lenses again. Vari-focals do not have the same functionality as the zoom lenses. Their classification should be in the fixed focal lenses group. They **are** practical in cases where the customer doesn't know what angle of coverage he or she requires, but they have to always be manually re-focused once the angle of view (i.e., the focal length) is changed.

A note of warning: be more critical of the optical quality of vari-focal lenses. It is more difficult to produce the same optical resolution due to additional movement when compared to fixed focal lenses. Of course, there will be situations where vari-focals may have quite sufficient quality for the application, but trials will always give you a better judgement.

C- & CS-mount and Back-focus

Back-focusing is very important in CCTV.

"Back-focusing" is what we call the adjustment of the lens back flange relative to the CCD image plane.

Currently, there are two standards for the distance between the back-flange of a lens and the CCD image plane:

- **C-mount**, represented with 17.5 mm (more precisely, 17.526 mm).

This is a standard mounting, dating from the very early days of tube cameras. It consists of a metal ring with a 1.00/32-mm thread and a front surface area at 17.5 mm away from the image plane.

- **CS-mount**, represented with 12.5 mm.

This is a new standard intended for smaller camera and lens designs. It uses the **same thread** of 1.00/32 mm as the C-mount, but it is approximately 5 mm closer to the image plane. The intention is to preserve compatibility with the old C-mount format lenses (by adding a 5-mm ring) and yet allow for cheaper and smaller lenses, to suit smaller CCD chip sizes, to be manufactured.

Since both of the above formats use the thread type of lens mounting, there might be small variations in the lens's position relative to the CCD chip when mounted (screwed in). Hence the need for a little variation of this position (back-focus adjustment).

In photography, for example, we never talk about back-focusing simply because most of the brands come with a bayonet mount, which has **only one fixed position of the lens relative to the film plane**. Camcorders, for that matter, come with lenses as an integral part of the unit, so the back-focus is already adjusted and never changes.

In CCTV, because of the modular concept of the camera/lens combination and the thread mount, it is a different story.

If a lens is C-mount and the camera CS, a C/CS adaptor ring is required

Back-focus adjustment is especially important and critical when zoom lenses are used. This is because the optics-to-CCD distance in zoom lenses has to be very precise **in order to achieve good focus throughout the zoom range**.

Obviously, the back-focusing adjustment applies to fixed lenses as well, only in that case we tend not to pay attention to the distance indicator on the lens ring when focusing. If we want to be more accurate, when the back-focus is adjusted correctly on a fixed lens, the distance indicator should show the real distance between the camera and objects. Most installers, however, do not pay attention to the indicator on the lens since all they want to see is a sharp image on the monitor. And this is fine, but if we want to be precise the back-focus adjustment should apply to *all* lenses used in CCTV. With zoom lenses this is more critical.

An important factor to be taken into account when doing back-focus adjustment is the effect of depth-of-field. The reason is very simple: if a CCTV camera is installed at daytime (which is most often the case) and if we are using an AI lens, it is natural to see the iris set at a high F-stop to allow for a good picture (assuming the AI is connected and works properly). Since the iris is at a high F-stop we have a very high depth-of-field. The image seems sharp no matter what position we set the focus ring at. At nighttime, however, the iris opens fully due to the low light level situation, and the operator sees the picture out of focus.

This is actually one of the most common problems with new installations. When a service call is placed, usually the installer comes during the day time to see what the problem is, and if the operator cannot explain exactly what he or she sees, the problem may not be resolved, since the picture looks great with a high F-stop.

Some cameras don't require C/CS adaptor

The moral of the above is: always do the back-focus adjustment with a low F-stop.

The following different methods are used:

- Adjust the back-focus at low light levels in the workshop (easiest).

- Adjust the back-focus in the late afternoon, on site.

- Adjust the back-focus at daytime, on site, by using external ND filters.

There is one exception to the above: if a camera with CCD-iris is used, then the optical iris can be opened fully even at daylight because the CCD-iris will compensate for the excessive light. This means, with CCD-iris cameras, the back-focus can easily be adjusted even at daylight without being confused with the depth of field and without a need for ND filters. Obviously, you should not forget to switch the CCD-iris off after the adjustment, should you decide to use auto iris.

Back-focus adjustment

In the following few paragraphs we will examine a procedure for proper back-focus adjustment. This is based on practical experience and is by no means the only procedure, but it will give you a good understanding of what is involved in this operation. We should also clarify that often, with a new camera and zoom lens setup, there might not be a need for back-focus adjustment. This can be easily checked as soon as the lens is screwed onto the C or CS ring, and the camera is connected to a monitor. Obviously, the zoom and focus functions have to be operational so that one can check if there is a need for adjustment. The idea is to get as sharp an image as possible, and if a zoom lens is used, once it is focused on an object, the object should stay in focus no matter what zooming position is used. If this is not the case, then there is a need for back-focus adjustment.

One will rightly ask: "What is so complicated about adjusting the back-focus?"

The answer is of a rather practical nature, and apart from of the depth-of-field problems. The reason for this is that no zoom lens in CCTV comes with a distance indicator engraved on the lens. For example, if a zoom lens had a distance indicator engraved, we could set the focus ring to a particular distance, then set an object at that distance and adjust for a perfectly sharp image (a monitor, of course, is required) while rotating the lens **together** with the C-mount ring, or perhaps adjusting the CCD chip back and forth by a screw mechanism on the camera. But, of course, the majority of zoom lenses do not come with these distances engraved, so the hard part is to determine where to start from.

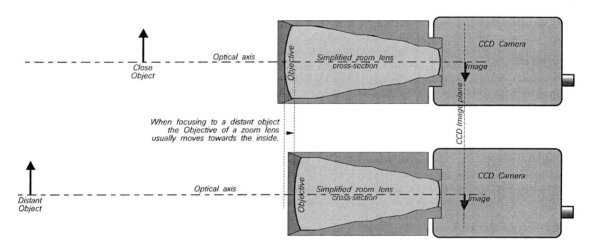

Zoom lens focusing at different distance objects

All lenses have two known points on the focus ring (the limits of the focus ring rotation):

-focus infinity "∞" (no lens focuses past this point) and

-focus at the minimum object distance (MOD).

The latter one varies with different lenses, i.e., we don't know what the minimum focusing distance of a particular lens would be, unless we have the manufacturer's specification sheet, which is usually not supplied with the lens or, quite often, lost in the course of installation.

This leaves us with only the focus infinity as a known point. Infinity is, obviously, not literally an infinite distance, but big enough to give a sharp image when the lens is set to the "∞" mark.

The longer the focal length of the lens, the longer the infinity distance that has to be selected. For a typical CCTV zoom lens of 10× ratio, which is usually 8-80 mm, 10-100 mm or 16-160 mm, this distance may be anything from 200-300 m onwards. From this, we can see it is impossible to simulate this distance in the workshop, so the technician working on the back-focus needs to point the camera out through a window, in which case **external ND filters** are required to minimize the effect of depth of field (unless a CCD-iris camera is used, of course).

The next step would be to set the focus to the infinity mark. To do this, a PTZ controller would be required, but this is obviously impractical.

I suggest, therefore, to simulate the zoom and focus control voltages by using a regular 9 V DC battery and applying it to the focus and zoom wires. Don't forget, the lens focus and zoom control voltages are from ±6 V DC to ±9 V DC, and the lens has a very low current consumption, usually below 30 mA. A 9 V battery has plenty of capacity to drive such motors for a considerable time, at least long enough for the adjustment procedure to be completed.

There is no standard among manufacturers for the lens wire color coding, but quite often, if no information sheet is supplied with the lens, the black wire is common, the zoom wire is red and the focus wire is blue. This is not a rule, so if in doubt it is not that hard to work it out by using the same battery and monitor. Instead of a monitor, an even more practical tool would be a **viewfinder**. Some

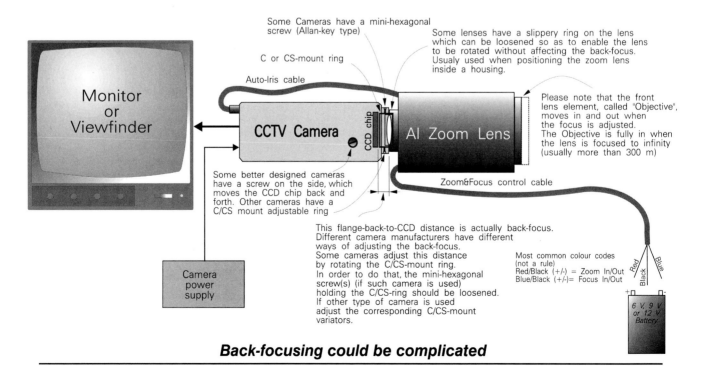

Back-focusing could be complicated

call it a focus adjuster. This is a little monitor, in fact, battery operated, with a rubber eyepiece to protect from excessive daylight. On a bright sunny day, if a normal monitor is used in the field, it will be almost impossible to see the picture on the screen, so it is highly recommended that you use a viewfinder instead.

If no monitor is available at the point of adjustment, a distinction should be made between which optical parts move when focusing and which when zooming. This is not so naive, since zoom lenses are enclosed in black (or beige) boxes and no moving parts are visible. A rule of thumb would be, however, zooming elements are not visible from the outside, while focusing is performed by the first group of lenses, called the **objective**. When focusing is done, the objective rotates around its optical axis and at the same time moves along the optical axis either towards the inside or the outside of the lens. All lenses have this common concept of the objective moving towards the outside when focusing to closer distances, and moving towards the inside of the lens when focusing to infinity. See the section on the focusing concepts for a detailed explanation.

On-camera C/CS ring

So, even if the zoom lens hasn't got any visible markings for distances and zoom factors, using the above logic we can start doing the back-focus adjustment.

With the battery applied to the focus wire, we need to focus the lens to infinity. Even if we don't have a monitor, this will be achieved when the **lens objective goes to the end position on the inside of the lens**.

The next step is to point the camera to an infinity object, at a distance we already spoke about. The infinity objects can be trees or antennas on the horizon.

Now, without changing the focus, zoom in and out fully. If the picture on the monitor looks sharp throughout the zooming range, **back-focusing is not necessary.**

If, however, the camera's C- or CS-mount ring is out of adjustment, we will not see a sharp picture on the monitor for all positions of the zoom.

Some CCD cameras use miniature hexagonal screws to secure the C-mount ring to the camera

Then, we proceed with adjustment by either rotating the lens together with the C-ring (if the camera is of such a type) or by shifting the CCD chip with a special back-focus adjustment screw or in some cameras by rotating a large ring with C & CS written on it.

The first type of camera is the most common. In this case, the C- or CS-mount ring is usually secured with miniature hexagonal locking screws. These need to be loosened prior to the adjustment, but after the zoom lens is screwed in tightly.

Then, when the focus is to be adjusted (after we did the battery focusing and pointing to infinity) we need to rotate the zoom lens but now **together** with the ring (that is why we have loosened the ring). Again, some cameras may have a special mechanism that shifts the CCD chip back or forth, in which case it's easier since we don't have to rotate the lens.

By doing one of the above, the distance between the lens and the CCD chip changes until the picture becomes sharp. Don't forget, because we have made the depth of field minimal by opening the iris as much as possible (with low light level simulation), the sharpness of the objects in the distance should be quite easily adjusted. Once we find the optimum we should stop there.

Please note, the focus wires are not used yet, i.e., we still need to have the zoom lens focused at infinity. We are only making sure that while zooming, the lens stays focused at infinity throughout the zoom range. Also, we need not be confused when the objects at infinity are getting smaller while zooming out, due to the image size reduction they might give the impression that they are going out of focus.

After this, the next step would be to zoom by using the 9 V battery. Watch the video picture carefully and make sure that the objects at infinity stay in focus while zooming in or out. If this is the case, our back-focus is nearly adjusted.

In order to confirm this, the next step would be to point the camera at an object that is only a couple of meters away from the camera. Then we zoom in on the object and use the focusing wires to focus on it. When focused precisely, use the zoom wires and zoom out. If the object stays in focus, that will be **confirmation** of a correct back-focus adjustment.

The last step would be to tighten the little hexagonal screws (if such a camera is used) and secure the C/CS-mount ring on the camera.

If the above procedure does not succeed from the very first go, a couple of iterations might be necessary, but the same logic applies.

As one can imagine, the mechanical design and robustness of the C-mount CCD-chip combination is very important, especially the precision and "parallelness" of the C-ring and the CCD chip plane. Little variations of only one-tenth of a millimeter at the image plane may make a focus variation of a couple of meters at the object. With bad designs, like locking the C-ring with only one screw or poor mechanical construction, problems might be experienced even if the

Focus adjusting tool

above procedure is correct. So it is not only the lens that defines the picture quality, but the camera's mechanical construction as well.

We have mentioned that a monitor is required when doing the back-focus adjustment, which is not a surprise. This is fine when the adjustments are done in the workshop, but when back-focusing needs to be performed on site it is almost impossible to use a normal CRT monitor. The reason for this is not so much the impracticality of the need for a main supply (240 VAC or whatever the country you are in has got), but more so because of the bright outdoor light compared to the brightness produced by a CRT monitor. That's why I've recommended the use of a viewfinder monitor (like the ones used on camcorders) with a rubber eyepiece that protects from external light and allows for comfortable use. Plus, these little viewfinder monitors are battery operated and very compact. Some manufacturers have viewfinder focus adjusters specially made with a flicker indicator to show when objects are in focus.

Little and practical tools like this make the difference between a good and bad CCTV system installation and/or commissioning.

Optical accessories in CCTV

Apart from fixed and zoom lenses in CCTV, we also have other optical devices.

One of the more popular is the **2× tele-converter** (also known as **an extender**). The tele-converter is a little device that is usually inserted between the lens and the camera. The 2× converter multiplies the focal length by a factor of 2. In fact, this means a 16 mm lens will become 32 mm, a zoom lens 8-80 mm will become 16-160 mm, etc. Important to note though, is that the F-number is also increased for one F-stop value. For example, if a 2× converter is used on a 16 mm/1.4 this becomes 32 mm/2. Back-focusing a lens with a 2× converter may be more complicated. It is recommended that you first do the back-focusing of the zoom lens alone, then just insert the converter. Some zoom lenses come with a tele-converter

Optical accessories   Photo courtesy of Fujinon

built-in but removable with a special control voltage. For this purpose the auxiliary output from a site driver can be used. In general, the optical resolution of a lens with a converter is reduced, and if there is not a real need for it, it should be avoided. It should be noted that 1.5× converters also exist.

Another accessory device is the **external ND filter**, which comes with various factors of light attenuation – 10×, 100× or 1000×. They can also be combined to give higher factors of attenuation. As we have already described, external ND filters are very helpful in back-focusing and AI adjustments. Since they come as loose pieces of glass, you may have to find a way of fixing them in front of the lens objective. Some kind of a holder could be made for better and more practical use of the filters.

Polarizing filters might sometimes be required when using a CCTV camera to view through a window or water. In most cases, reflections make it difficult to see what is beyond the glass or water surface. Polarizing filters can minimize such an effect. However, there is a little drawback in the practicality of this, since a polarizing filter requires rotation of the filter itself. If a fixed camera is looking at a fixed area that requires a polarizing filter, that might be fine, but it will be impossible to use it on a PTZ (Pan/Tilt/Zoom) camera because of constant camera repositioning and objective rotation when focusing.

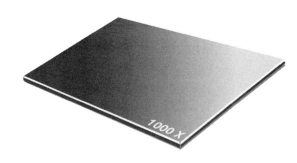

A 1000X Neutral Density filter

Extension rings

For special purposes, when the camera needs to have a close-up (macro) view of a very small object, it is possible to focus the lens on objects much closer than the actual MOD (Minimum Object Distance) as specified by the lens manufacturer. This can be achieved with special sets of **extension rings** that can be purchased through some lens suppliers. It is much easier and also more practical to use surplus CS-mount adaptor rings. By combining one or more of them, and depending upon the focal length in use, macro views can be obtained. This might be useful for inspecting surface-mount PCB components, stamps, detecting fake money, monitoring insect populations, or other miniature objects.

4. General Characteristics of TV Systems

This chapter discusses the theoretical fundamentals of video signals, their bandwidth and resolution. It is intended for technical people who want to know what the limits are of the TV system in general and CCTV in particular.

A little bit of history

In order to understand the basic principles of television we have to refer to the effect of persistency (see Chapter 2).

Television, like cinema, uses this effect to cheat our brain so by showing us still images at a very fast rate, our brain is made to believe that we see "motion pictures."

In 1903, the first film shown to the public was *The Great Train Robbery* which was produced in the Edison Laboratories. This event marked the beginning of the motion picture revolution. Although considered younger than film, the concept of television has been experimented with since the late 19th century. It all began with the discovery of the element selenium and its *photoelectricity* in 1817, by the Swedish chemist Jons Berzelius. He discovered that the electric current produced by selenium, when exposed to light, would depend on the amount of light falling onto it. In 1875, G.R.Carey, an American inventor, made the very first crude television system, where banks of photoelectric cells were used to produce a signal that was displayed on a bank of light bulbs, every one of which emitted light proportional to the amount of light falling onto the photo cells. A few minor modifications were made to this concept, like the "scanning disk" presented by Paul Nipkow in 1884, where elements were scanned by a mechanical rotating disk with holes aligned in a spiral. In 1923, the first practical transmission of pictures over wires was accomplished by Baird in England and later Jenkins in the United States. The first broadcast was transmitted in 1932 by the BBC in London, while experimental broadcasts were conducted in Berlin by the Fernseh company, led by the cathode ray tube (CRT) inventor, Prof. Manfred von Ardenne. A Russian-born engineer, Vladimir Zworykin, in 1931 developed the first TV camera known as the iconoscope, which was of the same concept as the later developed tube cameras and the cathode ray tube (CRT).

Both of these technologies, film and TV, produce many static images per second in order to achieve the motion effect. In TV, however, instead of projecting static images with a light projector through a celluloid film, this is achieved with electronic beam scanning. Pictures are formed line by line, in the same manner as when reading a book, for example, from left to right and from top to bottom (as seen from in front of the CRT).

An important role in the whole process is played by the persistency of the phosphor coating of the monitor's CRT. This depends on the type of phosphor coating and the brightness of the screen.

The very basics of television

There are a few different television standards used worldwide today. CCIR/PAL recommendations are used throughout most of Europe, Australia, New Zealand, most of Africa and Asia. A similar concept is used in the EIA/NTSC recommendations for the television used in the United States, Japan and Canada, as well as in the SECAM recommendations used in France, Russia, Egypt, some French colonies and Eastern European countries. The major difference between these standards is in the number of scanning lines and frame frequency.

Before we begin the television basics, let's first explain the abbreviation terminology used in various technical literature discussing television:

CCIR stands for *Committée Consultatif International des Radiotelecommuniqué.* This is the committee that recommended the standards for B/W television accepted by most of Europe, Australia and others. This is why we call equipment that complies with the B/W TV standards **CCIR compatible**. The same type of standard, but later extended to color signals, was called **PAL**. The name comes from the concept used for the color reproduction by alternate phase changes of the color carrier at each new line, hence, **phase alternate line (PAL).**

EIA stands for *Electronics Industry Association,* an association that created the standard for B/W television in the United States, Canada and Japan, where it is often referred to as **RS-170**, the recommendation code of the EIA proposal. When B/W TV was upgraded to color, it was named by the group that created the recommendation: **National Television Systems Committee (NTSC)**.

SECAM comes from the French "*Sequentiel à mémoire*" which actually describes how the color is transmitted, by a sequence of chrominance color signals and the need for a memory device in the TV receiver when decoding the color information.

All of the TV standards' recommendations have accepted the picture ratio of the TV screen to be 4:3 (4 units in width by 3 units in height). This is mostly due to the similar film aspect ratio of the early days of television.

The different number of lines used in different TV standards dictates the other characteristics of the system.

EIA recommends 525 lines, and PAL and SECAM use 625 (SECAM used to have 819 lines in the earlier versions).

Irrespective of these differences, all of the systems use the same concept of composing pictures with electron beam scanning lines, one after another.

When a video signal, as produced by a camera, comes to the monitor input, the voltage fluctuations are converted into current fluctuations of electrons in the electron beam that bombards the phosphor coating of the **CRT** as it is scanning line by line. The phosphor coating produces light proportional to the amount of electrons, which is proportional to the voltage fluctuation. This is, of course, proportional to the light information falling onto the CCD chip (the tube's target).

The phosphor coating of the monitor has some persistency as well, i.e., light produced by the beam does not immediately disappear with the disappearance of the beam. It continues to emit light for another few milliseconds. This means the TV screen is lit by a bright stripe that moves downwards at a certain speed.

This is obviously a very simplified description of what happens to the video signal when it comes to the monitor. We will discuss monitor operation in more detail in Chapter 6, but we will use the previous information as an introduction to the television principles for the readers who haven't got the technical background.

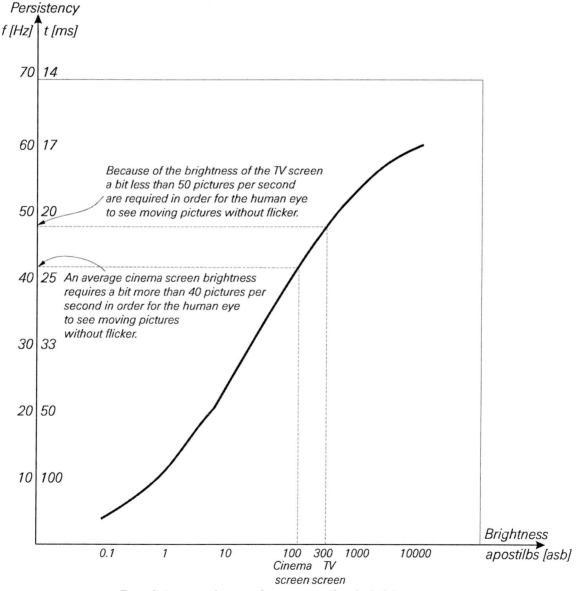

Persistency dependence on the brightness

Many factors need to be taken into account when deciding the number of lines and picture refresh rate to be used. As with many things in life, these decisions have to be a compromise – a compromise between as much information as possible, in order to see a faithful reproduction of the real objects, and as little information as possible in order to be able to transmit it economically and receive it by a large number of users who can afford to buy such a TV receiver.

The more lines used, combined with the number of pictures per second, the wider the frequency bandwidth of the video signal will be, thus dictating the cost of the cameras, processing equipment, transmitters and receivers.

The refresh rate, i.e., the number of pictures composed in 1 second, was decided on the basis of the persistency characteristic of the human eye and the luminance of the CRT. Theoretically, 24 pictures per second would have been ideal because of the compatibility between cinematography and television (used widely at the time of television's beginning). Practically, however, this was impossible because of the very high luminance produced by the phosphor of the CRT, which led to the flicker effect (relative to the viewing distance, see the diagram on the previous page).

With many experiments it was found that at least 48 pictures per second were required for the flicker to be eliminated. This would have been a good number to use because it was identical to the cinema projector frequency, and would be very practical when converting movies into television format. Still, this was not the number that was accepted. The television engineers opted for 50 pictures per second in CCIR, and 60 in EIA recommendations. These numbers were sufficiently high for the flicker to be undetectable with the human eye, but more importantly they coincided with the mains frequency of 50 Hz used all over Europe, and 60 in the United States, Canada and Japan. The reason for this lies in the electronic design of the TV receivers that were initially very dependent on the main frequency. Should the design with 48 pictures have been accepted, the 2-Hz difference for CCIR and 12-Hz for EIA, would have caused a lot of interference and irregularities in the scanning process.

The big problem, though, was how to produce 50 (PAL) or 60 (NTSC) pictures per second, without really increasing the initial camera scan rate of 25 (i.e. 30) pictures per second. Not that the camera scan rate could not be doubled, but the bandwidth of the video signal would have to be increased, thus increasing the electronics cost, as mentioned previously. Plus, broadcasting channels were taken into account, which would have to be wider and therefore fewer channels would be available for use, without interference, in a dedicated frequency area.

All of the above forced the engineers to use a trick, similar to the Maltese Cross used in film projection, where 50 (60) pictures would be reproduced without really increasing the bandwidth. The name of this trick is **interlaced scanning**.

Instead of composing the pictures with 625 (525) horizontal lines by progressive scanning, the solution was found in the alternate scanning of odd and even lines. In other words, instead of a single TV picture being produced by 625 (525) lines in one progressive scan, the same **picture was broken into two halves**, where one half was composed of only **odd lines** and the other of only **even lines**. These were scanned in such a way that they precisely fitted in between the lines of each other. This is why it is called interlaced scanning. All of the lines in each half, in the case of the CCIR signal 312.5 and in NTSC 262.5, form a so-called **TV field**. There are 25 odd fields, and 25 even fields in the CCIR and

SECAM systems, and 30 in the EIA system – a total of 50 fields per second, or 60 in EIA, flicking one after the other, every second.

An odd field together with the following even field composes a so-called *TV frame*. Every CCIR/ PAL and SECAM signal is thus, composed of 25 frames per second, or 50 fields. Every EIA/ NTSC signal is composed of 30 frames per second, which is equivalent to 60 fields.

The actual scanning on the monitor screen starts at the top left-hand corner with line 1, then goes to line 3, leaving a space in between 1 and 3 for line 2, which is due to come when even lines start

Interlaced scanning, simplified

scanning. Initially, with the very first experiments, it was hard to achieve precise interlaced scanning. The electronics needed to be very stable in order to get such oscillations that the even lines fit exactly in between the odd lines. But a simple and very efficient solution was soon found in the selection of an odd number of lines, where every field would finish scanning with half a line. By preserving a linear vertical deflection (which was much easier to ensure), the half line completes the cycle in the middle of the top of the screen, thus finishing the 313th line for CCIR (263rd for EIA), after which the **exact interlace was ensured for the even lines**.

When the electron beam completes the scanning of each line (on the right-hand side of the CRT, when seen from the front), it receives a **horizontal synchronization pulse** (commonly known as **horizontal sync**). This sync is embedded in the video signal and comes after the line video information. It tells the beam when to stop writing the video information and to **quickly** fly back to the left at the beginning of the new line. Similarly, when a field finishes a **vertical sync** pulse, it "tells" the beam when to stop writing the video information and to **quickly** fly back to the beginning of the new field. The fly-back

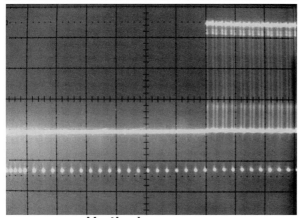

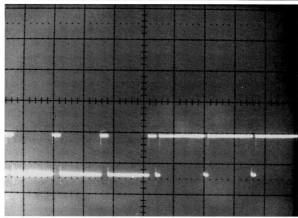

Vertical sync area
as seen on an oscilloscope

Vertical sync detail

period of the electron beam scanning is faster than the actual active scanning, and it is only positional, i.e., no electrons are ejected during these periods of the picture synthesis.

In reality, even though the scanning system is called 525 TV lines (or 625 for PAL), **not all of the lines are active, i.e., visible on the screen.** As can be seen on the NTSC and PAL TV Signal Timing Chart (next pages), some of the lines are used for vertical sync equalization, some are not used and others are practically invisible because of the overscanning effect (remember, no monitor or TV shows 100% of the camera video signal, except for the special broadcasting monitors).

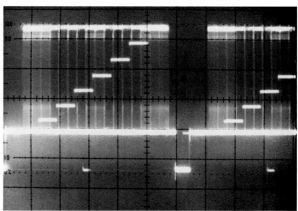

An oscilloscope view of TV signal
in line mode (with horizontal sync)

If we take into account the errors in the beam interlace, the thickness of the beam and so on in the CCIR system (and again, a similar logic applies to the other standards), we can hardly count more than 570 active TV lines in PAL, and not more than 480 in NSTC. For a more detailed explanation of the video signal limitations, please refer to page 131.

Some of the "invisible" lines are used for other purposes quite efficiently. In the PAL Teletext concept, for example, the CCIR recommends lines 17, 18, 330 and 331, where 8-bit digital information is inserted. The Teletext decoder in your TV or VCR can accumulate the fields' digital data, which contain information about the weather, exchange rates, Lotto, etc.

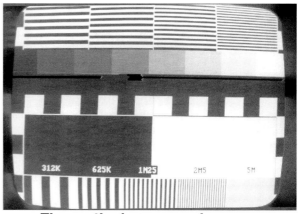

The vertical sync can be seen
on a monitor with V-Hold adjustment

In some NTSC systems line 21 carries closed captioning, i.e., subtitling information. Some of the other invisible lines are used for specially shaped video insertion test signals, known as **VITS,** which when measured at the receiving end, give valuable information on the quality of the transmission and reception in a particular area.   In CCTV, some manufacturers use the invisible lines to insert camera ID, time and date, or similar information. When recorded on a VCR, these lines are also recorded but they are not visible on the monitor screen. However, the information is always there, embedded in the video signal. This type of information is more secure and harder to tamper with. It can be retrieved with a

Timing intervals of TV signals	NTSC (μs)	PAL (μs)
Field period (V)	16,683	20,000
Line period (H)	63.5	64
Line blanking interval	10.7~11.1	11.8 ~ 12.3
Front porch interval	1.4~1.6	1.3 ~ 1.8
Line synchronizing pulse interval	4.6 ~ 4.8	4.5 ~ 4.9
Field blanking interval	20 H + 1 H	25 H + 1 H
Duration of field synchronizing pulse sequence	3 H	2.5 H
Duration of pre-equalizing pulse sequence	3 H	2.5 H
Duration of post-equalizing pulse sequence	3 H	2.5 H
Equalizing pulse interval	2.2 ~ 2.4	2.2 ~ 2.4
Interval between field synchronizing pulses	4.6 ~ 4.8	4.5 ~ 4.9
Start of color burst, from leading edge of line sync pulse	5.2 ~ 5.4	5.5 ~ 5.7
Color sub-carrier burst duration (NTSC 9 cycles, PAL 10 cycles)	2.5	2.0 ~ 2.5
Duration of burst blanking pulse (per field)	9 H	9 H

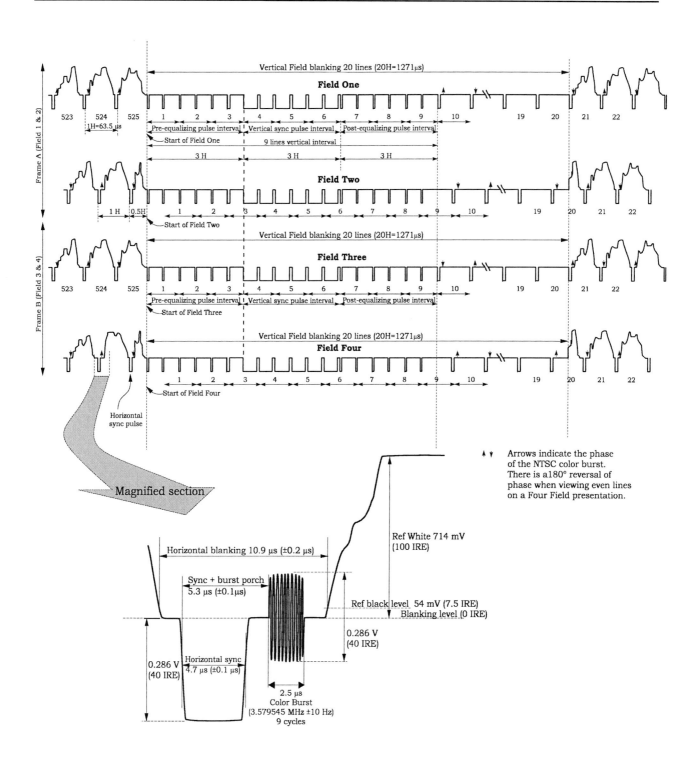

NTSC TV signal timing chart

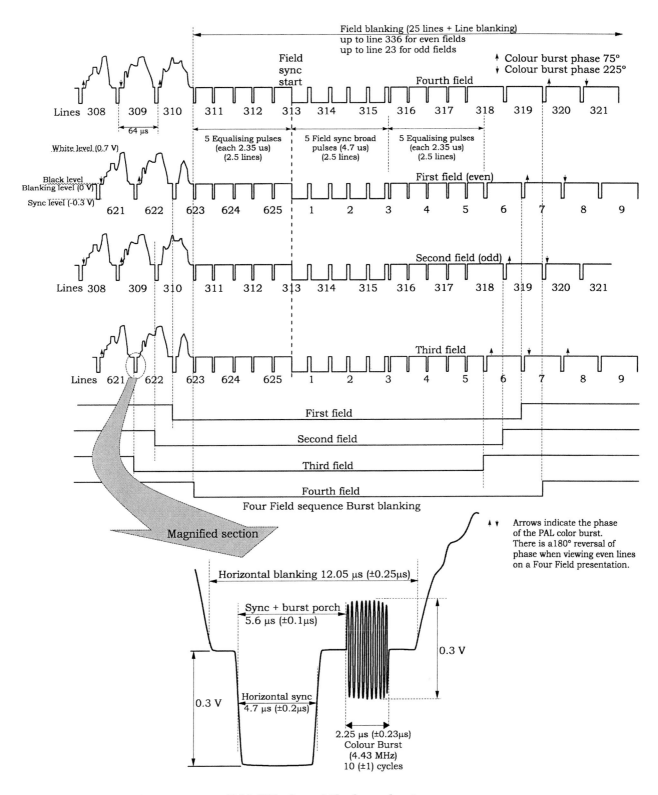

PAL TV signal timing chart

special TV line decoder and used whenever necessary, revealing the camera ID together with the time and date of the particular signal and, for example, the intruder in the picture.

The video signal and its spectrum

This heading discusses the theoretical fundamentals of the video signal's limitations, bandwidth and resolution. This is a complex subject with its fundamentals involving higher mathematics and electronics, but I will try to explain it in plain and simple language.

Most of the artificial electrical signals can be described mathematically. Mathematical description is very simple for signals that are periodical, like the main power, for example. A periodical function can always be represented with a sum of sinewaves, each of which may have different amplitude and phase. Similar to a spectrum of white light, this is called **spectrum of an electrical signal**. The more periodical the electrical signal is, the easier it can be represented and with fewer sinewave components. Each sinewave component can be represented with discrete value in the frequency spectrum of the signal. The less periodical the function is, the more components will be required to reproduce the signal. Theoretically, even a non-periodical function can be represented with a sum of various sinewaves, only that in such a case there will be a lot more sinewaves to summarize in order to get the non-periodical result. In other words, the spectral image of a non-periodical signal will have a bandwidth more densely populated with various components. The finer the details the signal has, the higher the frequencies will be in the spectrum of the signal. Very fine details in the video signal will be represented with high-frequency sine waves. This is equivalent to high-resolution information. A signal rich with high frequencies will have wider bandwidth. Even a single, but very sharp pulse, will have a very wide bandwidth.

The above describes, in a very simplified way, the very important **Fourier spectral theory,** which states that **every signal in the time domain has its image in the frequency domain**. The Fourier spectral theory can be used in practice – wide bandwidth periodical electrical signals can be more efficiently explored by analyzing their frequency spectrum. Without going deeper into the theory itself, CCTV users need to accept the concept of the spectrum analysis as very important for examining complex signals, such as the video itself. The video signal is perhaps one of the most complex electrical signals ever produced, and its precise mathematical description is almost impossible because of the constant change of the signal in the time domain. The video information (i.e., luminance and chrominance components) changes all the time. Because, however, we are composing video images by **periodical** beam scanning, we can **approximate** the video signal with some form of a periodical signal. One of the major components in this periodicity will be the line frequency – for CCIR and SECAM, $25 \times 625 = 15,625$ Hz; for EIA, $30 \times 525 = 15,750$ Hz.

It can be shown that the spectrum of a simplified video signal is composed of **harmonics** (multiples) of the line frequency around which there are companion components, both on the left- and right-hand sides (**sidebands**). The inter-component distances depend on the contents of the video picture and the dynamics of the motion activity. Also, it is very important to note that such a spectrum, composed of harmonics and its components, is **convergent,** which means the harmonics become smaller in amplitude as the frequency increases. One even more important conclusion from the Fourier spectral theory is that **positions of the harmonics and components in the video signal spectrum depend only on the picture analysis** (4:3 ratio, 625 interlaced scanning). The video signal energy distribution around the harmonics depends on the contents of the picture. The harmonics, though, are **at exact positions because they only depend on the line frequency**. In other words, the video signal dynamics and amplitude of certain components in the sidebands will vary, but the harmonics locations (as sub-carrier frequencies) will remain constant.

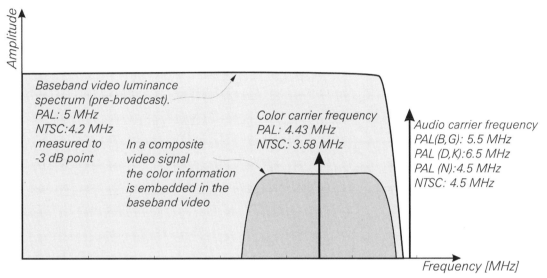

The spectrum of a baseband composite video signal

This is a very important conclusion. It helped find a way, in broadcast TV, to reduce the spectrum of a video signal to the minimum required bandwidth without losing too many details. There is always a compromise, of course, but since **the majority of the video signal energy is around the zero frequency and the first few harmonics, there is no need and no way to transmit the whole video spectrum**. Scientists and engineers have used all of these facts to find a compromise, to find how little of the video bandwidth need be used in a transmission, without losing too many details. As we already mentioned when discussing different TV standards, the more scanning lines that are used in a system the wider the bandwidth will be, and the higher the resolution of the signal is the wider the bandwidth will be.

Taking into account the electron beam's limited size (which also dictates the smallest reproducible picture elements), the physical size of the TV screens, viewing distances and the complexity and production costs of domestic TV sets, it has been concluded that for a good reproduction of a broadcast signal, 5 MHz of video bandwidth is sufficient. **Using a wider bandwidth is possible, but the quality gain factor versus the expense is very low**. As a matter of fact, in the broadcast studios, cameras and recording and monitoring equipment are of much higher standards, with spectrums of up to 10 MHz. This is for internal use only, however, for quality recording and dubbing. Before such a signal is RF modulated and sent to the transmitting stage, it is cut down to 5 MHz video, to which about 0.5 MHz is added for the left and right audio channels. When such a signal comes to the TV transmitter stage it is modulated so as to have only its vestigial side band transmitted, with a total bandwidth, including the separation buffer zone, of 7 MHz (for PAL). But please note that the actual usable video bandwidth in broadcast reception is only 5 MHz. For the more curious readers we should mention that in most PAL countries, the video signal is modulated with amplitude modulation (AM) techniques, while the sound is frequency modulated (FM).

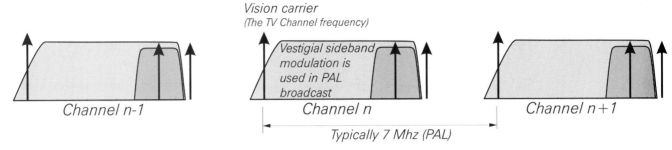

Broadcast TV channels frequency displacement example

Similar considerations apply when considering NTSC signals, where the broadcasted bandwidth is around 4.2 MHz.

In CCTV, with the majority of system designs, **we do not have such bandwidth limitations** because we do not transmit an RF-modulated video signal. We do not have to worry about interference between neighboring video channels. In CCTV, we use a raw video signal as it comes out of the camera, which is a **basic bandwidth video,** or usually called **baseband video**. This usually bears the abbreviation **CVBS**, which stands for composite video bar signal. The spectrum of such a signal, as already mentioned, ranges from 0 to 10 MHz, depending on the source quality.

The spectral capacity of the coaxial cable, as a transmission medium, is much wider than this. The most commonly used 75Ω coaxial cable RG-59B/U, for example, can easily transmit signals of up to 100 MHz bandwidth. This is applicable to a limited distance of a couple of hundred meters of course, but that is sufficient for the majority of CCTV systems. Different transmission media imply different bandwidth limitations, some of which are wider and some narrower than the coaxial one, but most of them are considerably wider than 10 MHz.

Color video signal

When color television was introduced, it was based on the monochrome signal definitions and limitations. Preserving the compatibility between B/W and color TV was of primary importance. The only way color information (chroma) could be sent together with the luminance without increasing the bandwidth was if the color information was modulated with a frequency that fell exactly in between the luminance spectrum components. This means that the spectrum of the chrominance signal is interleaved with the spectrum of the luminance signal in such a way that they do not interfere. This color frequency is called a **chroma sub-carrier** and the most suitable frequency, for **PAL**, was found to be **4.43361875 MHz**. In **NTSC**, using the same principle, the color sub-carrier was found to be **3.579545 MHz**.

At this point we need to be more exact and highlight that NTSC is defined with 29.97 frames exactly, not 30 (!). The reason for this is the definition of color signal in NTSC, as proposed by the RS170A video standard, which is based on the exact sub-carrier frequency of 3.579545 MHz. The horizontal scanning frequency is defined as 2/455 times the burst frequency, which makes 15,734 Hz. The vertical scanning frequency is derived from this one, and the NTSC recommends it as 2/525 times the horizontal frequency. This produces 59.94 Hz for the vertical frequency, i.e., the field rate. For the purpose of generalization and simplification, however, we will usually refer to NTSC as a 60-field signal in this book.

As we have already mentioned in the ***Color Television*** section, the basics of color composition lie in the additive mixing of three primary color signals: red, green and blue. So, for transmitting a complete color signal, theoretically, apart from the luminance information, another three different signals are required. Initially, in the beginning of the color evolution, this seemed impossible, especially when only between 4 and 5 MHz are used to preserve the compatibility with the B/W standards.

With a complex but clever procedure, this was made possible. It is beyond the scope of this book to explain such procedure, but the following facts are important for our overall understanding of the complexity of color reproduction in television.

In a real situation, apart from the **luminance** signal, which is often marked as $Y = U_Y$, **two more signals** (and not three) are combined. These signals are the so-called **color differences** $V = U_R - U_Y$, and $U = U_B - U_Y$, which means the difference between the red and the luminance signal and between the blue and the luminance. The reason why color differences are used instead of just plain values for R, B (and G) is because of the compatibility with the B/W system. Namely, it was found that when a white or grey color is transmitted through the color system, only a luminance signal needs to be present in the CRT. In order to eliminate the color components in the system, the color difference was introduced.

Having in mind the basic relationship among the three color signals:

$$U_Y = 0.3U_R + 0.59U_G + 0.11U_B \tag{34}$$

it can be shown that **all of the three primary color signals can be retrieved using the luminance and color difference signals**:

$$U_R = (U_R - U_Y) + U_Y \tag{35}$$

$$U_B = (U_B - U_Y) + U_Y \tag{36}$$

$$U_G = (U_G - U_Y) + U_Y \tag{37}$$

For white color $U_R = U_G = U_B$, thus $U_Y = (0.3 + 0.59 + 0.11)U_R = U_B = U_G$. The green color difference is not transmitted, but it is obtained from the following calculation (again using (34)):

$$U_G - U_Y = -0.51(U_R - U_Y) - 0.19(U_B - U_Y) \tag{38}$$

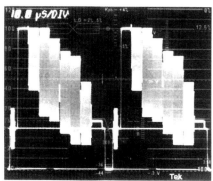

Color bars

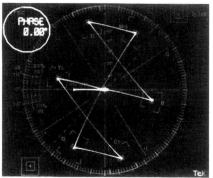

A vectorscope display of the color bars above (NTSC)

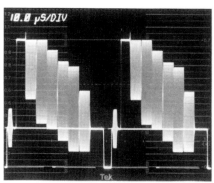

Color bars

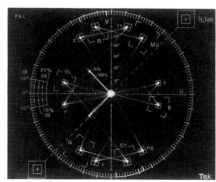

A vectorscope display of the color bars above (PAL)

This relation shows that in color television, apart from the luminance, only **two additional** signals would be sufficient for successful color retrieval. That is the red and the blue color difference (V and U), and they are embedded in the CVBS signal.

Because the R, G and B components are derived from the color difference signals by way of simple and linear matrix equations, which in electronics can be realized by simple resistor networks, these arrangements are called **color matrices**.

It should be noted here that the two discussed TV standards, NTSC and PAL, are basing their theory of color reproduction on two different exponents of the CRT phosphor (called *gamma*, which will be explained in the Monitors section). The NTSC assumes a gamma of 2.2, and PAL 2.8. This assumption is embedded in the signal encoding prior to transmission.

In practice, gamma of 2.8 is a more realistic value, which is also reflected in a higher contrast picture. Of course, the reproduced color contrast will depend on the monitor's phosphor gamma itself.

In order to combine (modulate) these color difference signals with the luminance signal for broadcast transmission, a so-called **quadrature amplitude modulation** is used where the two different signals (V and U) modulate a single carrier frequency (color sub-carrier). This is possible by introducing a phase difference of 90° between the two, which is the reason for the name quadrature modulation.

In the PAL color standard, we have another clever design to minimize the color signal distortions. Knowing that **the human eye is more sensitive to color distortions than to changes in brightness**, a special procedure was proposed for the color encoding so that distortions would be minimized, or at least made less visible. This is achieved by the color phase change, of 180°, in every second line. So, if transmission distortions occur, which is usually in the form of phase shifting, they will result in a color change of the same amount. But because **the electronic vector representation of colors is chosen so that complementary colors are opposite each other, the errors are also complementary and, when errored lines next to each other are seen from a viewing distance the errors would cancel each other out**. This is the reason for the name phase alternating line (PAL).

Resolution

Resolution is the property of a system to display fine details. The higher the resolution, the more details we can see. The resolution of a TV picture depends on the number of active scanning lines, the quality of the camera, the quality of the monitor and the quality of the transmitting media.

Since we use two-dimensional display units (CCD chips and CRTs), we distinguish two kinds of resolutions: vertical and horizontal.

The vertical resolution is defined by the number of vertical elements that can be captured on a camera and reproduced on a monitor screen. When many identical vertical elements are put together in the scanning direction, we get very dense horizontal lines. This is why we say **the vertical resolution tells us how many horizontal lines we can distinguish**. Both black and white lines are counted and the counting is done vertically. Clearly, this is limited by the number of scanning lines used in the system – we cannot count more than 625 lines in a CCIR system or 525 in an EIA system. If we take into account the duration of the vertical sync and the equalization pulses, the invisible lines and so on, **the number of active lines in CCIR comes down to 575 lines and about 475 in EIA.**

This is still not the actual vertical resolution. Usually, the resolution is measured with a certain patterned image in front of the camera, so there are a lot of other factors to take into account. One is that the absolute position of the supposedly high-resolution horizontal pattern can never exactly match the interlaced lines pattern. Also, the monitor screen overscanning cuts a little portion of the video picture, the thickness of the electronic beam is limited and for color reproduction the "grill mask" is limited.

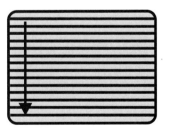

Vertical resolution

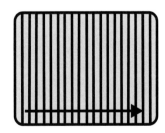

Horizontal resolution

As early as 1933, Kell and his colleagues found by experimenting that a **correction factor** of 0.7 should be applied when calculating the "real" vertical resolution. This is known as the **Kell factor** and it is accepted as a pretty good approximation of the real resolution. This means that 575 has to be corrected (multiplied) by 0.7 to get the **practical limits** of the vertical resolution for PAL, which is approximately 400 TV lines. The same calculation applies for the NTSC signal, which will give us approximately 330 TV lines of vertical resolution. This is all true in an ideal case, i.e., with excellent video signal transmission.

Horizontal resolution is a little bit of a different story. **The horizontal resolution is defined by the number of horizontal elements that can be captured by a camera and reproduced on a monitor**

screen. And, similar to what we said about the vertical resolution, **the horizontal tells us how many vertical lines can be counted.**

One thing is different though. Because of the TV aspect ratio of 4:3, the width is greater than the height. So, to preserve the natural proportions of the images, **we count only the vertical lines of the width equivalent to the height**, i.e., 3/4 of the width. This is why we don't refer to the horizontal resolution as just lines but rather **TV lines**.

The horizontal resolution of a monochrome (B/W) TV system is theoretically only limited to the cross section of the electron beam, the monitor electronics and, naturally, the camera specifications. In reality, there are a lot of other limitations. One is the video bandwidth applicable to the type of transmission. Even though we may have high-resolution cameras in the TV studio, we transmit only 5 MHz of the video spectrum (as discussed earlier); therefore, there is no need for television manufacturers to produce TV receivers with a wider bandwidth. In CCTV, though, the video signal bandwidth is mostly dictated by the camera itself, since B/W monitors have a very high resolution (up to 1000 TV lines), which is limited only by the monitor quality, of which the most important are the electron beam precision and cross section.

A color system has an additional barrier, and that is the physical size of the color mask and its pitch. The color mask is in the form of a very fine grille. This grille is used for the color scanning with the three primary colors, red, green and blue. The number of color picture elements (RGB dots) the grille has is determined by the size of the monitor screen and the quality of the CRT. In CCTV, anything from 330 TV lines (horizontal resolution) up to 600 TV lines is available. The most common are the standard 14" monitors with around 400 TV lines of resolution. Don't forget we are talking about TV lines, which in the horizontal direction gives us an absolute

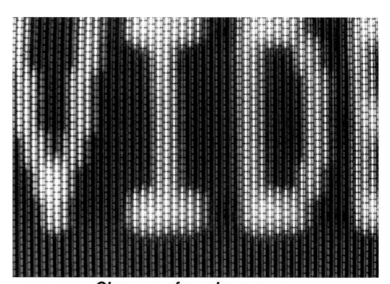

Close-up of a color screen

maximum number of 400 × 4/3 = 533 vertical lines, countable.

In CCTV, like in broadcast TV, we cannot change the vertical resolution since we are limited to the number defined by the scanning system. That's why we rarely argue about vertical resolution. **The commonly accepted number for realistic vertical resolution is around 400 TV lines for CCIR and 330 TV lines for EIA**. The horizontal resolution we can change and this will depend on the camera's horizontal resolution, the quality of the transmission media and the monitor. It is not rare in CCTV to come across a camera with 570 TV lines of horizontal resolution, which corresponds to a maximum of approximately 570 × 4/3 = 760 lines across the screen. This type of camera is considered

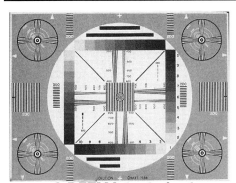

A RETMA test chart measures resolution

a high-resolution camera. A standard resolution B/W camera would have 400 TV lines of horizontal resolution.

There is a simple relation between the bandwidth of a video signal and the corresponding number of lines. If we take one line of a video signal, of which the active duration is 57 μs, and spread 80 TV lines across it, we will get a total of $80 \times 4/3 = 107$ lines. These lines, when represented as an electrical signal, will look like sinewaves. So, a pair of black and white lines actually corresponds to one period of a sinewave. Therefore, 107 lines are approximately 54 sinewaves. A sinewave period would be 57 μs /54 = 1.04 μs. If we apply the known relation for time and frequency, i.e., $T = 1/f$, we get $f = 1$ MHz. The following is a very simple rule of thumb, giving us the relation between the bandwidth of a signal and its resolution: **approximately 80 TV lines correspond to 1 MHz in bandwidth.**

Instruments commonly used in TV

It is very hard to determine any of the video signal properties with a typical electronic multimeter. There are, however, specialized instruments that, when used correctly, can describe the tested video signal precisely. These instruments include oscilloscopes, spectrum analyzers and vectorscopes. In most cases an oscilloscope will be sufficient, and I strongly recommend that a serious technician or engineer invest in it.

Oscilloscope

The change of a signal (timewise) can be slow or fast. What is slow and what is fast depends on many things, and they are relative terms. One periodical change of something in one second is defined as Hertz. Audio frequency of 10 kHz makes 10,000 oscillations in one second. The human ear can hear a range of frequencies from around 20 Hz up to 15,000-16,000 Hz. A video signal, as defined by the aforementioned standards, can have frequencies from nearly 0 Hz up to 5-10 MHz.

The higher the frequency, the finer the detail in the video signal.

How high we can go depends, first of all, on the pickup device (camera) but also on the transmission (coaxial cable, microwave, fiber optics), and the processing/displaying media (VCR, framestore, hard disk, monitor).

A time analysis of any electrical signal (as opposed to a frequency analysis) can be conducted with an electronic instrument called an **oscilloscope**. The oscilloscope works on principles similar to those of a TV monitor, only in this case the scanning of the electron beam follows the video signal voltage in the vertical direction, while horizontally, time is the only variable. With the so-called time-base adjustment, video signals can be analyzed from a frame mode (20 ms) down to the horizontal sync width (5 μs).

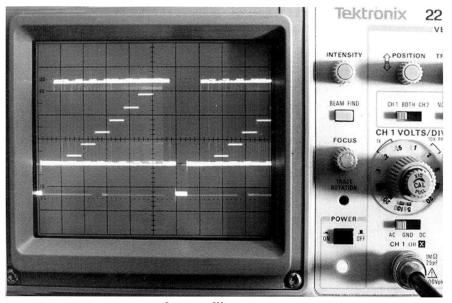

An oscilloscope

On the photo of an oscilloscope we can see the typical appearance of CCIR video signal displayed by an oscilloscope.

Oscilloscope measurements have the most objective indication of the video signal quality, and it is strongly recommended to anyone seriously involved in CCTV. First, with an oscilloscope it is very easy to see the quality of the signal, bypassing any possible misalignment of the brightness/contrast on a monitor. Sync/video levels can easily be checked and can confirm whether a video signal has a proper 75-Ω termination, how far the signal is (reduction of the signal amplitude and loss of the high frequencies)

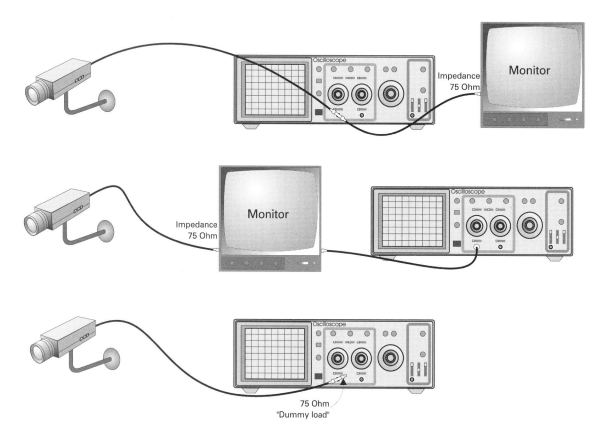

A few different methods of correct measurement with an oscilloscope

and whether there is a hum induced in a particular cable. Correct termination is always required for proper measurements, i.e., the input impedance of an oscilloscope is high and whichever way the signal is connected, it needs to see 75 Ω at the end of the line. A few examples of how an oscilloscope is to be connected for the purposes of correct video measurement are shown on the diagram on previous page.

Spectrum analyzer

Every electrical signal that changes (timewise) has an image in the frequency domain, as already discussed by the Fourier theory. The frequency domain describes the signal amplitude versus frequency instead of versus time. The representation in the frequency domain gives us a better understanding of the composition of an electrical signal. The majority of the contents of the video signal are in the low to medium frequencies, while fine details are contained in the higher frequencies. An instrument that shows such a spectral composition of signals is called a **spectrum analyzer**.

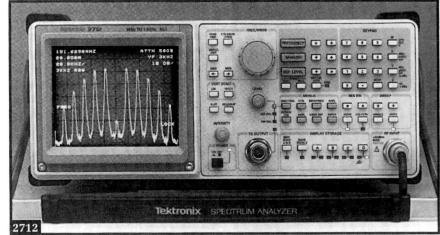

A spectrum analyzer

Photo courtesy of Tektronix

A spectrum analyzer is an expensive device, which is not so necessary in CCTV. However, if used properly, when combined with a test pattern generator with a known spectral radiation, a lot of valuable data can be gathered. Video signal attenuation, proper cable equalization, signal quality and so on can be precisely determined. In broadcast TV, the spectrum analyzer is a must for making sure that the broadcast signal falls within certain predefined standard margins.

Vectorscope

For measuring the color characteristics of a video signal an instrument called a **vectorscope** is used. A vectorscope is a variation of an oscilloscope, where the signal's color phase is shown. The display of a vectorscope is in the polar form, where primary colors have exact known positions with angles and radii. The vectorscope is rarely used in CCTV, but could be necessary when specific colors and lighting conditions need to be reproduced.

In most cases, a color CCD camera will have an automatic white balance that, as discussed earlier in the color temperature section, compensates for various color temperature light sources. Sometimes, though, with manual white balance cameras, a color test chart may need to be used, and with the help of a vectorscope, colors can be fine tuned to fall within certain margins, marked on the screen as little square windows. It should be noted that a vectorscope display of the same image in NTSC is different

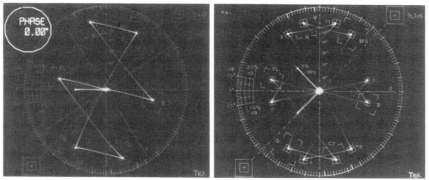

Vectorscope display of NTSC and PAL color bars

from the vectorscope display in PAL, and this is because of the difference of color encoding in the two systems. PAL has vertically symmetrical color vectors, as it can be on the photos below.

Tektronix 1781 Video Measurement Set

There are many other practical instruments (designed for the broadcast industry really) that can be used in CCTV. With a little bit of understanding and willingness to learn, many features of a video component, or a whole system, can be quantified. Some instruments combine more measuring devices into one box.

If you are serious about CCTV, these should be considered valuable tools of your trade.

Tektronix VM700 Video Measurement Set

Television systems around the world

There are a number of variations of the three major systems PAL, NTSC and SECAM. Various countries have accepted various broadcast bandwidths, color sub-carrier frequencies and sound carriers. These variations are usually referred to with a suffix next to the system a country uses.

The tables below show variations of the three major systems, and the next three pages list most of the countries of the world with their respective standards.

With many newly designed TV sets and VCRs there is no need to know what standard you have as the set will automatically find the standard, but as technical people it is a good idea to know what is in use.

With the new digital standards, hopefully, there will be much less variation around the world.

SYSTEM	PAL B,G,H	PAL I	PAL D	PAL N	PAL M
Line/Field	625/50	625/50	625/50	625/50	525/60
Horizontal Frequency	15.625 kHz	15.625 kHz	15.625 kHz	15.625 kHz	15.750 kHz
Vertical Frequency	50 Hz	50 Hz	50 Hz	50 Hz	60 Hz
Color Sub Carrier Frequency	4.433618 MHz	4.433618 MHz	4.433618 MHz	3.582056 MHz	3.575611 MHz
Video Bandwidth	5.0 MHz	5.5 MHz	6.0 MHz	4.2 MHz	4.2 MHz
Sound Carrier	5.5 MHz	6.0 MHz	6.5 MHz	4.5 MHz	4.5 MHz

SYSTEM	NTSC M
Lines/Field	525/60
Horizontal Frequency	15.734 kHz
Vertical Frequency	60 Hz
Color Subcarrier Frequency	3.579545 MHz
Video Bandwidth	4.2 MHz
Sound Carrier	4.5 MHz

SYSTEM	SECAM B,G,H	SECAM D,K,K1,L
Line/Field	625/50	625/50
Horizontal Frequency	15.625 kHz	15.625 kHz
Vertical Frequency	50 Hz	50 Hz
Video Bandwidth	5.0 MHz	6.0 MHz
Sound Carrier	5.5 MHz	6.5 MHz

COUNTRY	COLOR SYSTEM	VHF	UHF	MAINS ELECTRICITY
AFGHANISTAN	PAL/SECAM(H)	B	-	220 50Hz
ALASKA	NTSC	M	-	110/240 60Hz
ALBANIA	PAL	B	G	220 50Hz
ALGERIA	PAL	B	-	120/220 50Hz
ANDORRA	SECAM(V)/PAL	L	L	220 50Hz
ANGOLA	PAL	I	-	220 50Hz
ANTIGUA	NTSC	M	-	230 60Hz
ARGENTINA	PAL-N	N	N	220 50Hz
AUSTRALIA	PAL	B	B	240 50Hz
AUSTRIA	PAL	B	B	200 50Hz
AZERBAIJAN	SECAM(H)	D	K	220 50Hz
BAHAMAS	NTSC	M	-	110/240 60Hz
BAHRAIN	PAL	B	G	220 50/60Hz
BANGLADESH	PAL	B	-	220/230 50Hz
BARBADOS	NTSC	M	-	220 50Hz
BELARUS	SECAM	D	K	220 50Hz
BELGIUM	PAL	B	H	110/220 50Hz
BELIZE	NTSC	M	-	110 60Hz
BENIN	SECAM(V)	K1	-	220 50Hz
BERMUDA	NTSC	M	-	120/240 60Hz
BOLIVIA	NTSC M N	M	N	110/220 50Hz
BOSNIA HERZEGOVINIA	PAL	B	H	220 50Hz
BOTSWANA	PAL	-	-	220 50Hz
BRAZIL	PAL M	M	M	110/220 60Hz
BRITISH VIRGIN ISLANDS	NTSC	M	-	110/240 60Hz
BRUNEI	PAL	B	-	230 50Hz
BULGARIA	SECAM(H)	D	K	220 50Hz
BURMA	NTSC	-	-	120/240 60Hz
CANADA	NTSC	M	M	120 60Hz
CANARY ISLANDS	PAL	B	G	110/220 50Hz
CENTRAL AFRICAN REPUBLIC	SECAM	K1	-	220 50HZ
CHAD	SECAM(V)	D	-	220 50Hz
CHILE	NTSC	M	-	220 50Hz
CHINA (PEOPLES REPUBLIC)	PAL	D	-	220 50Hz
COLOMBIA	NTSC	M	-	110 60Hz
CONGO (PEOPLES REPUBLIC)	SECAM(V)	D	-	220 50Hz
COSTA RICA	NTSC	M	-	120 60Hz
CROATIA	PAL	B	G	220 50Hz
CUBA	NTSC	M	-	120 60Hz
CYPRUS (GREEK)	SECAM(H)	B	G	240 50Hz
CYPRUS (TURKISH)	PAL	B	G	240 50Hz
CZECH REPUBLIC	SECAM(H)	D	K	230 50Hz
DENMARK	PAL	B	G	220 50Hz
DOMINICAN REPUBLIC	NTSC	M	M	110 60Hz
ECUADOR	NTSC	M	M	220 60Hz
EGYPT	SECAM(H)	B	G	120/220 50Hz
EL SALVADOR	NTSC	M	-	120/230 60Hz
ESTONIA	SECAM(H)	D	K	220 50Hz
ETHIOPIA	PAL	B	-	220 50Hz
FIJI	NTSC	M	-	120 60Hz
FINLAND	PAL	B	G	220 50Hz
FRANCE	SECAM(V)	L	L	220 50Hz
GABON	SECAM(V)	K1	-	220 50Hz
GAMBIA	PAL	I	I	230 60Hz
GEORGIA	SECAM(H)	D	K	220 50Hz

COUNTRY	COLOR SYSTEM	VHF	UHF	MAINS ELECTRICITY
GERMANY	PAL	B	G	220 50Hz
GHANA	PAL	B	-	220 50Hz
GIBRALTAR	PAL	B	G	240 50Hz
GREECE	SECAM(H)	B	G	220 50Hz
GREENLAND	PAL	B	-	220 50Hz
GUATEMALA	NTSC	M	M	120/240 60Hz
GUINEA	PAL	K1	-	220 50Hz
HAITI	NTSC	M	-	220 60Hz
HAWAII	NTSC	M	-	120 60Hz
HOLLAND	PAL	B	G	220 50Hz
HONDURAS	NTSC	M	-	120 60Hz
HONG KONG	PAL	-	I	220 50Hz
HUNGARY	SECAM(H)	D	K	220 50Hz
ICELAND	PAL	B	G	240 50Hz
INDIA	PAL	B	-	240 50Hz
INDONESIA	PAL	B	-	110/220 50Hz
IRAN	SECAM(H)	B	-	220 50Hz
IRAQ	SECAM(H)	B	-	220 50Hz
IRELAND	PAL	I	I	220 50Hz
ISRAEL	PAL	B	G	220 50Hz
ITALY	PAL	B	G	220 50Hz
JAMAICA	NTSC	M	-	110 50Hz
JAPAN	NTSC	M	M	110 60Hz
JORDAN	PAL	B	G	220 50Hz
KAZAKHSTAN	SECAM(H)	D	K	220 50Hz
KENYA	PAL	B	G	230 50Hz
KOREA NORTH	SECAM	D	K	220 50Hz
KOREA SOUTH	NTSC	M	-	110 60Hz
KUWAIT	PAL	B	G	240 50Hz
LAOS	PAL-M	M	-	220 50Hz
LATVIA	SECAM(H)	M	-	220 50Hz
LEBANON	PAL	B	G	220 50Hz
LIBERIA	PAL	B	-	110/240 60Hz
LIBYA	SECAM	B	G	120/230 50Hz
LITHUANIA	SECAM(H)	D	K	220 50Hz
LUXEMBOURG	PAL/SECAM	B/L	G	220 50Hz
MACEDONIA	PAL	B	G	220 50Hz
MADAGASCAR	SECAM(V)	K1	-	120/220 50Hz
MALAYSIA	PAL	B	G	230 50Hz
MALTA	PAL	B	G	240 50Hz
MAURITANIA	SECAM(V)	B	-	230 50Hz
MAURITIUS	SECAM(V)	B	I	230 50Hz
MEXICO	NTSC	M	-	110-125 60Hz
MONACO	SECAM(V)/PAL	L	L,G	220 50Hz
MONGOLIA	SECAM(V)	D	-	120 50Hz
MOROCCO	SECAM(V)	B	-	110/220 50Hz
MOZAMBIQUE	PAL	B	-	220 50Hz
NAMIBIA	PAL	I	-	220 50Hz
NEPAL	PAL	B	-	220 50Hz
NETHERLANDS	PAL	B	G	220 50Hz
NEW CALEDONIA	SECAM(V)	K1	-	220 50Hz
NEW ZEALAND	PAL	B	G	230 50Hz
NICARAGUA	NTSC	M	-	220 60Hz
NIGER	SECAM(V)	K1	-	220 50Hz
NIGERIA	PAL	B	G	240 50Hz
NORWAY	PAL	B	G	220 50Hz

COUNTRY	COLOR SYSTEM	VHF	UHF	MAINS ELECTRICITY
OMAN	PAL	B	G	240 50Hz
PAKISTAN	PAL	B	-	230 50Hz
PANAMA	NTSC	M	-	120 60Hz
PAPUA NEW GUINEA	PAL	B	G	240 50Hz
PARAGUAY	PAL-N	N	-	220 50Hz
PERU	NTSC	M	M	220 60Hz
PHILIPPINES	NTSC	M	-	110 60Hz
POLAND	SECAM(H)	D	K	220 50Hz
POLYNESIA	SECAM(V)	K	-	220 50Hz
PORTUGAL	PAL	B	G	220 50Hz
PUERTO RICO	NTSC	M	M	110/240 60Hz
QATAR	PAL	B	-	240 50Hz
ROMANIA	SECAM(H)/PAL	D	K	220 50Hz
RUSSIA	SECAM	D	K	220 50Hz
SAMOA	NTSC	M	-	230 50Hz
SAUDI ARABIA	SECAM(H)/PAL	B	G	120/220 50Hz
SENEGAL	SECAM(V)	K1	-	120 50Hz
SERBIA	SECAM(H)	D	K	220 50Hz
SEYCHELLES	PAL	B	-	230 50Hz
SIERRA LEONE	PAL	B	-	230 50Hz
SINGAPORE	PAL	B	-	230 50Hz
SLOVAKIA	SECAM(H)	D	K	220 50Hz
SLOVENIA	PAL	B	G	220 50Hz
SOMALIA	PAL	B	-	220 50Hz
SOUTH AFRICA	PAL	I	I	230 50Hz
SPAIN	PAL	B	G	120/220 50Hz
SRI LANKA	PAL	B	-	230 50Hz
SUDAN	PAL	B	-	240 50Hz
SWEDEN	PAL	B	G	220 50Hz
SWITZERLAND	PAL	B	G	110/220 50Hz
SYRIA	PAL	-	G	110/220 50Hz
TAHITI	SECAM(V)	K	-	110/220 60Hz
TAJIKISTAN	SECAM	D	K	220 50Hz
TAIWAN	NTSC	M	-	110 60Hz
TANZANIA	PAL	B	G	230 50Hz
THAILAND	PAL	B	-	220 50Hz
TOGO	SECAM(V)	K1	-	220 50Hz
TRINIDAD & TOBAGO	NTSC	M	-	110/230 60Hz
TUNISIA	SECAM(V)	B	G	110/220 50Hz
TURKEY	PAL	B	G	110/220 50Hz
UKRAINE	SECAM	D	K	220 50Hz
UGANDA	PAL	B	-	240 50Hz
UNITED ARAB EMIRATES	PAL	B	G	220/240 50Hz
UNITED KINGDOM	PAL	-	I	240 50Hz
URUGUAY	PAL-N	N	-	220 50Hz
USA	NTSC	M	M	110 60Hz
UZBEKISTAN	SECAM	D	K	220 50Hz
VANUATU	PAL	-	-	220 50Hz
VATICAN	PAL	B	G	220 50Hz
VENEZUELA	NTSC	M	-	120/240 60Hz
VIETNAM	NTSC/SECAM(V)	M,D	-	220 50Hz
YEMEN	PAL	B	-	220 50Hz
YUGOSLAVIA	PAL	B	G	220 50Hz
ZAIRE	SECAM(V)	K1	-	220 50Hz
ZAMBIA	PAL	B	-	220 50Hz
ZANZIBAR	PAL	I	I	220 50Hz
ZIMBABWE	PAL	B	-	230 50Hz

HDTV

Although not officially, high-definition television (HDTV) has arrived. Many experiments and tests have been conducted, and most importantly, the technology is now developed to a stage where it can be mass produced.

Many countries have already adopted a program of introducing terrestrial broadcast HDTV and slowly phasing out the old analog TV. This is supposed to happen by the end of 2006 in the United States, and on a similar time frame for elsewhere in the developed world.

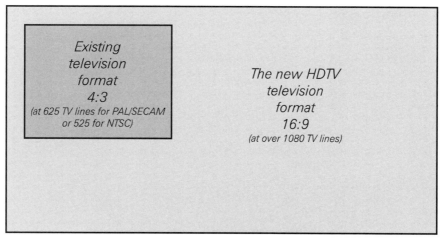

Existing television format 4:3 (at 625 TV lines for PAL/SECAM or 525 for NTSC)

The new HDTV television format 16:9 (at over 1080 TV lines)

HDTV and analog SDTV comparison

Hopefully, it won't take too long for CCTV to follow suit.

The idea of high definition is to have approximately twice as much resolution (horizontal and vertical, which produces four times more details) and a new aspect ratio of 16:9 as opposed to the existing 4:3. The reason for this widening of the TV screen is compatibility with the majority of movie formats.

HDTV offers approximately twice the vertical and horizontal resolution of a PAL signal, providing a picture quality close to 35-mm film and a sound quality close to that of a compact disc.

HDTV has been worked on for over a decade now, but without any global agreement among major video manufacturers. Test broadcasts have been conducted in Japan, Europe and the US, but again, based on the two strongest standards developed: PAL and NTSC. For both of these, an analog high-definition signal was used. Today though, most of the images are processed in digital format. This is why the newer HDTV can also be called digital television since all data is stored and transmitted in digital format.

In 1993 a group of institutions and companies was formed in order to evaluate the present technologies and decide on key elements that will be at the heart of the best HDTV system. This group was called the Grand Alliance and some of its members include AT&T™, General Instrument Corporation™,

Massachusetts Institute of Technology (MIT), Philips™, David Sarnoff Research Centre™, Thomson™ and Zenith™.

In 1995, the Alliance agreed to use the MPEG-2 video, audio and system multiplexing, which is the same format as in DVD.

Two display modes have been proposed: interlaced and progressive (or non-interlaced) scanning.

The video compression algorithm accepted is the MPEG-2 standard, while the audio compression will use some of the Dolby™ techniques. The transmission modulation technique proposed is to be a quadrature amplitude modulation with vestigial sideband. The selected audio technology is an eight-channel, CD-quality digital surround-sound system, using one of Dolby's cinema surround-sound techniques.

The draft defines a choice of picture frame update of 24, 30 and 60 frames per second with progressive, non-interlaced scanning. The display resolution will work at around 1080 scanning lines with 1920 samples per line. This defines an absolute picture resolution of 1920 × 1080 (16:9). Some minor changes of these numbers are still possible as of writing this book.

With this resolution it will be natural to see the development of bigger and better screens, but also a blending of most of the visual media into one large unity: film, TV, computer graphics and multimedia.

Digital terrestrial transmission broadcast (DTTB) brings to an end the direct relationship between one television program and one frequency. DTTB is capable of carrying either one HDTV program or up to six services using standard definition television (SDTV), or as many as ten services with lower definition formatting. As with computer technology, it is possible to trade off the bit rate, the channel width and picture quality.

Essentially, the type of picture determines how much of the channel's capacity is needed for transmission. A digital terrestrial broadcast channel can carry up to 20-Mbps of data. HDTV services would use most if not all of this capacity, but an SDTV service would use considerably less depending on the nature of the service, fast moving sports, for example, could require up to 10-Mbps data rate and hence possibly only two of these services could be delivered at the one time. By comparison, a talking-head picture would utilize about 5 Mbps of data.

DTTB systems can accommodate 6-, 7- and 8-MHz channel spacings with minimal or no apparent cost disadvantage. Australia uses 7-MHz channel spacing for analog services, the United States uses 6-MHz and Europe commonly uses 8-MHz, although there is also some 7-MHz use.

DTTB can be accommodated within the existing broadcasting frequency bands, generally in UHF but also in VHF bands, using vacant channels adjacent to analog services.

These channels often cannot be used for additional analog services, because of technical constraints inherent in analog systems, but they can be used for DTTB as such receivers are expected to tolerate higher levels of co-channel and adjacent channel interference.

The HDTV will naturally be more exciting to watch, and the clarity and resolution of the images will allow for much bigger screens. Initially, if such screens are based on CRT technology with which high resolution can be achieved, we cannot expect a diagonal size larger than 1 m. But with one of the new display technologies, such as the plasma display, the FED or DMD, and not excluding the LCD (all of which are discussed in *Monitors,* Chapter 6), we will certainly see larger screen sizes, most probably only limited by the room size and the viewing distance.

For CCTV, the HDTV size will not be so critical and CRT high-definition monitors are OK since the majority of security operators and users watch the screens from a very close distance. But this is not to say that new control room designs will not take a different approach where one or two large monitors at a room's distance will be the main control displays.

5. CCTV Cameras

The very first and most important element in the CCTV chain is the element that captures the images – the camera.

General information about cameras

The term "camera" comes from the Latin *camera obscura*, which means "dark room."

This type of room was an artist's tool in the middle ages. A lightproof room, in the form of a box, with a convex lens at one end and a screen that reflected the image at the other was used by the artists to trace images and later produce paintings.

In the 19th century, "camera" referred to a device for recording images on film or some other light-sensitive material. It consisted of a lightproof box, a lens through which light entered and was focused, a shutter that controlled the duration of the lens opening and an iris that controlled the amount of light that passed through the glass.

Joseph Nicéphore Niépce produced the first negative film image in 1826. This is considered as the birth of photography. Initially, such photographic cameras didn't differ much from the camera obscura concept. They were in the form of a black box, with a lens at the front and a film plate at the back. The initial image setup and focusing were done on an upside-down projection, which a photographer could see only when he or she was covered with a black sheet.

The first commercial photographic cameras had a mechanism for manual transport of the film between exposures and a viewfinder, or eyepiece, that showed the approximate view as seen by the lens.

Today, we use the term "camera" in film, photography, television and multimedia. Cameras project images onto different targets, but they all use light and lenses.

To understand CCTV you don't need to be an expert in cameras and optics, but it helps if you understand the basics.

Many things are very similar to what we have in photography, and since every one of us has been, or is, a family photographer, it will not be very hard to make a correlation between CCTV and photography or home video.

In photographic and film cameras, we convert the optical information (images) into a chemical emulsion imprint (film). In television cameras, we convert the optical information into electrical signals.

They all use lenses with certain focal lengths and certain angles of view, which are different for different formats.

Lenses have a limited resolution and certain distortions (or aberrations), but this is more obvious in the film cameras. This is because the film resolution is still far better than the electronic camera resolution although there are higher resolution chips coming out daily.

To illustrate, high-resolution CCD chips in CCTV these days have about 752 × 582 pixels (picture elements), while 100 ISO 35-mm color negative film has a resolution equivalent to 8000 × 6000 elements (film grains). This is based on a typical film resolution of 120 lpm.

In 1997, another type of camera emerged onto the market. This camera is used with computers for both video conferencing and digital image storage. A camera like this uses a CCD chip as an imaging device, but instead of producing analog electronic signal or projecting the image on film, it converts the image to digital format and stores it on a micro disk or RAM-card in the camera, so it can be transferred to a computer. Although most of such camera produce still images, models with real time video in digital format are already appearing.

Tube cameras

The first experiments with television cameras were made, as mentioned earlier, in the 1930s by the Russian-born engineer Vladimir (Vlado) Zworykin (1889-1982). His first camera, made in 1931, focused the picture onto a mosaic of photoelectric cells. The voltage induced in each cell was a measure of the light intensity at that point and could be transmitted as an electrical signal. The concept, with small modifications, remained the same for decades.

Those first cameras were made with a glass tube and a light-sensitive phosphor coating on the inside of the glass. We now call them **tube cameras**.

Tube cameras

Tube cameras work on the principles of **photosensitivity**, based on the photo-effect. This means the light projected onto the tube phosphor coating (called the **target**) has sufficient energy to cause electrons' ejection from the phosphor crystal structure. The number of electrons is proportional to the light, thus forming an electrical representation of the light projection.

There were basically two main types of tubes used in the early days of CCTV: Vidicon and Newvicon.

Vidicon was cheaper and less sensitive. It had a so-called *automatic target voltage control*, which effectively controlled the sensitivity of the Vidicon and, indirectly, acted as an electronic iris control, as we know it today on CCD cameras. Therefore, Vidicon cameras worked only with manual iris lenses. The minimum illumination required for a B/W Vidicon camera to produce a signal was about 5~10 lux reflected from the object when using an F/1.4 lens.

Newvicon tube cameras were more sensitive (down to 1 lux), more expensive and required auto iris lenses. Their physical appearance was the same as the Vidicon tube, and one could hardly determine which type was which by just looking at the two. Only an experienced CCTV technician could notice the slight difference in the color of the target area: the Vidicon has a dark violet color, while the Newvicon has a dark bluish color. The electronics that control these two types of tubes are different, and on the outside of the camera the Newvicon type has an auto iris connection.

All tube cameras use the principles of electromagnetism, where the electron beam scans the target from the inside of the tube. The beam is deflected by the locally produced EMF which is generated by

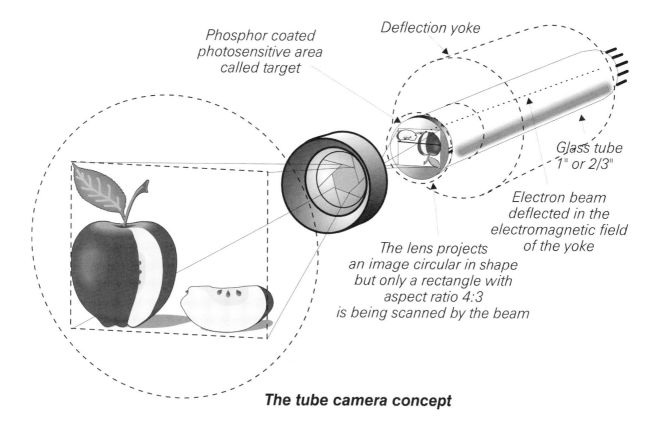

Phosphor coated
photosensitive area
called target

Deflection yoke

Glass tube
1" or 2/3"

Electron beam
deflected in the
electromagnetic field
of the yoke

The lens projects
an image circular in shape
but only a rectangle with
aspect ratio 4:3
is being scanned by the beam

The tube camera concept

the camera electronics. The more light that reaches the photo-conductive layer of the target, the lower its local resistance will be. **When an image is projected, it creates a potential map of itself by the photosensitivity effect**. When the analyzing electron beam scans the photosensitive layer, it neutralizes the positive charges created, so that a current flow through the local resistor occurs. When the electron beam hits a particular area of the potential map, an electrical current proportional to the amount of light is discharged. This is a very low current, in the order of pico-Amperes (pA = 10^{-12} A), which is fed into a very high input impedance video preamplifier, from which a video voltage signal is produced. For a tube camera, it is important to have a thin and uniform photo layer. This layer produces the so-called **dark current**, which exists even if there is no image projected by the lens (iris closed).

After a signal has been formed, the rest of the camera electronics add sync pulses, and at the output of the camera we get a complete video, known as a **composite video signal**.

There are a few important concepts used in the operation of tube cameras, which we need to briefly explain in order to appreciate the differences between this and the new, CCD, technology.

The first one is the **physical bulkiness of the camera** as such, due to the glass tube, electromagnetic deflection yoke around the tube and the size of the rest of the electronic components in the era when surface mount components were unknown. This made tube cameras quite big.

The second thing is the **need for a precise alternating electromagnetic field** (EMF) which will force the electron beam to scan the target area as per the television recommendations. To use an EMF to do the scanning means the external EMF of some other source may affect the beam scanning, causing picture distortions.

Third is the **requirement for a high voltage** (up to 1000 V), which accelerates the electron beam and gives it straight paths when scanning. Consequently, high-voltage components need to be used in the camera, which are always a potential problem for the electronic circuit's stability. Old and high-voltage capacitors may start leaking, moisture can create conductive air around the components and electric sparks may be produced.

The fourth thing to note is the need for a phosphor coating of the target, which converts the light energy into electrical information. The phosphor as such is subject to constant electron bombardment

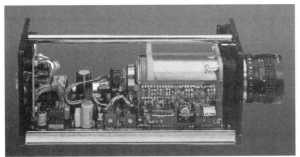

The inside of a tube camera

that wears it out. Therefore, **the life expectancy of a tube phosphor coating is limited**. With a constant camera usage, as is the case in CCTV, a couple of years will be the realistic life expectancy, after which the picture starts to fade out, or even get an imprinted image if the camera constantly looks at the same object. As a result, we can see pictures from a tube camera where, when people move, they appear as ghostlike figures, since they are semitransparent to the imprinted image.

And the fifth feature, conceptually different from the CCD cameras used today (and, again, this feature can be considered as a drawback) and inherently part of the tube camera design itself, are the **geometrical distortions** due to the beam hitting the target at various angles. Namely, the path of the electron beam is shorter when it hits the center of the target as compared to when it scans the edges of the tube. Therefore, certain distortions of the projected image are present. In a lot of tube camera designs, we'll find some magnetic and electronic corrections for such distortions, which means every time a tube needs to be replaced, all of these adjustments have to be remade.

With the new CCD technology, none of the above problems exist in cameras. One tube's feature, however, was very hard to beat in the early days of the CCD technology. This was the resolution of a good tube camera.

Vertical resolution is dependent on the scanning standard, and this would be, more or less, the same at both, CCD and tube cameras, but the horizontal resolution (i.e., the number of vertical lines that can be reproduced) depends on the thickness of the electron beam. Since this can be quite successfully controlled by the electronics itself, very fine details can be reproduced, i.e., analyzed while scanning.

Comparison of the physical size of a tube and a CCD chip

Initially, with the CCD design, microelectronics technology was not able to offer picture elements (pixels) of the CCD chip smaller than the beam cross section itself. This means that in the very beginning of CCD technology, the resolution lagged well behind that of the tube cameras.

Very soon, however, it was improved to match the tube camera's resolution quality.

CCD Cameras

CCD stands for charge-coupled device.

In the 1970s, when personal computers were born, experiments were made with solid-state electronic elements called **charge-coupled devices**, which were initially intended to be used as memory devices.

Very soon it was found that CCDs are very sensitive to light, so they could be used more effectively as imaging devices than as memory devices.

The basic principle of CCD operation is the storing of the information of electrical charges in the elementary cells and then, when required, to shift these charges to the output stage.

CCD Camera

When a CCD chip is used as an imaging device, the shifting concept stays the same, but instead of injecting charge packets as digital information (which would be the case if the CCD chip is used as a memory device), we have a **photo-effect generating electrons proportional to the amount of light falling on the imaging area**, and then, these charges are shifted out vertically and/or horizontally, in the same manner as shift registers in digital electronics shift binary values.

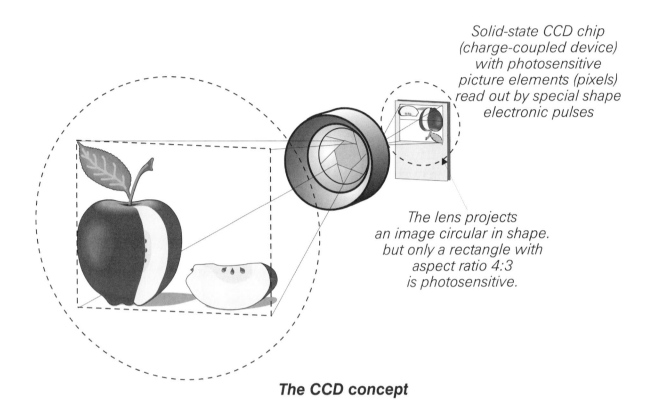

Solid-state CCD chip (charge-coupled device) with photosensitive picture elements (pixels) read out by special shape electronic pulses

The lens projects an image circular in shape. but only a rectangle with aspect ratio 4:3 is photosensitive.

The CCD concept

So, in effect, we have charge packets, once they have been collected in each photosensitive cell, "sliding down" to the output stage by using charge-coupling methods. Thus, an electrical coupling is done by means of voltage and timing manipulation of each cell, called a picture element (or **pixel**).

One of the pioneers of CCD technology, Gilbert Amelio, in his article written in 1974, describes charge coupling as "a collective transfer of all the mobile electric charge stored within a semiconductor storage element to a similar, adjacent storage element by the external manipulation of voltages. The quantity of the stored charge in this mobile packet can vary widely, depending on the applied voltage and on the capacitance of the storage element. The amount of electric charge in each packet can represent information."

The construction of CCD chips is either in the form of a line area (linear CCD) or in the form of a two-dimensional matrix (array CCD). It is important to understand that **they are composed of discrete pixels, but CCDs are not digital devices**. Each of these pixels can have any number of electrons, proportional to the light that falls onto it, thus representing **analog information**.

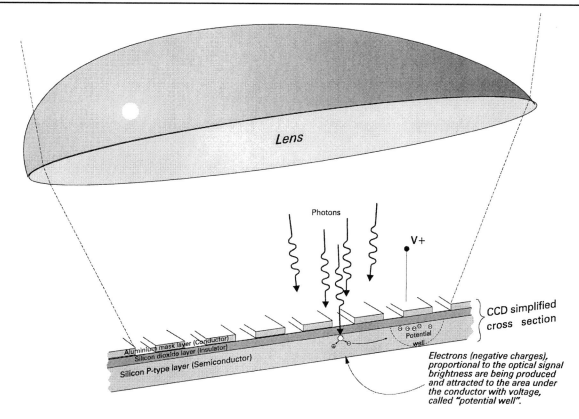

Lens

Photons

V+

CCD simplified cross section

Aluminium mask layer (Conductor)
Silicon dioxide layer (Insulator)
Silicon P-type layer (Semiconductor)

Potential well

Electrons (negative charges), proportional to the optical signal brightness are being produced and attracted to the area under the conductor with voltage, called "potential well".

Electrons in a CCD chip are produced by photons

These discrete packets of electrons are then transferred (once the exposure time is over), by simultaneous shifting of row and column packets, to the output stage of the chip.

This is why we can say **CCDs are, in essence, analog shift registers sensitive to light.**

Today, CCDs are not used as memory devices, but mostly as imaging devices. They can be found in many objects of daily use: facsimile machines use linear CCD chips; picture and OCR scanners also use linear CCDs; many auto-focusing photographic cameras use CCD chips for auto-focusing; geographic aerial monitoring,

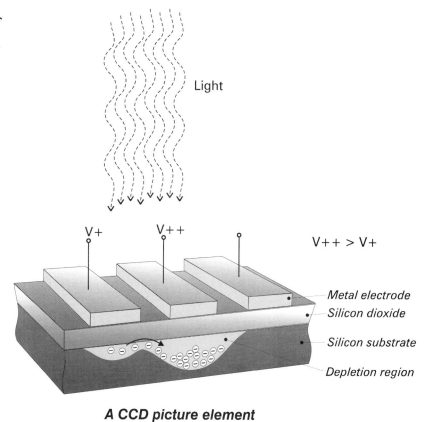

Light

V+   V++   V++ > V+

Metal electrode
Silicon dioxide
Silicon substrate
Depletion region

A CCD picture element

spacecraft planet scanning and industrial inspection of materials also use linear CCD cameras and last, but not least, most of the television cameras these days, both in broadcast and CCTV, use CCD chips.

CCD cameras have many advantages (in design) over the tube cameras, although, as mentioned earlier, in the beginning it was hard to achieve high-resolution similar to what the tube cameras had. These days, however, the technology is at such a level that high resolution is no longer a problem.

Various types of CCD chips <small>Photo courtesy of Dalsa</small>

The main advantages that the CCD cameras have over tube cameras are:

- Very low minimum illumination performance (in B/W down to 0.1 lx at the object);

- No geometrical distortions due to a precise two-dimensional construction;

- Low power consumption;

- No need for high voltage for beam acceleration;

A fixed camera dome with tinted glass

- Small size;

- No influence of external EMFs; and, most importantly,

- Unlimited lifetime of electrons generated by photo-effect.

Installation of dome cameras is simple

As we said earlier, CCDs come in all shapes and sizes, but the general division is into linear and two-dimensional matrices. Linear chips are used in applications where there is only one direction of movement by the object (like with facsimile machines or scanners).

In CCTV we are only interested in two-dimensional matrices, the so-called 2/3", 1/2", and 1/3" sizes.

As mentioned earlier, these numbers are **not the diagonal sizes of the chips**, as many assume, but rather they are the sizes people use to refer to the diameter of the tube that would produce such an image.

PCB CCD cameras are very small

Sensitivity of the CCD chips

Comparing sensitivities will show us the advantage of CCD chips relative to the Vidicon and Newvicon tubes, but also relative to a film emulsion.

The 100 ISO film is the mo st commonly used in photography, although we can buy 200 ISO film (twice as sensitive), or 400 ISO (four times more sensitive than the 100 ISO film). Sometimes, we may even come across 1600 ISO film, and this is usually used for extremely low light level situations (at least in photographic terms).

It can be shown that an average B/W CCD chip has a very high light sensitivity compared to a film emulsion. On a full sunny day, a typical 100 ISO film camera will require a setting of 1/125 s and F-16. When the same scene is observed by a CCD camera, of which the normal CCIR exposure speed is 1/50 s, a lens with approximately F-1000 needs to be used (give or take an F-stop or two, since the camera's AGC plays a role too). If we convert the 1/50 to 1/125 (2.5 times shorter), in order to have the same exposure the lens needs to have an opening 2.5 F-stops wider to compensate for the shortening of the exposure. This brings us from F-1000 to approximately F-400 (remember the F-numbers: 1.4, 2, 2.8, 4, 5.6, 8, 11, 16, 22, 32, 44, 64, 88, 128, 180, 250, 360, 500, 720, 1000, 1400, etc.). Now, in order to convert the sensitivity of the film emulsion to get from the 100 ISO settings of 1/125 and F-16 to the equivalent settings of a higher film sensitivity, and knowing that double sensitivity occurs with doubling the ISO number, we get 9.5 F-times from F-16 to F-400. And this is approximately $2^{9.5} = 720$ times. So, **the average B/W CCD chip sensitivity, expressed in photographic ISO units, is approximately 100 ISO × 720 = 72,000 ISO!**

Similarly, we will find that **a color CCD camera has the equivalent sensitivity of approximately 5000 ISO**, which is still very high compared to the photographic standards.

Chemical (film) photography is slowly merging with electronic cameras. Having in mind the computerization and digitalization of the photographic techniques, as well as the introduction of various photo CD standards, it should be noted that photographic cameras are also undergoing a revolution and we will see more CCD-based still cameras with increased light sensitivity.

Array CCD chips come in various sizes

Photo courtesy of Dalsa

Such still cameras are not dependent on the TV standard; therefore, there is no practical limitation on the number of pixels and aspect ratio. Even as this book is being written, manufacturers are producing chips with an area size as small as 62 mm × 62 mm, with no less than 5120 × 5120 picture elements. As already mentioned, these are still cameras and should not be confused with CCTV cameras.

The spectral sensitivity of CCD chips varies with various silicon substrates, but the general characteristic is a result of the photo-effect phenomenon: **longer wavelengths penetrate deeper into the CCD silicon structure**. This refers to the red and infrared light. A typical CCD chip spectral curve is shown on the drawing below.

Even though this "penetration" may seem beneficial (CCD chips seem more sensitive), there are reasons for preventing some of the longer waves from getting too deep inside the chip. Namely, such wavelengths might be so strong that they could produce electron carriers in areas that are not supposed to be exposed to light. As a result the picture may lose details because the next door pixels will melt their content into each other, losing high-resolution components and causing a blooming effect. The masked areas, which are supposed to only temporarily store charges and are not supposed to be exposed to light, can also be affected, so that noise and smear increase significantly. Because of these reasons, special **optical infrared cut filters** have been introduced as part of a

A CCTV camera CCD chip

well-designed CCD camera. These filters are optically precise plan-parallel pieces of glass, mounted on top of the CCD chips. As the name suggests, they behave as optical low pass filters, where the cutting frequency is near 700 nm, i.e., near the color red.

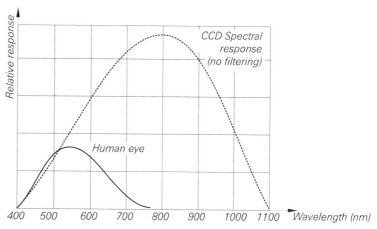

The eye's and the CCD chip's spectral sensitivity

There are a number of manufacturers of B/W cameras, though, that prefer not to put such filters on their chips, to make their cameras more sensitive. This might be acceptable, especially when cameras for lower light levels need to be used or if infrared illuminators are to be part of the system; however, from a theoretical point of view **cameras *with* infrared cut filters will show better resolution** (compared to the same chip without an IR cut filter), **better S/N ratio and more natural color-to-gray conversion**, at the expense of a not so low minimum illumination response.

Color CCD cameras, on the other hand, *must* use an IR cut filter, as the CCD chip's spectral response, which we saw is different to that of the eye, must be made similar to the human eye's spectral sensitivity. This is also one of the reasons why color CCD cameras are less sensitive than B/W.

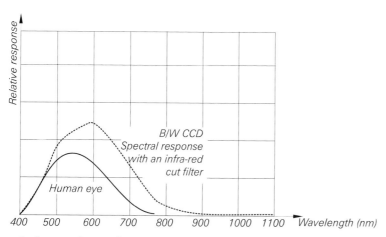

Infra-red cut filter modifies the CCD response

A typical B/W CCD chip, without an infrared cut, can produce a reasonable

level of video signal at as low as 0.01 lx. The same camera with a filter will be quoted 0.1 lx for the same object illumination.

Color cameras these days are quoted to have 2-lx minimum illumination at the object, with an F/1.4 producing a video signal of a reasonable level (0.3 to 0.5 V).

The IR cut filter is a must for color CCD cameras

Types of charge transfer in CCDs

Matrix (array) CCD chips, as used in CCTV, can be divided into three groups based on the techniques of charge transfer.

The very first design, dating from the early 1970s, is known as **frame transfer** (FT). This type of CCD chip is effectively divided into two areas with an equal size, one above the other, an imaging and a masked area.

The **imaging area is exposed to light for 1/50 second** for a CCIR standard video (1/60 second for EIA). Then, **during the vertical sync period, all photo-generated charges** (electronically representing the optical image that falls on the CCD chip) **are shifted down to the masked area** (see the simplified drawing on the next page). Basically the whole "image frame" comes down.

Note the upside-down appearance of the projected image, since that is how it looks in a real situation, i.e., the lens projects an inverted image and the bottom right-hand pixel is re-created in the top left-hand corner when displayed on a monitor.

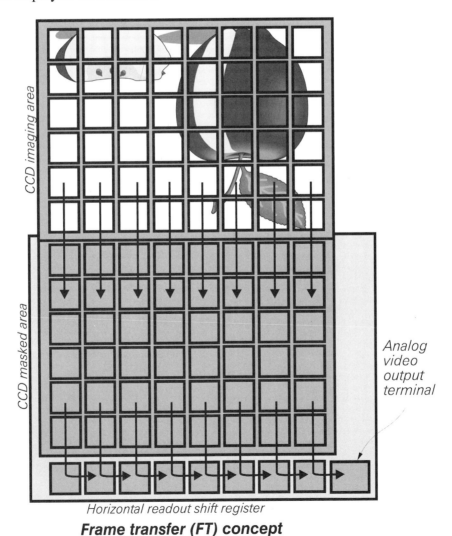

Frame transfer (FT) concept

For the duration of the next 1/50 second, the imaging area generates the electrons of the new picture frame, while the electron packets in the masked area are shifted out horizontally, line-by-line. The electron packets (current) from each pixel are put together in one signal and converted into voltage, creating a TV line information.

Technically, perhaps, it would be more precise to call this mode of operation "field transfer" rather than "frame transfer," but this has been used since the early days of CCD development and we'll accept it as such.

This first design of the CCD chip was good. It had surprisingly better sensitivity than Newvicon tubes and much better than Vidicon, but it came with a new problem that was unknown to tube cameras: **vertical smearing**. Namely, in the time between subsequent exposures when the charge transfer was active, **nothing stopped the light from generating more electrons**. This is understandable since electronic cameras do not have a mechanical shutter mechanism as photographic or film cameras do. So where intense light areas were present in the image projection, vertical bright stripes would appear.

To overcome this problem, design engineers have invented a new way of transference called **interline transfer** (IT). The difference here is (see the simplified drawing) that the exposed picture is not transferred down during the vertical sync pulse period, but it is **shifted to the left masked area columns**. The imaging and masked columns are next to each other and interleave, hence the name, interline. Since the masked pixel columns are immediately to the right of the imaging pixel columns, the shifting is considerably faster; therefore, there is not much time for bright light to generate an unwanted signal, the smear.

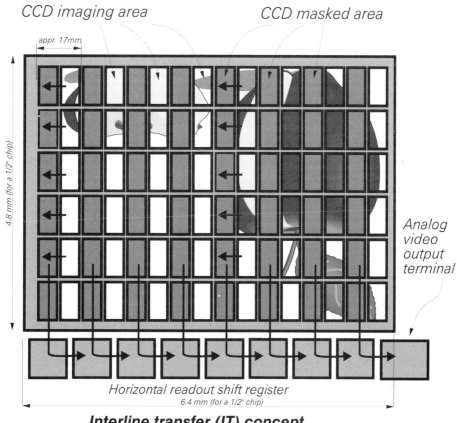

Interline transfer (IT) concept

To be more precise, the smear is still generated, but in a considerably smaller amount. As a result, we also have a much higher S/N ratio.

There is one drawback to the IT transfer chips, which is obvious from the concept itself: in order to add the masked columns next to the imaging columns on the same area as the previous FT design, the size of the light-sensitive pixels had to be reduced. This reduces the sensitivity of the chip. Compared to the benefits gained, however, this drawback is of little significance.

One new and interesting benefit is the **possibility of implementing an electronic shutter in the CCD design**. This is an especially attractive feature, where the natural exposure time of 1/50 second (1/60 for NTSC) can be electronically controlled and reduced to whatever shutter speed is necessary, still producing a 1 V_{pp} video signal.

Initially, with the IT chip, manual control of the CCD-shutter was offered, but very soon an automatic version came out. This type of control is known as an automatic **CCD-iris**, or **electronic iris**. The electronic iris replaces the need for AI controlled lenses. So an MI lens can be used with an electronic iris camera even in an outdoor installation. It should be noted, however, that an **electronic iris cannot substitute the depth of field function** produced by the mechanical iris in a lens. Also, it should be remembered that when the electronic iris switches to higher shutter speeds, and due to lower charge transfer efficiency, the smear increases.

So, when the electronic iris is enabled, it switches from a normal exposure speed of 1/50 (1/60) to a higher one (shorter duration), depending upon the light situation. Theoretically, exposures longer than 1/50 second (1/60 for EIA) could not be used because of loss of motion. With some CCD cameras, longer exposures are possible, and this mode of operation is called **integration**. With some of the latest camera

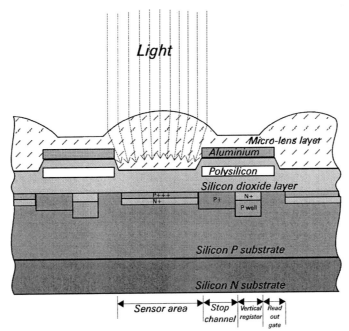

**A typical structure of the cross-section of a CCD chip
with micro lens design**

designs incorporating digital signal processing, integration is automatically turned on when object illumination falls below a certain level. This is especially helpful with color cameras, where low light level pictures are produced, until now possible only with B/W cameras. The price paid for this is the loss of smoothness in motion (in integration mode we cannot have 50 fields), which is substituted with a motion appearance similar to a playback from a TL VCR.

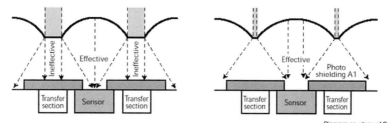

Diagram courtesy of Sony

Comparison between a conventional on-chip micro lens and the new Sony's Exwave concept

Reducing the pixel size in the IT design, we said, indirectly reduces the chip's minimum illumination performance. This problem can be solved with a very simple concept (technologically not as easy though) of putting micro lenses on top of every pixel. Micro lenses concentrate all of the light that falls on them to a smaller area, which is actually the pixel itself, and effectively increase the minimum illumination performance. The most common types of CCD cameras in CCTV today have IT chips.

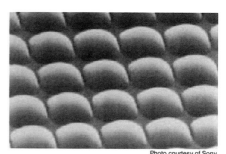

Photo courtesy of Sony

An electronic microscope photo of the on-chip microlens structure

A typical cross section of an IT CCD chip with a micro lens on top of every pixel is shown in the drawing on the next page. As it can be seen, the micro structure of the chip becomes quite complex when a high-quality signal needs to be produced.

The best design so far is the latest **frame interline transfer** (FIT) chip, offering all the features of the interline transfer plus even less smear and a better S/N ratio. As it can be concluded from the simplified drawing, the FIT CCD works as an interline transfer in the top part of the chip, thus having the electronic iris control, but instead of holding the image in the masked columns for the duration of the next field exposure, it is shifted down to the better protected masked area.

This is the reason for even less smearing in the FIT design, but there is also gain in the S/N ratio. Micro lenses are also used here to increase the minimum illumination performance. FIT chips have an even further advanced micro structure, with a lot of cells and areas designed to prevent spills of excessive charges to the area around, trap the thermally generated electrons and so on. With all these fine tune-ups, FIT chips have a very high dynamic range, low smear and high S/N ratio, which makes them ideal for external camera shooting and news gathering in broadcast TV. These types of cameras, in broadcast TV, are usually referred to as **electronic news gathering** cameras (ENG).

So, as it can be seen, these chips are expensive for CCTV, and their main use is in broadcast TV.

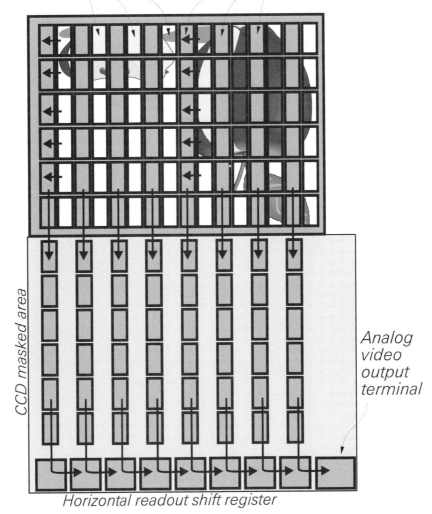

Light-sensitive pixels, CCD imaging area

Vertical shift registers, CCD masked area

CCD masked area

Analog video output terminal

Horizontal readout shift register

Frame interline transfer (FIT) concept

In the end we should point out that no matter how good the camera electronics are, if the source of information – the CCD chip – is of an inferior quality, the camera will be inferior too. The opposite statement is also true, i.e., even if the CCD chip is of the best quality, if the camera electronics cannot process it in the best possible way, the total package becomes second class.

It should also be noted that most of the handful of chip manufacturers have CCD products of the same type divided into a few different classes, depending on the pixel quality and uniformity. Different camera manufacturers may use different classes of the same chip type. This is in the end reflected not only in the quality but also in the price of the camera.

Pulses used in CCD for transferring charges

The quality of a signal as produced by the CCD chip depends also on the pulses used for transferring charges. These pulses are generated by an internal crystal oscillator in the camera. This frequency depends on many factors, but mostly on the number of pixels the CCD chip has, the type of charge transfer (FT, IT or FIT), as well as the number of phases used for each elementary shifting of charges, namely, the elementary shifting can be achieved with a two-phase, three-phase or four-phase shift pulse. In CCTV, cameras with three-phase transfer pulses are the most common.

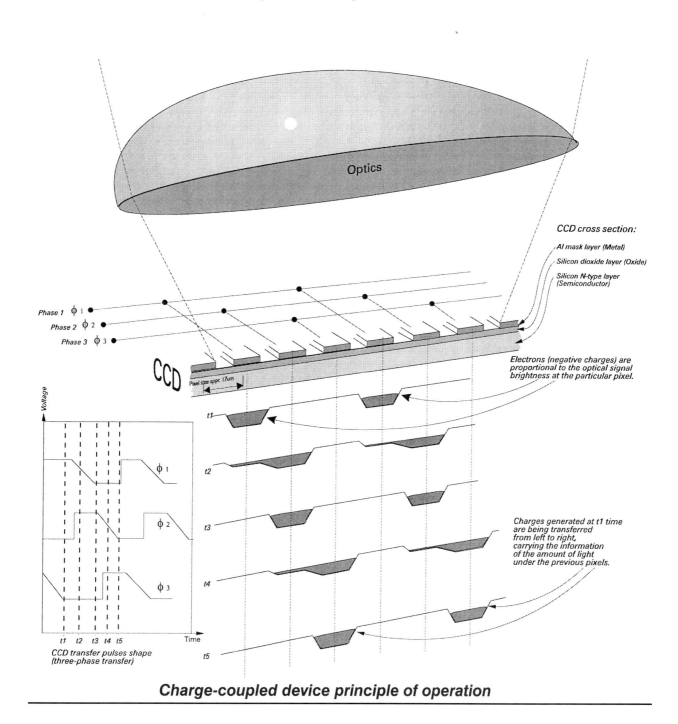

Charge-coupled device principle of operation

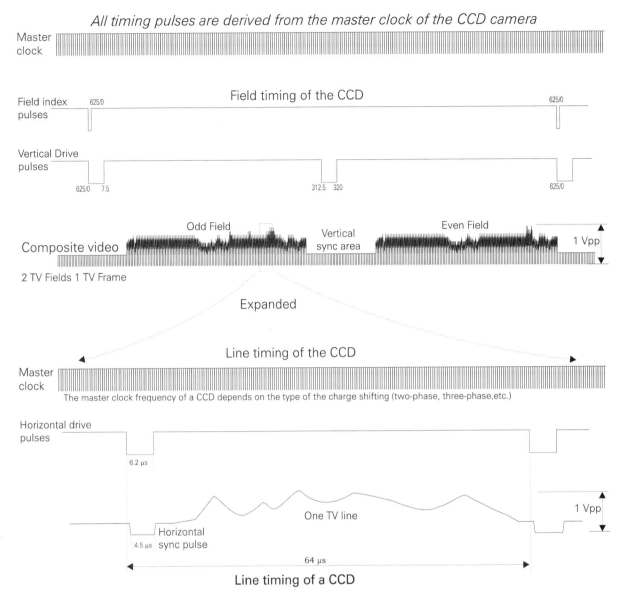

Timing pulses in a CCD chip are derived from a master clock

As you can imagine, the camera's crystal oscillator needs to have a frequency at least a few times higher than the signal bandwidth that a camera produces. All other syncs, as well as transfer pulses are derived from this master frequency. The drawing shows how this charge transfer is performed with the three-phase concept.

The pulses indicated with ϕ_1, ϕ_2 and ϕ_3 are low-voltage pulses (usually between 0 and 5 VDC), which explains why CCD cameras have no need for high voltage, as was the case with the tube cameras.

The above schematic shows how video signal sync pulses are created using the master clock.

This is only one of many examples, but it clearly shows the complexity and number of pulses generated in a CCD camera.

CCD chip as a sampler

As we said earlier, the CCD chip used in CCTV is a two-dimensional matrix of picture elements (*pixels*). The resolution that such a matrix produces depends on the number of pixels and the lens resolution. Since the latter is usually higher than the resolution of the CCD chip, we tend to not consider the optical resolution as a bottleneck. However, as mentioned in the heading on MTF, lenses are made with a resolution suitable for a certain image size, and care should be taken to use the appropriate optics with various chip sizes.

There is another important aspect of the CCD resolution to be taken into account, and this is the TV line non-continuity. Namely, a TV line produced by a tube camera is obtained by a **continuous** beam scanning along the line. A CCD chip has **discrete** pixels and therefore the information contained in one TV line is composed of **discrete** values from each pixel. This method does not produce digital information but rather discrete samples. In a way, the CCD chip is an **optical sampler**.

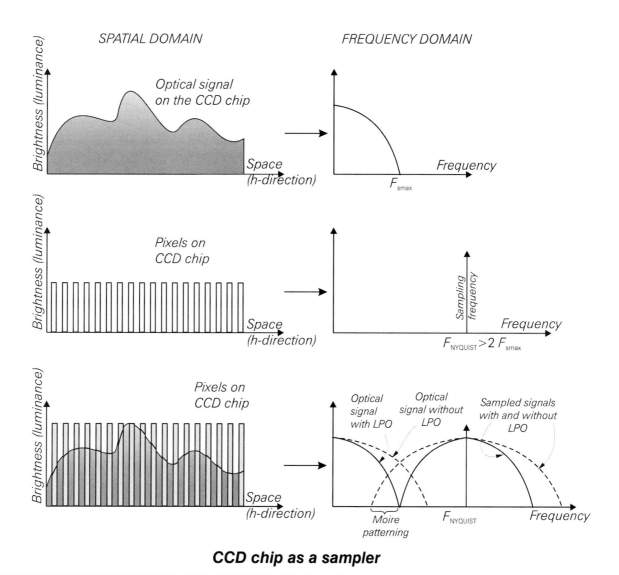

CCD chip as a sampler

Like with any other sampler, we don't get the total information of each line, but only discrete values at positions equivalent to the pixel positions.

To some, it may seem impossible to reproduce a continuous signal from only portions of the same. In 1928, however, Nyquist showed that a signal can be reconstructed perfectly, without any loss of information, if the sampling frequency is at least twice the bandwidth of the signal. **Samples of the signal in between the sampled points are not necessary**. This is a great theory, proven correct and used in many electronic samplers such as in CD-audio, video, etc. The sampling frequency, which is equivalent to two times the bandwidth, is called **the Nyquist frequency**.

There is, however, an unwanted by-product of the CCD sampling. This is the well-known **Moiré pattern** that occurs when taking shots of higher-resolution objects. This is usually obvious with, for example, a news reader wearing a coat or shirt with a very fine pattern. This can mathematically be described as a fold-over frequency around the sampling one. Since the spatial sampling frequency should be twice the highest frequency in the optical image F_{smax}, we can represent it, in the frequency domain, with a single frequency located at the Nyquist frequency $F_{NYQUIST}$. The basic bandwidth spatial spectrum of the optical signal will be modulated around this frequency, very similar to an amplitude modulation sideband's spectrum. If a high spatial frequency exists in the optical image projected on the CCD chip, and if this frequency is higher than half of the $F_{NYQUIST}$ frequency, the side bands (after the sampling is done) will fold over into the visible basic bandwidth and we will see the result as an unwanted pattern, known as Moiré pattern. The Moiré frequency is lower than the highest frequency of the camera ($F_{NYQUIST}/2 - F_{smax}$).

To minimize this unwanted effect, **low-pass optical (LPO) filtering** has to be done. These filters are usually part of the CCD chip glass mask and are formed by combining several birefringent quartz plates. The effect is similar to blurring the fine details of an optical image.

Correlated Double Sampling (CDS)

The noise in a CCD chip has several sources. The most significant is the thermally generated noise, but a considerable amount can be generated by the impurities of the semiconductors and the quality of manufacture.

High noise reduces the image sensor's dynamic range, which in turn degrades image quality.

A careful CCD device design and fabrication can minimize the noise. Also, low operating temperature can reduce thermally generated noise. The user, unfortunately, rarely has control over these parameters.

There is, however, a signal processing technique that can be implemented in the design of the CCD camera that reduces this noise considerably. This technique is called **correlated double sampling (CDS)**. The term *sampling* here refers to the CCD signal output sampling.

The concept of CDS is based on the fact that the same noise component is present in the valid video as in the reference signal in between charge transfers. Namely, when the output stage of the CCD chip transfers packets of electrons, they are converted to an output voltage. To do this, CCD devices typically use a floating sensing diffusion to collect signal electrons as they are shifted out of the chip. As the electrons are transferred out of the CCD, the voltage on the sensing diffusion area drops. This voltage represents the valid data, and is amplified on-chip by a thermally compensated amplifier. Before the next packet of signal electrons can be transferred into the diffusion area, it must be cleared from the previous packet. This represents a reference reset signal that has a thermal noise component of the same type. By extracting these two values a less noisy signal is obtained.

CDS is best accomplished using two high-speed sample and hold circuits connected to the image sensor's output signal through a low pass filter.

We will not go into more details on how these circuits are designed, as it is beyond the scope of this book, but it should be remembered that the CDS circuits are part of the camera electronics and not of the CCD chip.

Camera specifications and their meanings

The basic objective of the television camera is, as already explained, to capture images, break them up into a series of still frames and lines, transmit and display them onto a screen rapidly so that the human eye perceives them as motion pictures.

There are a number of characteristics we should take into account when choosing a camera. Some of them are important, others not so much, depending on the application.

It is impossible to judge a camera on the basis of only one or two characteristics from a brochure.

A modern, Digital Signal Processing CCD camera

Different manufacturers use different criteria and evaluation methods, and in most cases, even if we know how to interpret all of the numbers from a specification sheet, we still have to evaluate the picture ourselves, relative to the picture taken with another camera.

Comparison tests are quite often the best and probably the only objective way to check camera performance, such as smear, noise, sensitivity, etc.

Don't forget, the general impression of a good quality picture is a combination of many attributes: resolution, smear, sensitivity, noise, gamma, etc.

On the left a camera with visible smear and on the right almost invisible smear

The human eye is not equally sensitive to all of these factors.

People with no experience would be amazed to find that a 50-line difference in resolution is sometimes of less importance to picture quality than a correct gamma setting or a 3-dB difference in the S/N figure, for example.

We will go through some of the most important features:

* Camera sensitivity

* Minimum illumination

* Camera resolution

* S/N ratio

* Dynamic range

Other, less important but not wholly insignificant, features include: gamma settings, dark current, spectral response, optical low pass filtering, AGC range in dB, power consumption, physical size, etc.

Sensitivity

The sensitivity of a camera, although clearly defined in broadcast TV, is quite often misunderstood in CCTV and is usually confused with minimum illumination.

Sensitivity is represented by the minimum iris opening (maximum F-stop) that produces a *full* **$1V_{pp}$ (1 V peak-to-peak) video signal of a test chart, when that same test chart is lit by exactly 2000 lx at 3200° K color temperature of the source.** The test chart has to have a gray scale with tones from black to white, and an overall reflection coefficient of 90% for the white portion of the gray scale.

One of the standard test charts used for such purposes is the EIA gray scale chart. The white peak level needs to be 700 mV and the pedestal level around 20 mV. Gamma also plays a role in the proper reproduction of the grays and needs to be set at 0.45. In order to establish the sensitivity of the camera, a manual iris lens, usually of 25 to 50 mm, is required. In order to get a realistic measurement, the camera's AGC should be switched off.

The Gray Scale Test Chart

When all of the above is done, the manual iris lens is closed just until the white peak level drops from 700 mV, relative to the blanking level. The reading obtained from the lens's iris setting, like F/4 or F/5.6, represents the camera sensitivity. The higher the number is, the more sensitive the camera is. It is important to consider using the same light source and gray scale chart when comparing different cameras.

Minimum illumination

A camera's minimum illumination, contrary to the sensitivity, is not clearly defined in CCTV. It usually refers to **the lowest possible light at the object at which a chosen camera gives a recognizable video signal**. It is therefore expressed with luxes at the object, at which such a signal is obtained. The term *recognizable* is very loosely used, and depending on the manufacturer, it may or may not be defined. This represents one of the biggest loopholes in CCTV. Most manufacturers, especially the Taiwanese, do not specify what video level we should get at the camera output for the light amount specified as the minimum illumination. This level could be 30% (of the 700 mV), sometimes 50% and, for some, even 10 % might be acceptable.

The usual wording when describing minimum illumination would be, for example: "0.1 lx at the object with 80 % reflectivity using an F/1.4 lens."

Have in mind, though, that with high AGC circuitry in the camera, even 10% of video (70 mV) could be pumped up to appear as a much higher value than what it really is. This could obviously be misleading.

Let's say, for example, we have specifications that say 0.01 lx at the object with an F/1.4 lens, which presumes (but does not tell you) the AGC is switched to on. Another manufacturer may be very modest in their specs, stating, let's say, minimum illumination (where 50% of the video signal is obtained with the AGC set to off) of 0.1 lx with an F/1.4 lens. Clearly, on paper, the first case would seem to be a much more promising camera than the second one, although the second, in reality, is much better.

Another matter for discussion is when some manufacturers state the minimum illumination at the object, while others may refer to the minimum illumination at the CCD chip itself. This is not the same and there is a big difference as well.

When the minimum illumination of a camera (with the illumination at the object) is stated, we should also read to what F-stop it applies. Also, another important factor to know is the reflectivity percentage of the object when the illumination is stated.

If the minimum illumination is stated at the CCD chip, then not all the factors (such as reflectance and lens transmittance) have been taken into account. So, we have to compensate for all those factors when calculating the equivalent object illumination that is projected onto a CCD chip.

There is a rule of thumb (which I have elaborated in the **Calculating the amount of light** section) that, with an F/1.4 lens, the minimum illumination at the chip is usually 10 times higher (lower lux number) than the sensitivity at the object. For example, an illumination of 1 lx at the object with a reflectivity of 75% @ F/1.4 is equal to 0.1 lx illumination at the CCD chip.

As it can be concluded from the above, the real characteristics of a camera can be obscured quite easily by simply not stating all of the factors. **Read the specs carefully**.

A known fact is that B/W CCD cameras always have got a much lower minimum illumination than color CCD cameras.

One reason for this is the infrared cut filter on the CCD chip. As described earlier, it corrects the spectral response of the CCD chip so that it can be closer to the human eye's sensitivity, but it also reduces the amount of light that falls on the chip.

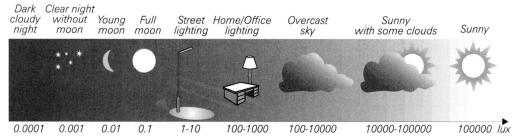

Some typical levels of illumination

The other reason is the primary color construction of a single color chip, as used in CCTV. A single pixel of a color CCD chip is composed of three sub-pixels, sharing the same physical space of a single B/W pixel.

The size will be no more than 1/3 of a B/W pixel, indirectly reducing the sensitivity.

At the time of writing the third edition of this book, new designs of CCD cameras and chips have arrived where a color camera is converted into B/W when light levels fall below a certain low level. There are a number of different ways such dual function has been achieved. One is by introducing physically two CCD chips in the camera and have some sort of switching electromechanical that is activated by the low light signal. Another is have the IR cut filter of the color chip removed and convert the color functionality of the chip into monochrome. And, finally, there is a complete new design of the chip itself performing this function, without the need for an electromechanical device.

The most common application of these cameras would be in areas where nighttime viewing with infrared light is required while preserving the color operation at full daylight.

Camera resolution

Camera resolution is very simple, but quite often misunderstood. **Vertical resolution** is the maximum number of horizontal lines that a camera is capable of resolving. This number is limited, by the CCIR/PAL standard, to 625 horizontal lines and to 525 by the EIA/NTSC recommendations. The real vertical resolution (in both cases), however, is far from these numbers.

If we take into account the vertical sync pulses, equalization lines, etc., the maximum for vertical resolution appears to be 575 lines for CCIR/PAL and 470 for EIA/NTSC. This needs to be further corrected by the Kell factor of 0.7, to get the maximum realistic vertical resolution of 400 TV lines for CCIR/PAL (see "Resolution" under Chapter 5 "General characteristic of TV systems" for more in-depth study). Similar deduction can be applied to the EIA/NTSC signal, where the maximum realistic vertical resolution is 330 TV lines.

Horizontal resolution is the maximum number of vertical lines that a camera is capable of resolving. This number is limited only by the technology and the monitor quality. These days, we have CCD cameras with horizontal resolution of more than 600 TV lines.

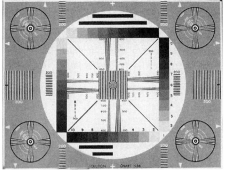
A RETMA Test chart measures resolution

The horizontal resolution of CCD cameras is usually 75% of the number of horizontal pixels on the CCD chip. As explained earlier, this is a result of the 4:3 aspect ratio. Namely, when counting vertical lines in order to determine horizontal resolution, we count only the horizontal width equivalent to the vertical height of the monitor. The idea behind this is to have equal thickness of lines, both vertically and horizontally. So if we count the total number of vertical lines across the width of the monitor, we have to then multiply this by 3/4, which is equal to 0.75. Because this is an unusual counting, we always refer to horizontal resolution as **TV lines and not just lines**.

There are a number of test charts on the market that can be used to evaluate a camera's resolution. The most popular is the EIA RETMA chart, but others can serve the purpose equally well. On the inside of the back cover of this book you will find a test chart specifically designed for the CCTV industry.

The important thing to know is, when measuring the resolution, the video signal must be properly terminated with 75 Ω, and the image must be seen in full, without the picture being overscanned (as is the case with most monitors). To do this, a special high-resolution monitor with the underscanning feature needs to be used.

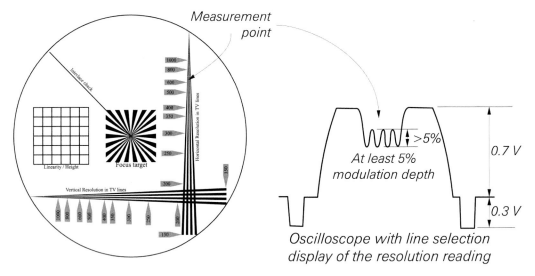

Measuring resolution

The camera is then set to the best focus possible (usually at a middle F-stop, 5.6 or 8) having the test chart fully in the field of view. Also, all internal camera correcting circuits (AGC, gamma, CCD-iris) need to be switched off.

Resolution can then be checked by measuring where the four resolution lines (in the form of a sharp triangle) stop being distinguishable. If this is done visually only, it will represent an approximate conclusion.

For a more precise reading, a high-quality oscilloscope, with TV line selection feature, should be used. The measurement is then narrowed down to selecting a line where the four lines modulation depth is equal or better than 5% (relative to 0.7 V signal). Using an oscilloscope in such a case enables us to

Resolution measurement

disregard the monitor's resolution limits. It should also be noted that due to optical resolution differences between the center and the corners of an image (center is always better than the corners), resolution measurements are best if made in the central area of the image.

Resolution is closely related to the signal bandwidth a camera is capable of reproducing. Their correlation was explained in the earlier section about resolution.

The test chart on the back cover of this book, which I have prepared for testing resolution as well as other important video signal features, can be used in a similar way. Please refer to the heading **The CCTV Test Chart** for a more detailed explanation of what else you can test with it.

Practical experience shows that the human eye can hardly distinguish a resolution difference of less than 50 lines. This is not to say that the resolution is an unimportant factor in determining camera quality but that small resolution differences are often hardly noticeable, especially if the resolution difference is smaller than 10% of the total number of pixels.

Single chip color CCD cameras (as used in CCTV) have lower resolution than B/W, again because of the separation into three color components, yet they still have the same size chips as B/W cameras. Three-chip color cameras, as used in broadcast TV, may have much higher resolution. There are now high-definition cameras where the three 1" chips produce horizontal resolution close to 1000 TV lines.

Signal/Noise ratio

S/N ratio is an expression that shows how good a camera signal can be, especially in lower light levels. Noise cannot be avoided, but only minimized. It depends mostly on the CCD chip quality, the electronics and the external electromagnetic influences but also very much on the temperature of the electronics. The camera's metal enclosure offers significant protection from external electromagnetic influences. Internal noise sources include both passive and active components of the camera, their quality and circuit design, and it very much depends on the temperature. This is why when stating S/N ratio, a camera manufacturer should indicate the temperature at which this measurement is taken.

The image noise is very similar in nature to the noise present in audio tapes, only it is part of a video and not of an audio signal. On the screen, noisy picture appears grainy or snowy, and if color signal is viewed, sparkles of colors may be noticeable. Extremely noisy signals may be difficult for equipment to synchronize to, and the picture may suffer from blurriness or lack of resolution. A noisy picture from a camera gets even worse if the light reduces and if high-gain AGC circuitry is used.

The units for expressing the S/N ratios are called *decibels* and are written as dB.

Decibels are only relative units. Instead of expressing the ratio as an absolute number, a logarithm is calculated. The reasoning behind this is simple: logarithms can show big ratios as only two- or three-digit numbers, but more importantly, signal manipulation (like when calculating the attenuation of a medium or amplification of a system) is reduced to simple addition and subtraction. Another reason for using decibels, i.e., logarithms, is the more natural understanding of sound and vision quantities. Namely, the human ear, as well as the eye, hears and sees sound and light quantities (respectively) by obeying logarithmic laws.

When a ratio of any two numbers with the same units is calculated, the units are in dB only. If, however, a relative ratio is calculated – for example, a voltage level relative to 1 mV – the units are called **dBmV**. If the power value is shown relative to 1 μW, the units are called **dBμW**.

The general formula for voltage and current ratios is:

$$S/N = 20 \log(V_s/V_n) \tag{39}$$

where: V_s is the signal voltage and V_n is the noise voltage. Current values are used when a current ratio needs to be shown.

If a power ratio is the purpose of a comparison, the formula is a little bit different:

$$S/N = 10 \log(P_1/P_2) \tag{40}$$

We won't go into explaining why this is different (10 and 20), but remember that it comes from the relation between the voltage, current and power.

In CCTV, we use decibels mostly for calculating voltage ratios, which means the first formula will be the one we would use.

The table below gives some dB values of voltage (current) and power ratios. Please note the difference between the two. While a 3-dB voltage difference means only a 41% higher value of the compared volts relative to the referred one, in terms of power this 3 dB means twice as much power (100% increase) of the compared relative to the reference power.

dB	0	0.1	0.2	0.3	1	2	3	10	20	30	60
Voltage/current ratio	1	1.012	1.023	1.035	1.122	1.259	1.413	3.162	10	31.62	1000
Power ratio	1	1.023	1.047	1.072	1.259	1.585	1.995	10	100	1000	1,000,000

Decibels table

The S/N ratio of a CCD camera is measured differently from that of a broadcast or transmitted signal.

In a broadcast TV signal the S/N ratio is the signal versus the accumulated noise from the transmission to the reception end. This is defined as the ratio (in dB) of the luminance bar amplitude to the RMS voltage of the superimposed random noise measured over a bandwidth of frequencies between 10 kHz and 5 MHz. There are special instruments that are designed to measure this value directly from the signal, by using some of the video insertion test signal (VITS) lines.

The S/N ratio in a CCD camera is defined as the ratio between the signal and the noise produced by the chip combined with the camera electronics. In order to get a realistic value for the S/N ratio of a camera, all internal circuits (that modify the signal in one way or another) need to be switched off or disabled. This includes gamma, AGC, CCD-iris and back light compensation circuitry. The temperature, as already mentioned, should be kept at room level. Of the few different methods used to measure camera video noise, the easiest one is to use a special instrument called a video noise meter. This unit selects the noise in the band between 100 kHz and 5 MHz and reads the S/N directly in decibels.

Practically, a S/N ratio of more than 48 dB is considered good for a CCTV CCD camera.

Don't forget, a 3-dB higher S/N ratio means approximately 30% less noise, since the video level doesn't change. So when comparing a 48-dB camera with a 51-dB camera, for example, the latter one will show a considerably better picture, more noticeable at lower light levels. We should always assume that the AGC is off when stating S/N ratios.

Keeping the camera as cool as possible reduces the noise.

For comparison purposes, let's just mention that broadcast CCD cameras have a ratio of more than 56 dB, which is extremely good for an analog video signal.

Dynamic range of a CCD chip

Dynamic range (DR) is not very often mentioned in CCTV camera specification sheets. It is, however, a very important detail of the camera performance profile.

The dynamic range of a CCD chip is defined as the maximum signal charge (saturation exposure) divided by the total RMS (root-mean-square) noise equivalent exposure. DR is similar to S/N ratio, but it only refers to the CCD chip dynamics when handling low to bright objects in one scene. While the S/N ratio refers to the complete signal including the camera electronics and is expressed in dB, the DR is a pure ratio number, i.e., not a logarithm.

This number actually shows the light range a CCD chip can handle, only this light range is not expressed with the photometric units but with the generated electrical signal. It starts from the very low light levels, equal to the CCD chip RMS noise, and goes up to the saturation levels. Since this is a ratio of two voltage values, it is a pure number, usually in the order of thousands. Typical values are between 1000 and 100,000. External daylight can easily saturate the CCD chip since the dynamic range of the light variation in an outdoor environment is much wider than the range a CCD chip can handle. A bright sunny day, for example, can easily saturate a CCD chip, especially if a camera hasn't got AGC, auto iris lens or a CCD-iris function. An auto iris lens optically blocks the excessive light and reduces it to whatever upper level the CCD chip can handle, while CCD-iris does that by electronically reducing the exposure time of the chip (which in normal circumstances is 1/50 s for CCIR/PAL signal and 1/60 s for EIA/NTSC signal).

When saturation levels are reached during a CCD exposure (1/50 s for PAL, or 1/60 s for NTSC), the **blooming** effect may become apparent, when excessive light saturates not only the picture elements (pixels) on which it falls but the adjacent ones as well. As a result, the camera reduces the resolution and detail information of the bright areas. To solve this problem, a special **anti-blooming** section is designed in most CCD chips. This section limits the amount of charges that can be collected in any pixel. When anti-blooming is designed properly, no pixel can accumulate more charges than what the shift registers can transfer. So, **even if the dynamic range of such a signal is limited, no details are lost in the bright areas of the image**. This may be extremely important in difficult lighting conditions such as looking at car headlights or perhaps looking at people in a hallway against light in the background.

Some camera makers, like Plettac, have introduced a special design that blocks the oversaturated areas during the digital signal processing stage. The video signal AGC circuitry then does not see extremely bright areas as a white peak reference point, but much lower levels are taken as white peaks, thus making the details in the dark more recognizable.

Photo courtesy of Plettac Electronics

Peak light blanking by Plettac

Others, like Panasonic, have patented new methods of CCD chip operation where, instead of having one field exposure every field time (1/50 s for PAL, or 1/60 s for NTSC), two exposures are done during this period. One at a very short time, usually around 1/1000 s and the other at the normal time that will depend on the amount of light. Then, the two exposures are combined in one field so bright areas are exposed with short exposure duration giving details in the very bright, and the darker areas exposed with the lower speed

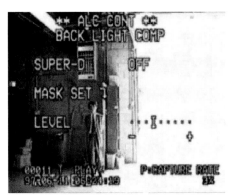

Images courtesy of Panasonic

The Panasonic superdynamic effect
(The images are captured from a compressed CD-ROM video clip)

giving details in the dimmer part of the same picture. The overall effect is of the dynamic range of the camera being increased 40 times (as claimed by Panasonic).

We should mention that, apart from the CCD design itself, and as with the S/N ratios, the operating temperature plays a big role in the dynamic range of a chip. Lower temperatures, in any electronic device, produce less noise; thus, the DR range will improve. In scientific applications, where every little bit of noise is unwanted, specially cooled CCD heads are used, where the operating temperature of the CCD chip is kept well below –50° C. For such applications, cameras are available where the CCD block has provision for a coolant to be attached to it.

So, it should be remembered, if in a CCTV system we do not use good quality cameras, the temperature can play a significant role in lowering the picture quality. Keeping the camera housing temperature as low as possible thus is very important.

Color CCD cameras

Color television is a very complex science in itself. The basic concept of producing colors in television is, as earlier described, by combining the three primary colors: red, green and blue. The color mixing actually happens in our eyes when we view the monitor screen from a certain distance. The discrete colors (R, G and B) are so small that we actually see a resultant color produced by the additive mixing of the three components. As mentioned earlier, this is called additive mixing, as opposed to subtractive, because by adding more colors we get more luminance, and with a correct mixture of the primary colors, a white can be obtained.

Most broadcast color TV cameras are made with three CCD chips, each of which receives its own color component. The white light's separation into R, G and B components is done with a special **optical split-prism,** which is installed between the lens and the CCD chips.

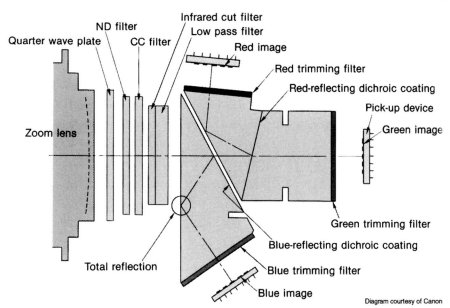

Three-chip CCD color cameras use
split prism for color separation

The split-prism is a very expensive and precisely manufactured optical block with dichroic mirrors. These are called three-chip color cameras and are not very commonly used in CCTV as they are considerably more expensive than one chip cameras. They do, however, offer a very high resolution and superior technical performance.

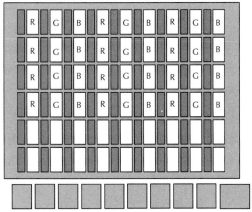

**RGB stripe filter of a
single-color CCD chip**

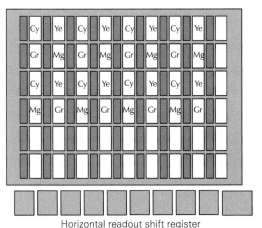

**Complementary (Cy, Ye, Mg, Gr)
mosaic filter of a
single-color CCD chip**

In CCTV, single-chip color cameras are the most common. They produce a composite color video signal, known as CVBS. As already discussed in Color Video Signal in Chapter 4 (see equation (35)), the three components of the signal that are embedded in the CVBS composition are luminance (Y), the color difference for red (V = R – Y) and for Blue (U = B – Y). These are quadrature modulated and, together with the luminance, combined in a composite color video signal. Then, the color monitor circuit processes these components and obtains the pure R, G and B signals.

In single-chip CCD color cameras, the color separation may be done using one of the two filtering methods:

- RGB stripe filter, where three vertical pixel columns (stripes) are next to each other: red, green and blue.

- Complementary colors mosaic filter, where the CCD chip pixels are not made sensitive to R, G and B colors, but to the complementary colors of cyan, magenta, yellow and green, ordered in a mosaic.

The first type of single-chip color CCD camera has a very good color reproduction and requires simpler circuits to achieve the same. However, it suffers from very low horizontal resolution, which is usually on the order of 50% of the total number of pixels in the horizontal direction of the chip. The vertical resolution, however, achieves the full number of vertical pixels. This type of color camera can easily produce RGB color signals.

The mosaic type single-chip color CCD camera requires more complex camera-electronics and it may lag in color reproduction quality compared to the RGB models (because of the color transformation needed to be applied to the Cy, Mg, Ye and Gr components), but it offers a much higher horizontal resolution of over 65% of the horizontal number of pixels.

Since the latter is the most common type of camera in CCTV, we will devote a bit more space to explaining how color components are converted to obtain a composite color video signal.

The mosaic filter, which is usually called **color filter array** (CFA), splits the light into magenta, cyan, yellow and green components. As mentioned, these colors are selected as complementary colors. So, in practice, this type of single-chip CCD color camera uses Mg, Cy, Ye and Gr color components to produce the luminance signal Y, and the color differences V = R – Y and U = B – Y.

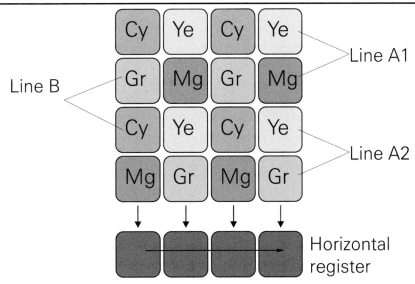

Color filter array (CFA)
of a color, single-chip, CCD camera

It should be noted (and we will mention it for clarity) that the single-chip color CCD cameras have light-sensitive pixels of the **same** silicon structure, and not different for different colors as some may think. It is the CFA filter that splits the image into color components.

In order to understand how is this produced, see the diagram of the color filter array above.

This type of CFA refers to a standard field integration camera, i.e., a camera where the exposure time is 1/50 s for PAL or 1/60 s for NTSC.

As it can be seen from the diagram, the four cells of the horizontal shift register contain signals of (Gr + Cy), (Mg + Ye), (Gr + Cy) and (Mg + Ye), respectively. By proper processing of these four signals we can get the three components that make a composite color video signal: the luminance (Y), the red color difference (R – Y) and the blue color difference (B – Y).

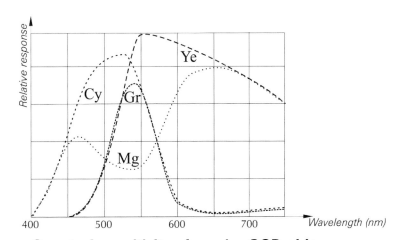

Spectral sensitivity of a color CCD chip
camera with Cy-Mg-Gr-Ye mosaic CCD filter

First, the luminance signal is obtained by the relation:

$$Y = \tfrac{1}{2}\left[(Gr + Cy) + (Mg + Ye)\right] = \tfrac{1}{2}(2B + 3G + 2R) \tag{41}$$

In order to understand the above, see the spectral sensitivity characteristic of a single-chip color CCD, shown on the bottom of the previous page.

The red color difference is similarly obtained through line A1:

$$R - Y = \left[(Mg + Ye) - (Gr + Cy)\right] = (2R - Gr) \tag{42}$$

The blue color difference is composed of line A2 values:

$$B - Y = \left[(Gr + Ye) - (Mg + Cy)\right] = (2B - Gr) \tag{43}$$

So, these are the two signals that, together with the luminance, are embedded in the composite video signal and represent a PAL (or NTSC) color video signal, as per standards.

Color printed circuit board camera

White balance

From color cameras we require, apart from the resolution and minimum illumination, a good and accurate color reproduction.

The first color CCD cameras had an external color sensor (usually installed on top of the camera) whose light measurement would influence the color processing of the camera. This was called **automatic white balance (AWB)**, but lacked precision due to the discrepancy of the viewing angle between the white sensor and the camera lens. In modern cameras we have a **through-the-lens** automatic white balance **(TTL-AWB)**.

Generally, the initial calibration of the camera is done by exposing the CCD chip to white on power up. This is achieved by putting a white piece of paper in front of the camera and then turning the camera on. This stores correction factors in the camera's memory that are then used to modify all other colors. In a way, this depends very much on the color temperature of the light source in the area the camera is mounted.

A lot of cameras have an AWB reset button that does not require camera powering down. How good, or sophisticated, these corrections are really depends on the CCD chip itself and the white balance circuit design.

Although the majority of cameras today have AWB, there are still models with **manual white balance** (MWB) adjustments. In MWB cameras there are usually two settings (switch selectable): indoor and outdoor. Indoor is usually set for a light source with a color temperature of around 2800° K - 3200° K, while the outdoor is usually around 5600° K - 6500° K. These correspond to average indoor and outdoor light situations. Some simpler cameras, though, may have potentiometers accessible from the outside of the camera for continuous adjustment. Setting such a color balance might be tricky without a reference camera to look at the same scene. This gets especially complicated when a number of cameras are connected to a single switcher, quad or multiplexer.

Newer design color cameras have, apart from the AWB, an **automatic tracking white balance** (ATWB), which continually adjusts (tracks) the color balance as the camera's position or light changes. This is especially practical for PTZ cameras, and/or areas where there is a mix of natural and artificial light. In a CCTV system where pan and tilt head assemblies are used, it is possible while panning for a camera to come across areas with different color temperature lights, like an indoor tungsten light at one extreme and an outdoor natural light at the other. ATWB tracks the light source color temperature dynamically, i.e., while the camera is panning. Thus, unless you are using ATWB color cameras, you have to be very wary of the lighting conditions at the camera viewing area, not only the intensity but the color temperature as well.

Last, and as mentioned earlier, don't forget to take into account the monitor screen's color temperature. The majority of color CRTs are rated as 6500° K, but some of them might have higher (9300° K) or even lower (5600° K) color temperature.

CMOS cameras

CCD technology is about 25 years old. CCDs have matured to provide excellent image quality with low noise. Although CCD chip operational fundamentals are based on MOS electronics (metal-oxide-semiconductor) the actual manufacturing of CCD chips requires a special type of silicon technology with its own customized fabrication line.

It is technically feasible, but not economically, to use the CCD process to integrate other camera functions, like the clock-drivers, timing logic, signal processing, etc. These are therefore normally implemented in secondary chips. Thus, most CCD cameras are comprised of several chips.

Apart from the need to integrate the other camera electronics into a separate chip, the Achilles heel of all CCDs is the clock requirement. The clock amplitude and shape are critical for successful operation. Generating correctly sized and shaped clocks is normally the function of a specialized clock-driver chip, and leads to two major disadvantages: multiple nonstandard supply voltages and high power consumption. If the user is offered a simple single voltage supply input, then several regulators will be employed internally to generate these supply requirements.

In the last couple of years a new type of image chip has appeared on the market called CMOS chips.

CMOS sensors are manufactured on standard CMOS processes using the so-called very large scale integration (VLSI) technique. This is a much cheaper and more standardized method of chip manufacturing than is the case with CCDs.

A major benefit of CMOS cameras over CCDs lies in the high level of product integration that can be achieved through **implementing virtually all of the electronic camera's functions onto the same chip**. CMOS technology is ideal for this, and with its timing logic, exposure control and A/D conversion can be put together with the sensor to make complete one-chip cameras.

CMOS imagers sense light in the same way as CCD, but from the point of sensing onwards, everything is different. The charge packets are not transferred, but they are instead detected as early as

Photo courtesy of Marshall Electronics Inc.

A single-chip color CMOS camera

possible by charge-sensing amplifiers, which are made from CMOS transistors. In some CMOS sensors, amplifiers are implemented at the top of each column of pixels – the pixels themselves contain just one transistor which is used as a charge gate, switching the contents of the pixel to the charge amplifiers.

These passive pixel CMOS sensors operate like analog dynamic random access memory (DRAM).

The weak point of CMOS sensors is the problem of matching the multiple different amplifiers within each sensor. Some manufacturers have overcome this problem by reducing the residual level of fixed-pattern noise to insignificant proportions. With the initial CMOS designs and prototype cameras, there were problems with low-quality, noisy images that made the technology somewhat questionable for commercial applications. Chip process variations produce a slightly different response in each pixel, which shows up in the image as snow. In addition, the amount of chip area available to collect light is also smaller than that for CCDs, making these devices less sensitive to light.

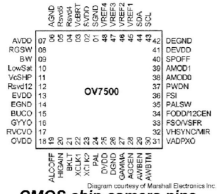

Diagram courtesy of Marshall Electronics Inc.

CMOS chip-camera pins

There are many advancements as we write this text, and improvements include on-chip image-processing functions that allow application builders to program image processing, including noise reduction, direct on-chip A/D conversion, etc. Although there are not many CMOS cameras in the security industry at the moment, they are clearly going to attract attention, if nothing else than due to their low price and integrated electronics processing.

Special low light intensified cameras

The CCD chips happen to have better minimum illumination performance than the image tubes, but there is still a limit to how low they can see. A reasonably good approximation would be that a B/W CCD camera can see, in low light levels, as much as the human eye. Described in a technical way, normal B/W CCD cameras can cover a light range from 10^5 lx, to 10^{-2} lx. This range of light intensity is called a **photopic vision** area.

Sometimes, for special purposes, there is a need for an even lower light level camera. The light range lower than 10^{-2} lx belongs to the **scotopic vision** area. Although the human eye cannot see this low, it is possible to get images from light levels much lower than 10^{-2} lx with the use of the integration function available on some cameras. This is a function where exposure time longer than 1/50 s (1/60 s for EIA) is used. Obviously, in such a case we lose the real-time effect and the camera actually becomes a kind of storage device. This might not be acceptable for viewing moving objects in low light levels, but it is a good alternative for viewing slow-moving objects in the dark. If we want to see

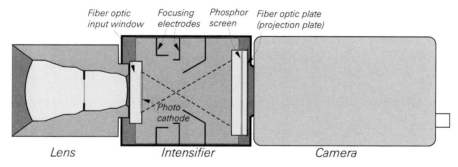

Low light level intensifier camera

real movement in the scotopic vision area, a special type of camera called **intensified,** or **low light level (LLL)** can be used.

Intensified cameras have an additional element, called a **light intensifier,** usually installed between the lens and the camera. The light intensifier is basically a tube that converts the very low light, undetectable by the CCD chip, to a light level that can be seen by it. First, the lens projects the low light level image onto a special faceplate that acts as an electronic multiplying device, where literally every single photon of light information is amplified to a considerable signal size. The amplification is done by an **avalanche** effect of the electrons, which light photons produce when attracted to a high-voltage static field. The resultant electrons hit the phosphor coating at the end of the intensifier tube, causing the phosphor to glow, and thus producing visible light (in the same manner as when an electron beam produces light onto a B/W CRT). This now visible image, is then projected onto the CCD chip, and that's how a very low light level object is seen by the camera. Because of the very specific infrared wavelengths of low light levels, as well as the monochrome phosphor coating of the intensifier, the LLL cameras will only display monochrome images.

Photo courtesy of Pulnix

An LLL camera

It is to be expected that, having a phosphor coating inside the intensifier, the lifetime, or more correctly, the MTBF (mean time between failure) of an intensifier tube is short. It's usually in the vicinity of a couple of thousand hours.

In order to prolong this lifetime, high F-stop lenses are necessary (with at least F-1200), especially if the camera is to be used day and night. Also, lenses with infrared light correction should be more adequate.

More advanced and purposely built LLL cameras have a fiber optic plate for coupling the phosphor screen of the intensifier tube to the CCD chip. This technique avoids any further light losses and improves picture sharpness.

Needless to say, the intensifier requires a power source in order to produce the high-voltage static field for the electrons' acceleration.

This type of intensifier can be bought separately and installed onto a camera, but specifically made integrated cameras have much better performance.

Another interesting and innovative design has been offered by PixelVision Inc. with their back-illuminated CCD camera that operates without an image intensifier. This camera, the manufacturer claims, is capable of acquiring quality images at low light levels previously attainable only with image intensifier tubes. Conventional video cameras use front-illuminated CCDs that impose some limitations on performance. The design of their special device illuminates and collects charge through the back surface, permitting the image photons to enter the CCD unobstructed, allowing for high-efficiency light detection in the visible and ultraviolet wavelengths. The manufacturer claims greater resolution under low light conditions through increased sensitivity, better target identification through superior contrast and resolution, lower cost and a longer lifespan through increased reliability.

Photo courtesy of Pixel Vision

A different concept of low light level camera by back illumination

Camera power supplies and copper conductors

A typical CCD camera consumes between 3 and 4 W of energy. This means a 12 V DC camera needs no more than 300 mA of current supply. A 24 V AC camera needs no more than 200 mA. As the technology improves cameras will consume less current.

When powering a number of cameras from a central power supply, it is important to take the voltage drop into account and not to overload the supply.

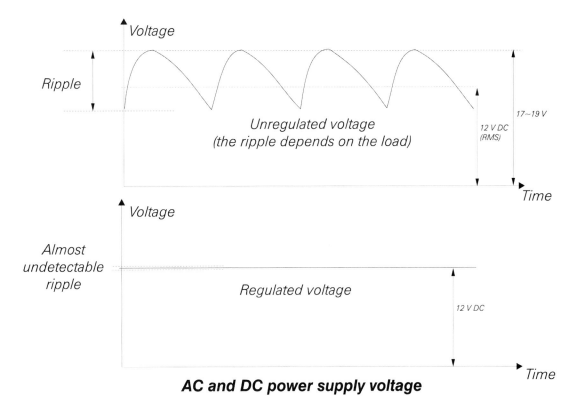

AC and DC power supply voltage

Another very important factor to check with DC power supplies is whether they are regulated or not. For example, if a power supply of 12 V DC/2 A is used, it is advisable to have approximately 25%-30% of spare capacity to minimize overheating. Be very critical when choosing a power supply. When some manufacturers quote 12 V/2 A, the 2 A may only be a maximum rating. This is usually defined with short lengths of peak deliveries. In other words, you cannot count on a constant load of 2 A with any 2-A supply. It really depends on the make and model. Very often, 12 V DC power supplies are actually made with a 13.8 V output used for charging batteries on security panels. Take this fact into account to minimize camera overheating, especially if there is only a short-run power cable between the camera and the power supply. Usually no intervention is required for a couple of hundred meters of power cable run, because of the voltage drop, but if the camera is in the vicinity of the power supply, the excessive power must be dissipated somewhere, and this is usually in the camera itself. To put it simply, the 12 V DC camera gets hotter if it is powered from a 13.8 V rather than a 12 V power supply, and this influences the camera's S/N performance.

Unregulated DC power supplies (usually in the form of plug-packs) are not very healthy for the CCD cameras. Firstly, there is a high probability of blowing the camera's fuse when the power is switched on, due to voltage spikes created when turning the load on (the camera in this instance) and second, there is an extra power dissipation that occurs in the camera when more than 12 V DC are applied.

Finally, if the camera does not have any further voltage regulations inside (DC/DC conversion), or if the regulations are of a bad quality, the unregulated voltage ripples may get into the readout pulses, thus affecting the video signal.

On the other hand, in most of the regulated power supplies there is a short circuit protection. That means, even if the installer makes a mistake with the polarities or termination, the power supply will cutoff the output, thus protecting the supply and the camera from further damage. Also, with regulated power supplies, the voltage can be adjusted to compensate for voltage drops.

This is not the case with unregulated supplies.

Copper wire size in AWG (cross section)	#24 (0.22 mm²)	#22 (0.33 mm²)	#20 (0.52 mm²)	#18 (0.83 mm²)
Resistance Ω/m	0.078	0.050	0.030	0.018
Resistance Ω/ft	0.257	0.165	0.099	0.059
Current rating (A)	1.5	2.0	3.0	6.0

Voltage drop has to be taken into account when powering distant cameras. This is especially critical with 12 V DC cameras since the voltage drop at lower DC voltages is more evident. This is a result of the $P = V \cdot I$ formula, where for a certain camera power consumption level, the lower the voltage is the higher the current will be, indirectly increasing the voltage drop through a long run power cable.

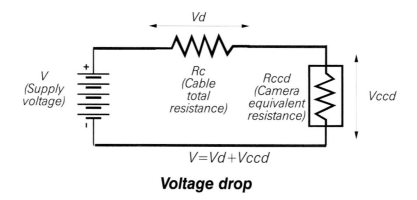

Voltage drop

Nearest AWG	Stranding (No./diam. in mm)	Copper area (mm²)	Resistance (Ω/km)
10	65/0.30	4.59	4.0
12	41/0.30	2.90	6.0
14	26/0.30	1.84	9.4
14	50/0.25	2.45	7.0
16	7/0.50	1.37	13.0
16	16/0.30	1.13	15.3
16	30/0.25	1.47	12.0
17	32/0.20	1.00	20.0
18	16/0.25	0.78	23.5
18	24/0.20	0.75	26.0
19	1/0.90	0.65	27.0
20	1/0.80	0.50	35.0
20	7/0.30	0.49	35.0
20	9/0.30	0.64	28.0
20	10/0.25	0.49	35.0
20	16/0.20	0.50	39.0
21	1/0.70	0.40	46.0
21	14/0.20	0.44	44.0
22	1/0.64	0.32	54.8
22	7/0.25	0.34	54.5
24	1/0.50	0.20	89.2
24	7/0.20	0.22	84.3
26	1/0.40	0.13	136.0
26	7/0.16	0.14	139.4
28	7/0.127	0.08	221.5

Very similar logic applies when using numerous 24 V AC cameras powered from a single source (transformer). When calculating the total amount of current required for all the cameras, always leave at least 25% – 30% of spare capacity.

When AC cameras are used, attention should be paid first of all to the voltage rating (24 V is what the majority of AC-powered cameras require). Very often, power transformers can be purchased that have secondary voltage stated with the transformer fully loaded, like with halogen lamps. This might be misleading, since with big and constant loads, transformers may show lower voltage than they would really have if only one camera is connected to it.

An AC camera's current consumption is very minimal (200 to 300 mA), so you should look for transformers with an open circuit of 24 V AC rating. Not by any means least important is the sinewave appearance, which can be especially critical when uninterruptable power supplies (UPS) are used. If a step-sinewave UPS is used, it may interfere with the camera electronics and phase adjustment. If a UPS is part of the CCTV system, a true sinewave is what we should always intend to use.

We will see in the following, a very basic calculation for the voltage drop which occurs in the so-called *figure-8* cable that powers a single 12 V DC camera.

The typical copper wire resistance, together with the cross section and the AWG (American Wire Gauge) is shown in the table below:

The popular figure-8 cable is, in most cases, a 14/0.20 type. The first number indicates the number of strands per conductor, and the second indicates the diameter of each strand in mm. The cross-section area of this cable is $14 \times (0.1)^2 \times 3.14 = 0.44$ mm^2. The resistance for a copper figure-8 wire, per meter, is approximately 0.04 Ω. A typical manufacturer's specification for the 14/0.20 states approximately 8 Ω / 100 m DC loop resistance (loop, meaning 2 × 100 m). Using these numbers we can calculate the average voltage drop when powering a 12 VDC camera via a 300 m cable run, using the very simple Ohm's Law.

A realistic assumption would be that our 12 V CCD camera consumes 250 mA.

This means that the camera is seen by the power supply as 12 V/0.25 A = 48 Ω resistor.

For 300 m of 14/0.20 cable we will have a total loop resistance of 24 Ω. The supply voltage will now see a total resistance of 72 Ω. The 12 V will be divided between the R_c and R_{ccd} proportional to the resistance, i.e., we will have a voltage divider. The calculation will show V_d to be 4 Volts.

With a 4 V voltage drop, the camera will most likely not work.

Therefore, we have to increase the voltage (and a plug pack cannot do this) to at least 16 V, according to this calculation.

In practice, however, depending on the camera, we may only need as much as 13 V, as our camera under test may work properly with as low as 9 V (if we still assume around 4 V drop). This would be the case if the camera's internal minimum requirement (due to further DC/DC regulations inside) is no higher than 9 V.

If we were to use a 24/0.20 cable instead, we would have a 15 Ω total loop resistance, and using the same calculations we'd get only a 2.8 V voltage drop.

The conclusion is: **The thicker the cable we use, the smaller the loop resistance will be, thus a smaller voltage drop**. Increasing, or pumping-the-voltage-up, with a regulated power supply unit (PSU) may help, since the regulation range of such supplies is usually from 10 V to 16 V DC.

A similar principle applies to 24 V AC cameras, only then, we are talking about RMS voltages (Root Mean Square), therefore it may look as though there is a smaller voltage drop.

Ohm's Law is valid for both AC and DC voltages, so if we try to calculate the voltage drops for when the camera is powered with, let's say 24 V AC, we have to consider two things: the current consumption is lower (since the voltage is higher), and the 24 V AC we refer to are really RMS, i.e., $24 \times 1.41 = 33.84$ V_{zp} (volts zero-to-peak). So, applying Ohm's Law, a mathematical calculation will obtain a lower voltage drop compared to the 12 V DC power, but this is only due to the different current and voltage numbers. In other words, a lower voltage drop with 24 V AC (and even lower with 110 or 240 V AC) is not because different laws apply to AC cameras, but simply because the voltage is higher. This is in fact the same reason why power used in households is not distributed from power stations at the level it is used in the household, but it is raised to tens of thousands of volts, so the current and voltage drop, due to the power cables' resistance with long distances, becomes acceptable.

For the purposes of easy calculation and further reference, located on the previous page is a table of the typical copper wires found on the market, showing the relation between the nearest AWG number, the most common stranding technique, the area in mm² and the resistance in ohms.

V-phase adjustment

AC-powered cameras are usually line-locked. This means that the vertical video frequency is synchronized with the mains frequency. If all cameras in a system are locked to the same power supply, i.e., to the same phase (don't forget we can have three different phases, each of them displaced at 120° relative to the other two), then we will (indirectly) have synchronized cameras.

For the purpose of fine adjusting the vertical phase of each and separate line-locked camera a V-phase adjustment is available. V-phase adjustment cannot only align the vertical sync of the cameras relative to their mains frequency zero crossing, but it can compensate even when different phase mains is used.

In order to do this, an oscilloscope with two channels is required. One camera is then taken as a reference, to which a monitor's vertical adjustment is set, so as to have no picture roll. The V-phase of the camera being adjusted is set so as to coincide with the V-phase of the referenced camera.

It should be noted that not necessarily all AC cameras are line-locked. That really depends on the camera design and provision in the electronics for such locking. If in doubt check with your supplier.

Camera checklist

In order to help people involved in installations, I have put together a list of things to be checked before the camera is installed in its position. Some may find this list very helpful and others may even like to add a few more things, specific to their particular system. Many integral cameras (fixed and PTZ) made in recent years do not require all of the things listed below since many things are factory preset. However, there are still many camera setups that may require your thorough checking.

So, the following are things which are advisable to be checked before a camera is installed:

■ Auto iris plug. This usually comes with the camera, not with the lens. Unfortunately, there is no standard among manufacturers, and AI connectors of all shapes and sizes are available. Keep the connector with the camera. It might be very hard to find a spare if you lose it. Also, keep the AI pin-wiring diagram that usually comes with the camera instructions.

■ If a DC camera is used, be sure to work out which is the positive and which is the negative end of the power plug. Sometimes the tip is positive, and sometimes it's negative. There are some DC cameras where there is no need for polarity to be known.

■   Do the back-focus in the workshop, especially if a zoom lens is used. Doing the back-focus on site will be at least ten times harder. Follow the procedure described in the back-focus section, until you get more practice.

■   Select a suitable lens for the angle of coverage required. For this purpose you can use focal-length viewfinders, hand calculators, tables, etc. Take into account the CCD chip size, as well as, whether you have a C-mount or CS-mount camera/lens combination.

■   Adjust the optimum picture for the estimated distance when the camera is installed. This is not so critical for a fixed lens, but installers tend to forget to adjust the camera focus on site, or unintentionally change the focus ring, and if any out-of-focus problems appear they will not be noticed during the daytime when the depth of field is big. They will become obvious and problematic at nighttime, when the depth of field is minimal.

■   Make sure that the level setting of the auto iris is good for day and night situations. ALC adjustment is important only if a very high-contrast scene needs to be monitored. The level may need some adjusting depending on the picture contrast.

■   Get the mounting screws for the camera (if installed in a housing) and the bracket. These are 1/4" imperial thread screws, usually 10 to 15 mm in length. Sometimes trivial things like this will slow your installation.

■   Make sure the camera/lens combination fits in the housing. If a zoom lens is used, take into account the focusing objective protrusion when focused to the minimum object distance (MOD). This should not add more than 10 mm to the lens length.

■   Set the ID of the camera if such a model is used.

■   If a camera with a CCD iris is used, along with an auto iris, switch the CCD iris off. Alternatively, use a manual iris or remore controlled iris lens. Auto iris and CCD-iris don't go together very well.

■   Set a higher shutter speed if the application requires. This is usually the case when high speed traffic is observed and the signal is rocorded on a VCR or framestore. Have in mind though, with higher shutter speeds you will need more light on the object, and the CCD smear may become more apparent.

■   Set the power supply voltage value to what is required, i.e. take into account voltage drop. Also, consider the current required by all cameras connected to the supply.

■   If a 24 V AC camera is used and synchronization needs to be achieved, a V-phase adjustment may be necessary. You will need a two-channel oscilloscope and a reference camera for this purpose.

■   If a color camera is used, check the white-balance setting. Some cameras have selectable indoor and outdoor white balance. Among the automatic white balance models you will find cameras with A WB (automatic white balance) and ATWB (automatic tracking white balance) selectable. In most situations ATW is the better choice.

■   If a digital signal processing camera is used, set the parameters to suit the application.

6. Monitors

Monitors are often considered an unimportant investment in CCTV, compared to the other parts of a CCTV system. It is, however, very clear that if a monitor is not of equal or better quality than a camera, the overall system quality will be diminished. Simple, but worthwhile advice is: pay equal attention to your monitor as you do to your camera selection.

General about monitors

Monitors display a video signal from a camera after it has gone through the transmission and switching media. The camera might be of excellent quality and resolution, but if the monitor does not reproduce equally or better than it, the whole system loses in quality.

In CCTV, as in broadcast TV, the majority of monitor display units are CRTs, that means they use cathode ray tube technology, designed to convert the electrical information contained in the video signal into visual information. Today, there are many alternatives to CRTs, such as liquid crystal display (LCD) monitors, plasma display, rear projection monitors, and similar, but still the most popular are the CRT monitors.

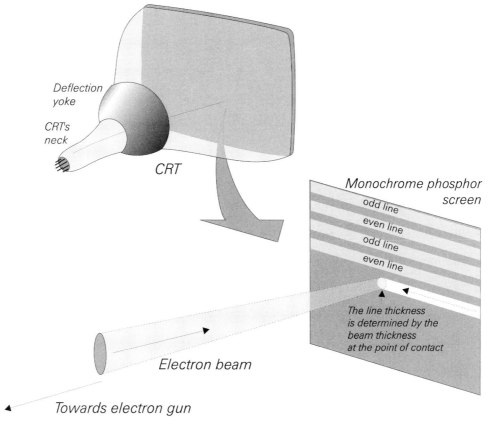

Monochrome monitor operation

The CRTs are coated on the inside with a phosphor layer that, when bombarded with electron beams, converts the kinetic energy of the electrons into light radiation. Different compositions of phosphor produce different colors. This is defined as the **phosphor spectral characteristic**.

For a monochrome (or B/W) CCTV system, a phosphor layer that produces neutral color is used.

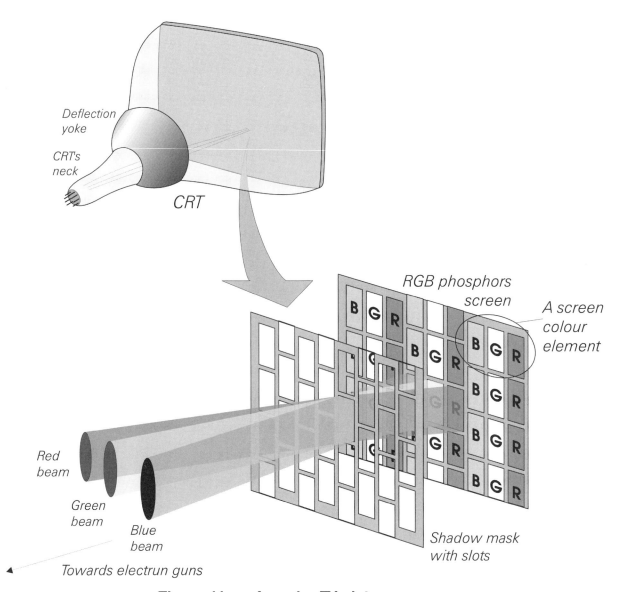

The making of a color TV picture

Color CRTs use a mosaic of three different phosphors that produce **red, green and blue**, that are called **primary colors**. These are little pixels (limited by the physical size of the mask) that, when viewed from a distance, mix into a secondary (resultant) color.

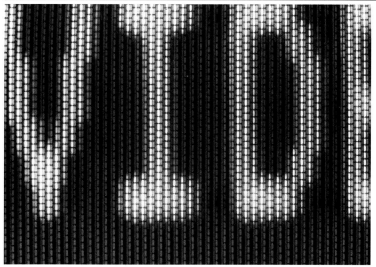

It has been proven that with the red, green and blue primaries the majority of natural colors can be simulated. This kind of color mixing is called **additive mixing** because light is added by each of the primary components to produce the resultant color. This is contrary to the subtractive color mixing as in painting and printing, where the term subtractive is used because these colors are produced by reflecting the light, in that case we have an absorption of certain colors (depending on the color pigmentation), thus a passive method of producing the resultant color.

Close-up of a color screen

Apart from the **spectral characteristics**, other important properties of the phosphor used in TV monitors are the **efficiency** and the **persistency**.

The **efficiency** is defined by the ratio between the produced light flux and the electron beam power. The electron beam power depends on the acceleration produced by the CRT's high voltage and the electron beam itself. Different phosphors have different efficiencies, i.e., they can produce different luminance with the same amount of electrons and high voltage. In color TV, the phosphor that produces green color, for example, has the highest efficiency and the red one has the lowest. Hence, the equation:

$$U_Y = 0.3\ U_R + 0.59\ U_G + 0.11\ U_B \tag{44}$$

is applied to the electron beams of the R, G and B colors in color television sets.

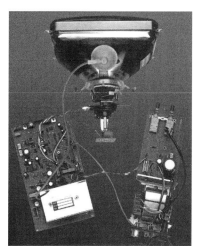

The **persistency** of the phosphor layer is described as the duration of the luminance after the electron bombardment has stopped. Since the light produced does not disappear abruptly, but decreases slowly, persistency is measured until the time when the luminance produced decreases to 1% of its initial value. Phosphor persistency is a useful feature because it helps minimize the flicker, but it should not be longer than the TV frame duration (40 ms), as we want reproduction of dynamic images, whose movements would be blurred if the persistency is too long. The persistency of the majority of CRTs used these days is around 5 ms. This is a bit more complicated with color monitors, since not all the phosphors have the same persistency (the blue phosphor has the shortest), but they are all around 5 ms.

Parts of a monochrome monitor

The basic division of monitors in CCTV is made into: B/W and color. Due to the TV standard's recommendations there must be a compatibility between B/W and color. In other words, a B/W video signal can be displayed on a color monitor and a color signal can be displayed on a B/W monitor. B/W monitors have better resolution (since they have only one continuous phosphor coating), but color monitors offer very important information about the colors of objects. That factor is more important depends on the application. In, for example, a number plate recognition CCTV system, good resolution is more important therefore a high resolution B/W camera/monitor would be the better choice, while in other systems, for example, where person identification is required, color will be the better choice.

Monitor sizes

Monitors are referred to by their diagonal screen size, that is usually expressed in inches, but sometimes in centimeters. B/W monitors have a variety of sizes, of that most often used are 9" (23 cm) and 12" (31 cm). Smaller sizes, such as 5" (13 cm) and 7" (18 cm), are not very practical apart from, perhaps, in vehicle rear vision systems, video intercoms, back-focus adjustments. Bigger ones are most often used with multiplexers and sizes like 15" (38 cm), 17" (43 cm) and 19" (48 cm) are available.

A 23cm (9") color monitor

The most popular color monitor size in CCTV is 14" (36 cm). There are 9" monitors (some manufacturers make 10" CRTs as well), that quite often are more expensive than the 14" ones. This is due to the massive production of 14" CRTs for the domestic market, that has brought the tube prices down. Larger color monitors are also available, like 17"or 20", but they are of a better quality, and therefore more expensive.

A B/W monitor

A lot of installers prefer to use a 14" TV receiver instead of a proper monitor. This is usually due to the price advantage. TV receivers are produced by the hundreds of thousands and they have become very cheap. When such a display is used, you will need a TV receiver with an audio/video input since, as we said earlier, in CCTV we use basic bandwidth video signals. In order to display the image on the screen the A/V channel has to be selected, i.e., bypass the TV tuner. If the TV doesn't have an A/V input, this might be possible through the VCR A/V inputs, since VCR modulates the video signal at its output to the VHF or UHF band (usually channels 2, 3, 4 or 36).

The picture quality of a TV receiver, when compared to a monitor's display, may or may not be of equal quality.

This depends on the CRT, the receiver quality and the input bandwidth, that are usually made to suit a 5 MHz broadcast signal. Another important factor to consider, TV receivers are usually housed in a plastic shell and are not protected against electromagnetic radiation from another set next to it. As we know, in CCTV a few monitors may be positioned next to each other and that is why CCTV monitors are usually housed in metal cabinets.

A 36 cm (14") color CCTV monitor

Monitor adjustments

CCTV monitors usually have four adjustments at the front of the unit: **horizontal hold, vertical hold, brightness and contrast.**

The **horizontal hold** circuit adjusts the phase of the horizontal sync of the monitor circuit relative to the camera signal. The effect of adjusting the horizontal hold is like shifting the picture left or right. When the horizontal phase goes too far to either end, the picture becomes unstable and horizontal scanning lines break. A similar effect may appear when the horizontal sync pulses are too low or deformed, that usually

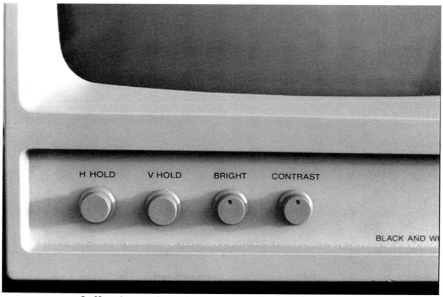

Adjustment pots on a typical B/W monitor

happens with long coaxial cable runs (voltage drop due to significant resistance, and high frequency losses due to significant capacitance). The last effect cannot be compensated by the horizontal hold adjustments. By adjusting the horizontal hold the picture can only be centered.

The **vertical hold** adjusts the vertical sync phase. This has an effect of compensating for various cameras' vertical syncs. Usually a monitor is adjusted for only one video signal, and so the picture stays stable. However, when more non-synchronized video signals are sequentially switched onto a monitor, an unwanted effect called **picture roll** occurs. This is, perhaps, the most unwanted effect in CCTV. It occurs due to the monitor's inability to quickly lock to the various signals as they are switched through a sequential or a matrix switcher (this is also discussed in the switcher section). This also means that various monitor designs have various locking times. Better monitors lock to vertical syncs quicker.

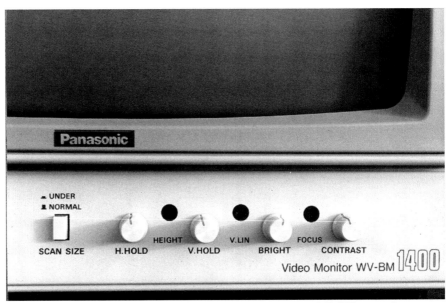

The front controls of a more advanced B/W monitor

In CCTV, switching numerous cameras onto one monitor is the most common system design. This is why we will devote some more space to explain the synchronization techniques used in CCTV. Very rarely, systems are designed where each camera goes onto its own monitor. Not only do the system costs become prohibitive, but the practicality of such systems is not sustained. First of all, physical space is required for more monitors, but more importantly no security operator can concentrate for long periods on so many different monitors.

Contrast adjusts the dynamic range of the electron beam thus making the picture with higher or lower contrast (a difference from black to white). It is usually used when lighting conditions in the room (where the monitors are) change.

Brightness is different from the contrast adjustment because it raises or lowers the DC level of the electron beam, whilst

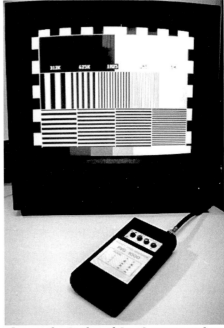

A pocket-sized test generator could be very handy

preserving the same dynamic range. It is adjusted when the video signal tone reproduction is not natural.

A simple rule of thumb is to have the brightness and contrast adjusted so that the viewer can see **as many picture details as possible**. The less light in the monitor room, the lower the contrast setting can be. By reducing the contrast, picture sharpness improves (smaller electron beam cross-section) and the CRT lifetime is prolonged. Sometimes, brightness and contrast are hard to adjust properly, especially when switching different cameras with different video signals. In order to have an objective setting for the brightness and contrast, a test pattern generator that produces an electronic gray scale should be used, i.e., where the gray levels are equally spaced. Then, the contrast and brightness are adjusted so as to distinguish all of the steps equally well. After such an adjustment is made, the camera brightness and contrast can be judged more objectively. Consequently, we can decide whether a certain camera needs to have its iris level or ALC adjusted.

With time, the phosphor coating of a monitor's CRTs wears out. This is due to constant bombardment of the phosphor layer with electrons. The lifetime expectancy of a B/W CRT is around 20,000 to 30,000 hours. This means about a couple of years of constant operation. Worn out CRT phosphor reproduces images with very poor contrast and sharpness. Color monitors should last a little longer due to the smaller amount of electrons (don't forget there are three separate beams for the three primary colors) used to excite each of the three phosphors. In any case, after a few years of constant use, contrast and brightness adjustment can no longer compensate for the CRT's ageing, and that means the monitors need replacement.

A more sophisticated pocket test signal generator

Sometimes, when a monitor is displaying one camera all the time, an imprinted image effect becomes noticeable (as was the case with tube cameras). If brightness and contrast adjustment are used carefully and in accordance with the ambient light, the monitor's life can be prolonged. The same applies to the domestic TV receivers.

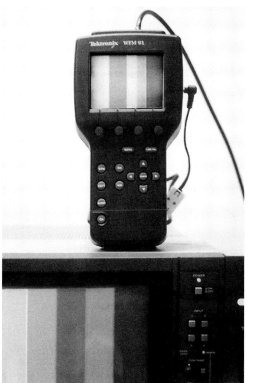

A pocket test generator with built-in monitor

Linearity and **picture height** are two other adjustments, and are usually located at the back of the monitor.

Linearity adjusts the vertical scanning linearity, that is reflected in the picture's vertical symmetry. If the linearity is not properly adjusted, circles appear egg-shaped. In order to adjust monitor linearity, a test pattern generator with a circular pattern is required. Sometimes a CCD camera can be used instead (CCDs do not have geometrical distortions), by positioning it to look perpendicularly at a perfectly circular object.

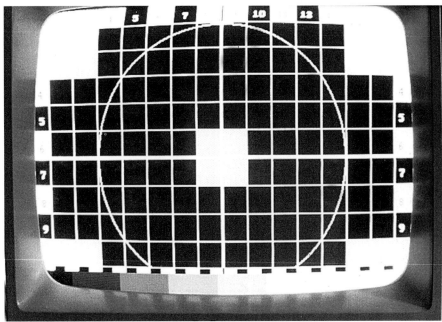

Linearity test signal

Picture height, as the name suggests, adjusts the height of the picture. With an improper picture height adjustment, the circles may appear elliptical. The scanning raster is also affected (increased or decreased), that indirectly changes the picture's vertical resolution.

Most of the monitors have electron beam **focus** adjustment, that is usually inside the monitor and close to the high voltage unit. This adjustment controls the thickness of the electron beam when it hits the phosphor coating, indirectly affecting the sharpness of the picture. On some monitors, this adjustment may be located at the front of the monitor and could also be called **aperture**.

Color monitors have **color** adjustment as well, that increases or decreases the amount of color in a color signal. This is different to brightness control. Color monitors are especially sensitive to static and other external magnetic fields, because the color reproduction depends very much on the proper dynamic positioning of the three electron beams (red, green and blue).

Even a slight presence of another magnetic field, like a loudspeaker next to the CRT, may affect one of the beams more than the other two. This then results in unnatural colored spots in certain areas of the screen that are close to the magnetic field. In order to combat such effects, color TV monitors have an additional element in their design that is called a **degaussing coil**. The degaussing coil is a conductor loop around the CRT, through that, every time the monitor is turned on, a strong current pulse is injected. This creates short but strong electromagnetic pulse that clears any residual magnetic fields. If the external field is very strong and permanent, the degaussing coil might not be capable of clearing it.

There are professional monitors (designed for the broadcast industry) that are quite often used in bigger and better CCTV systems. They are equipped with sophisticated electronics and high resolution

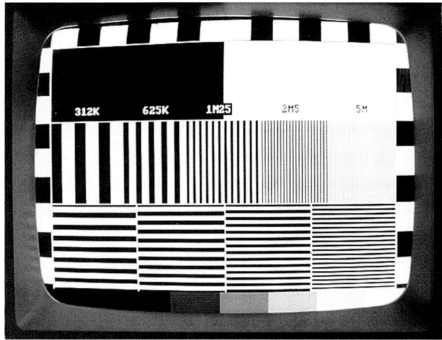

Bandwidth test signal

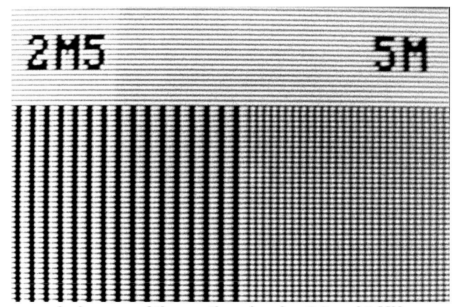

A close up of the section showing 2.5 and 5 MHz

CRTs whose horizontal resolution exceeds 600 TV lines. They quite often have some additional adjustments along with the ones mentioned above. These may include **hue** (that is actually the color itself: red, green, orange, etc.), **saturation** (represents the purity of the color, i.e., how much white is mixed into it, where 100% saturated color has no white additives), **H-V delay** (a very useful feature where horizontal and vertical syncs are delayed so that the CRT will show the signal broken up into four areas, similar to a quad, so that horizontal and vertical syncs can be visually checked) and **underscan** (where the monitor shows 100% of the video signal, that is especially important when testing camera resolution).

Impedance switch

At the back of most CCTV monitors there is an impedance switch next to two BNC connectors. The purpose of the impedance switch is to allow for either terminating the video coaxial cable with 75 Ω (when the monitor is the last element) or leaving it to high position if the monitor is not the last component in the video signal path.

As we have already discussed earlier, the video sources used in CCTV are all designed to have 75 Ω output impedance, that requires the same impedance from the signal receivers (monitors in this case).

Only then, we will have 100% energy transfer and perfect picture reproduction.

If however, the monitor is not the last element in the signal path, but perhaps another monitor is using the same signal, we then have to set the

Back of a typical monitor includes looping BNC input and impedance switch (75/High)

impedance of the first monitor to high (looping monitor) and set 75 Ω on the last one (terminating monitor).

Most CCTV monitors have passive video inputs. There are monitors and other devices, like VCRs, video printers, video distribution amplifiers and so on, where the video input is active. Active means the video signal is going through an amplifier stage and the signal is split into two or more components that are electronically matched with their impedances. In such case, we don't have any switches to switch because there is no need for them. In other words, don't be confused if you cannot see an impedance switch on some professional monitors or VCRs. This will simply mean that the video input is already terminated with 75 Ω, and the output of it should be treated as a new signal coming out of a camera.

Viewing conditions

In a CCTV system the number of monitors can be quite large. It is very important to know how many monitors can be used in a place without going overboard, as well as how to position them and what will

Large number of switching monitors may cause headaches

be the correct viewing distance for the users. Even with one monitor in the system, there are certain facts and recommendations to be aware of. This is especially important when the operators are spending the majority of their time in front of the monitors.

CONDITION	50 Fields (CCIR)	60 Fields (EIA)
Peak luminance on the screen	70 lx	70 lx
Viewing distance / picture height	6	4 ~ 6

The CCIR Recommendation 500 states that the preferred viewing conditions are affected by the field frequency of the TV system, the size of the screen and the distance, relative to the screen size.

Converted into practical numbers, for the most common monitor sizes, we have the following table:

MONITOR SIZE	RECOMMENDED VIEWING DISTANCE (CCIR)	RECOMMENDED VIEWING DISTANCE (EIA)
9´´ (23 cm)	0.9 m	0.6 ~ 0.9 m
12´´ (31 cm)	1.2 m	0.8 ~ 1.2 m
14´´ (36 cm)	1.6 m	1.0 ~ 1.6 m
17´´ (43 cm)	1.8 m	1.2 ~ 1.8 m
21´´ (53 cm)	2.2 m	1.4 ~ 2.2 m

The last table shows recommendations only, and one should be flexible when applying these in various circumstances. With big systems, where perhaps a dozen monitors need to be mounted in front of the operator(s), viewing distances may vary. It is also very important to plan and suggest the number of operators needed for a given number of monitors and control points. CCTV systems are made, in the end, to satisfy the customer's requirements.

It is a known fact that the vertical flicker is noticeable with the peripheral vision of the eye. In other words, if you have many monitors to view, the vertical refresh rate of the surrounding monitors is affecting your vision even though you may be watching a monitor directly in front of you with easy comfort. Because of this reason some manufacturers are now coming up with 100 Hz monitors for CCTV (this is more critical with PAL and SECAM due to their lower vertical frequency). The 100 Hz monitors simply double up the 50 fields refresh rate and the display looks rock-steady. Sitting in front of such monitors for a longer period is a definite advantage, and I would suggest such monitors where the display has to be of a bigger size. Namely, the bigger the monitor screen, the more noticeable the flicker.

*A 100 Hz CCTV monitor
with low MPRII radiation*

Another important consideration we should have is the electrostatic radiation of larger monitors. Although this is a negligible amount, when walls of monitors are in one room they may have a significant influence on the environment. This can usually be confirmed by the amount of dust collected by such a large number of monitors. There is a low radiation standard accepted in the medical science called MPR II. This is also being accepted by some CCTV manufacturers and would clearly give an advantage to systems designed with such monitors.

With big systems, visual display management is of vital importance. For example, not all the monitors need to display images all the time. It may be much more effective if the operator(s) is/are concentrating on one or two active monitors (usually larger sized) and the rest of them are blank. In case of activity, i.e., an alarm activation, motion detection or perhaps video fail detection, a blank monitor can be programmed to bring the image of a pre-programmed camera. In such a case, the operator's attention is immediately drawn to the new image and the system becomes more efficient. As an additional bonus, the monitor's life time will also be prolonged. Most of the video matrix switchers can be programmed to do such blanking and display alarmed camera's only when necessary.

Another subject concerning the viewing conditions is the size of the monitor and its effect on the picture resolution. Clearly, whether a 9", 12" or 17" monitor is used, the resolution would still be more or less the same (assuming that the same quality of electronics is inside). The impression of picture sharpness though, may be different. So, a 9" monitor will be quite OK when a single operator views it at about 1 meter distance. But if a 17" monitor is viewed from the same distance (and this is usually for the reasons of viewing a quad picture, for example) when a full screen is displayed it will appear as if the picture resolution is lower than with the 9" monitor. This is only an illusion due to the different viewing distance relative to the monitor's size.

Gamma

The CRT phosphor doesn't have a linear characteristic. This means, if a linear signal is displayed (continuous rising ramp from black (0 V) to white (0.7 V)) it will not have the same rate of luminance rise. The monochrome monitor's characteristic of the electron beam current versus luminance produced by the beam, is a parabolic function with a power exponent of 2.2.

Ideally, we would like to have a linear CCTV system. This would mean linear reproduction of the gray levels and colors. But since the CRT phosphor coating is, naturally, without a linear characteristic, we have to somehow compensate for it. This compensation is easiest done at the camera end. If the CCD camera's characteristic luminance-versus-voltage (usually linear) is electronically modified to have an inverse characteristic of the CRT (1/2.2 = 0.45), we will get a linear camera-monitor system.

When these two curves (of the monitor and camera) are put together on a single diagram they are symmetrical around a straight line of 45°. This resembles the mathematical symbol γ (gamma), hence the name.

In practice, if you have a camera with a gamma setting that is not complementary to the monitor's characteristic, the picture quality will not be as good. This is reflected in the unnatural reproduction of grey levels where the picture has high contrast, lacking details in the middle gray range.

Most B/W monitors have a 2.2 gamma value, therefore 0.45 should be the common default setting for a B/W camera. Naturally, CCD cameras have a linear gamma value (1).

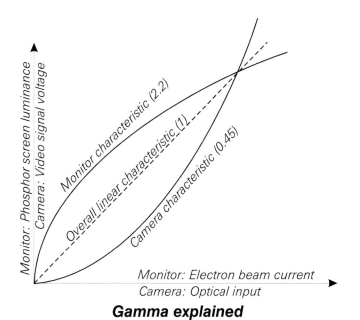

Gamma explained

Color monitors are especially sensitive to the gamma effect, and as mentioned earlier in the *Color Television* section, the NTSC and PAL systems are designed with two different assumptions for the color phosphors gamma values. Theoretically, as assumed in NTSC gamma should be 2.2, but in practice most of the phosphor coatings are close to 2.8, as proposed by PAL. Higher values of gamma have appearance of higher contrast images. Clearly, this depends not only on the standard (NTSC or PAL) but also on the type of phosphor coating inside the monitor's CRT.

LCD monitors

Liquid crystal display (LCD) monitors are still at an early stage of use in CCTV. They are becoming more and more popular for notebook computers, and they could also be used in CCTV as well. As this book is being written, there are already 10" and 14" color LCD TV receivers with audio/video inputs, that means they could also be used for basic bandwidth video signals.

The concept of LCD operation is quite different to the CRT principles. Perhaps, the best description, or analogy, would be that LCD monitors compared to CRT monitors are what CCDs are to tube cameras. Namely, the image is not formed by electron beam scanning, but by addressing liquid crystal cells, that are polarized in different directions when voltage is applied to their electrodes. The amount of voltage determines the angle of polarization, that as a result determines the transparency of each pixel, thus forming an element of the video picture.

Photo courtesy of Sharp

A 100 cm (40") TFT LCD TV

The advantages of the LCD are: no need for high voltage EHT elements; no phosphor layer wear, i.e., unlimited lifetime of the screen; a flat and miniature appearance; no geometrical distortions; low power consumption; no effect from electromagnetic fields as is the case with CRTs, and similar.

There are many variations of LCD technologies. One of the well-known, although now superceded, technology is the so-called **passive LCD**, where the actual crystal matrix is composed of passive liquid that polarizes on the basis of the voltage applied. The other, that uses better technology, uses thin film transistors on each LCD cell, and, since transistors are active components, it is called **active matrix TFT LCD** screen.

The major disadvantage is the fact that the picture is formed by reflected light and not by generating-light as is the case with the CRTs. Some LCDs, especially color LCDs, use a backlit area, but this is still different to generating-light as is the case with the CRTs. Another disadvantage is the effect of smearing that occurs due to slow LCD pixel response to the line scanning process, that is seen as a vertical smear. And lastly, the pixel size defines the maximum resolution and it is limited to the achievements in LCD technology. Although S-VGS resolution is easily achieved with smaller size LCD displays, that is evident from the PC industry, the increase in overall size of such displays is difficult to achieve due to the delays associated with the very fast control signals addressed to each of the pixels. There are definitely daily advancements and many variations to the liquid materials used in the LC technology. Sharp, one of the major R&D companies for LCD, claims to have achieved contrast ratios of 300:1 with its Super-V technology, that is based on phase difference compensation combined with picture element segmentation technology. Not long ago they released their 40" LCD TV. We should expect such displays to become an affordable part of CCTV sooner or later.

Projection monitors

Although CRT monitors are the most widely used they can only be so big as their physical size is limited primarily with the high voltage required to accelerate electrons over their size. The biggest CRTs used in CCTV are hardly bigger than 68 cm (27"). But there are other ways of producing a bigger picture and this is usually by projection methods. Some years ago, projection monitors were extremely big, expensive and complicated for use and setup. They would usually consist of three separate optical systems each projecting their own primary color.

Today, video projectors are much smaller, cheaper, brighter and easier to use and setup. In most cases, they would accept a range of video inputs such as composite video, RGB (or Component) video, Y/C, computer video S-VGA and similar. Most of the projectors are single-lens color projectors that filter the light through an LCD film.

Projectors cannot have the same brightness as CRT, but technology advances very rapidly and brighter and brighter projectors are on the market. The brightness is usually expressed in lumens, and a typical LCD projector would have up to 500 lumens. Their resolution advances with the LCD technology advancement and today we can get projectors with resolution

Photo courtesy of Philips

An LCD projector

well over what the CCTV cameras can offer. The projected brightness is even stronger with the new digital micro-mirror based projectors.

Digital micromirror display (DMD) technology

Very often, a big screen projection is required from a video signal. With the current technology, there are some CCTV systems intended for public use (like shopping centers) that display the cameras on a big screen so as to be viewed by many people. So far, this was usually done with a three tube projector (RGB), or a wall of monitors (called *Video-wall*) made up of 4×4 or 5×5 monitors in a mosaic. Lately, projectors incorporating color LCD screen filters can be seen more often. These types of projectors are big, expensive and don't offer very bright and high resolution images. All of the above are based on CRT, i.e., LCD technology, that are well suited for small screens, or close viewing distance applications.

New and innovative displays are needed for the upcoming HDTV and/or multimedia presentations, and probably CCTV in the near future. There are requirements for higher resolution, better brightness, better color quality, better contrast and larger sizes.

One of the ideas, developed by Texas Instruments™, called digital micro-mirror device (DMD) technology may fulfill all of the above requirements. The concept is based on a memory chip with a matrix of millions of

Photo courtesy of NEC

A DMD projector

microminiature mirrors (similar size and appearance as CCD chips). Then, a light source projects an image to the DMD chip so as to have the mirrors reflect the image onto virtually any size screen. The

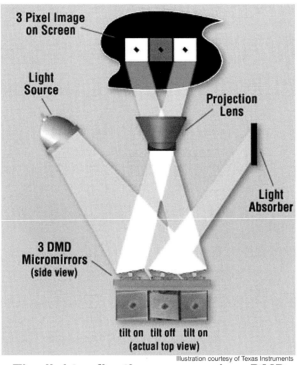

size of each mirror is 26 millionths of a millimeter. The mirrors are so small that a grain of salt could obscure hundreds of them. Each mirror represents a screen pixel. All are controlled and switched on and off by the on-chip circuitry, and every one of the hundreds of switches per second is performed with great precision and accuracy. The mirrors are programmed to remain at designated reflective angles for various time periods within a single frame of motion. This permits gray-scale projection or correct color presentation. For color projection the light is beamed through a condenser lens and then through a red, green, and blue color sequential filter. The filter switching is synchronized to the video information fed to the DMD chip at a rate three times that of the video (that results in 150 Hz switching for PAL and 180 Hz for NTSC signals).

Filtered light is then projected onto the DMD integrated circuit, whose mirrors are switched on or off according to the digital video information written

The light reflection process in a DMD

into the chip's memory circuits. Light shined on these mirrors is then reflected into a lens to project images from the DMD surface. The full color digitized video image created on the DMD, displays onto either a front or rear projection screen. Depending on whether one or three DMDs are used, high brightness projection screen size can range anywhere from 1.5 m to 5 m (diagonally). By applying a zoom lens projection, the image size can be increased or decreased to virtually any screen size. But the

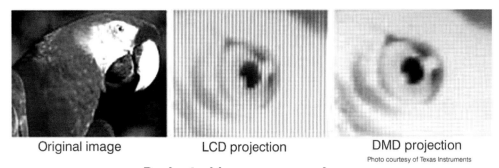

Original image   LCD projection   DMD projection
                                          Photo courtesy of Texas Instruments

Projected image comparison

most important benefits (apart from the miniature physical size itself) include equal high resolution, brightness and color fidelity, regardless of the screen size.

We should point out that because of the individual digital processing of each DMD pixel, this technology and these type of projectors are also known as digital light processing, or DLP projectors.

Plasma display monitors

Some scientists refer to plasma as the fourth state of matter (the first three being solid, gas and liquid). Often plasma is defined as an ionized gas. The theory of plasma is beyond the scope of this book, but we would like to mention the usage of plasma in display monitors.

Such monitors are made of an array of pixels, each composed of three phosphor sub-pixels, red, green and blue. As opposed to CRTs where light radiation was caused by electron bombardment, in the

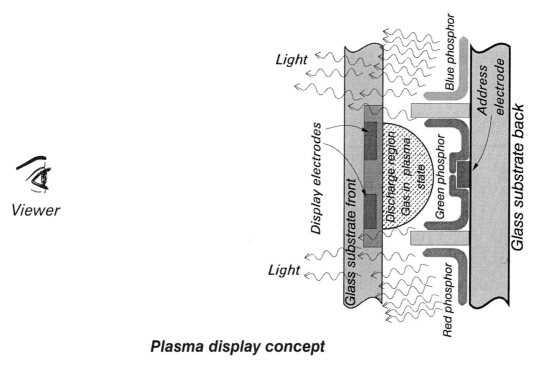

Plasma display concept

plasma displays, gas in plasma state is used to react with phosphors in each sub-pixel. In plasma displays each sub-pixel is individually controlled in order to get 16.7 million colors.

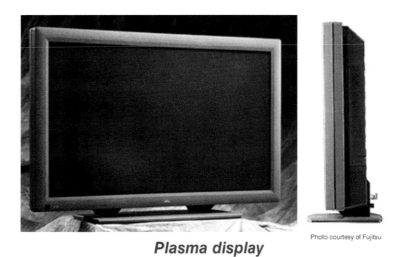

Photo courtesy of Fujitsu

Plasma display

Because of the fact that each pixel is excited with the plasma process individually there are no geometrical distortion as is the case in CRTs and the picture sharpness and color richness is brought up to new heights. The picture contrast is also high, typically over 400:1, making the plasma displays suitable for bright areas.

Since the plasma display does not require high voltage as is the case with CRT, larger displays are possible. Typical plasma display sizes are from 105 cm (42") up to 125 cm (50"). More importantly though, the thickness of plasma displays is minimal, ranging from 10 to 15 cm (4-6"). This is especially attractive for aesthetic reasons, but also for rooms with limited space.

It should be noted that since plasma displays are based on phosphor coating they also fade with time. Manufacturers usually claim 30,000 hours for the brightness to get reduced to 50% of its original quantity. This is equivalent to about 3 years of constant operation, that is more or less the same as what the CRT monitors are quoted as.

Field emission technology displays

Another alternative for better image displays, but on a standard screen size and not a projection screen, was presented by Motorola™ recently. The concept is a flat display with active light emission called field emission device (FED) technology. Instead of a single cathode ray source, as is the case with a standard CRT display, the FEDs rely on hundreds of little cathode ray sources for each pixel. FEDs are composed of two sheets of glass separated by a vacuum. The back glass, or cathode, is made up of millions of tiny tips, that form the source of electrons that accelerate across the vacuum. The front glass, or anode, has layers of standard CRT phosphors.

The FED display, it is claimed, offers many of the anode glass benefits of a CRT display, but it is thinner, lighter, uses less power and has no geometrical distortions. The addressable x-y emitter layout eliminates the non-linearity and pincushion effects associated with standard CRT images. The companies developing the FED are claiming that these type of display devices will be cheaper and easier to manufacture than LCDs, and considering there is no need for a single RGB gun that dictates the equivalent CRT size and appearance, the FED display will be larger, yet thinner and lighter.

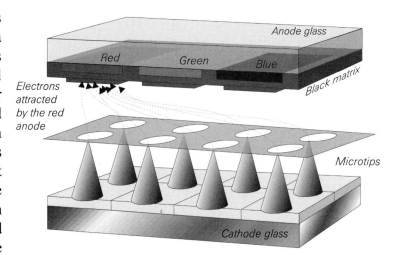

The field emission display concept

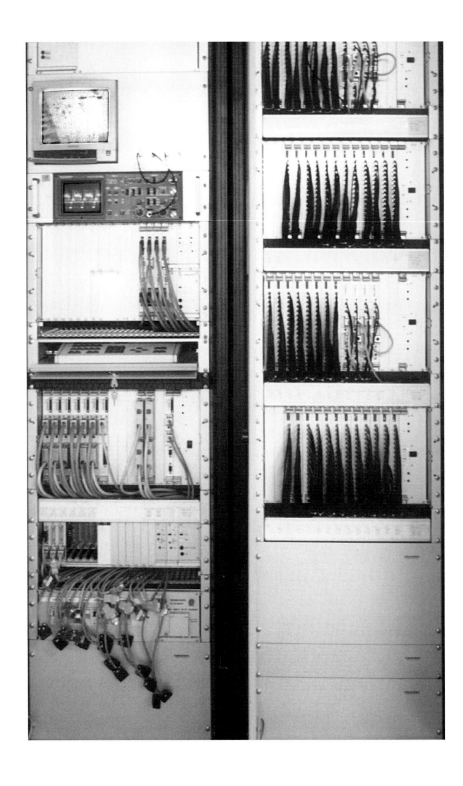

7. Video Processing Equipment

Only very small CCTV systems use the simple camera-monitor concept. Most of the bigger ones, in one way or another, use some kind of video switching or processing equipment before the signal is displayed on a monitor.

The term video processing equipment here refers to any electronic device that processes the video signal in one way or another, such as switching between multiple video inputs, compression into one quadrant of the screen, boosting of the higher frequencies, etc.

Analog switching equipment

The simplest and most common device found in very small to medium-sized CCTV systems is the video sequential switcher.

Video sequential switchers

Since in the majority of CCTV systems have more cameras than monitors on which to view them, there is a need for a device that will sequentially switch from one camera signal to another. This device is called a **video sequential switcher**.

Sequential switchers come in all flavors. The simplest one is the 4-way switcher, then we have 6-way, 8-way, 12-way, 16-way and sometimes 20-way. Other numbers of inputs are not excluded, although they are rare.

On the switcher's front panel, there are usually a set of buttons for each input and beside the switch position for manual selection of cameras, there is a switch position for including a camera in the sequence or bypassing it. When a sequence is started, the dwell time can be changed, usually by a potentiometer. The most common and practical setting for a dwell time is 2-3 seconds. A shorter scanning time is too impractical and eye-disturbing for the operator, while a longer scanning time may result in the loss of information for the non-displayed cameras. So, in a way, sequential switchers are always a compromise.

A simple, 8-channel video sequential switcher

Apart from the number of video inputs, sequential switchers can be divided into switchers with and without alarm inputs.

When a sequential switcher has alarm inputs, it means external normally opened (N/O) or normally closed (N/C) voltage-free contacts can halt the scanning and display the alarmed video signal. Various sources can be used as alarm devices. For indoor applications the choice of suitable sensors is often straightforward, but outdoor alarm sensors are more critical and harder to select. There is no perfect sensor for all applications. The range of site layouts and environmental conditions can vary enormously. The best help you can get in selecting a sensor is from a specialized supplier that has both the knowledge and the experience.

Most common are the passive infrared (PIR) detectors, door reed switches, PE beams, video motion detectors (VMD) and similar. Care should be taken, when designing such systems, about the switcher activity after the alarm goes off, i.e., how long the alarmed video input remains displayed, whether it requires manual or automatic reset; if the latter, how many seconds does the automatic reset activate for; what happens when a number of alarms activate simultaneously; and so on. The answers to all of these questions are often decisive for the system's efficiency and operation. There is no common answer and it should be checked with the manufacturer's specifications, or even better, test it yourself.

It is not a rule, but quite often simple sequential switchers (i.e., without alarm inputs) have only one video output. The alarming sequential switchers, on the other hand, quite often have two video outputs: one for video sequencing and the other for the alarmed picture. The first output is the one that scans through all the cameras, while the second one is often called the alarmed or spot output, because it displays the alarmed picture (when the alarm activates).

Video sequential switchers (or just switchers for short) are the cheapest thing that comes between multiple cameras and a video monitor. This does not mean that more sophisticated sequential switchers are not available. There are models with text insertion (camera identification, time and date) multiple configuration options via RS-485 or RS-422 communications, etc.

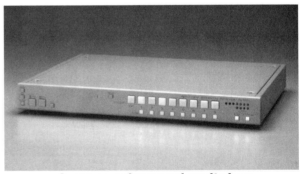

A more advanced switcher

Some models like these either have the power down coaxial cable function, or they send synchronization pulses to the camera via the same cable that brings video signals to the switcher. All this is with the intention of synchronizing cameras, which will be discussed next. Most of these more sophisticated sequential switchers can easily be expanded to the size of a miniature matrix switcher.

Synchronization

One of the more important things relevant to the switchers, irrespective of how many inputs they have, is the switching technique used. Namely, when more than one camera signal is brought to the switcher inputs, it is natural to have them with various video signal phases. This is a result of the fact that every camera is, in a way, a self-contained oscillator producing the line frequency of the corresponding TV system (i.e., for CCIR 625×25 = 15625 Hz and for EIA 525×30 = 15750 Hz) and it is hard to imagine that half a dozen cameras could have a coincidental phase. This is unlikely even for only two cameras. We call such random phase signals **non-synchronized**. When non-synchronized signals are switched through a sequential switcher, an unwanted effect appears on the monitor screen: **picture-roll**. A picture-roll appears due to the discrepancies in the vertical synchronization pulses at various cameras that results in an eye-disturbing picture-roll when the switcher switches from one camera to another. The picture, roll is even more obvious when recording the switched output to a VCR. The reason for having the roll more obvious with the VCR is that the VCR's head needs to mechanically synchronize to the different cameras' vertical sync pulses, while the monitor does it electronically. The only way to successfully combat the rolling effect is to synchronize the sources, i.e., the cameras.

The most proper way of synchronizing cameras is by use of an **external sync generator** (*sync-gen*, for short). In such a case, cameras with an external sync input have to be used (please note: not every camera can accept external sync). Various cameras have various sync inputs, but the most common are:

- Horizontal sync pulses (usually known as horizontal drive pulses or HD)

- Vertical sync pulses (usually referred to as vertical drive pulses or VD)

- Composite sync pulses (include both HD and VD in one signal, usually referred to as composite video sync or CVS)

In order to do the synchronization, an extra coaxial cable has to be used between the camera and the sync-gen (besides the one for video transmission) and the sync-gen has to have as many outputs as there are cameras in use.

Clearly, the above is a very expensive exercise, although theoretically, it is the most proper way to synchronize. There are camera manufacturers that produce models where sync pulses are sent from the switcher to the camera via the same coax that sends the video signal back. The only problem here is the need to have all the equipment of the same make.

There are cheaper ways to resolve the picture-roll problems and one of the most accepted is with **line-locked cameras**. Line-locked cameras are either 24 V AC or 240 V AC (110 V AC for the US, Canada and Japan)

A line-locked camera (24 VAC) which also has an external vertical sync input terminal

powered cameras. The 50 Hz (60 for the US, Canada and Japan) mains frequency is the same as the vertical sync rate, so these cameras (line-locked) are made to pick up the zero crossings of the mains sinewave and the vertical syncs are phased with the mains frequency. If all of the cameras in a system are powered from the same source (same phase is required), then all of the cameras will be locked to the mains and thus synchronized to each other.

The above method is the cheapest one, although it sometimes offers instability of the mains phase due to heavy industrial loads that are turned off and on at unpredictable intervals. Still, it is the easiest way. There is even a solution for different phases powering different cameras in the form of the so-called *V-phase* adjustment. This is a potentiometer on the camera body that will allow the camera electronics to cope with up to 120° phase difference. It should be noted that the low voltage AC-powered cameras (i.e., the 24 V AC) are more popular and more practical than the high voltage ones and the main reason is that they are safer.

Some cameras are designed to accept the video signal of the previous camera and lock to it. This is called **master-slave** camera synchronization. By daisy-chaining all of the cameras in such a system, synchronization can be achieved, where one is the master camera and the others are slave cameras. A coaxial cable is required between all of the cameras for this purpose, in addition to the coax for video transmission.

Still, not every sequential switcher could use the benefits of synchronized cameras. The switcher also needs to be a **vertical interval switcher**. Only vertical interval switchers can switch synchronized signals at the moment of the vertical sync pulse so that the switching is smooth and without roll. Non-vertical interval switchers switch on a random basis, rather than at a specific moment relative to the video signals. With the vertical interval switcher, when a dwell time is adjusted to a particular value, the switcher switches with this specific dwell time, but only **when the vertical sync period occurs**. By doing so, **the switching is nice and clean and happens in the vertical blanking period**, i.e., there is no picture break on the monitor screen.

Normal switchers, without this design, will switch anywhere in the picture duration and this means it could be in the middle of a picture field. So if the cameras are synchronized, there will be no picture roll, but there will still be picture breaking visible to the operator **due to abrupt transition from one signal to another in the middle of the visible picture field**.

The same concept of vertical interval switching applies to the sequential switcher's big brother the video matrix switcher.

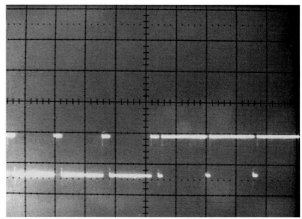

Vertical sync detail

Video matrix switchers (VMS)

The **video matrix switcher** is the big brother of the sequential switcher. The bigger CCTV systems can only be designed with a video matrix switcher (VMS) as the brain of the system.

The name matrix switcher comes from the fact that the number of video inputs plotted against the number of video outputs makes a matrix, as it is known in mathematics. Quite often, video matrix switchers are called video cross-point switchers. These cross-points are actually electronic switches that select any video input onto any video output at any one time preserving the video impedance matching. Thus, one video signal can simultaneously be selected on more than one output. Also, more video inputs can be selected on one output, only in this case we would have a sequential switching between more inputs, since it is not possible to have more than one video signal on one output at any single point in time.

A sophisticated video matrix switcher

VMS are, in essence, big sequential switchers with number of advancements:

- A VMS can have more than one operator. Remember that the sequential switchers usually have buttons at the front of the unit, thus only one operator can effectively control the system at any one time. Matrix switchers can have up to a dozen operators, sometimes even more, all of whom can concurrently control the system. In such a case, every operator controls (usually) one video output channel. A certain intelligent control can be achieved, depending on the VMS in use. Different operators may have equal or different priorities, depending on their position in the security structure of the system.

- VMS accept much more video inputs and accommodate for more outputs, as already mentioned and more importantly, these numbers can easily be expanded at a later date, by just adding modules.

- VMS have pan, tilt and lens digital controllers (usually referred to as PTZ controllers). The keyboard usually has an integral joystick, or buttons, as control inputs and at the camera end, a so-called PTZ site driver (sometimes called PTZ decoder) within a box which is actually part of the VMS. The PTZ site driver talks and listens to the matrix in digital language and drives the pan/tilt head together with the zoom lens and perhaps some other auxiliary device (such as wash/wipe assembly).

- VMS generate camera identification, time and date, operator(s) using the system, alarm messages and similar on screen information, superimposed on the video signal.

- VMS have plenty of alarm inputs and outputs and can be expanded to virtually any number required. Usually any combination of alarms, like N/O, N/C and logical combinations of them (OR, NOR, AND, NAND), is possible.

- In order for the matrix switchers to perform the very complex task of managing the video and alarm signals, a microprocessor is used as the brain. With the ever-increasing demand for power and processing capacity, microprocessors are becoming cheaper and yet more powerful. These days, full blown PCs perform these complex processes. As a consequence, a VMS setup becomes programming in itself, complex but with immense power and flexibility, offering password protection for high security, data logging, system testing and re-configuring via modem and similar. The latest trend is in the form of graphical user interface (GUI), using Windows™ or OS/2™ environment, with touch sensitive screens, graphical site layout representation that can be changed as the site changes and much more.

- The VMS might be very complex for the system designer or commissioner, but they are very simple and user friendly for the operator and, more importantly, faster in emergency response.

There are only a handful of manufacturers of VMS in the world, the majority of which come from the United States, England, Denmark, Germany, Japan and Australia. Many of them have stayed with the traditional concept of cross-point switching and a little bit of programmability, usually stored in a battery backed EPROM. Earlier concepts with battery backed EPROMs, without recharging, could only last for a few weeks. But many have accepted clever and flexible programming, with the system

**The Maxpro video matrix at Sydney's Star City Casino
handles over 1000 cameras and over 800 VCRs**

configuration stored on floppy disks or hard drives, preventing loss of data even if the system is without power for more than a couple of months.

The demand for compatibility has forced many systems to become PC based, making the operation familiar to the majority of users and at the same time, offer compatibility with many other programs and operating systems that may work in conjunction.

The large Plettac CCTV matrix at the Frankfurt Airport

The new designs of matrix switchers take almost every practical detail into account. First of all, configuring a new system, or even re-configuring an old one, is as easy as entering details through a setup menu. This is, however, protected with high levels of security which will not allow anyone to play around with the setup, but only authorized people that know the appropriate access code and procedures.

Next, the VMS became so intelligent and powerful that controlling other complex devices became possible. These include lights in buildings, air conditioning, door access control, boom gates in car parks, power and other regular operations done at a certain time of the day or at certain detectable causes.

Unfortunately there is no standard design or language for configuring and programming matrix switchers. Different manufacturers use different concepts and ideas, so it is very important to choose a proven expert for a particular system.

Matrix switchers usually come with their basic configurations of 16 or 32 video inputs and 2 or 4 video outputs. Other combinations of numbers are possible, but the above mentioned are most common.

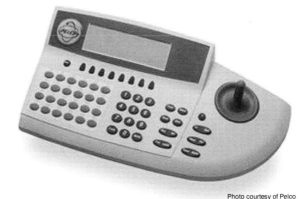

Photo courtesy of Pelco

An intelligent, ergonomic and re-configurable matrix keyboard

Cabling by Wegtech Services. Courtesy of Pacific Communications
**Some larger matrices by
Pacific Communications
come neatly prewired**

Many of them would come with a certain number of alarm inputs and outputs. Almost all of them, in their basic configuration, will have a text insertion feature incorporated and a keyboard for control. A basic operator's manual and other technical information should be part of the switcher.

Most suppliers would need a separate notice to incorporate PTZ control modules, as in many systems only fixed cameras are used, so it is not considered a must to have PTZ control. Some makes though, may include PTZ control as standard.

The latter does not mean PTZ site drivers will be a compulsory part of the VMS. Since the number of PTZs may vary from system to system, it is expected for the number to be specified when ordering. How many you can actually use in a system depends on the make and model. In most cases, VMS use digital control which has a limited number of sites it can address. This number depends on the controlling distances as well and it can be anything between 1 and 32 PTZ sites. For a higher number of sites, additional PTZ control modules need to be used.

I will repeat again that, until now, there has been no compatibility between products of different manufacturers, so you cannot use, for example, a matrix switcher of one brand and PTZ site drivers of another. In most cases, when a CCTV system with a matrix switcher needs to be upgraded you need to replace the whole system, with the exception of the cameras, lenses, monitors and cables. It is fair to say though, that in the period between the last edition of the book and the present one I have seen an increased number of matrix manufacturers that have produced multi-functional driver boards so that you can control at least a couple of different brands. Furthermore, there are now protocol converter boxes available that will allow the users, if they know the protocol of the PTZ camera and the matrix switcher, to have them talk to each other.

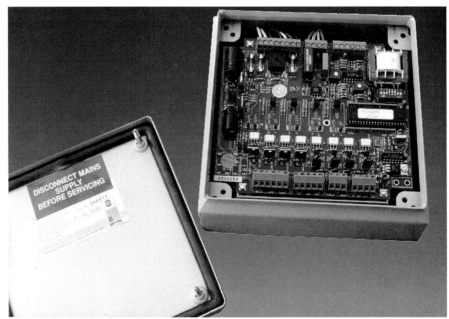

A typical PTZ site driver (receiver)

Small systems with up to 32 cameras can easily be configured, but when more inputs and outputs are required from a matrix switcher it is better to talk to the manufacturer's representative and work out exactly what modules are required. This selection can make a big difference between an affordable and an expensive system, as well as between a functional and nonfunctional system.

Due to their capability and potential to do many things other than just video switching, video matrix switchers are often referred to as CCTV management systems. This is not to say that VMS can also perform quad processing or multiplexing of signals. Quad compressors and multiplexers would still be required in addition, if such functions are to be performed.

Digital switching and/or processing equipment

Quad compressors

Sequential switchers' inability to view all of the cameras simultaneously and other synchronization worries, have appealed to the CCTV designers to come out with a new device called a *quad compressor*, or sometimes known as a **quad splitter**.

Quad compressors, as the name suggests, put up to four cameras on a single screen by dividing the screen into four quadrants (hence the name quad). In order to do that, video signals are first digitized and then compressed to corresponding quadrants. The quad's electronics does the time base correction, which means all of the signals are synchronized, so when the resultant video signal is produced all of the four quadrants are actually residing on one signal and **there is no need for external synchronization**.

Quad compressors are digital image-processing devices with an analog input and output.

As with any digital image-processing device there are a few things we should know about that define the system quality: framestore resolution expressed by the number of pixels (horizontal × vertical) and the image processing speed.

The typical framestore capacities found in today's quads are 512×512 or 1024×1024 pixels. The first one is fine compared to the camera resolution, but don't forget that we split these 512×512 into four images, hence every quadrant will have 256×256 pixel resolution, which might only be acceptable for an average system. So, if you have a choice of quads, opt for the higher framestore resolution. Apart from this detail, every pixel stores the gray level information (monochrome quads) the color information (color quads). A typical good quality B/W quad will have 256 levels of gray, although 64 levels are sufficient for some. However, 16 levels of gray are too little and the image appears too digitized. Color quads of the

A typical B/W compressor

highest quality will have over 16 million colors, which corresponds to 256 levels of each of the three primary colors, i.e., 256^3.

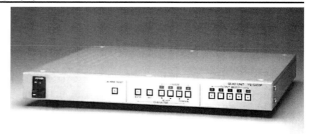

A dual-quad compressor

The next important thing about quads is the image processing time. In the early days of quads, the digital electronics were not fast, so quite often you would notice jerky movements, because the quad could only process a few images every second. Slow processing quads are still available today. In order to see smooth movements we need electronics that will process every image at the vertical frequency rate of the TV system (1/50 s or 1/60 s). Then, we will not have motion delays in the picture and the digitized effect will be less noticeable. We call these fast processing quads, **real time quads**. Real time and high resolution quads are more expensive. Color quads are more expensive than monochrome as there is a need for three framestores for each channel (the three primary colors). If more than four cameras are in the system, the solution can be found in the **dual quads,** where up to 8 cameras can be switched onto two quad images alternating one after the other. On most of these quads the dwell time between the two switching quads is adjustable.

Another very handy feature that most of the quads have is the alarm input terminal. On receiving an alarm, the corresponding camera is switched from quad mode to a full screen. Usually, this is a live mode, i.e., an analog signal is shown without being processed through the framestore. This full screen alarm activation is especially important when recording. No matter how good the quad video output may look on the monitor, when recorded onto a VHS VCR the resolution is reduced to the limits of the VCR. These limits are (discussed later in the VCR section) 240 TV lines for a color signal and about

300 for B/W. When a quad picture is replayed from the VCR, it is very hard to compare details to what was originally seen in live mode. For this reason, a system can be designed to activate on alarm that will switch from quad to full screen mode. The details of the activity recorded can then be examined much better. Various things can be used as an activation device, but most often they are passive infrared detectors (PIR), infrared beams, video motion sensors, duress buttons and reed switches.

Photo courtesy of Gyyr

A quad compressor with alarm inputs

As with alarming sequential switchers, it should be determined what happens after alarm activation, i.e., how long the quad stays with the full image and whether it requires manual acknowledgment or not. These are minor details, but they make a big difference in the system design and efficiency.

Sometimes a customer might be happy with quad images recorded as quad, in which case a plain quad, without alarm inputs, might suffice.

However, when full-screen recordings are required, care should be taken in choosing quad compressors that have zoom playback. They may appear the same as the alarming input quads, but in fact they do not record full-screen images as might be expected, rather they electronically blow up the recorded quadrants into a full screen. The resolution of such zoomed images is only a quarter (1/2 vertical and 1/2 horizontal) of what it is after being recorded.

Multiplexers (MUX)

The natural evolution of digital image-processing equipment made video multiplexers a better alternative to quads, especially when recording. Multiplexers are devices that perform **time division multiplexing** with video signals on their inputs and produce two kinds of video outputs: one for viewing and one for recording.

The output for live viewing shows all of the cameras on a single screen simultaneously. This means, if we have a 9-way multiplexer with 9 cameras, all of them will be shown in a 3×3 mosaic of multi images. The same concept also applies to 4-way multiplexers and 16-way multiplexers. Usually, with the majority of multiplexers, single full-screen cameras can also be selected. While the video output shows these images, the multiplexer's VCR output sends the time division multiplexed images of all the cameras selected for recording. This time division multiplexing looks like a very fast sequential switching, with the difference being that all of these are now synchronized to be recorded on a VCR in a sequential manner. Some manufacturers produce multiplexers which only perform fast switching (for the purpose of recording) and full-screen images, but no mosaic display. These devices are called **frame switchers** and when recording is concerned they work like multiplexers.

In order to understand this, we should mention a few things about the VCR recording concept (also discussed later in this book). The video recording heads (usually two of them) are located on a 62 mm rotating drum, which performs a helical scanning of the videotape that passes around the drum. The rotation depends on the TV system: for PAL this is 25 revolutions per second and for NTSC it's 30. By using the two heads, positioned at 180° opposite each other on the video drum, the helical scanning can read or write 50 fields each second for PAL and 60 for NTSC. This means, every TV field (composed of 312.5 lines for PAL and 262.5 for NTSC) is recorded in slanted tracks on the videotape that are densely recorded next to each other. When the VCR plays back the recorded information, it does it with the same speed as the TV standard requires so we once again reproduce motion pictures.

Clearly though, because the VCR heads are electromechanical devices the rotation speed precision is critical. Due to the electromechanical inertia the VCRs have a longer vertical lock response time than monitors. This is the main reason for even bigger picture-roll problems when non-synchronized cameras are recorded through a sequential switcher.

With normal recordings and playback, the video heads are constantly recording or reading field, after field, after field. There are 50 (60 for NTSC) of them every second.

Instead of recording one camera a few seconds, then another a few seconds and so on (which is what a sequential switcher produces), the multiplexer

Photo courtesy of Dedicated Micros

Uniplex was one of the first multiplexers

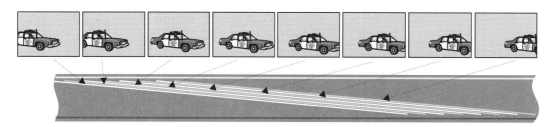

Real time recording of a video signal means
50 fields (tracks) for PAL (60 for NTSC) per second of the same signal.

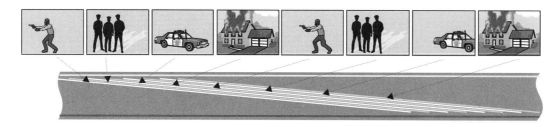

Multiplexed recording of four video signals, for example, means
the 50 fields (60 for NTSC), every second, are split among the four.

Explaining the multiplexed recording

processes video signals in such a way that every TV field sent to the VCR is another camera (usually the next one in order of inputs).

So, in effect, we have a very fast switching signal coming out of the multiplexer that **switches with the same speed that the recording heads are recording**. This speed depends on the type of VCR and the recording mode (as is the case with time lapse VCRs, which will be discussed later in the book). This is why it is very important to set the multiplexer to an output rate suitable for the particular VCR. This selection is available on all multiplexers in their setup menu. If the particular VCR model is not available on your multiplexer, there is either the generic selection you can try, or if nothing else, go by the method of trial and error to find an equivalent VCR. The major difference in TL VCRs is that some are field recorders and some are frame recorders.

Apart from this output synchronization (MUX-VCR), theoretically there is also the need for an input synchronization (cameras-MUX), but because multiplexers are digital image-processing devices, this synchronization, i.e., the **time base correction** (TBC) of the cameras, happens inside the multiplexer. This means, different cameras can be mixed onto a

Photo courtesy of Dedicated Micros

An 8-channel multiplexer

multiplexer and there is no need for them to be gen-locked, i.e., synchronized between themselves.

There are, however, multiplexer models on the market that are made to synchronize the cameras by sending sync pulses via the same coaxial cable that brings the video signal back and then multiplex the synchronized cameras. These multiplexers don't waste time on TBC and, therefore, are supposed to be faster.

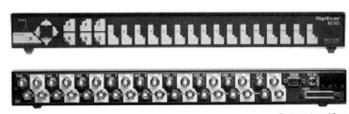

Photo courtesy of Gyyr

16-input looping multiplexer

When playback is needed, the VCR video output goes first to the multiplexer and then, the multiplexer extracts the selected camera only and sends it to the monitor. The multiplexer can display any one camera in full screen, or playback all of the recorded cameras in the mosaic mode (multiple images on one screen).

Recording time delays

It should be understood that the number of shots (images) taken from every camera during the recording depends on the total number of cameras connected to the multiplexer and the time lapse mode of the VCR. This means, **it is not possible to record real time images from all the cameras simultaneously**, because, as the name suggests, this is a time division multiplexing.

There are however, ways to improve performance by using external alarm triggers, usually with a built-in activity detector (to be explained later) in the multiplexer. The best way though, is to record in as short a time lapse mode as practically possible and also by keeping the number of cameras as low as possible. Translated into plain language, if your customer can change tapes at least once a day, don't use more than a 24-hr time lapse recording mode. If the system is unattended over weekends, then a 72-hr time lapse mode should be selected. And, if the budget allows, instead of using a 16-way multiplexer for more than 9 cameras, it would be better to use two 9-way (some manufacturers have 8-way and some 10-way) multiplexers and two VCRs. The recording frequency will then be doubled and two tapes need to be used instead of one.

This is how you can calculate the time gaps between the subsequent shots of each camera. Let's say we have a time lapse VCR that records in 24-hr time lapse mode. We earlier stated that normal (real time) recording VCRs make 50 shots every second in PAL and 60 in NTSC. If you open the TL VCR technical manual, you will find that when the VCR is in 24-hr mode it makes a shot every 0.16 s and even if you haven't got a manual with the VCR, it is easy to calculate: When a PAL VCR records in real time it makes a field recording every $1/50 = 0.02$ s. If the TL VCR is in 24-hr time lapse mode it means $24 \div 3 = 8$ times slower recording frequency. If we multiply $0.02 \times 8 = 0.16$ s. Same exercise for NTSC VCR will obtain a field recording every $1/60 = 0.0167$ s. For a 24-hr time lapse mode, when using T120 tape, i.e., $24 \div 2 = 12$. This means in 24-hr time lapse mode in the NTSC format, the TL VCR moves 12 times slower to fit 24 hr on one 2-hr tape. Thus the update rate of each recorded field in 24-hr mode is $12 \times 0.0167 = 0.2$ s.

All of the calculations are referring to a single camera signal, and therefore, if the multiplexer has only one camera, it will make a shot every 0.16 s in PAL and every 0.2 s in NTSC. If more cameras are in the system, in order to calculate the refresh rate of each camera, we need to multiply by the number of cameras, plus add a fraction of the time the multiplexer spends on time base correction due to non-synchronized cameras (which will usually be the case). So if we have, for example, 8 cameras to record, $8 \times 0.16 = 1.28$ s (PAL) and $8 \times 0.2 = 1.6$ s (NTSC). Adding to it the time spent on sync correction and

the realistic time gaps between the subsequent shots of **each** camera, should result in, approximately 1.5 to 2 s. This is not a bad figure when considering that **all 8 cameras are recorded on a single tape**. If we have to identify an important event that happened at 3 PM, for example, we can either view all of the cameras in a mosaic mode and see which cameras have important activity, or select each one of them separately in full screen.

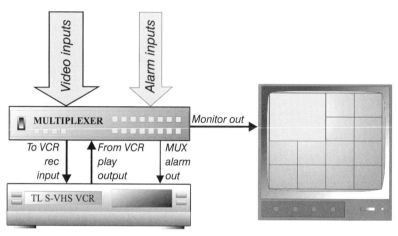

A typical multiplexer – TL VCR interconnection

For some applications, 2 s might be too long a time to waste and this is where the alarm input or the motion activity detection can be very handy. Most of the multiplexers have alarm input terminals and with this we can trigger the **priority encoding** mode. **The priority encoding mode is when the multiplexer encodes the alarmed camera on a priority basis**. Say we have an alarm associated with camera 3. Instead of the normal time division multiplexing of the 8 cameras in sequence 1, 2, 3, 4, 5, 6, 7, 8, 1, 2, it goes 1, 3, 2, 3, 4, 3, 5, 3, 6, 3 and so on. The time gap in such a case is prolonged for all cameras other than 3. But since number 3 is the important camera at that point in time, the priority encoding has made camera 3 appear with new shots every $2 \times 0.16 = 0.32$ s, or in practice almost 0.5 s (due to the time base correction). This is a much better response than the previously calculated 2 s for the plain multiplexed encoding. It should be noted, though, when more than one alarm is presented to the multiplexer inputs, the time gaps between the subsequent camera shots are prolonged and once we get through all of the alarmed camera inputs, we get plain multiplexed encoding.

In case a system cannot be designed to use external alarm triggers, it should be known that most of the multiplexers have an **activity motion detection** built-in. This is a very handy feature where every channel of the multiplexer analyzes the changes in the video information in each of the framestore updates. When there is a change in them (i.e., something is moving in the field of view), they will set off an internal alarm, which in turn will start the priority encoding scheme. This can be of great assistance when replaying intrusions, or events and determining the activity details.

A typical multiplexer display

Usually, the activity motion detection can be turned on or off and when turned on, on some MUX models, it will allow you to configure the shape of the detection area in order to suit various areas or objects.

Real-time time lapse recorders have appeared on the CCTV market that might confuse the issue of calculating the refresh rate. These are faster recording machines where the TL VCR's mechanics is modified so as to record 16.7 fields per second in PAL (a field every 0.06 s) for 24-hr relative to E240 tape. In the case of NTSC, around 20 fields per second (a field every 0.05 s) can be recorded for 24 hrs on a T160 tape. Understandably, to calculate the refresh rate of multiplexed cameras on such a TL VCR, you would need to multiply the number of cameras with the above mentioned field update.

If we wanted to be fair, this is not really real time recording, but defintely better than the ordinary time lapse mode. To the best of my knowledge there is only one CCTV manufacturer that makes real 24-hr recordings at 50 fields per second for PAL and 60 for NTSC and that is Elbex.

The NTSC system uses tape at a higher recording speed (2 meters/minute) than PAL or SECAM (1.42 meters/minute). To confuse this issue even more, VHS tapes are marked in playing times as opposed to tape length. Therefore, a T120 (2-hour) tape bought in the United States is not the same as an E120 (2-hour) tape bought in the UK. The US T120 tape is 246 meters in length and will give 2 hours of play time on an NTSC VCR. This same tape used on a PAL VCR will give 2 hour & 49 minutes of play time. Conversely, a UK E120 tape is 173 meters in length and will give 2 hours of play time on a PAL VCR. The same tape used on an NTSC VCR will give only 1 hour & 26 minutes of play time. The chart compares the recording times of each tape in PAL, SECAM and NTSC.

Tape label	Tape length (m)	NTSC time (min)	PAL time (min)
E30	45	22	30
E60	88	44	60
E90	130	65	90
E120	173	86	120
E180	258	129	180
E240	346	173	240
T20	44	20	28
T30	64	30	42
T45	94	45	63
T60	125	60	84
T90	185	90	126
T120	246	120	169
T160	326	160	225

Simplex and duplex multiplexers

Most multiplexers will allow you to view images of any selected camera in a mosaic mode while they are encoding. When a recorded tape needs to be viewed, as we already mentioned, the VCR output does not go directly to a monitor, but it has to go through the multiplexer again in order for the images to be decoded. While doing this, the multiplexer cannot be used for recording. So, if recording is very important and the playback needs to be used in the meantime, another multiplexer and VCR are required. These multiplexers that can do only one thing at a time are called **simplex** multiplexers.

There are also **duplex** multiplexers, which are actually two multiplexers in the one unit, one for recording and one for playback. Still, two VCRs will be required if both recording and playback are required at the same time.

Some manufacturers even make multiplexers which they refer to as **triplex**. These are multiplexers with the same functionality as the duplex ones, with the addition of displaying a mixture of live and playback images on one monitor.

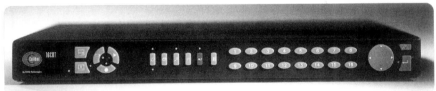

A 16-channel triplex multiplexer   Photo courtesy by Calibur

As with quad compressors, we can get B/W and color multiplexers. We also have a limited amount of framestore resolution available. Needless to say, the bottleneck in the resolution reproduction will still be the VCR itself. Many newer CCTV systems are being installed with Super VHS VCRs, that offer an improved resolution of 400 TV lines as opposed to 240 with the ordinary VHS format.

Multiplexers can successfully be used in applications other than just recording. This might be especially useful if more than one video signal needs to be transmitted over a microwave link, for example. By using two identical simplex multiplexers, one at each end of the link, we can transmit more than one image in a time division multiplexed mode. In this instance, the speed of the refresh rate for each camera is identical to what it would be if we were to record those cameras in real (3-hr) mode on a VCR.

Video motion detectors (VMD)

A video motion detector (VMD) is a device that analyzes the video signal at its input and determines whether its contents have changed and consequently, produces an alarm output.

With the ever-evolving image processing technology, it became possible to store and process images in a very short period of time. If this processing time is equal to or smaller than 1/50 (PAL) or 1/60 (NTSC) s, which as we know, is the live video refresh rate, we can process images without losing any fields and preserve the real time motion appearance.

In the very beginning of the development of VMDs, only analog processing was possible. Those simple VMDs are still available and perhaps still very efficient relative to their price, although they are incapable of sophisticated analysis and, therefore, high rates of false alarms are present. The principles of operation of the analog VMDs (sometimes called video motion sensors) are very simple: a video signal taken from

a camera is fed into the VMD and then onto a monitor, or whatever switching device might be used. In the analyzed video picture, little square marks (usually four) are positioned by means of a few potentiometers on the front of the VMD unit. The square marks actually indicate the sensor areas of the picture and the video level is determined by the VMD's electronics. As soon as this level is changed to a lower or higher value, by means of someone or something entering the field of view at the marked area, an alarm is produced. The sensitivity is determined by the amount of video luminance level change required to raise an alarm (usually 10% or more of the peak

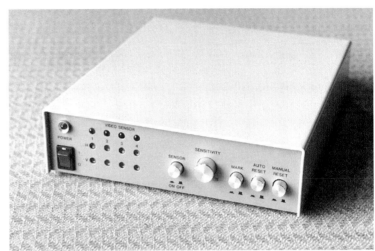

A simple non-intelligent single-channel video motion detection unit

video signal). The alarm is usually audible and the VMD produces relay closure, which can be used to further trigger other devices. The alarm acknowledgment can be either automatic (after a few seconds) or manual. There is also a VMD sensitivity potentiometer on the front panel in such devices and with the proper adjustment it can bring satisfactory results. There will always be false alarms activated by trees swaying in the wind, cats walking around or light reflections, but at least the reason for the alarm can be seen when the VCR is played back (assuming the VMD is connected to a VCR).

A PC-based VMD system by Dindima

VMDs are often a better solution than passive infrared motion detectors (PIR), not only because the cause of the alarm can be seen, but also because it analyzses exactly what the camera sees, no less and no more. When using a PIR, its angle of coverage has to match the camera's angle of view if an efficient system is to be achieved.

When a number of cameras are used, we cannot switch signals through the VMD as it will cause constant alarms, so therefore one VMD is required per camera. In systems where further processing of the video signal is done, the sensing markers can be made invisible, but they are still active.

The next step up in VMD technology is the digital video motion detector (DVMD), which is becoming even more sophisticated and popular. This, of course, is associated with higher price, but the reliability is also much higher and the false alarm rate is lower.

One of the major differences between various DVMD manufacturers is the software algorithm and how motion is processed. These concepts have evolved to the stage where tree movement due to wind can be ignored, car movement in the picture background can also be discriminated against and excluded from the process deciding about the alarm activity. In the last few years, DVMDs that take the perspective into account have been developed. This means that as the objects move away from the camera, thus getting smaller in size, the VMD sensitivity increases in order to compensate for the object's size reduction due to the perspective effect. This effect, we should point out, also depends on the lens.

Many companies now produce a cheaper alternative to a full blown stand-alone system in a form of PC card(s). The cards come with specialized software and almost any PC can be used for VMD. Further more, image snapshots can be stored on a hard disk and transmitted over telephone line connected to the PC. With many options available in the VMDs a lot of time needs to be spent on a proper setup, but the reward will be a much more reliable operation with fewer false alarms.

A special method of recording called *pre-alarm history* is becoming very standard in most of the VMD devices. The idea behind this is very simple, but extremely useful in CCTV. When an alarm triggers the VMD, the device keeps a number of images recorded after the alarm occurrence, but also a few of them before. The result is a progressive sequence of images showing not only the alarm itself, but also what preceded it.

One of the latest developments in this area has brought to light an Australian company, among a few other successes, with their (original) concept of three dimensional video motion detection. This concept offers extremely low rates of false alarms by using two or more cameras to view objects from different angles. Thus, a three dimensional volumetric protection area is defined, which like the other VMDs is invisible to the public, but it is quite distinguishable to the image-processing electronics. With this concept, movement in front of any of the cameras

PC-based 3-dimensional VMD by Practel

will not trigger an alarm until the **protected volume area**, as seen by **both cameras,** is disturbed. Using this concept, valuable artworks in galleries, for example, can be monitored so that the alarm doesn't activate every time someone passes in front of the artwork, but only when the artwork is removed from its position.

Quite often, very useful alarm detection is not when someone or something moves in the field of view, but rather when something fixed is removed from its location. This can be done with a **video non-motion detector** (VNMD). This is a unit very similar to the VMD, only that additional information is collected for objects put in the field of view

Photo courtesy of Vision Systems

A sophisticated multi-channel video motion detection unit

that are stationary for a longer period. Movements around the **selected** object do not cause alarms, only when the protected object is removed from the stationary position does the alarm activate.

In the last couple of years, some modern DSP cameras offer VMD circuitry built inside the camera itself. This could be quite practical in systems where recording and/or alarm is initiated only when a person or object moves inside the camera's field of view.

All of the above mentioned VMDs, used as an alarm output, produce a closure of relay contacts that can trigger additional devices in the CCTV chain, like VCRs, or matrix switchers, framestores, sirens, or similar. If you decide to use one, make sure you clarify the type of alarm output with the supplier, as it can be anything from voltage free N/O contacts, to a logic level voltage (5 V) N/C output.

We should also mention VMDs that, apart from the motion detection, also dial remote receiving stations and send images via telephone lines. With such devices, remote monitoring is possible from virtually anywhere in the world. Images are sent to a receiver station only when the VMD detects movement, indirectly saving on long distance telephone calls.

Framestores

Framestores are, conceptually, very simple electronic devices used to temporarily store images. Two important parts of a framestore device are the analog-to-digital (A/D) conversion (ADC) section and the random access memory (RAM) section. The ADC section converts the analog video signal into digital which is then stored in the RAM memory, for as long as it is powered.

Photo courtesy of Vision Systems

A framestore device

The main advantage of the framestores compared to VCRs is their response time. Since they do not have any mechanically moving parts, the storage of the alarmed picture is instant on activation. This is then fed back, usually, to a video printer or a monitor for viewing or verification purposes.

More sophisticated framestores are usually designed to have a few framestore pages which constantly store and discard a series of images using the first in first out (FIFO) principle until an alarm activates. When that happens, it is possible to view not only the alarmed moment itself, but also a few frames taken before the alarm event took place giving a short event history. This is the same concept as the "Pre-alarm history" used in VMDs.

Another application of the framestores is the **frame lock device**. This device constantly processes video signals present at its input and also does the time base correction to be in sync with the master clock inside. Since this processing is done at a very fast real time rate and the framestore has a high resolution, there is no perceptible degradation of the video signal. This is a very practical and useful device for showing (switching) non-synchronized cameras on a single monitor. In cases like this, the frame lock device acts as a synchronizer, i.e., eliminates picture-roll while cameras are scanning.

The major division of framestores, as used in CCTV, is into B/W and color. The quality of a framestore is determined, first of all, with the framestore resolution, i.e., the number of pixels that can be stored and, secondly, with the gray level's bit-resolution or, in the case of color, the number of bits used to store colors. A typical good quality framestore has more than 400×400 pixels and the usual resolution is 752×480 pixels and 256 levels of gray (2^8). For a color framestore (with three color channels) we would have over 16 million colors ($256 \times 256 \times 256$).

Video Printers

Video printers are commonly used in bigger systems where a hard-copy printout of a live or recorded image is necessary for evaluation or evidence. There are two types of video printers: monochrome and color. The monochrome video printers usually use thermal paper as an output medium, but some more expensive ones can print on plain paper. The thermal-paper video printers, used for monochrome signals, are similar in operation to the facsimile machine and they print out images with a size and resolution dependent on the printer's resolution. With thermal printers the output is not as durable and stable (due to thermal paper aging) and the printouts need to be photocopied for longer duration.

Color video printers print on special paper and the process of printing is similar to dye-sublimation printing, using cyan, magenta, yellow and black filters. The printing quality produced by such technology is excellent, but the number of copies that can be produced is limited, i.e., the cartridge needs to be replaced with every new set of paper.

Photo courtesy of Panasonic

A color video printer

More sophisticated video printers have a number of controls including titling, sharpening, duplication into more copies and storing the images in their framestores until a printout is necessary.

In many instances, CCTV users don't want to invest in a video printer, so often there is the need to use the specialized services of some bureaus. The videotape is taken to them and the certain event(s) is/ are extracted and printed out.

8. Video Recorders

The framestore/VCR relation is very similar to the RAM/tape backup relation in computers. That is to say, framestores are used to store images temporarily, for as long as there is power, whereas VCRs store images on a more permanent basis, even without power.

Video recorders are a very important and very special part of a CCTV system. So special that a particular type has been developed exclusively for CCTV called time lapse VCR (TL VCR).

A little bit of history and the basic concept

The era of tape recording really began in 1935 with the appearance of AEG's first commercial sound tape recorder, called *Magnetophone*. The tape used was a cellulose acetate tape, coated with carbonyl iron powder. The performance of these sound recording machines, even though it was very good for its time, steadily improved during the 1930s and 1940s to the point where at the end of the 1940s much of the radio broadcast material was off tape and indistinguishable from live programs.

The basics of magnetic tape recording are familiar to most of us from the good old audio cassette recorders. An alternate current (AC) signal, passing through an audio head winding, produces alternate magnetic flux through a magnetically permeable metal ring, called a head. In order for the magnetic flux to come out of the ring (otherwise, the magnetic flux will stay inside the core) a little slit is made at one end of the core. This slit will now act as an exhaust for the magnetic field that exits the core and closes it through the air going back to the other end of the slit. But if we put a magnetic tape very close to the head, the flux will pass through the tape itself, thus closing the circle. The magnetic tape is a very thin tape coated with magnetic powder, whose microscopic particles act as little magnets. By applying an external magnetic field, these little particles can be polarized in various directions, depending on the current intensity and its direction.

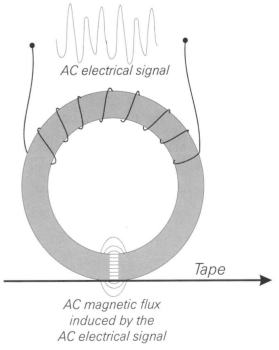

AC electrical signal

Tape

AC magnetic flux induced by the AC electrical signal

If the magnetic tape is stationary, no information will be recorded, except for the last state of the magnetic field. In order for an audio recording to be performed, **the tape needs to move at a constant speed**. At what speed, depends on the resolution, i.e., the highest frequency needed to be recorded. **The faster the tape moves and the smaller the gap in the ring is, the higher the frequency can be recorded.**

The concept of magnetic recording

An analogy to the above would be like having a fountain pen with a sharp tip and another one with a calligraphic tip. With the sharper tip we can write more details and smaller fonts, on the same space, than with the calligraphic tip.

This is a simplified description of how audio recording is done. In real life, the audio signal is not recorded directly as it is, but rather it is amplitude modulated with a sinewave. It has been found that the linearity of the recorded signals is then better. The tape speed, in the case of an audio cassette, was chosen to be 4.75 cm/s. So, a half-hour recording made on one side of a C-60 cassette, will take about 86 m ($4.75 \times 60 \times 30 = 8550$ cm) of tape. With a good quality tape an audio bandwidth of approximately 50 Hz to 15,000 Hz can be recorded with a clean head. With such audio characteristics, the recording is not impressive when compared to today's digital CD standards. Obviously, with bigger audio tape recorders (reel-to-reel) and a quadrupled tape speed of 19 cm/s, the recorded and reproduced bandwidth is much better.

A similar concept to audio tape recording was initially tried on video signals, back in the 1950s, when strange machines were designed with tape speeds close to 1000 cm/s and extraordinarily big reels. The theory behind the tape recording showed that in order to record a monochrome video signal with a bandwidth of only 3 MHz (for a reasonable picture quality, as opposed to only 15 kHz in audio), a tape speed of around 3 m/s (300 cm/s) is required. For such a speed, one can calculate that for only a one hour recording, $3 \times 60 \times 60 = 10,800$ m of tape is required. The quality of such a **longitudinal** recording was still very poor and the equipment extremely large and difficult to deal with.

Knowing the size of a C-60 tape (86 m), one can imagine the physical size of reels having 10 km of tape. Since this was very impractical, a solution was sought for in a different way of achieving the tape speed relative to the video head. In the 1950s, a couple of Ampex™ engineers came up with a **transverse-scan** system which had 4 video heads rotating while the tape passed at an incredible speed of 40 m/s. This system was capable of recording up to 15 MHz of signal bandwidth and was sufficient in quality for broadcast television. For the commercial and CCTV markets this was a far too expensive product, so other alternatives and solutions had to be developed.

The early VCR concepts

By the end of the 1950s, the concept of the **helical scanning** was proposed. This was a much simpler system compared to the transverse scanning, although initially all of the manufacturers offered open reel designs, incompatible with each other. The recorders were not using cassettes yet and were not for domestic use.

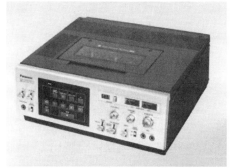

In the 1970s, Sony™ proposed its U-matic standard, which became well established in the broadcast industry, having very good performance for its time and introducing cassettes instead of open reels.

It was 1972 when Philips™ came out with their first machine aimed at the domestic market called N1500, which was a real

An early model VHS VCR

milestone in VCR development, but unfortunately, it didn't sell very well. It offered one hour of recording and had a built-in tuner, timer and RF modulator. This led to the development of the System 2000 design, but unfortunately, it happened at the time when color television appeared and a lot of people were saving money to buy color TVs instead of VCRs.

In the early 1970s, Matsushita™ and JVC™ came out with their rivalling proposals, i.e., with the video home system (VHS), while Sony™ proposed the Beta. So there was actually a bitter competition between the System 2000, Beta and VHS. They were similar in concept, but unfortunately, totally incompatible.

In time, VHS crystallized itself as the most popular and widely accepted by the domestic market. Technically speaking, VHS was initially the poorest in quality, but it was much simpler and cheaper to make.

Over the years, a lot of improvements have made it of a much better quality than it was originally and today in CCTV, as is the case with the domestic market, in more than 90% of cases, VHS is used. Once VHS was widely accepted, Sony came out with their **8 mm** format and then **Hi 8 mm**, offering much smaller tapes and better recording quality, but JVC™ released their **Super VHS** which matched the Hi 8 quality.

As we have already mentioned, a special type of VHS VCR was developed for CCTV, called a time lapse VCR. That is why in this book we will only cover the VHS concept. We are, perhaps, being a little bit unfair to the other formats which may also be in use, like the U-Matic, Beta, or 8, but we only have time and space to concentrate on the equipment used in the majority of systems today.

The video home system (VHS) concept

Helical scanning is the concept where the heads are located on a tilted drum which rotates with a speed equal to the video frame frequency, 25 revolutions per second for PAL and 30 for NTSC. **The required tape-relative-to-head speed is achieved mainly with the head drum rotation.**

With the initial video home system (VHS) design there were actually two video heads used, 180° opposite each other. They are mounted on a rotating cylinder, called a video drum. So when a recording or playback happens, each head records or plays back one TV field. The video tape is wound around the drum for 180°, thus **one of the two video heads is always in contact with the tape.** The actual speed of the tape relative to the stationary parts of the VCR's tape

A VHS video drum with two video heads

compartment is 2.339 cm/s (PAL), i.e., approximately half the speed of an audio cassette. For NTSC speed is a bit higher, 3.33 cm/s.

The VHS tape format is 1/2" (12.65 mm) wide and as it can be seen from the drawing below, the thickness of each of the slanted tracks is approximately 0.049 mm and their length is approximately 10 cm. In so little space, information for 312.5 lines for PAL (and 262.5 for NTSC) has to be recorded.

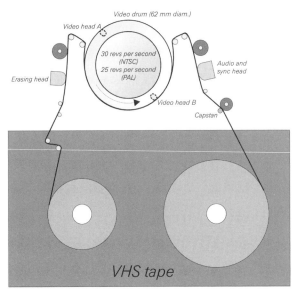

The VHS tape alignment

When you have this in mind, it becomes understandable how important the quality of the tape is, both with its magnetic coating and its mechanical continuity and durability.

Apart from the video signal, which is recorded on slanted tracks, audio is also recorded on the tape, with a stationary audio head on the top part of the tape and control tracks on the bottom.

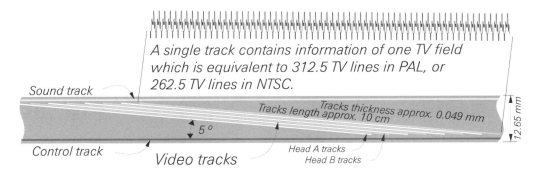

1:1 scaled and simplified drawing of a VHS tape and recording

There are certain limitations imposed on the video signal when it gets inside the VCR electronics. For starters, the design of the VHS recording, including the size of the video drum, the rotation speed and the videotape quality, determine how wide a bandwidth can be recorded on the videotape.

When the video signal gets to the video input stage of the VCR, it goes through a very sharp-edged low-pass filter with a high frequency end of 3 MHz. This filter passes only the luminance information, while the chrominance is extracted from the high-pass filtered portion of the same signal. The reason for such a cutoff of the luminance is simply that more cannot be recorded. Those are the limits of the VHS concept.

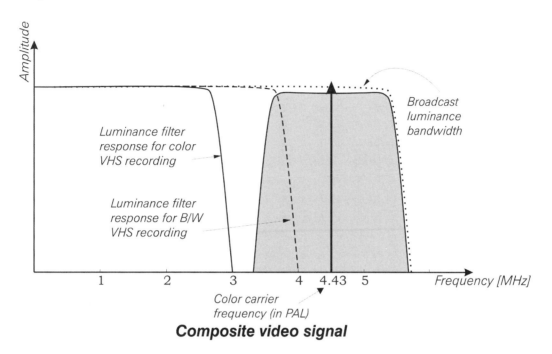

Composite video signal

From the simple relation we introduced earlier, 3 MHz corresponds to 240 TV lines of horizontal resolution. This is the practical limitation for a color video signal when played back. Clearly, this indicates that the VCR is almost always the bottleneck in achieving a good quality playback picture in today's CCTV systems.

When recording only monochrome signals, the low-pass filtering can be bypassed since we don't have a color carrier. In such cases, the actual resolution will be a bit higher and depending on the tape and VCR quality, it can be close to 300 TV lines. Many VCRs have an automatic switch for this bypass, but on most time lapse VCRs there is a manual switch for this.

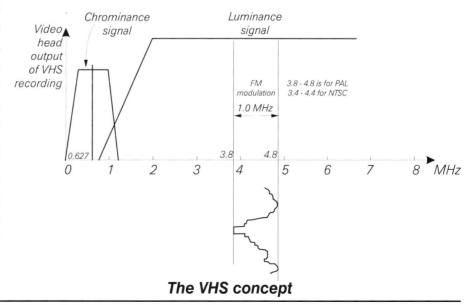

The VHS concept

The actual video luminance signal is not recorded directly as it is, but it is modulated, as is the case with the audio recording. In VHS, the luminance is frequency modulated (FM) with frequency deviations starting from 3.8 MHz (corresponds to lowest sync peak) up to 4.8 MHz (corresponds to white peaks). The chrominance information, which is extracted from the VCR input, is directly recorded with a down-converted carrier of 627 kHz and occupies the 0~1 MHz spectrum range. This is possible because the luminance is frequency modulated above this area.

With the further development of the VHS concept a lot of improvements were introduced. Models with four heads were produced, long play mode was offered and pause mode stability improved considerably. Also, audio recording, which was initially very poor with low speed transversal recording, was improved in the Hi-Fi models. Instead of the initial 40 Hz ~ 12 kHz audio bandwidth, a high fidelity sound is recorded with audio heads located on the video drum itself, rotating with the same speed as the video heads. Having such a high speed tape-relative-to-heads recording the audio bandwidth was widened to 20 Hz ~ 20 kHz and the signal/noise ratio dramatically increased from 44 dB to over 90 dB. The Hi-Fi audio channels are not recorded on separate tracks along the video but rather in the deeper layer of the tape and with a different azimuth angle of the recorded FM signal. So, this type of recording is called Depth Multiplex Recording.

Even though better tapes and video heads were manufactured, the video bandwidth could not be improved considerably, due to the limitations of the concept itself. Having this in mind, the VHS inventors introduced a new and improved format called Super VHS.

Super VHS, Y/C and comb filtering

The next major advancement in the development of VHS VCRs came in 1987 with the introduction of the **Super VHS** concept. The Super VHS format improved the luminance and chrominance quality of the recorded video signals, yet preserved downward compatibility with the VHS format. This means the same type of video heads, rotating with the same speed at the same angle.

S-VHS recorders differ from the VHS basically by their wider bandwidth. This is achieved by separating the color and luminance from the composite video signal with a special comb filter and then modulating the luminance signal with a higher and wider FM band, whose frequency now deviates from 5.4 MHz to 7 MHz. This means that a video luminance bandwidth

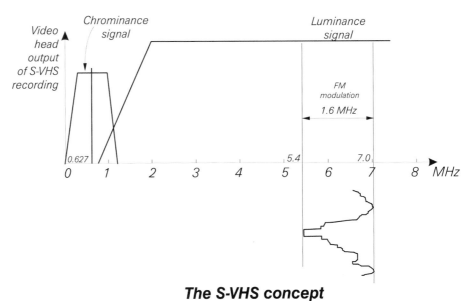

The S-VHS concept

of over 5 MHz can be recorded, giving 400+ TV lines resolution. Video heads of the same physical dimensions are used, but they have better characteristics. Also, although the same sized videotapes are used, the magnetic coating is of a much better quality.

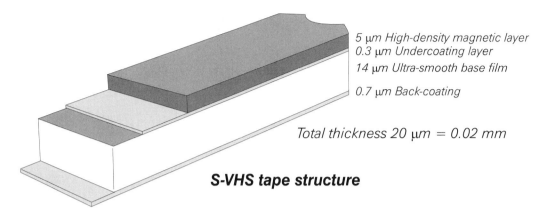

5 μm *High-density magnetic layer*
0.3 μm *Undercoating layer*
14 μm *Ultra-smooth base film*

0.7 μm *Back-coating*

Total thickness 20 μm = 0.02 mm

S-VHS tape structure

S-VHS VCRs can record and play back VHS and S-VHS. For a S-VHS recording to be activated a S-VHS tape must be used (the S-VHS recorder recognizes a S-VHS tape by a little slot on the cassette box). A VHS VCR cannot playback S-VHS tapes.

When color and luminance signals are combined in a composite video signal, there is always a visible cross-color and cross-luminance artifacts. In order to minimize such deterioration, S-VHS recorders permit direct input and output of the uncombined luminance and chrominance components. This pair is called **Y/C** (Y stands for luminance and C for chrominance) and is found at the back of S-VHS VCRs in the form of miniature DIN (Deutsche industrie norme) connectors.

If you have a video source that produces Y/C signals (like some multiplexers, VCRs or framestores), they can be connected to the S-VHS VCR with a special Y/C cable that is composed of two miniature coaxial cables.

There is a misinterpretation among some users that we can only record a high quality video when a Y/C signal is brought to the S-VHS. This is not true, since the S-VHS was designed primarily for recording composite video signals. For this purpose, a special adaptive comb filter was designed for S-VHS, where the color information is separated from the composite video signal **without losing significant luminance resolution** (as is the case with the low-pass filter in VHS).

An early solution to the Y/C separation problem was to put a low pass filter on the composite signal and filter out the color signal above about 2.5 MHz in NTSC (above 3 MHz in PAL) to recover the Y signal. The reduced bandwidth of the Y signal dramatically limited the resolution in the picture. A bandpass filter was used to recover the color signal but it was still contaminated by high frequency luminance crosstalk and suffered serious cross-color effects.

It is known though that the basic composite video signal is periodic in nature as a result of the horizontal and vertical scanning and blanking processes. This means that when such signal is represented in the frequency domain (a Fourier analysis is applied) it will be represented by **harmonics in precise locations, rather than have an uniform spectrum throughout the whole spectrum** of the video signal. This is a very important and fundamental fact in television signal analysis.

By picking the horizontal and vertical scanning rates and the color sub-carrier frequency in particular harmonic relationships, the Y/C separation process can be simplified. The color sub-carrier frequency in NTSC (and similar logic can be applied to PAL), Fsc, is chosen to be 3.579545 MHz (usually referred to as simply 3.58 MHz). This corresponds to the 455th harmonic of the horizontal scanning frequency, Fh, divided by two (as per the NTSC definitions).

Fh = 15,734.26 Hz

Fsc = 455 × Fh/2 = 3.579545 MHz

Since there are 525 lines in a video frame and a frame consists of two interlaced fields, there are 262.5 lines in a field. Therefore, the vertical field rate is:

Fv = Fh/262.5 = 59.94 Hz.

There are also two fields in a frame, so the frame rate is Fv/2 = 29.97 Hz.

Since the video signal is periodic in nature, the spectral distribution of the video frequencies are grouped together in clusters. The Fourier analysis of a static video signal shows that the energy spectrum is concentrated in clusters separated by 15.734 kHz, which is the horizontal scan rate. Each cluster has sidebands with 59.94 and 29.97 Hz spacing. Therefore, the luminance signal does not have a continuous distribution of energy across its bandwidth. Instead, it exists as clusters of energy, each separated by 15.734 kHz. These clusters are not very wide so **most of the space between them is empty**.

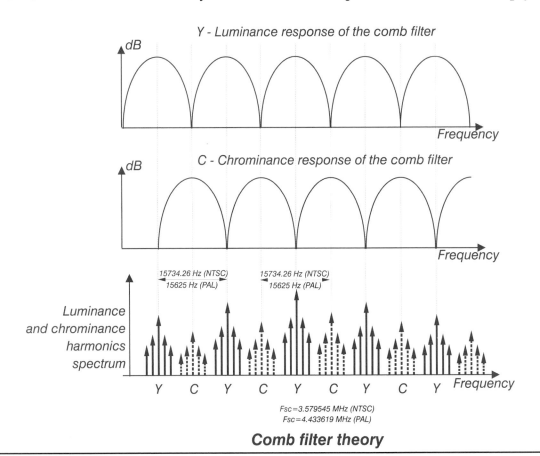

Comb filter theory

The chrominance signal is also periodic in nature, since it appears on each horizontal scan and is interrupted by the blanking process. Therefore, the **chrominance signal will also cluster** at 15.734 kHz intervals across its bandwidth. By picking the color sub-carrier at an odd harmonic (455) of Fh/2, the chroma signal clusters are **centered exactly between the luminance signal clusters**. Therefore, the Y and C signals can occupy the same frequency space by this process of frequency interleaving.

This is the idea behind the comb filters design. A comb filter can be designed to have a frequency response with nulls at periodic frequency intervals. At the center frequency between the nulls, the comb filter passes the signal. If the comb filter is tuned to be periodic at the same 15.734 kHz intervals as the Y/C frequency interleaving, it will **pass the Y signal while rejecting the C** signal or visa versa.

When using Y/C cables between S-VHS components there is minimal cross-luminance and cross-color interference, but for CCTV this is quite impractical since it requires two coaxial cables. The miniature Y/C cable that comes with some S-VHS VCRs is a twin-coaxial cable designed for short runs only, as it has a much higher attenuation than the popular RG-59/U. The main intention of such Y/C connections is for dubbing purposes.

It should also be noted that the technology of comb filtering is improving daily. Today the most advanced comb filters are imployed not only in S-VHS VCRs but also in high quality monitors and television sets.

First it was the 2D-comb filter where not only one line in the video signal but the previous and the next one was used to compare the color content and decide on the optimum filtering (thus 2D). Further improvement brough the 3D comb filtering and digital comb filtering, where not only information in one TV field, but the previous and next fields are processed for the color content (thus 3D). New developments are further improving the resolution and color fidelity.

It is possible that of the units you might have, an S-VHS recorder, for example, and a TV monitor, both of them have comb filters but not necessarily of equal type and quality. It is worth experimenting as it may happen that a better picture quality will be reproduced if a composite video signal is brought from the recorder and let the TV extract the color information with it's own comb filter (if it is of a better design), rather than having Y/C cable connection between the S-VHS VCR and TV monitor.

So, using S-VHS recorders in CCTV with high resolution color cameras and a single coaxial cable for composite color video signal is still far superior than using VHS VCRs. The quality of the recorded signal is ensured by the high quality adaptive comb filter built in the S-VHS VCR and the played back signal will be as good as the monitor can show. If a high resolution color monitor is used, which would also have its own comb filter, the quality will be much better than using TV monitors designed for commercial use. If we assume a camera has 470 TV lines of horizontal resolution, the S-VHS VCR has about 400 and the monitor is 600 TV lines, the VCR will still be the bottleneck for the played back resolution and the played back signal should have around 400 TV lines (providing, of course, S-VHS tape is used).

Another minor note not found in many technical topics related to S-VHS VCRs, is in regards to the LP/SP (long play/standard play) modes. The S-VHS quality is achievable in LP mode as well as in SP mode. There is a very minor deterioration of the higher frequencies recorded because of the closer video tracks and slower tape movement, but this is almost undetectable.

Using consumer model VCRs for CCTV purposes

A very trivial question that I have often been asked by nontechnical people is Can I connect a CCTV camera to my VCR at home and record and view it on my TV? The answer is yes, although you should be aware of the reduction in recorder quality when compared to dedicated CCTV equipment.

A typical domestic VCR, apart from the RF (antenna) input, also has the audio/video inputs. In most cases they are in the form of phono sockets (some call them RCA connectors), one for a basic bandwidth video (this is, as we said earlier, what the CCTV camera gives us) and the other for an audio signal. So, a CCTV camera video signal should be connected directly to the video input of the VCR, with an appropriate adaptor (BNC-RCA). Then, the video output terminal of the VCR (the same type of RCA connector) has to be connected to the video input of the TV receiver. Both the VCR and the TV **have to be switched to A/V channel** and then the CCTV camera should appear on your TV screen.

However, if your TV receiver **doesn't have an A/V input**, then the RF output of the VCR should be taken to the RF input (or the antenna input) of the TV set. Understandably, **the TV now has to be tuned to the VCR channel**, which in most cases should be UHF (36-39), as this is a dedicated area for VCRs, but some older models may modulate their signal in the low VHF channels 0, 1, 2 or 3. Also in this case, the VCR has to be set to the A/V channel in order to pass the CCTV camera signal from its video input to the RF output. In both of the above cases, **the VCR is in between the camera and the TV**. When viewing a live signal or recording, the picture is displayed on the TV and when playing back a recorded signal, the VCR cuts the incoming live signal and shows the recorded image on the same TV.

**Walls of VCRs in Sydney's Star City Casino record all cameras
in real time mode, fully managed by the matrix switcher**

When compared to the CCTV dedicated time lapse VCRs, discussed in the next heading, the disadvantage of the domestic models of VCRs are manyfold: there is no time and date inserted in the recorded video signal, there are no external alarm trigger inputs and maximum recording time can be achieved in long play mode, which is not longer than 10 hrs for PAL or over 8 hrs for NTSC. There are, however, some clear advantages: the price of a normal VCR is very low and affordable and the images are recorded in full motion, i.e., 50 fields per second for PAL and 60 fields per second for NTSC.

Because of the latter, some matrix manufacturers have designed special hardware and software interface devices for their matrix switchers so as to be able to intelligently control VCRs. This is usually done by intercepting the infrared control section of the VCR and full control over the recorders is taken from the matrix. In large systems it is almost as expensive, if not more, to incorporate MUX-es and TL VCRs instead. Because of this reason and because of the requirement for real time recording all the time, this solution has been especially attractive for large casino installations. With a properly designed and programmed matrix system, it is possible to fully automate and control hundreds and hundreds of VCRs except for when tapes need to be changed.

At this point, we should also mention that due to the different recording speeds in the two television standards discussed in this book (PAL and NTSC) we also have different videotape length, and consequently, slightly different recording/playback time. The table below should give sufficient information for such discrepancies. Please note that international tape marking for PAL system machines is with "E" and for NTSC machines with "T."

Tape label	Tape length (m)	NTSC time (min)	PAL time (min)
E30	45	22	30
E60	88	44	60
E90	130	65	90
E120	173	86	120
E180	258	129	180
E240	346	173	240
T20	44	20	28
T30	64	30	42
T45	94	45	63
T60	125	60	84
T90	185	90	126
T120	246	120	169
T160	326	160	225

Time lapse VCRs (TL VCRs)

Time lapse VCRs are a special category of video recorders, developed specifically for the security industry.

The main difference between the TL VHS VCR and domestic models is in the following:

- TL VCRs can record up to 960 hrs on a single 180-minute tape (PAL) or 120-minute tape (NTSC). Other time lapse modes between 3 and 960 are available: 12, 24, 48, 72, 96, 120, 168, 240, 480 and 720 hrs. This is achieved by the time lapse stepper motor that moves the tape in discrete steps, while the video drum rotates constantly. Usually up to the 12-hr mode, the tape moves with continuous speed, after which, starting from 24, it moves in discrete steps. The time lapsed between subsequent shots increases as the mode increases. Typical times are shown in the table on the next page.

The modes mentioned refer to a 180-minute tape or 120-minute tape, depending on the television system in question. If a 240-minute tape is used instead, the corresponding TL mode increases by 1/3, i.e., 24 hrs becomes 32, 72 becomes 96 and so on. The same logic applies when a 300-minute tape is used, where TL modes are increased by 2/3, i.e., 24 hrs becomes 40, 72 becomes 120 and so on. Please refer to the table on next page for more details.

Clearly, when a TL VCR is recording in TL mode, no real time movement is recorded, because there are not 50 fields (60 for NTSC) recorded each second. The playback looks like a video playback in pause mode, advancing at short but regular intervals, as per the table. TL VCRs can record and playback in any mode, irrespective of which it was recorded in. In pause mode, still frames (fields) have exceptionally good quality. When unstable, a special still lock adjustment potentiometer, not available on commercial VCRs, can stabilize the picture to a perfectly still frame. This is of great importance for verification purposes.

- TL VCRs have no tuners, i.e., normal RF reception is not possible.

- TL VCRs can be triggered by an external alarm, which will cause the unit to switch instantly from TL mode into real time for a preset duration (15 s, 30 s, 1 min, 3 min) or until the alarm is cleared, after which it goes back into TL mode. Usually, voltage free N/O (normally open) contacts are expected as the alarm input. This is a very powerful function of TL VCRs. When an alarm is recorded, most TL VCRs index the tape so that a quick search of the alarmed area is possible. Some makes offer search by time, date and hour and some offer alarm scan as well, which could be very convenient when more than one alarm has to be reviewed every day.

- TL VCRs pass the incoming alarms out in a form of alarm voltage output which can be used to trigger an additional device such as a buzzer, strobe light or similar.

- TL VCRs can be programmed to recycle-record, which is very useful when the tape duration expires earlier than expected and there's no operator to replace it.

- The MTBF of a video head used in TL VCRs is, usually, about 10,000 hrs, which is equivalent to about one year of constant play/record operation. After this, head replacement is recommended. All TL VCRs have some form of indication of the head's hourly usage. This is either displayed on a mercury-based indicator or electronically when the setup is performed.

- Some TL VCRs can be programmed to record only one shot with each alarm input. Using this type of recording, more than 960 hrs can be fitted on a single tape.

TL VCRs also have, as the standard VCRs, timer settings, which means they can be programmed to record only at certain times and on certain days.

TL VCRs are very important devices in CCTV, even though they are the weakest link in the resolution chain. Apart from their use in multiplexed recording, one of the most important features is their ability

NTSC			PAL		
Tape hours	Fields per second	Refresh rate (sec)	Tape hours	Fields per second	Refresh rate (sec)
002	60.0	0.0167	003	50.0	0.02
012	10.0	0.1	012	12.5	0.08
018	6.66	0.15	018	8.33	0.12
024	5.0	0.2	024	6.25	0.16
048	2.5	0.4	048	3.125	0.32
072	1.7	0.58	072	2.083	0.48
120	1.0	1.0	120	1.25	0.8
168	0.7	1.403	168	0.89	1.12
240	0.5	2.0	240	0.625	1.6
360	0.33	3.0	360	0.416	2.4
480	0.25	4.0	480	0.3125	3.2
600	0.20	5.0	600	0.25	4.0
720	0.16	6.25	720	0.208	4.8
960	0.12	8.0	960	0.156	6.4

to switch to real time recording when an external alarm is received. Most of the models available on the market can be switched from stop mode to real time recording, but it is more advantageous when the same alarm switches the VCR to real time while it is already recording in time lapse mode. The reason is very simple, VCRs being electromechanical devices have inertia. This means a few parts of a second (and sometimes even more than a second) might be lost until the video head starts spinning and the tape is wound around the drum. If a TL VCR is already recording in time lapse mode, it takes only a few milliseconds to change to real time recording because the tape is in place and the video heads are already spinning. If tape wastage is of concern (due to the low hours of time lapse recording that are not necessary), the longest time lapse mode can be selected.

Some TL VCRs, or even domestic models referred to as Quick Start, have the tape already wound around the heads and are ready to record even in stop mode. They have a better response than other VCRs, when the record button is pressed. Be aware that on most domestic models there is a certain time delay during which the machine will be in standby mode, after which the tape unwinds. This could be only a minute or two or sometimes up to ten.

Photo courtesy of Gyyr (an Odetics company)

A Time Lapse recorder

Many installers have modified domestic model VCRs for alarm recording, which is reasonably easy to do. The record button contacts are paralleled and connected to a relay which is controlled by an external alarm. Have in mind that in such cases, the VCR's warranty will be void. Another important detail is that there is no time and date stamping when an alarm triggers such a VCR.

VHS VCRs' horizontal resolution limitations (vertical is still defined by the TV system in use) are, as mentioned earlier, 240 TV lines for a color signal. Because CCTV still uses a lot of B/W cameras, most TL VCRs have a switch for selecting between B/W and color. When set to B/W, the video signal bypasses the low-pass filtering used for extracting the color information from a color signal, thus allowing for an improved horizontal resolution for a B/W signal, in excess of 300 TV lines (which also depends very much on the tape quality and how clean the heads are).

If we want an even better recording quality than what the VHS format offers, there are time lapse Super VHS models we can use. They offer the same flexibility and programmability as the VHS TL VCRs, only they are of better picture quality and more expensive.

Whichever type of video recorder you use (and this also refers to domestic VCRs), the video signal resolution should not be taken for granted. It could be much worse than in theory, if any of the following requirements are not met:

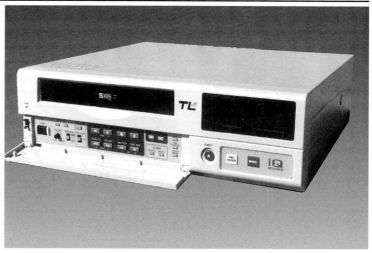

A S-VHS time lapse VCR

- For starters, connect a good video signal to the VCR input. This is especially important for the horizontal sync pulses of the signal since they are reproduced from the tape as part of the video signal. If the camera is very distant, with distorted syncs and color bursts (voltage drop and high frequency losses), the video playback will be very unstable, with picture breaking across the top and unstable colors. Because the tape and the heads limit the resolution even further, the sync pulses' quality is affected too. How these distortions are reproduced on a monitor screen, depends very much on the monitor's sync handling capability, but if the sync pulses (and video information) are recorded poorly, there is little else that can be done by the monitor.

- Always use good quality tapes. The uniformity of the magnetic coating and the film base quality is very important. Good tapes not only improve the recording quality, but prolong the life of the video heads and VCR mechanics in general. Bad tapes (or imitations of known brands) have a nonuniform magnetic layer, which quite often peels off and microscopic particles accumulate on the video heads, causing more damage than saving dollars.

- Video heads need regular cleaning, but do it only with approved cleaning kits. The best thing to do is to consult your local video shop or service. They have valuable practical experience in VCRs which you could apply to CCTV. If you don't clean your VCR for a long period, snowy playback is what you will see. To confirm that it is a dirty head and not a bad tape or signal (which may look similar), take a tape of a known brand and make sure it has been properly recorded, then play it back. If the snowy picture is still there, the video heads need cleaning. Don't confuse the snow produced by dirty heads with when the VCR needs tracking adjustment. The difference is in the amount of snow. The tracking usually needs adjustment if the bottom of the monitor shows picture breaking.

Typical connections at the back of a TL VCR

The table on page 231 gives the number of fields recorded every second with different TL settings, in both of the major TV systems, NTSC and PAL. The refresh rate represents the time gap between the subsequent fields.

Digital video

So far, most of the discussions in this book have referred to analog video signals.

The very few components in CCTV that work with digital video are the framestores, quad compressors, multiplexers, the internal circuits of the digital signal processing (DSP) cameras and now the increasingly popular digital video recorders (DVR). Complete digital video is the new development which everyone is looking forward to.

In the period between this edition of the book and the previous one (that is from 1996 till 1999) there have been revolutionary developments in the digital video processing. Very soon digital video broadcast (DVB) will become widely accepted as a new television standard. In fact it is already recommended by various countries' broadcast regulatory authorities. Closed circuit television will definitely follow suit with such advancements, although majority of the video devices are still analog.

One of the most important differences between an analog and a digital signal, apart from the form itself, is the immunity to noise. A digital signal, having an electronic form, is also affected by noise as is the analog signal. Digital signals, however, can only have two values: zeros and ones. Noise will only affect the signal when it's value reaches levels that may interfere with the digital circuit margins that decide whether a signal is zero or one. This means, digital signals allow noise accumulation to an extent unimaginable with analog video signals. As a result, this means longer distances, high immunity to external EMIs and no signal degradation, i.e., better picture quality.

The same photo with 50×50, 100×100 and 200×200 pixels

The other important advantage of a digital video signal is the possibility for digital processing and storage. This includes image enhancement, compression, various corrections and so on. Most importantly, there is no difference in image quality between the copies and the original.

Since most of the CCTV cameras produce analog signals, prior to processing or storing the signal in digital format, the first stage is an Analog to Digital conversion (ADC). This is a stage where the analog signal is sampled and quantized (broken into discrete values). The sampling rate and levels of quantization depend on the electronics quality and speed and they define the resolution and refresh rate of the digital framestore.

Once the video signal is converted into digital format it can be processed in many different ways, depending on the algorithms built in the processor. Some of them may do a simple division and recalculation in order to put the images in smaller screens (as is the case with quad compressors or multiplexers), some may perform sharpening (which is actually an algorithm where every pixel value of the image is changed on the basis of the values of the pixels around it), others may reduce the noise in the signal and so on. These digital functions could be especially useful in CCTV, where we often manipulate recorded images that are difficult to recognize.

At the time of writing this book, digital CCD cameras are available but they are used mainly in video conferencing over the Internet or in industrial and specialized scientific applications. Also, the modern Mini DV camcorders have digital audio/video outputs in the form of IEEE1394.

It seems that CCTV has to follow suit. The obvious problem we would have initially is the cables required for longer distances, as we require in CCTV installations. The data rate for a good quality live video is very high and such data rate, requires better cables. The present IEEE1394 cables (also known as *fire wire*) as used with the Mini DV camcorders are good for only a couple of meters. No doubt, new cabling technologies are already on the designers' boards, one of which is a cheaper, plastic version of fiber optics.

IEEE 1394 (fire wire) connector

Fast local area networks (LAN) and wide area networks (WAN) are also becoming attractive for distributing live video images. Some large companies are already installing CCTV systems whose components are interconnected via the existing company networks rather than with coaxial cables.

Only a few years ago the price of high speed digital electronics capable of live video processing was unaffordable and uneconomical. Today, however, with the ever increasing performance and speed of memory chips, processors and hard disks and their decrease in prices, digital video signal processing in real time is not only more affordable, but it has become a natural evolution of the video technology.

Digital video recorders (DVR)

Recording images on a VCR tape is economical, but lacks a few things which have led us to search for new, usually digital, methods of storage. First of all, with the VCR's analog method there is no direct and quick access to the desired image shot, except when using a reasonably quick alarm search mode (available on most TL VCRs). In VCRs the information is stored in an analog format and cannot be further processed. And finally, the played back picture quality is always lower than the actual original source.

The following are the main advantages of digital video recording:

■   Digital signals are more immune to noise.

■   Digital signals can be reproduced many times with the same excellent picture quality as the first time.

■   Digital signals can be protected against tampering (water-marking).

Initially, in CCTV, there have been attempts to implement digital video recording on a digital audio tape (DAT) format. Although digital, such recorded material still requires a sequential search mode and that is not as attractive as the random access when a hard disk is used.

Hard disks have a much higher through-output than other digital storage media and better than S-VHS quality images are achievable without any problems. The main problem with the hard disks is that their capacity is still insufficient for multi-day recordings, such is the case with the time lapse VCRs. It is, however, a reasonably good combination to have a hard disk as a primary recording media, which upon reaching its full capacity automatically dumps the contents onto a backup DAT, JAZ drive, DVD-RAM, DV tape or similar large media. Such backup can be automated so as not to require operator's manual intervention. Then, the hard disk can be instructed to continue recording by overwriting the earlier recorded video data.

Photo courtesy of Panasonic

**A digital video recorder
with DVD-RAM storage**

Hard-disk drives (HDD) have a reasonably fast access time and by using some caching and a good compression, it is possible to retrieve real time images. As it can be seen from the diagram on the next page, MPEG-2 data transfer rate is around 5 Mbps and this can easily be achieved with the faster hard disks, providing you have sufficient space. The hard disk prices are falling daily and at the time of writing this book, single 3.5" HDD with the capacity of nearly 36-GB are becoming available. How many video images can be stored on 36 GB depends firstly on the type of compression and the quality of images elected for such compression, but it would usually be sufficient for over 24 hours of time lapse video of multiple cameras with excellent quality.

One way to increase the above mentioned capacity of one HDD to a much higher value is by use of SCSI drives, where up to 15 devices can be daisy-chained.

As it can be seen from the diagram below, data transfer rates of over 5 Mbps are required for real time image storage and playback. It should be taken into account though that the numbers below are for ideal conditions and therefore, a little bit of spare capacity should be planned for.

Photo courtesy of Sony

A digital video recorder for up to 16 cameras and built-in DV tape backup

For special applications, one of which could be CCTV, arrays of hard disks are used in a configuration known as RAID (redundant arrays of independent disks). RAID storage technology increases the capacity, speed and reliability of on-line data storage by connecting or grouping two to more disks into an array. For the user, these disks appear as a single mass storage device.

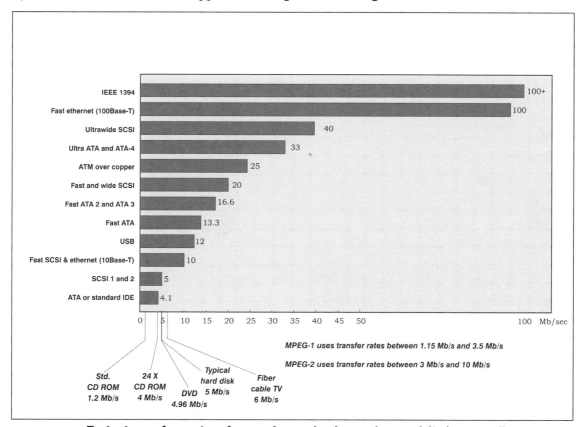

Data transfer rates for various devices (megabits/second)

All of the above leads us to various considerations we have to have in mind when selecting a digital storage media and data transfer rate. This is why we have to understand the theory of digital data and image representation with various compression techniques. The following few headings will try to explain some of the basics.

Digital image size and compression

In order to understand the reason and the concept of various image compression techniques, let's work out the size of a typical high resolution digitized video.

If we take a high resolution color camera in CCTV, the number of picture elements, or pixels, we would have in one TV frame is determined from:

752×582 picture elements = 437,664 pixels

This is valid for 1 TV frame = 2 fields

Each of these pixels is represented by 8 bits of luminance quantization, i.e., $2^8 = 256$ levels, thus 437,664 pixels luminance are represented by 437,664 bytes of information (important to remember is that 8 bits = 1 byte).

If the image is in color, there are 3 primary colors to be encoded with 256 levels, making 16 million color combinations (this comes from $256^3 = 16,777,216$).

So the total number of bytes required to digitally describe each of the possible three primary colors for every pixel is $437,664 \times 3 = 1,312,992$ bytes = 1,282 kB. This is a **digital representation of a full TV frame with no compression**. This file size could have been an uncompressed BMP file of one TV frame since the bitmap is an image format where every pixel is represented with a byte without compression. Now, if we want a real time recording and playback of files this size, for PAL we would have to have 1,282 kB $\times$ 25 frames per second = 32,050 kBs = 31 MBs.

For NTSC such calculation will bring more or less the same number since we have got more frames per second, but the vertical resolution is smaller. Please note this is 31 Mbps. The data flow in computer language is usually measured in megabits per second. Even if we accept that 1 byte is 8 bits (but it can also be 16 bits, depending on the application) the 31 MBs will be equivalent to 250 Mbps.

This is a very high number of data flow indeed, even for today's standards. The maximum data flow we can have inside a computer is limited, usually, by the hard disk mechanical limitations. The fastest hard disks we know about, using the ultrawide SCSI have theoretical maximum transfer rate of 40 Mbps, but realisticly this is half this value.

So, from the above it is clear that video images cannot be recorded (stored) in their raw format since the computers cannot cope with the amount of data required for a real time video. The only **practical solution** would then be **to compress the video images**. There are two basic approaches for compression: lossless and lossy.

Lossless compression can retrieve the compressed image without any losses. The only problem is that maximum compression factors for lossless is 4:1. This type of compression is used in some broadcast and high quality video processing equipment, but it is far too expensive for CCTV applications.

Lossy compression throws away non-critical image information thus achieving much higher compression factors (between 10 and 300). The difference between various methods is in what is considered non-critical data. If correctly selected, compression can be high without losing noticeable details of the image.

The following are the most common video image compression types in CCTV today:

- MPEG-1 (also known as motion predictable, works up to 3.5 Mbps)

- MPEG-2 (motion predictable, works up to 20 Mbps)

- JPEG and motion-JPEG (DCT transformation)

- Wavelet (wavelet transformation, different compression encoding)

- Others (proprietory compressions)

MPEG-1

Different compression algorithms have been proposed for motion pictures, which are handled by the MPEG (**motion pictures experts group** of the ISO). There are a couple of different variations of this, such as MPEG-1 and MPEG-2, the latter being widely accepted for multimedia, digital video (or versatile) disk (DVD) and high definition digital television (HDDTV).

MPEG works with motion pictures.

It should be noted that **MPEG does not define compression algorithms, but rather the compressed bit stream, i.e., the organization of digital data for recording, playback and transmission**. The actual compression algorithms are up to the individual manufacturers and they may vary in their quality.

MPEG-1 is targeted at processing real time images at bit rates from 1.5 Mbps up to 3.5 Mbps. This is the speed that is easily achievable, but initially was designed for laser disk speeds, hard disk and the CD-ROMs. It is possible to have MPEG-1 running at higher bit rates, but the real intention is to have images of equal or better than VHS quality and up to the resolution quality of S-VHS.

The practical application of MPEG-1 is most often in storing video clips on CD-ROMs, but also for cable television and video conferencing. There are, however, some digital recorders designed specially for CCTV applications where real time video is recorded using MPEG-1 technique. These are applications where real time video is more important than having high resolution video at a lower rate.

MPEG-1 files usually come on CD ROMs

MPEG-2

MPEG-2 is not a next generation MPEG-1 but rather another **standard targeted for higher quality digital motion pictures and audio**. It was accepted by the ISO in 1993.

The MPEG-2 standard specifies the coding formats for multiplexing high quality digital video, audio and other data into a form suitable for transmission or storage. So, MPEG-2, like MPEG-1, does not limit its recommendations to video only. It should be highlighted again, **MPEG-2 is not a compression scheme or technique** (as thought by many), but rather a standardization of handling and processing digital data in the fastest and most optimized way. MPEG-2 encoding can produce data rates between 3.5 Mbps and 10 Mbps.

There are two data stream formats defined by MPEG-2: the **transport stream**, which can carry multiple programs simultaneously and which is optimized for use in applications where data loss may be likely and the **program stream**, which is optimized for multimedia applications, and for performing fast processing in a system's software. As a compatible extension, MPEG-2 video builds on the MPEG-1 video standard, by supporting interlaced video formats and a number of other advanced features.

For us, in CCTV, the most interesting is the transport stream as it is well suited for transmission of digital television over telephone lines, fiber, coaxial and non-coaxial cable, ISDN lines, as well as storage on tape, magnetic media and optical disks.

The DVD has the same physical size as the CD ROM, but the data storage can be anything from 4.7 GB for a single layer up to 17 GB for the double-sided, double-layer DVD

MPEG-2 is used in services like DBS (direct broadcast satellite), CATV (cable television) and most importantly HDTV (high definition television). Also the DVD format (which was standardized between the two editions of this book) uses MPEG-2 encoding for its high quality video and audio. Thanks to MPEG-2 compression, a single-layer, single-sided DVD has enough capacity to hold two hours and 13 minutes of spectacular video, surround sound and subtitles. The MPEG-2 nominal average video data rate is 3.5 Mbps for video only. When audio and subtitles are added to this data stream, the total average data rate becomes 4.962 Mbps. The picture quality, as many readers have already had a chance to see, is better than S-VHS.

The MPEG encoding (in both MPEG-1 and MPEG-2) relies on picture content before and after the actual frame. In essence, MPEG works by analyzing the video picture for repetition, called redundancy.

*A DVD stores a whole movie
with 500 lines of video and surround sound*

It is a fact that over 90% of the digital data that represent a video signal is redundant and can be compressed without visibly harming the picture quality.

In CCTV, we prefer to have still shots at a reasonably frequent schedule over a longer period of time (such is the case with the time lapse VCRs) than have real time images at a shorter period of time. This is why in CCTV we are more interested in compression techniques where single-image frames are independently compressed and decompressed, at a fast rate. This type of data manipulation will allow for random selection and playback faster than MPEG can do (as it will be discussed a little bit later in more detail), but also playback in reverse direction, which MPEG cannot do and finally easy extracting of images or sequence of images on other removable media (floppy disks, ZIP disks, CD-ROMs, etc.) without the need for having MPEG decoders.

No doubt, CCTV will be using MPEG-2 in the near future in one form or another, but at this stage we are more interested in frame independent compression techniques. JPEG is one such technique.

JPEG

JPEG stands for joint photographic experts group, which is the original name of the committee that recommended the standard. **JPEG is a standardized image compression mechanism. It refers only to still digital images**. Such still images in video can be either TV fields or TV frames.

There is a JPEG derivative in CCTV that some like to refer it to as **motion JPEG.** Motion JPEG does not exist as a separate standard but rather it is a rapid flow of JPEG images that can be played back at a sufficiently high rate to produce an illusion of motion.

Although JPEG has a subgroup recommendation for lossless compression (of about 2:1) we are more interested in the lossy compression JPEG, where compression factors of over 10× are possible without noticeable degradation. JPEG works by transforming blocks of 8×8 picture elements using the discrete cosine transformation (DCT). The DCT is based on Fourier transformation of time signals into frequency domain signals. The Fourier transformation (as

Photo courtesy of Dallmeier

*Actual digital image (JPEG)
from a real CCTV system*

already mentioned in the light section) is a very good method for analyzing signals in frequency domain, the only problems is it always works with an assumption of time domain signals being periodical and infinite. This is not the case in reality and this is why an altrenative to Fourier transformation was introduced in the 1960s and called fast Fourier transformation (FFT). The DCT is based on FFT.

When a highly compressed image is enlarged a blocky appearance is evident. Compressions of up to 100× can be achieved. JPEG is also known as a lossy compression, meaning that once the image is compressed it cannot be decompressed to exactly the same quality as the original. However, the compression factors achieved with JPEG compression are quite high (over 10 times) and the picture quality loss appears insignificant to the human eye. JPEG is designed to exploit the known limitations of the human eye, like the fact that fine chrominance details aren't perceived as well as fine luminance details in a given picture.

For each separate color component, the image is broken into 8×8 blocks that cover the entire image. These blocks form the input to the DCT. Typically, in the 8×8 blocks, the pixel values vary slowly. Therefore, the energy is of low spatial frequency. A transformation that can be used to concentrate the energy into a few coefficients is the two-dimensional, 8×8 DCT. This transformation, studied extensively for image compression, is extremely efficient for highly correlated data.

JPEG stores full-color information: 24 bits/pixel (16 million colors) compared to GIF, for example, (another popular compression technique among PC users) which can store only 8 bits/pixel (256 or fewer colors). Gray-scale images do not compress by such large factors with JPEG because the human eye is much more sensitive to brightness variations than to hue variations and JPEG can compress hue data more heavily than brightness data. An interesting observation is that a gray-scale JPEG file is generally only about 10% to 25% smaller than a full-color JPEG file of similar visual quality. Also it should be noted that JPEG is not suitable for line art (text or drawings) as the DCT is not suitable for very sharp B/W edges.

JPEG can be used to compress data from different color spaces such as RGB (video signal), YCbCr (converted video signal) and CMYK (images for the printing industry) as it handles colors as separate components. The best compression results are achieved if the color components are independent (noncorrelated), such as in YCbCr, where most of the information is concentrated in the luminance and less in the chrominance.

Hard disk uses circular magnetic plates for random access

Since JPEG files are independent of each other, when used in CCTV recording, they can be easily played back in reverse direction, playback speed can be increased or reduced and copied as single files or group of files.

A known property of JPEG is that the degree of detail losses can be varied by adjusting compression parameters, usually made on a computer when saving images or in the video recording software. Thus, if higher quality of compression is wanted at the expense of a higher image file size, it can be done by selecting the appropriate quality factor. Compressions of up to 100× are achievable with JPEG.

The author of the book with the digital video recorder designed for Star City Casino

Below are some sample images of a high resolution color camera (unfortunately only B/W can be shown here) with various degree of compression. The blocky artifacts of the JPEG compression are visible in the last image with compression of 100×.

Wavelet

For many decades, scientists have wanted more appropriate functions than the sines and cosines which comprise the bases of Fourier analysis to approximate choppy signals. By their definition, sines and cosines are non-local functions (they stretch out to infinity). This is the main reason that they do a very poor job of approximating sharp changes, such as high resolution details in a finite, two-dimensional picture. This is the type of picture we most often have in surveillance time lapse recording, as opposed to a continuous stream of motion images in broadcast television.

Wavelet analysis works differently. With wavelet we can use approximating functions that are contained in finite domains. Wavelets are functions that satisfy certain mathematical requirements and are used in representing data or other functions in wavelet analysis. The main difference compared to the FFT analysis is that the **wavelets analyze the signal at different frequencies with different resolutions**, i.e., many small groups of waves, hence the name Wavelets. The wavelet algorithms process data at different scales or resolutions. The wavelet analysis tries to see **details and the global picture**, or as some wavelet authors have said, "see the forest and the trees" as opposed to Fourier analysis which "sees just the forest."

Wavelets are well-suited for approximating data with sharp discontinuities. The wavelet analysis procedure is to adopt a wavelet prototype function, called an analyzing wavelet or mother wavelet. Time analysis is performed with a contracted, high-frequency version of the prototype wavelet, while frequency analysis is performed with a dilated, low-frequency version of the prototype wavelet. Because the original signal or function can be represented in terms of a wavelet expansion (using coefficients in a linear combination of the wavelet functions), data operations can be performed using just the corresponding wavelet coefficients. Wavelet compression transforms the entire image as opposed to 8×8 sections in JPEG and is more natural as it follows the shape of the objects in a picture. Main advantage of Wavelets over JPEG is higher compression factors (up to 300×) for equal or better picture quality.

A high resolution CCD camera image with 752X582 pixels creates a file size of 1,312,992 bytes (1,282 kB)

10 X compressed JPEG image file size 128 kB

50 X compressed JPEG image file size 26 kB

100 X compressed JPEG image file size 13 kB

As a compression wavelet has been in use in scientific data compression such as in astronomy and seismic research for quite some time now, but it's a relatively new compression algorithm in CCTV and it is very attractive.

The pictures shown with different JPEG and wavelet compression should give you an idea of the quality of the two methods. Unfortunately, their original quality cannot be seen in B/W, but also the

A high resolution CCD camera image with 752X582 pixels creates a file size of 1,312,992 bytes (1,282 kB)

10 X compressed Wavelet image file size 128 kB

50 X compressed Wavelet image file size 26 kB

100 X compressed Wavelet image file size 13 kB

2X enlargement of a section   **2X enlargement of a section**
100X JPEG compression   **100X wavelet compression**

book printing quality may deteriorate them further. You can, however, check the CCTV Labs web site and download full-size pictures of each of these and compare for yourself.

The playback quality of digitally recorded video signal

The playback image resolution of a digital video recorder (DVR) is not necessarily the same as the image digitization resolution. It depends on the type of compression, but also on the factor of compression. Also the operating system is one of the key factors in the use of the system. The immense amount of data being processed in large chunks while the DVR unit is recording and/or playing back requires a very stable platform.

The best indication of the DVR's quality is to play back a recorded image of the camera(s) you intend to use. It is wrong to assume that if one DVR uses more picture elements in the digitization process that it provides better picture quality than another unit with a smaller number of digitized pixels. It is also wrong to assume that one compression technique is better than the other, as this really depends on the picture content as well as the compression setting for the particular application.

I would suggest that testings be done with various camera settings. My own personal experience has found that a good camera may produce a better picture on a DVR if the image is slightly defocussed, this will depend on the type of compression used. In low light level situations, it is often better to have AGC switched off as the noise amplification by the AGC is compressed and decompressed with artifacts which are detrimental to picture quality. This means nothing should be taken for granted, but proper trials and testings need to be conducted before deciding on a particular digital recorder.

DVRs usually perform two functions, they multiplex/demultiplex multiple video signals and they also record/playback them. This is clearly what the multiplexer + TL VCR combination performed in the analog recording system. With the DVRs though it is a bit more difficult to calculate the number of images taken every second by each camera. This is due to the fact that we have many variables:

- The number of cameras recorded

- The original file size before the compression

- The compression factor (selected image quality)

- The hard disk capacity

Most of the DVRs are designed to automaticaly dump the hard disk recorded contents onto some sort of archiving media. This is usually on DAT tape, but it could also be another hard disk, DVC Pro tape, DVD recordable, etc. The archiving is usually transparent to the continuous recording, i.e., the DVR performs duplex function.

D-VHS format

This is a digital variation of the VHS format which will be available soon and is especially attractive for CCTV. Again, the manufacturer has preserved the compatibility with the VHS and S-VHS format for playback and added an ADC circuit for recording a video signal in digital format. This recorder will not produce a picture itself, but it will have to be used in conjunction with another piece of equipment to provide digital to analog conversion.

D-VHS uses virtually the same head mechanism as the existing VHS, so D-VHS VCRs will still be able to play and record analog material, although there will be no crossover between the two modes.

JVC™ claims that a 4-hour videotape can record (store) 44 gigabytes of video information. Depending on the resolution selected, the duration of 44 GB of recorded material will vary. Starting from 49 hours (which is very interesting for CCTV!) when recording in long-play mode with only 2 Mbps rate, then 7 hours when recording in standard mode with 14.1 Mbps which is suitable for MPEG-2 (higher quality than S-VHS) compression and the high definition quality of 3.5 hours when recording with 28.2 Mbps mode. The picture quality of a D-VHS recording will depend on the compression algorithm offered by the analog-to-digital converters, but going back to the previous heading on compression, we can see that S-VHS quality can be achieved with a signal composed of 512×512 pixels.

An even more interesting fact (at least on the basis of the information provided by D-VHS designers) for CCTV users is that D-VHS can store up to 6 simultaneous data streams, without loss of time (i.e., no time lapse effect), provided they are multiplexed before reaching the recorder. So, at least 6 cameras can be simultaneously recorded in digital format on a D-VHS recorder.

DV format and the fire wire

DV is the digital video recording system used as a basis for the Mini DV, DVCAM™ (Sony) and DVCPRO™ (Panasonic) videotape formats. It uses Y:Cr:Cb = 4:1:1 encoding (luminance Y : crominance red : Chrominance blue) and 5:1 Discrete Cosina Transformation (DCT) interfield motion compression.

The Mini DV is becoming increasingly popular among home video enthusiast as it offers a major leap in quality and size compared to the previous analog recording formats, such as VHS, S-VHS and 8 mm.

More importantly, although there are some differences in the professional broadcast formats DVCAM™ and DVCPRO™, there is, luckily, an agreement among most manufacturers about the Mini DV format.

The Mini DV cassette is smaller than the VHS-C and the 8 mm videotapes - measuring only 66 mm × 48 mm × 12.2 mm and tape thickness of only 6.35 mm. The recording and playback is done with helical scanning of the magnetic tape, but instead of recording analog signals it does it with digital encoding.

Although the Mini DV cassette looks miniature (it's half the size of the audio cassette) it still uses 8-bit digital compression recording and delivers superb picture quality with 500-line resolution and a S/N ratio of over 54 dB. The audio recorded in Mini DV format is also of excellent quality and equals the CD quality.

During the writing of this book, Mini DV digital camcorders have become the preferred consumer video camcorder. The small size of these camcorders should not fool anyone as they can deliver broadcast quality images in digital format. Furthermore, it is now possible to use specialized software and hardware on a PC in order to video edit such recorded material, all in digital domain.

The majority of Mini DV camcorders use the IEEE 1394 digital interface, which is also known as *Fire Wire* (Sony calls it *i-Link*). Using this type of connection, digital video, audio and control data can be sent between a camcorder and editing device,

Size comparison between audio, mini DV and VHS tapes

which could be a PC. The DV manufacturers claim data rate of the Mini DV format (to tape and/or IEEE 1394 output) to be 3.56 Mbps. Please note this is megabytes, not megabits.

A Mini DV tape can store up to 60 minutes of video in standard mode, or 90 minutes in long-play mode. The amount of video and audio data stored is equivalent to around 20 GB of data.

Many camera manufacturers are coming up with PC desktop cameras for Internet video conferencing, which are connected directly to the PC via fire wire and can be controlled by the recipient of the video image.

The fire wire connection is a fast serial digital data transmission format, first proposed by Apple™. It consists of three pairs of shielded cable, two pairs for data and one for power. The maximum achievable distances at the moment are up to 4 m and up to 16 devices can be connected in a series.

The fire wire can carry data up to and over 100 Mbps. This data transfer rate is more than sufficient for a number of digital streams to travel along the cable at the same time. In fact the idea behind the fire wire was to have a much faster alternative to SCSI.

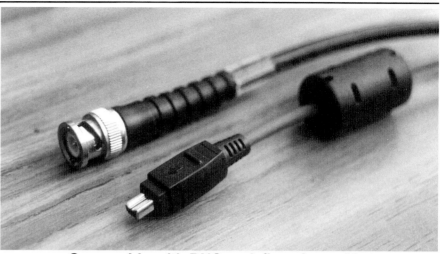

Coax cable with BNC and fire wire cable

A slower alternative to the fire wire is the USB standard (universal serial bus) for Intel PCs, which is designed to have a data rate of up to 12.2 Mbps. This rate is also sufficient for live video transmission, but USB is not intended to have many devices daisy-chained.

The short distances for fire wire are mostly imposed by the capacitance in copper cables, but there are new developments with plastic and optical fiber that might considerably increase this distance to something that could be used in CCTV designs.

9. Transmission Media

Once the image has been captured by a lens and a camera and then converted into an electrical signal, it is further taken to a switcher, a monitor, or a recording device.

In order for the video signal to get from point A to point B, it has to go through some kind of transmission medium. The same applies to control-data signal.

The most common media for video and data transmission in CCTV are as follows:

- Coaxial cable

- Twisted pair cable

- Microwave link

- RF open-air transmission

- Infrared link

- Telephone line

- Fiber optics cable

For video tra nsmission, a coaxial cable is most often used, but fiber optics is becoming increasingly popular with its superior characteristics. Mixed means of transmission are also possible, such as video via microwave and PTZ control data via twisted pair, for example.

We'll go through all of them separately, but we'll pay special attention to the coaxial cable and fiber optics transmission.

Coaxial cables

The concept

The coaxial cable is the most common medium for transmission of video signals and sometimes video and PTZ data together. It is also known as **unbalanced** transmission, which comes from the concept of the coaxial cable (sometimes called "coax" for short).

A cross section of a coax is shown to the left. It is of a symmetrical and coaxial construction. The video signal travels through the center core, while the shield is used to common the ground potential of the end devices – the camera and the monitor, for example. And it not only commons the ground potential, but also serves to protect the center core from external and unwanted electromagnetic interference (EMI).

Cross section of a coaxial cable

The idea behind the coaxial concept is to have all the unwanted EMI induced in the shield only. When this is properly grounded, it will discharge the induced noise through the grounds at the camera and monitor ends. Electrically, the coaxial cable closes the circuit between the source and the receiver, where the coax core is the signal wire, while the shield is the grounding one. This is why it is called an unbalanced transmission.

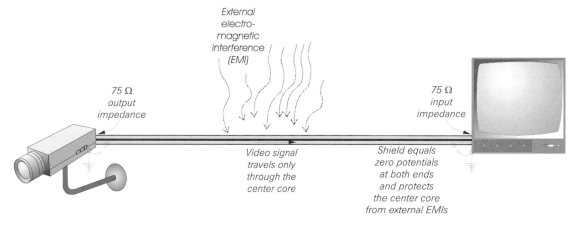

Video transmission over coaxial cable

Noise and electromagnetic interference

How well the coax shield protects the center core from noise and EMI depends on the percentage of the screening. Typically, numbers between 90 and 99% can be found in the cable manufacturer's specifications. Have in mind, though, even if the screening is 100%, it is not possible to have 100% protection from external interference. The penetration of EMI inside the coax depends on the frequency.

Theoretically, only frequencies above 50 kHz are successfully suppressed and this is mostly due to the skin-effect attenuation. All frequencies below this will induce current in smaller or bigger form. How strong this current is depends on the strength of the magnetic field. Our major concern would be, obviously, the mains frequency (50 or 60 Hz) radiation, which is present around almost all artificial objects.

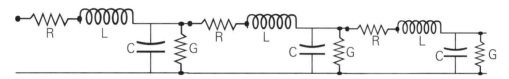

Theoretical representation of a coaxial cable

This is why we could have problems running a coaxial cable parallel to the mains. The amount of induced electromagnetic voltage in the center core depends first on the amount of current flowing through the mains cable, which obviously depends on the current consumption on that line. Second, it depends on how far the coax is from the mains cable. And last, it depends on how long the cables run together. Sometimes 100 m might have no influence, but if strong current is flowing through the mains cable, even a 50-m run could have a major influence. When installing, try (whenever possible) not to have the power cables and the coaxial cables very close to each other, at least 30 cm would be sufficient to notably reduce the EMI.

The visual appearance of the induced (unwanted) mains frequency is a few thick horizontal bars slowly scrolling either up or down. The scrolling frequency is determined by the difference between the video field frequency and the mains frequency and can be anything from 0 to 1 Hz. This results in stationary or very slow moving bars on the screen.

Other frequencies will be seen as various noise patterns, depending on the source. A rule of thumb is that the higher the frequency of the induced unwanted signal, the finer the pattern on the monitor will be. Intermittent inducting, like lightning or cars passing by, will be shown as an irregular noise pattern.

Characteristic impedance

Short wires and cables used in an average electronic piece of equipment have negligible resistance, inductance and capacitance, and they do not affect the signal distribution. If a signal, however, needs to be transmitted for a longer distance, a lot of factors add up and contribute to the complex picture of such transmission media. This especially influences high frequency signals. Then, the resistance, inductance and capacitance play a considerable role and visibly affect the transmission.

A simple medium like the coaxial cable, when analyzed by the electromagnetic theory, is approximated with a network of resistors (R), inductors (L), capacitors (C) and conductors (G) per unit length (as shown on the diagram on the previous page). For short cable runs this network has a negligible influence on the signal, but for longer runs it becomes noticeable. In such a case the network of R, L and C elements becomes so significant that it acts as a crude low pass filter that, in turn, affects the amplitude and phase of the various components in the video signal. The higher the frequencies of the signal are, the more they are affected by these non-ideal cable properties.

Each cable is **uniformly** built and has its own characteristic impedance, which is defined by the R, L , C and G per unit length.

The main advantage of the unbalanced video transmission (which will be shown a little bit later) is based on the fact that **the characteristic impedance of the medium is independent of the frequency** (refers mainly to the mid and high frequencies), while the phase shift is proportional to the frequency.

The amplitude and phase characteristics of the coax at low frequencies is very dependent on the frequency itself, but since the cable length in such cases is reasonably short compared to the signal wavelength, it results in negligible influence on the signal transmission.

When the characteristic impedance of the coaxial cable is matched to the video source output impedance and the receiving unit input impedance, it **allows for a maximum energy transfer between the source and the receiver.**

For high-frequency signals, as is the video, impedance matching is of paramount importance. **When the impedance is not matched, the whole or part of the video signal is reflected back to the source, affecting not only the output stage itself, but also the picture quality.** A 100% reflection of the signal occurs when the end

Coaxial cable braiding machine

of the cable is either short circuited or left open. The total (100%) energy of the signal (voltage x current) is transferred only when there is a match between the source, transmission media and the receiver. This is why we insist that **the last element in the video signal chain should always be terminated with 75 Ω** (the symbol Ω stands for Ohms).

In CCTV, 75 Ω is taken as a characteristic impedance for all the equipment producing or receiving video signals. This is why the coaxial cable is meant to be used with 75 Ω impedance. This does not exclude manufacturers producing, say, 50 Ω equipment (which used to be the case with some broadcast or RF equipment), but then impedance converters (passive or active) need to be used between such sources and 75 Ω recipients.

Impedance matching is also done with the twisted pair transmitters and receivers, which will be discussed later in the media section.

The 75 Ω of the coax **is a complex impedance, defined by the voltage/current ratio at each point of the cable. It is not a pure resistance, and therefore it cannot be measured with an ordinary multimeter.**

To calculate the characteristic impedance, we will make use of the electromagnetic theory as mentioned earlier and we will represent the cable with its equivalent network, composed of R, L, C and G per unit length. This network, as shown on the schematic diagram previously, has an impedance of:

$$Zc = \sqrt{\frac{R + j\omega L}{G + j\omega C}} \qquad\qquad (42)$$

where, as already explained, R is the resistance, L is the inductance, G is the conductance and C is the capacitance between the center core and the shield, per unit length. The symbol j represents the imaginary unit (square root of -1), which is used when representing complex impedance, $\omega = 2\pi f$, where f is the frequency.

If the coaxial cable is of a reasonably short length (less than a couple of hundred metres), R and G can be ignored, which brings us to the simplified formula for the coax impedance:

$$Zc = \sqrt{\frac{L}{C}} \qquad\qquad (43)$$

This formula simply means that the **characteristic impedance does not depend on the cable length and frequency but on the capacitance and inductance per unit length**. This is not true, however, when the length of a cable like RG-59/U exceeds a couple of hundred meters. The resistance and the capacitance then become significant and they **do affect** the video signal. **For reasonably short lengths though, the above approximation is pretty good.**

The cable limitations we have are mainly a result of the accumulated resistance and capacitance, which are so high that the approximation (43) is no longer valid and the signal is distorted considerably. This is basically in the form of voltage drop, high-frequency loss and group delay.

The most commonly used coaxial cable in CCTV is the RG-59/U, which can successfully and without in-line correctors, transfer B/W signals up to 300 m and color up to 200 m.

The other popular cable is the RG-11/U, which is thicker and more expensive. Its maximum recommended lengths are up to 600 m for a B/W signal and 400 m for a color signal. There are also

Physical size comparison between RG-59 and RG-11 coax

thinner coaxial cables with 75 Ω impedance, with only 2.5-mm diameter or even coax ribbon cables. They are very practical for crowded areas with many video signals, such as matrix switchers with many inputs. Their maximum cable run is much shorter than the thicker representatives, but sufficient for links and patches. Note that these numbers may vary with different manufacturers and signal quality expectations.

The difference between the B/W and color signal maximum run is due to the color sub-carrier of 4.43 MHz for PAL or 3.58 for NTSC. Since a long coaxial cable acts as a low pass filter, the color information will obviously be affected sooner than the lower frequencies, so the loss of color information will happen before the loss of details in the lower frequencies.

If longer runs are required, additional devices can be used to equalize and amplify the video spectrum. Such devices are known as **in-line amplifiers**, **cable equalizers, or cable correctors**. Depending on the amplifier (and cable) quality, double or even triple lengths are possible.

In-line amplifiers are best if they are used in the middle of the cable run because of the more acceptable S/N ratio, but this is quite often impossible or impractical due to the need for power supply and storage. So, the majority of in-line amplifiers available in CCTV are

Miniature coaxial cable can save a lot of space and improve accessibility

designed to be used at the camera end, in which case we actually have **pre-equalization** and **pre-amplification** of the video signal. There are, however, devices that are used at the monitor end and they have $1V_{pp}$ output with **post-equalization** of the video bandwidth.

Starting from the above theoretical explanation of the impedance, it can be seen that the cable uniformity along its length is of great importance for fulfilling the characteristic impedance requirements. **The cable quality depends on the precision and uniformity of the center core, the dielectric and the shield. These factors define the C and L values of the cable, per unit length. This is why careful attention should be paid to the running of the cable itself and its termination.** Sharp loops and bends affect the cable uniformity and consequently the cable impedance. This results in high-frequency losses, i.e., fine picture detail loss, as well as double images due to signal reflections. So, if a short and good quality cable is improperly run, with sharp bends and kicks, the picture quality will still be far from perfect.

Bends no smaller than 10 times the diameter of the coax are suggested for best performance. This is equivalent of saying "bending radius should not be smaller than 5 times the diameter, or 10 times the radius of the cable." This means an RG-59/U cable should not be bent in a loop with a diameter smaller than 6 cm (2.5") and an RG-11/U should not be bent in a loop smaller than 10 cm (4") in diameter.

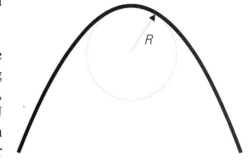

Minimum bending radius

Copper is one of the best conductors for a coaxial cable. Only gold and silver will show a better performance (resistance, corrosion), but these are too expensive to be used for cable manufacturing. A lot of people believe that copper-plated steel makes a better cable, but this is not correct. Copper-plated steel can only be cheaper and perhaps stiffer, but for longer lengths, in CCTV, copper would be the better choice. Copper-plated steel coaxial cables are acceptable for master antenna (MATV) installations, where the transmitted signals are RF modulated (VHF or UHF). Namely, with higher frequencies the so-called skin effect becomes more apparent where the actual signal escapes on the copper-plated surface of the conductor (not the shield, but the center conductor). CCTV signals are, as explained, in the basic bandwidth, and this is why a copper-plated steel coaxial cable might be OK for RF signals but not necessarily for CCTV. So always look for a copper coaxial cable.

BNC connectors

A widely accepted coaxial cable termination, in CCTV, is the BNC termination. BNC stands for **Bayonet-Neil-Concelman** connector, named after its designers. There are three types: screwing, soldering and crimping.

Crimping BNCs are proven to be the most reliable of all. They require specialized and expensive stripping and crimping tools, but it pays to have them. Of the many installations done in the industry, **more than 50% of problems are proven to be a result of bad or incorrect termination**. An installer doesn't have to

BNC connector

know or understand all the equipment used in a system (which will be commissioned by the designer or the supplier), but if he or she does proper cable runs and terminations, it is almost certain that the system will perform at its best.

Male and female crimping BNC elements

There are various BNC products available on the market, of which the male plug is the most common. Female plugs are also available, as well as right angle adaptors, BNC-to-BNC adaptors (often called "barrels"), 75 Ω terminators (or "dummy loads"), BNC-to-other-type of video connection and so on.

Breaking the cable in the middle of its length and terminating it will contribute to some losses of the signal, especially if the termination and/or BNCs are of a bad quality. A good termination can result in as small as 0.3 to 0.5 dB losses. If there are not too many of them in one cable run, this is an insignificant loss.

There are silver-plated and even gold-plated BNC connectors designed to minimize the contact resistance and protect the connector from oxidation, which is especially critical near the coast (salt water and air) or heavily industrialized areas.

Various BNC connectors and adaptors

A good BNC connector kit should include a gold-plated or silver-plated center tip, a BNC shell body, a ring for crimping the shield and a rubber sleeve (sometimes called a "strain relief boot") to protect the connector's end from sharp bends and oxidation.

Coaxial cables and proper BNC termination

Never terminate a coaxial cable with electrical cutters or pliers. Stripping the coaxial cable to the required length using electrical cutters is very risky. First, small pieces of copper fall around the center core and one can never be sure that a short circuit won't happen. Also, the impedance changes even if they do not short circuit the core and the shield. Second, using normal pliers for fixing the BNC to the coaxial cable is never reliable. All in all, these are very risky tools to terminate crimping BNCs and they should only be used when no other tools are available (remember to always take utmost care when using them).

If you are an installer, or a CCTV technician that regularly terminates coaxial cables, get yourself a proper set of tools. These are: precise cutters, a stripping tool and a crimping tool.

Make sure you have the crimping and stripping tools for the right cable. If you are using RG-59/U (overall diameter 6.15mm) don't get it confused with RG-58/U (overall diameter 5mm) even though they look similar. For starters, they have a different impedance, i.e., RG-59/U is 75 Ω, compared to RG-58/U which is 50 Ω. Next, RG-59/U is slightly thicker, both in the center core and the shield. There are BNC connectors for the RG-58/U which look identical externally, but they are thinner on the inside.

Samples of bad BNC terminations

The best thing to do is to waste one and try terminating it before proceeding with the installation. Sometimes a small difference in the cable's dimensions, even if it is RG-59/U, may cause a lot of problems fitting the connectors properly.

Technically, a solid center core coaxial cable is better, both from the impedance point of view (the cable is stiffer and preserves the "straightness") and from the termination point of view. Namely, when terminating the solid core cable it is easier to crimp the center tip, than compared to the stranded core cable which is too flexible. Some people may prefer a stranded center core coax, mainly because of its flexibility, in which case care should be taken when terminating as it is very easy to short circuit the center core and the shield because of its flexibility.

If there are no other tools available, it is best to get the soldering type BNC connectors and terminate the cable by soldering. Care should be taken with the soldering iron's temperature, as well as the

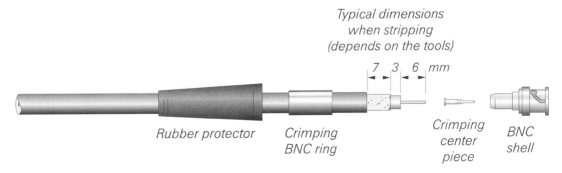

Suggestions for a correct BNC termination
(dimensions depend on stripping tool)

Tools for good termination

quality of the soldering, since it can easily damage the insulation and affect the impedance. In this instance, a multi-stranded core coax would be better.

If you have a choice of crimping connectors, look for the ones that are likely to last longer in respect to physical use and corrosion, like silver-plated or gold-plated BNCs. A good practice would be to use "rubber sleeves" (sometimes called "protective sleeves") for further protection of the interior of the BNC from corrosion and to minimize bending stress from plugging and unplugging.

In special cases, like with pan/tilt domes, there might be a need for a very thin and flexible 75 Ω coaxial cable (due to constant panning and tilting of the camera). Such cables are available from specialized cable manufacturers, but don't forget that you need special BNCs and tools for them.

Even if such a cable could be as thin as 2.5 mm, as is the case with the RG-179 B/U cable, the impedance would still be 75 Ω, which is achieved by the special dielectric and center core thickness. The attenuation of such a cable is high, but when used in short runs, it is negligible.

For installations where much longer runs are needed, other 75 Ω cables are used, such as RG-11B/U with an overall diameter of more than 9 mm. Needless to say, an RG-11 cable also needs special tools and BNCs for termination. Some installers use machines purposely built to strip or label coaxial

Coaxial cable	Impedance (Ω)	Overall diameter (mm)	Typical attenuation @10MHz (dB/100m)
RG-179B/U	75	2.5	17.4
RG-59B/U	75	6.15	3.3
RG-6B/U	75	6	2.2
RG-11B/U	75	10	1.3

A properly terminated RG-59 coaxial cable

cables. Although these machines are expensive and hard to find they do exist and if you are involved in very large installations they are worthwhile investment.

In the table on the previous page, typical attenuation figures are shown for various coax cables. Please note that the attenuation is shown in decibels and it refers to the voltage amplitude of the video signal. If we use the decibel table shown under the section of S/N for cameras it can be worked out that 10 dB is equivalent to attenuation of the signal to 30%, ie. 0.3Vpp. The RG-59 will attenuate the signal for 10 dB after 300m. Such low signal amplitude may be insufficient for a monitor or VCR to lock onto. This is the point of attenuation where we would usually require an amplifier to boost the signal.

Installation techniques

Prior to installation, it should be checked what cable length can be obtained from the supplier. Rolls of approximately 300 m (1000 feet) are common, but 100 m and 500 m can also be found. Naturally, it is better to run the cable in one piece whenever possible. If for some reason the installers need a longer run than what they have, the cable can be extended by terminating both, the installed and the extension cable. In such a case, although it is common practice to have a BNC plug connected to another BNC plug with a so-called "barrel" adaptor, it is better to minimize joining points by using one BNC plug and one socket (i.e., "male" and "female" crimping BNCs).

Before cable laying commences, the route should be inspected for possible problems such as feed-through, sharp corners, clogged ducts and the like. Once a viable route has been established, the cable lengths should be arranged so that any joints, or possible in-line amplifier installation, will occur at accessible positions.

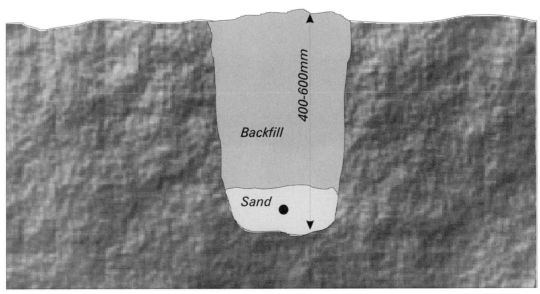

Trenching and burying recommendations

At the location of a joint it is important to leave an adequate overlap of the cables so that sufficient material is available for the termination operation. Generally, the overlap required doesn't need to be more than 1 m.

Whenever possible, the cable should be run inside a conduit of an adequate size. Conduits are available in various length and diameters, depending on the number of cables and their diameters. For external cable runs, a special conduit with better UV protection is needed. In special environments, like railway stations, special metal conduits need to be used. These are required because of the extremely high electromagnetic radiation that occurs when electric trains pass.

Similar treatment should be applied when a coaxial cable is run underground. When burying a cable, foremost consideration should be given to the prevention of damage due to excessive local loading points. Such loading may occur when backfill

Courtesy of Pacific Communications

Automatic coax cable stripping machine

material or an uneven trench profile digs into the cable. The damage may not be obvious instantly but the picture will get distorted due to the impedance change at the point of the cable's distortion. No matter what, the cost of digging up the cable and repairing it makes the expenditure of extra effort during laying well worthwhile.

Cabling by John Wishart. Ultrak Asia Pacific

It takes a lot of time and labor to have thousands of cables neatly organized and labelled

The best protection against cable damage is laying the cable on a bed of sand approximately 50-150 mm deep and backfilling with another 50-150 mm of sand. Due care needs to be exercised in the cutting of the trench so that the bottom of the trench is fairly even and free of protrusions. Likewise, when backfilling, do not allow soil with a high rock content to fall unchecked onto the sand and possibly put a rock through the cable, unless your conduit is extremely tough.

The trench depth is dependent on the type of ground being traversed as well as the load that is expected to be applied to the ground above the cable. A cable in solid rock may need a trench of only 300 mm or so, whereas a trench in soft soil crossing a road should be taken down to about 1 m. A general purpose trench, in undemanding situations, should be 400-600 mm deep with 100-300 mm total sand bedding.

Placing a coaxial cable on cable trays and bending it around corners requires observing the same major rule: **minimum bending radius.** As mentioned, the minimum bending radius depends on the coaxial cable size, but the general rule is **the bending radius should not be smaller than 5 times the diameter of the cable (or 10 times the radius)**. The minimum bending radius must be observed even when the cable tray does not facilitate this. The tendency to keep it neat and bend the coaxial cable to match power and data cables on the tray must be avoided. Remember, bending coax more than the minimum bending radius affects the impedance of the cable and causes a video signal quality loss.

Cabling and termination by Wegtech Services. Courtesy of Pacific Communications.

A briliant example of very neat cabling practises

The pulling of coaxial cables through ducts is performed by using a steel or plastic leader and then joining and securing all the cables that need to go through. Some new, tough plastic materials, called "snakes," are becoming more popular.

The types of cable ties normally used to tie the cables together are generally satisfactory, but remember, excessive force should not be applied, as it squashes the coax and therefore changes the impedance again.

Should a particular duct require the use of a lubricant, it is best to obtain a recommendation from the cable manufacturer. Talcum powder and bean-bag-type polystyrene beans can also be quite useful in reducing friction.

In some conditions the cable may already be terminated by connectors. These must be heavily protected while drawing the cable. The holes in such a case need to be bigger.

Automatic coax labeling machine
Courtesy of Pacom

Between the secured points of a cable it is wise to allow a little slack rather than leaving a tightly stretched length that may respond poorly to temperature variations or vibration.

If the cable is in some way damaged during installation, then leave enough extra cable length around the damaged area so that additional BNC joiners can be inserted.

Time domain reflectometer (TDR)

When a very complex and long coaxial cable installation is in question, it would be very useful to get a time domain reflectometer to help determine the location of bad cable spots.

The TDR works on a very basic principle in that it inserts short and strong pulses and measures the reflected energy. By determining the delay between the injected and the reflected signals, a pretty accurate localization of bad termination points and/or sharp bends can be made. This could be especially important if the cable goes through inaccessible places.

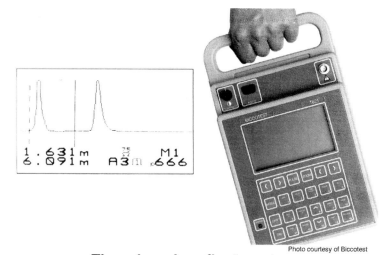

Time domain reflectometer
Photo courtesy of Biccotest

Twisted pair video transmission

Twisted pair cable is an alternative to the coaxial cable. It is useful in situations where runs longer than a couple of hundred meters have to be made. It is especially beneficial when only two wires have already been installed between two points.

Twisted pair cable is reasonably cheap when used with normal wires, but if a proper cable (as per the recommendations by the manufacturers) is used, with at least 10-20 twists per meter and with shielding, the price becomes much higher.

Twisted pair transmission is also called **balanced video transmission**.

The idea behind this is very simple and different to the unbalanced (coaxial) video transmission. Namely, to minimize the external electromagnetic interference, the twisted pair trick is to have a signal converted into balanced mode and sent via twisted wires. All the unwanted electromagnetic interference and noise will eventually induce an equal amount of current in both of these wires. This is why we need a proper twisted pair – the idea is to have **both of the wires equally exposed to the interference** and the voltage drop. Unlike the coaxial transmission, where the shield is grounded and commons the zero potential between the two points, **the twisted pair video transmission concept does not common the zero potential between the end points**. So when the signal arrives at the twisted pair receiver end it first comes to a differential amplifier input, with a well-balanced and good common mode rejection ratio (CMRR) factor. This differential amplifier reads the **differential signal between the two wires**.

If the two wires have similar characteristics and enough twists per meter (the more the better), they will be **equally affected** by noise, voltage drops and induced signals. With a good CMRR amplifier at the receiver end most of the unwanted noise will be eliminated.

The output impedance of the twisted pair transmitters is usually 100 Ω.

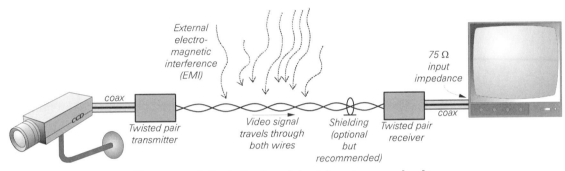

Balanced (twisted pair) video transmission

The drawback of this type of transmission is that one transmitting and one receiving unit is necessary in addition to the cable. They not only increase the cost of the system but also the risk of having the signal lost if either of the two components fails.

If the correct cable is used, however, much longer distances can be achieved than what is possible with an RG-59 or even an RG-11 cable. Manufacturers usually quote over 2000 m for B/W signals and more than 1000 m for color, without any in-line repeaters. Furthermore, when balanced transmission is used, no ground loops are apparent as with coax. Termination of the twisted pair cable does not require special tools and connectors. All these facts make such transmission even more attractive.

I must admit I have always preferred coax installation. But after seeing a major installation at the Frankfurt airport done with twisted pair video, the signal quality was, to my surprise, as good as with coax. I am now convinced that with a proper equipment selection, both cable and transmitter/receiver pair, this might be a very good alternative to coax.

Twisted pair video receiver modules in a 19" rack

Microwave links

Microwave links are used for good quality wireless video transmission.

The video signal is first modulated with a frequency that belongs in the microwave region of the electromagnetic spectrum. The wavelengths of this region are between 1 mm and 1 m. Using the known equation between the frequency and the wavelength:

$$\lambda = c / T \qquad [m] \qquad\qquad (44)$$

where c is the speed of light 300,000,000 m/s, we can find out that the microwave region is between 300 MHz and 3000 GHz. The upper region actually overlaps with the infrared frequencies that are defined as up to 100 GHz. Therefore, the lower part of the infrared frequency spectrum is also in the microwave region. In practice, though, the typical frequencies used for microwave video transmission are between 1 GHz and 10 GHz.

Since artificial frequencies are used by many services, like the military, the police, ambulances, couriers and aircraft radars, there is a need for some regulation of what frequency. This is done on an international level by the International Communications Union (ITU) and by the local authorities in your respective country. For Australia this was the Department of Transport and Communications, which was recently

Microwave wireless video transmission

renamed to the Spectrum Management Agency. Thus, a very important fact to consider when using microwave links in CCTV, is that each frequency and microwave power needs to be approved by the local authority in order to minimize interference with the other services using the same spectrum. This is to protect the registered users from new frequencies, but it is also a downfall (at least in CCTV) for using microwaves and one of the reasons why a lot of CCTV designers turn to microwaves only as a last resort.

Microwave links transmit a very wide bandwidth of video signals as well as other data if necessary (including audio and/or PTZ control). The transmission bandwidth depends on the manufacturer's model. For a well-built unit, a 7 MHz bandwidth is typical and sufficient to send high-quality video signals without any visible degradation.

Photo courtesy of Mitec
**Microwave antennas
and Tx/Rx modules**

Microwaves are usually **unidirectional** when a CCTV video signal is sent from point A to point B, but they can also be **bidirectional** when a video signal needs to be sent in both directions, or video in one and data in the other. The latter is very important if PTZ cameras are to be controlled.

The encoding technique in video transmission is usually frequency modulation (FM), but amplitude modulation (AM) can also be used. If audio and video are transmitted simultaneously, usually the video signal is AM modulated and the audio FM, as is the case with broadcast TV signals.

A line of sight is needed between the transmitter and the receiver. In most cases, the transmitting and receiving antennas are parabolic dishes, similar to those used for satellite TV reception.

The distances achievable with this technology depend on the transmitter output power and on the diameter of the antenna that contributes to the gain of the transmitter and the sensitivity of the receiver.

Obviously, atmospheric conditions will affect the signal quality. The same microwave link that has an excellent picture during a nice day may have considerable signal loss in heavy rain if it is not designed properly. Fog and snow also affect the signal. If the parabolic antenna is not anchored properly, wind may affect the links indirectly by shaking it, causing an intermittent loss of line of sight.

Many parabolic antennas come with a plastic or leather cover that protects the actual inner parabola. This protector simultaneously breaks the wind force and protects the sensitive parts from rain and snow.

The fitting and stability of a microwave antenna are of paramount importance to the links. The longer the distance that is required, the bigger the antenna and more secure fittings that are required.

Microwave transmitter

The initial line-of-sight alignment is harder to achieve for longer distances, although better quality units have a field strength indicator built in, which helps to make the alignment easier.

Maximum achievable transmitting distances of up to 30 km are quoted by most specialized manufacturers. In most cases a typical CCTV application will require only a couple of hundred meters, which is often not a problem as long as there is a line of sight.

The transmitting power and the size of the antenna required for a specific distance need to be confirmed with the manufacturer.

For shorter distances, microwave links may use rod or other types of non-parabolic antennas, which become very practical if dimensions are in question. The obvious security problem in such a case would be the omnidirectional radiation of the signal, but the advantage would be a fairly wide area of coverage.

One very interesting application that was initially developed in Australia was to use an omnidirectional microwave with a transmitting antenna fitted on top of a race car roof, which would send signals to a helicopter above the race track. From there it would be redirected to a TV broadcast van. With such a setup, the so-called Race Cam allowed the television audience to see the driver's view.

Most microwave manufacturers have RS-232 links available for camera and other remote control data, but also have in mind that some CCTV manufacturers offer their controls in audio bandwidth, so you can actually use an audio channel of the microwave (in the opposite direction of the video signal) to control PTZ cameras.

RF wireless (open air) video transmission

RF video transmission is similar to the microwave transmission in the way the modulation of signals is done. The major differences, however, are the modulation frequency in the VHF or UHF bands and the transmission of the signal, which is usually omnidirectional. When a directional Yagi antenna is used (similar to the domestic ones used for reception of a specific channel), longer distances can be achieved and there will be less distraction to the surrounding area. It should be noted, though, that depending on the regulations of your country, the radiated power cannot be above a certain limit, after which you will require approval from your respective frequency regulatory body.

RF transmitters are usually made with video and audio inputs and the modulation techniques are similar to those of the microwaves, i.e., video is AM modulated and audio is FM. The spectrum transmitted depends on the make, but generally it is narrower than the microwave. This usually means 5.6 MHz, which is sufficient to have audio and video mixed into one signal.

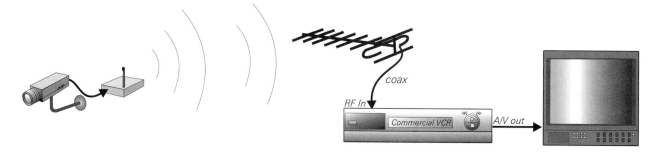

Wireless (RF) video transmission

Consumer products with similar characteristics to the above listed, are found in the so-called RF senders, or wireless VCR links. The RF modulator is fed with the audio and video signals of the VCR outputs and re-modulates and then transmits them so they can be picked up by another VCR in the house. Devices like these are not made with CCTV in mind, so the distances achievable are in the vicinity of a household area. Sometimes this might be a cheap and easy way out of a situation where a short distance wireless transmission is required.

Since VHF and UHF bands are for normal broadcast TV reception, you should check with your local authority and use channels that do not interfere with the existing broadcasting. In most countries, UHF

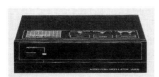

An RF modulator

channels 36 to 39 are deliberately not used by the TV stations because they are left for VCR-to-TV conversion, video games and similar.

The downfall of such an RF CCTV transmission is that any TV receiver at a reasonable distance can pick the signal up. Sometimes, though, this might be exactly what is wanted. This includes systems in big building complexes, where the main entrance cameras are injected through the MATV system so the tenants can call the camera on a particular channel of their TV receivers.

The RF frequency is such that, when compared to the microwave links, it does not require line of sight, as the RF (depending upon whether it is UHF or VHF) can penetrate through brick walls, wood and other nonmetal objects. How far one can go with this depends on many factors and the best bet is to test it out in the particular environment (in which the RF transmitter will be used).

Infrared wireless (open air) video transmission

As the heading suggests, an infrared open air video transmission uses optical means to transmit a video signal. An infrared LED is used as a light carrier. The light carrier is **intensity modulated with a video signal**. Effectively, this type of transmission looks like a hybrid between microwave and fiber optics transmission (to be discussed a little bit later). Instead of the microwave frequencies being used, it is the infrared that are used (infrared frequencies are higher). And instead of sending such light modulation over a fiber optics cable (such is the case in fiber optics, using the principles of total reflection), open space is used. **We therefore have to have line of sight.** The obvious advantage of the infrared light radiation is that you don't need a special license.

Infra red (wireless) video transmission

In order to have the infrared light concentrated into a narrow beam to minimize dispersion light losses, a lens assembly is required at the transmitter end to concentrate the light into a narrow beam and a lens assembly at the receiver end to concentrate the light onto the photosensitive detector.

Both color and B/W as well as audio, can be transmitted over distances of more than 1 km. Bigger lens assemblies and more powerful LEDs, as well as a more sensitive receiving end, will provide for even longer distances.

An infrared video Tx/Rx

Special precautions have to be taken here for the temperature around the transmitter so that the receiver doesn't detect those infrared frequencies radiated by hot walls, roofs and metal objects.

Photo courtesy of Plettac

Infrared video transmission between trains and station cameras

Understandably, weather conditions like rain, fog and hot wind will affect infrared links more than microwave transmission.

Transmission of images over telephone lines

First there was the *slow-scan* TV. That was a system that would send video pictures over a telephone line at a very slow speed, usually many tens of seconds for a full-frame B/W picture.

The slow-scan concept originates from the late 1950s, when it was used by some amateur radio operators. It was later applied to CCTV. The concept is very simple: There are units at both ends of the transmission path, like with any other transmission, a transmitter and a receiver. An analog video signal of a camera is captured and converted into digital format. It is then stored in the random access memory (RAM) of the slow-scan transmitter. This is usually triggered by an external alarm or upon the receiver's request. The stored image, which is at this stage in a digital format, is usually frequency modulated with an audio frequency that can be heard by the receiving phone. This frequency is usually between 1 and 2 kHz, i.e., where the phone line attenuation is lowest. When the receiver receives the signal, it reassembles the picture line by line, starting from the top left-hand corner until the picture at the receiving end is converted into an analog display (a steady picture).

This concept was initially very slow, but considering the unlimited distances offered by telephone lines (provided there was a transmitter compatible with the receiver), it was a very attractive concept for remote CCTV monitoring.

The slow-scan transmitter would usually have more cameras attached to it, so the viewer could browse through all of them. Also, any camera could send an image automatically when triggered by an external alarm associated with it. More transmitters could thus report to one or more receiving stations, with each one protected by a password to eliminate unwanted listeners.

One way of increasing the speed of transmission was to reduce the digitized picture resolution or to use only a quarter of the screen for each camera. So the initial 32 seconds could effectively be reduced to 8 seconds for when one picture update was required, or perhaps, have a 32-second update of a quad screen with blocks of four cameras. Considering that other signals could be added to this, like audio or control signals for remote relay activation, a better picture can be attained for these historic beginnings.

Older-generation slow scan systems would take 32 seconds to send a single low-quality picture from an alarmed site to the monitoring station. Dial-up and connecting time should be added to this, totalling to more than a minute for the completion of the first image transmission. The slow-scan, however, was very popular and ahead of its time. Today we have much more advanced techniques when video signals need to be transmitted over the telephone line.

The new technology, using the same concept but much faster image processing and compression algorithms, is called *Fast Scan* and can achieve speeds of less than 1 s for a full-color picture update. The image manipulation is digital and various compression techniques are used to even further increase the transmission speed, yet preserving the image quality.

Photo courtesy of Vision Systems

**Fast-scan transmitter
and receiver unit**

The most important details to take into consideration when choosing a fast-scan system are:

- The framestore resolution (in pixels),

- B/W or color,

- Whether other signals can be transmitted simultaneously (often PTZ control is required, or perhaps some relays activation) and

- The transmission speed.

For the last consideration you have to be very flexible because different telephone lines and different modems will give different and unfair comparisons.

Sometimes, for the customer it may be more important just to see very roughly what is happening at the other end of the line, as long as it is fast. Other customers may require a very good definition (resolution), irrespective of the time delay.

It is also important to know what else can be connected to the system in the future. Is there a need for more than one camera input, or perhaps one of the cameras should have a PTZ control?

Don't forget, if you require a PTZ control, you have to accept the delay between the command issued from the keyboard and the picture update in order to see where the camera is pointing. This might be a bit unusual or unacceptable for some, but a lot of manufacturers offer intelligent updates. Namely, when a joystick is used, the picture automatically selects a smaller viewing area that remains sharp (which will have a faster update), so you can see where the camera is pointing. It then upgrades to a full screen as soon as the joystick is released.

Another type of system offers an additional integrated feature: video motion detection. The system automatically sends images as soon as activity is detected in the video signal.

PSTN

The normal PSTN (public switched telephone network) line has a very narrow bandwidth of usually 300 to 3000 Hz, which is considered a standard (measured at 3-dBm points, where dBm are measured relative to 1 mW across 600 Ohms, the telephone line impedance). Some people call this type of line plain old telephone service (POTS).

Theoretically, it is impossible to send live video images of 5 MHz over such a narrow channel. It is possible, however, to compress and encode the signal to achieve faster transmission and this can be done today by most of the fast-scan transmitters. The technological explosion of the PCs, compression algorithms, fast modems and better telephone lines, in the last few years has made it possible to transmit video images over a telephone line at rates unimaginable when the first slow-scan transmitters were developed.

As mentioned earlier, the concept remained the same as that of the slow scan, but the intelligence behind the compression schemes (what and how it transmits) has improved so much that today **a color video signal with very good resolution can be sent in less than 1 s per frame**. In addition to this, with many models, other control and audio signals can be sent.

The more sophisticated fast-scan systems use a method of image updating called "conditional refresh." After the initial image is sent, only the portion that changes needs to be resent. This allows a much more rapid update rate than that with the basic fast-scan systems. Other manufacturers stick to the full image transmission but use proprietary compression algorithms to achieve similar speeds.

In order to understand the PSTN telephone line video transmission rates, let's consider this simplified exercise:

A typical B/W video signal with 256×256 pixels resolution will have $256 \times 256 = 65,536$ bits of information, which is equal to 64 kB of digital information (65,536/1024). (Note the digital numbers $64 = 2^6$, $256 = 2^8$.)

To send this amount of uncompressed information over a telephone line using a normal 2400 bits per second modem (as was the case in the early days of slow scan), it would take about 27 s (65,536/2,400).

If the signal is compressed, however (compressions of 10, 20 or even more times are available), by say 10 times, this gets reduced to 3 s. Most fast-scan transmitters will only send the first image at this speed, after which they only send the difference in the pictures, thus dramatically reducing the subsequent images' update time to less than a second.

A color picture with the same resolution will obviously require more. A high-resolution picture of quality better than S-VHS, is usually digitized in a 512×512 frame with 24-bit colors (8 bits of each R, G and B) will equal $512 \times 512 \times 3 = 786,432$ bytes, or 768 kB. If this is compressed by 10 times, it becomes 76 kB, which is not that hard to transmit with a 14,400-bps modem at approximately $76,000/14,400 = 5$ s. It all depends on the compression algorithm.

In practice, add another few seconds to the dialling time, which is faster with DTMF (dual tone multi-frequency) and slower with pulse dialing lines.

Most of the high security systems have a dedicated telephone line, which means that once the line is established, it stays open and there is no further time loss for the modem's handshake and initial picture update delay.

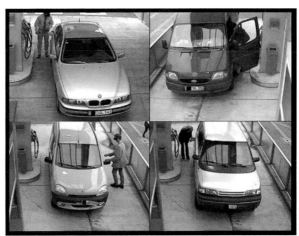

In the end, we should highlight that the maximum speed of transmission that can be achieved with a POTS or PSTN line is somewhere around 14,400 bps. Higher speeds are possible only with the compression algorithms of modern modems. Nowadays, 28.8-kbps modems are very common, but if you require even faster transmission, you'd better look at the ISDN or B-ISDN technology.

Fast-scan images can also be transmitted in quad mode for faster update

ISDN

For the fastest possible transmission, ISDN (Integrated Services Digital Network) telephone lines should be used, which are available in many industrialized countries.

ISDN lines were proposed and started to be implemented in the mid-1970s, almost at the same time when CCD chips appeared.

The basic ISDN channel offers a rate of 64 kb/s, which dramatically improves the update speed of fast scan. In comparison, a normal PSTN line, as mentioned above, can go up to 14.4 kb/s when the lines are in a very good condition. Some new modems can increase this even further (up to 28.8 kb/s) by using hardware compression techniques.

The ISDN is a **digital network and transmits signals in digital format**; hence, the bandwidth is not given in Hz but in b/s. For special purposes, like video conferencing and cable TV (available via telephone lines), ISDN can be used combined in **broadband ISDN** (B-ISDN) links, where even higher speed rates (multiples of 64 kb/s) of at least 128 kb/s can be achieved by intelligent multiplexing of more channels into one.

The units used to connect a device to an ISDN line is usually called a Terminal Adapter (TA), and the function, as well as the appearance of such device, is very similar to a modem with PSTN lines. Intelligent TA for B-ISDN links are also known as aggregating terminals adapters.

Don't forget that, in order to benefit from a wider ISDN, both ends (the transmitting and the receiving) need to have an ISDN connection. In most countries, ISDN connection is charged per time of use.

Cellular network

Transmitting images over mobile phones is an attractive possibility with the technology available today. A mobile phone with a modem socket, combined with a notebook computer, can easily be equipped with the software and hardware needed for wireless and mobile image transmission.

The same principles and concepts as previously discussed apply, with the exception of the transmission speed, which is much slower via the cellular network.

The digital network offers better noise immunity, although the coverage at the moment is not as good as with the analog mobile service. The digital cellular network is very rapidly growing, though, and worldwide ROAM-ing is already possible in the majority of industrialized countries. This means when users are overseas they can divert their calls to the digital network in the country they are visiting and make calls without going through an operator. Understandably, to activate ROAM-ing, the user needs to inform their major carrier.

With the digital cellular network speed of up to 9600 kb/s can be achieved when using the modem mode. There are advancements in the hardware and software of the GSM technology where boosting data speeds from the current 9.6 kb to 14.4 kb in a single traffic channel is now possible. By multiplexing up to four channels into a single time slot, operators will be able to offer transmission rates up to 57.6 kb, six times more than currently available and with the help of compression technology data speeds can be increased even higher.

Photo courtesy of Netcomm

A GSM modem card

Fiber optics

Fiber optics, if correctly installed and terminated, is the best quality and most secure transmission of all. Even though it has been used in long distance telecommunications, even across oceans, for over thirty years, it has been avoided or neglected in CCTV.

The main excuse installers have used was the fear of unknown technology, often labelled as "touchy and sensitive" and also considered "too expensive."

Fiber optics, though, offers many important advantages over other media and although it used to be very expensive and complicated to terminate, it is now becoming cheaper and simpler to install.

Most important advantages of all are immunity to electromagnetic interference, more secure transmission, wider bandwidth and much longer distances without amplification. We will, therefore, devote more space to it.

Why fiber?

Fiber optics is a technology that uses light as a carrier of information, be it analog or digital. This light is usually infrared, and the transmission medium is fiber.

Fiber optic signal transmission offers many advantages over the existing metallic links. These are:

- Very wide bandwidth.

- Very low attenuation, on the order of 1.5 dB/km compared to over 30 dB/km for RG-59 coax (relative to 10-MHz signal).

- The fiber (which is dielectric) offers electrical (galvanic) isolation between the transmitting and receiving end; therefore, no ground loops are possible.

- Light used as a carrier of the signal travels entirely within the fiber. Therefore, it causes no interference with the adjacent wires or other optical fibers.

- The fiber is immune to nearby signals and electro-magnetic interferences (EMI); therefore, it is irrelevant whether the fiber optics passes next to a 110 V AC, 240 V AC or 10,000 V AC or whether it is close to a megawatt transmitter. Even more important, lightning cannot induce any voltage even if it hits a centimeter from the fiber cable.

- A fiber optics cable is very small and light in weight.

- It is impossible to tap into the fiber optics cable without physically intercepting the signal, in which case it would be detected at the receiving end. This is especially important for security systems.

Fiber cables are very small and fragile but enclosed in tough jackets

- The cost of fiber is becoming cheaper every day. A basic fiber optics cable costs anywhere from $1 to $5 per meter, depending on the specific type and construction used.

There are also some not so attractive features of fiber optics, but they are being improved:

- Termination of fiber optics requires special tools and better precision of workmanship than with any other media.

- Switching and routing of fiber optics signals are difficult.

Fiber optics offers more advantages than other cables.

Fiber optics has been used in telecommunications for many years and is becoming more popular in CCTV and security in general.

As the technology for terminating and splicing fiber improves and at the same time gets cheaper, there will be more CCTV and security systems with fiber optics.

The concept

The concept of fiber optics lies in the fundamentals of light refraction and reflection.

To some it may seem impossible that a perfectly clear fiber can constrain the light rays to stay within the fiber as they travel many kilometers, yet not have these rays exit through the walls along the trip. In order to understand this effect, we have to refresh our memory about the physical principle of total reflection.

Physicist Willebrord Snell laid down the principles of refraction and reflection in the early 17th century. When light enters a denser medium, not only does the speed reduce, but the direction of travel is also corrected in order for the light to preserve the wave nature of propagation (see the Optics section). Basically, the manifestation of this is a light ray sharply bent when entering different media. We've all seen the broken straw effect in a glass of water. That is refraction.

A typical glass has an index of refraction of approximately 1.5. The higher the index, the slower the speed of light will be, thus the bigger the angle of refraction when the ray enters the surface.

The main reason for the beauty of a diamond is the rainbow of colors we see due to its high index of refraction (2.42). This is explained by the fact that a ray of light (natural light) has all the colors (wavelengths) a white light is composed of.

Fiber optics uses a special effect of refraction under a maximum incident angle; hence, it becomes a **total reflection**. This phenomenon occurs at a certain angle when a light ray **exits** from a dense medium to a sparser medium.

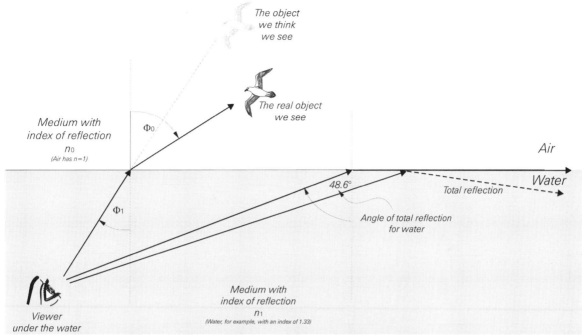

The effect of total reflection

The drawing above shows the effect of a diver viewing the sky from under the water. There is an angle below which he can no further see above the water surface. This angle is called the **angle of total reflection**. Beyond that point he will actually see the objects inside the water and it will seem to him like looking through a mirror (assuming the water surface is perfectly still).

For the index of refraction of water (1.33), using Snell's Law, we can calculate this angle:

$$\sin \Phi_T = 1.00/1.33 = 0.752 \;\; \rightarrow \Phi_T = 48.6° \tag{45}$$

The concept of fiber optics transmission follows the very same principles.

The core of a fiber optics cable has an index of refraction higher than the index of the cladding. Thus, when a light ray travels inside the core it cannot escape it because of the total reflection.

So, what we have at the fiber optics transmitting end is an LED (light emitting diode) or LD (laser diode) that is modulated with the transmitted signal.

In the case of CCTV the signal will be video, but similar logic applies when the signal is digital, like a PTZ control or other security data.

So, when transmitting, the infrared diode is **intensity modulated** and pulsates with the signal variations. At the receiving end, we have basically a photodetector that receives the optical signal and converts it into electrical.

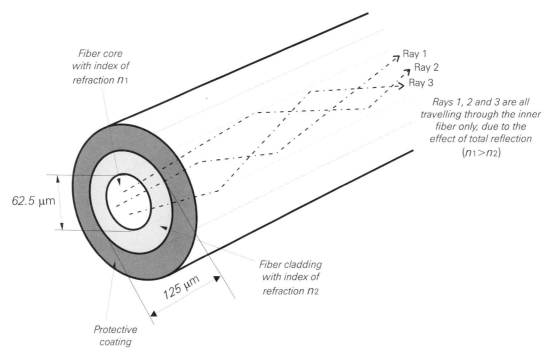

Fiber core
with index of
refraction n1

Ray 1
Ray 2
Ray 3

Rays 1, 2 and 3 are all
travelling through the inner
fiber only, due to the
effect of total reflection
(n1>n2)

62.5 μm

125 μm

Fiber cladding
with index of
refraction n2

Protective
coating

Fiber optics usage is based on the effect of total reflection

Fiber optics used to be very expensive and hard to terminate, but that is no longer the case, because the technology has improved substantially. Optical technology has long been known to have many potential capabilities, but major advancements are achieved when mass production of cheap fundamental devices like semiconductor light emitting diodes, lasers and optical fibers are made.

Nowadays, we are witnessing a conversion of most terrestrial hard-wired copper links to fiber.

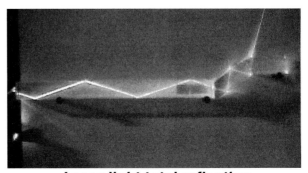

Laser light total reflection
inside a fiber channel

Types of optical fibers

There are a few different types of fiber optics cables. This division is based on the path light waves take through the fiber.

As mentioned in the introduction, the basic idea is to use the total reflection effect that is a result of the different indices of refraction ($n_2 > n_1$, where n_2 is the index of the internal (**core**) fiber and n_1 is the index of the outer (**cladding**) fiber).

A typical representation of what we have just described is the **step index** fiber optics cable. The index profile is shown on the next page, as well as how light travels through such a cable. Note the input pulse deformation caused by the various path lengths of the light rays bounced from the cylindrical surface that divides the two different index fibers. This is called a **modal distortion**.

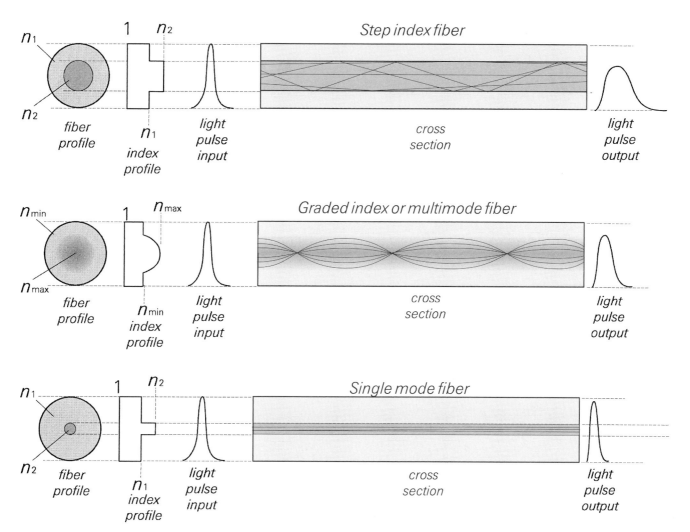

Three different types of fibers

In order to equalize the path lengths of different rays and improve the pulse response, a **graded index** (or **multimode**) fiber optics cable was developed. Multimode fiber makes the rays travel more or less at an equal speed, causing the effect of optical standing waves.

And finally, a **single mode** fiber cable is available with even better pulse response and almost eliminated modal distortion.

This latter one is the most expensive of all and offers the longest distances achievable **using the same electronics**. For CCTV applications, the multimode and step index are adequate.

The index profiles of the three types are shown above.

Numerical aperture

The light that is injected into the fiber cable may come from various angles.

Due to the different indices of the air and the fiber, we can apply the theory of refraction where Snell's law gives us:

$$\sin\phi_0 \; n_0 = \sin\phi_1 \; n_1 \tag{46}$$

understandably, n_1 is the index of the fiber core and n_0 is the index of air, which is nearly 1.

Further, this gives us:

$$\sin\phi_0 = \sin\phi_1 \; n_1 \tag{47}$$

The left-hand side of the above is accepted to be a very important fiber cable property, called **numerical aperture (NA)**.

NA represents the light-gathering ability of a fiber optics cable.

In practice, NA helps us to understand how two terminated fibers can be put together and still make a signal contact.

The realistic value of a typical NA angle, for a step index fiber cable is shown on the drawing.

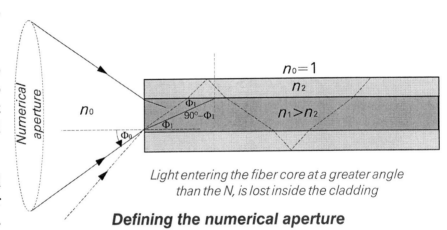

Light entering the fiber core at a greater angle than the N, is lost inside the cladding

Defining the numerical aperture

To calculate NA (basically the angle ϕ_0) it is not necessary to know the angle ϕ_1.

The following are some basic trigonometric transformations that will express NA using only the fiber indices.

Applying Snell's law and using the drawing, we get:

$$\sin(90° - \phi_1) \; n_1 = \sin(90° - \phi_2) \; n_2 \tag{48}$$

For a total reflection we have $\phi_2 = 0°$, therefore, the above becomes:

$$\sin(90° - \phi_1) \; n_1 = n_2 \tag{49}$$

Since $\sin(90° - \phi_1) = \cos\phi_1$, we can write:

$$\cos\phi_1 = n_2 / n_1 \tag{50}$$

Knowing the basic rule of trigonometry,

$$\sin^2\phi + \cos^2\phi = 1 \tag{51}$$

and using equation (50), we can convert (47) into a more acceptable relation without sine and cosine:

$$\sin^2\phi_0 / n_1^2 + n_2^2/n_1^2 = 1 \tag{52}$$

$$\sin^2\phi_0 = n_1^2 - n_2^2 \tag{53}$$

$$NA = \sin\phi_0 \quad = \text{SQRT}\,(n_1^2 - n_2^2) \tag{54}$$

Formula (54), is the well-known formula for calculating the numerical aperture of a fiber cable, based on the two known indices, the core and the cladding. SQRT stands for square root.

Obviously, **the higher this number is, the wider the angle of light acceptance will be of the cable.**

A realistic example would be with n_1=1.46 and n_2=1.40, which will give us NA=0.41, i.e., ϕ_0=24°.

For a graded index fiber this aperture is a variable and it is dependent on the radius of the index we are measuring, but it is lower than the step index multimode fiber. A single-mode 9/125-μm fiber has NA = 0.1.

Light levels in fiber optics

Light output power is measured in watts (like any other power), but since light sources used in fiber optics communications are very low, it is more appropriate to compare an output power relative to the input one, in which case we get the well-known equation for **decibels**:

$$A_r = 10 \log (P_o/P_i) \qquad \text{[dB]} \tag{55}$$

However, if we compare a certain light power relative to an absolute value, like 1 mW, then we are talking about dBm-s, i.e.:

$$A_a = 10 \log (P/1\ mW) \qquad \text{[dBm]} \tag{56}$$

Working with decibels makes calculation of transmission levels much easier.

Negative decibels, when A is calculated, mean loss and positive decibels mean gain.

In the case of A_a a negative number of dBm represents power less than 1 mW and a positive number is more than 1 mW.

The definition of dB, when comparing power values, is as shown in equation (55), but, remembering from earlier, there is a slightly different definition when voltage or current is compared and expressed in decibels:

$$B_r = 20 \log (V_o/V_i) \qquad \text{[dB]} \qquad (57)$$

Without going into the theory, it should be remembered that power decibels are calculated with 10 and voltage (and current) decibels are calculated with 20 times in front of the logarithm.

Light, when transmitted through a fiber cable, can be lost due to:

- Source coupling

- Optical splices

- Attenuation of the fiber due to inhomogeneity

- High temperature and so on.

When designing a CCTV system with fiber optics cables, the total attenuation is very important to know since we work with very small signals. It is therefore better to work with worst case estimates rather than using average values, which will help design a safe and quality system.

For this purpose it should be known that in most cases an 850-nm LED light power output is between 1 dBm and 3 dBm, while a 1300-nm LED has a bit less power, usually from 0 dBm to 2 dBm (note: the power is expressed relative to 1 mW).

The biggest loss of light occurs in the coupling between the LED and the fiber.

It also depends on the NA number and whether you use step or graded index fiber.

A realistic number for source coupling losses is around −14dB (this is relative to the source power output).

Light sources in fiber optics transmission

There are two basic electronic components used in producing light for fiber optics cables:

- LEDs

- LDs

Both of these produce frequencies in the infrared region, which is above 700 nm.

The light generating process in both LEDs and LDs results from the recombination of electrons and holes inside a P-N junction when a forward bias current is applied. This light is actually called **electroluminescence**.

The recombined electron/hole pairs have less energy than each constituent had separately before the recombination. **When the holes and electrons recombine, they give up this surplus energy difference, which leaves the point of recombination as photons (basic unit carriers of light).**

Photo courtesy of Laser Diode

Laser diode

The wavelength associated with this photon is determined by the equation:

$$\lambda = hc/E \tag{58}$$

where:

> h is the Planck's constant, a fundamental constant in physics: 6.63×10^{-34} Joules

> c is the speed of light (300×10^6 m/s)

> E is the band gap energy of the P-N material

Since h and c are constant, it means that **the wavelength depends solely on the band gap energy, i.e., the material in use**. This is a very important conclusion.

For pure gallium arsenide (GaAs) λ is 900 nm. For example, by adding some small amounts of aluminium, the wavelength can be lowered to 780 nm. For even lower wavelengths, other material, such as gallium arsenide phosphate (GaAsP) or gallium phosphate (GaP) is used.

The basic differences between an LED and an LD are in the generated wavelength spectrum and the angle of dispersion of that light.

An LED generates a fair bit of wavelength around the central wavelength as shown below. An LD has a very narrow bandwidth, almost a single wavelength.

An LED P-N junction not only emits light with more frequencies than an LD, but it does so in all directions, i.e., with no preferred direction of dispersion. This dispersion will greatly depend on the mechanical construction of the diode, its light absorption and reflection of the area. The radiation,

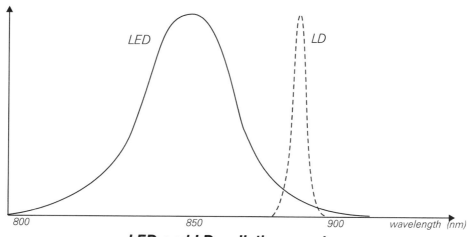

LED and LD radiation spectrum

however, is omnidirectional, and in order to narrow it down, LED manufacturers put a kind of focusing lens on top. This is still far too wide an angle to be used with a single-mode fiber cable. So this is the main reason why LEDs are not used as transmitting devices with single-mode fiber cables.

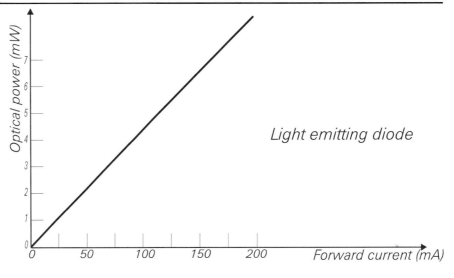

An LD is built of a similar material as an LED and the light generating process is similar, but the junction area is much smaller and the concentration of the holes and electrons is much greater. The generated light can only exit from a very small area. At certain current levels, the photon generation process gets into a **resonance** and the number of generated photons increases dramatically, producing more photons with the same wavelength and in phase. Thus, **the optical gain is achieved in an organized way and the generated light is a coherent (in phase), stimulated emission of light**. In fact, the word LASER is an abbreviation for *light amplification by stimulated emission of radiation.*

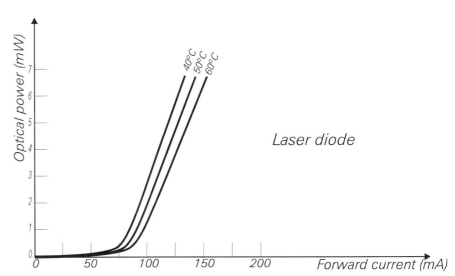

Light output dependence on current for LED and LD

In order to start this stimulated emission of light, an LD requires a minimum current of 5 to 100 mA, which is called a **threshold current**. This is much higher than the threshold with normal LEDs. Once the emission starts, however, LDs produce a high optical power output with a very narrow dispersion angle.

For transmitting high frequencies and analog signals, it is important to have a light output linear with the applied drive current, as well as a wide bandwidth.

LEDs are good in respect to linearity, but not so good in high-frequency reproduction compared to the LDs, although, they do exceed 100 MHz, which is, for us in CCTV, more than sufficient.

Laser diodes can easily achieve frequencies in excess of 1 GHz.

The above can be illustrated with the same analogy as when discussing magnetic recording: Imagine the light output spectrum of an LED and LD to be tips of pencils. The LED spectrum will represent the thicker and the LD the thinner pencil tip. With the thinner pencil you can write smaller letters and more text in the same space, i.e., the signal modulated with an LD will contain higher frequencies.

LEDs, however, are cheaper, linear and require no special driving electronics. An LED of 850 nm costs around $10, while 1300 nm is around $100. Their MTBF is extremely high ($10^6 \sim 10^8$ hr).

LDs are more expensive, between $100 and $15,000. They are very linear once the threshold is exceeded. They often have a temperature control circuit because the operating temperature is very important, so feedback stabilization for the output power is necessary. Despite all of that, they have a higher modulation bandwidth, a narrower carrier spectral width and they launch more power into small fibers. Their MTBF is lower than the LEDs', although still quite high ($10^5 \sim 10^7$ hr).

Recently, a new LED called a super luminescent diode has been attracting a great deal of attention. The technical characteristics of the SLDs are in between those of the LEDs and LDs.

For CCTV applications, LEDs are sufficiently good light sources. LDs are more commonly used in multichannel wide bandwidth multiplexers or very long run single-mode fibers.

Light detectors in fiber optics

Devices used for detecting the optical signals on the other side of the fiber cable are known as **photo diodes**. This is because the majority of them are actually one type of a diode or another.

The basic division of photo diodes used in fiber technology is into:

- P-N photo diodes (PNPD)

- PIN photo diodes (PINPD)

- Avalanche photo diodes (APD)

The PNPD is like a normal P-N junction silicon diode that is sensitive to infrared light. Its main characteristics are low response and high rise times.

The PINPD is a modified P-N diode where an intrinsic layer is inserted in between the P and N types of silicon. It possesses high response and low rise times.

The APD is similar to the PINPD, but it has an advantage that almost each incident photon produces more than one electron/hole pair, as a result of an internal chain reaction (avalanche effect). The APD is consequently more sensitive than the PIN diode, but it also generates more noise.

All these basic devices are combined with amplification and "transimpedance" stages that amplify the signal to the required current/voltage levels.

Frequencies in fiber optics transmission

The attenuation of the optical fibers can be grouped in attenuation due to material and external influences.

Material influences include:

- Rayleigh scattering. This is due to the inhomogeneities in the fiber glass, the size of which is small compared to the wavelength. At 850 nm, this attenuation may add up to 1.5 dB/km, reducing to 0.3 dB/km for a wavelength of 1300 nm and 0.15 dB/km for 1550 nm.

- Material absorption. This occurs if hydroxyl ions and/or metal ions are present in the fiber. Material absorption is much smaller than the Rayleigh scattering and usually adds up to 0.2 dB/km to the signal attenuation.

The external effects that influence the attenuation are:

- Micro-bending. This is mainly due to an inadequate cable design, i.e., inconsistency of the fiber cable precision along its length. It can amount up to several dB/km.

- Fiber geometry. Similar to the above, but basically due to the poor control over its drawn diameter.

The diagram below shows a very important fact: that not all the wavelengths (frequencies) have the same attenuation when sent through a fiber cable.

The wavelengths around the areas indicated with the vertical dotted lines are often called **fiber optics windows**. There are three windows:

- First window at 850 nm,

- Second window at 1300 nm and

- Third window at 1550 nm.

The first window is not really with minimum attenuation compared to the higher frequencies, but this frequency was first used in fiber transmission. The LEDs produced for this use were reasonably efficient and easy to make.

For short distance applications, such as CCTV, this is still the cheapest and preferred wavelength.

The 1300 nm wavelength is becoming more commonly used in CCTV. This is the preferred wavelength for professional telecommunications as well as CCTV systems with longer cable runs, where higher light source cost is not a major factor. The losses at this frequency are much lower, as can be seen from

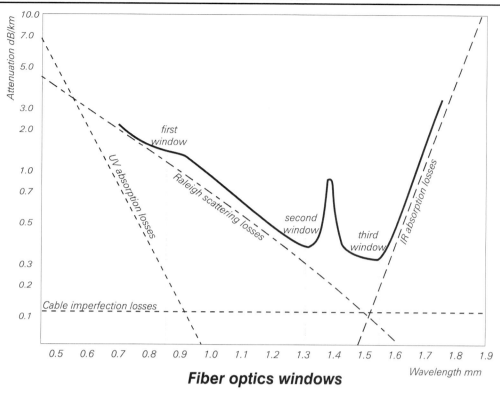

Fiber optics windows

the diagram above. The difference between 850 nm and 1300 nm in attenuation is approximately 2-3 dB/km.

The 1550 nm wavelength has even lower losses, and therefore, more future systems will be oriented towards this window.

For illustration purposes, a typical attenuation figure of a multimode 62.5/125-μm fiber cable, for an 850-nm light source, is less than 3.3 dB per kilometer. If a 1300-nm source is used with the same fiber, attenuation of less than 1 dB can be achieved. Therefore, **longer distances can be achieved with the same fiber cable, by just changing the light source**. This is especially useful with analog signals, such as the video.

When an 850-nm light source is used with 62.5/125-μm cable we can easily have a run of at least a couple of kilometers, which in most CCTV cases is more than sufficient. However, longer distances can be achieved by using graded multimode fiber and even longer when a 1300-nm light source is used instead of 850 nm.

The longest run can be achieved with a single-mode fiber cable and light sources of 1300 nm and 1550 nm.

A typical attenuation figure for a 1300-nm light source is less than 0.5 dB/km and for 1550 nm it is less than 0.4 dB/km.

Passive components

Apart from the previously mentioned photo diodes and detectors, which can also be considered as **active devices**, there are some **passive components** used in fiber optics systems.

These are:

    - Splices: permanent or semipermanent junctions between fibers.

    - Connectors: junctions that allow an optical fiber to be repeatedly connected to and/or disconnected from another fiber or to a device such as a source or detector.

    - Couplers: devices that distribute optical power among two or more fibers or combine optical power from two or more fibers into a single fiber.

    - Switches: devices that can reroute optical signals under either manual or electronic control.

Fusion splicing

Two fibers are welded together, often under a microscope. The result is usually very good, but the equipment might be expensive.

The procedure of fusion splicing usually consists of cleaning the fiber, cleaving and then positioning the two fibers in some kind of mounting blocks.

The precision of this positioning is improved by using a microscope, which is quite often part of the machine. When the alignment is achieved, an electric arc is produced to weld the two fibers. Such process can be monitored and repeated if an unsatisfactory joint is produced.

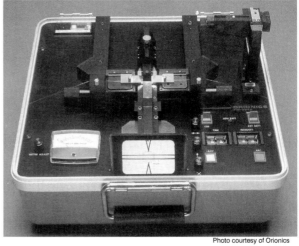

Photo courtesy of Orionics

A fusion splicing machine

Losses in fusion splicing are very low, usually around 0.1 dB.

Mechanical splicing

This is probably the most common way of splicing, due to the inexpensive tools used with relatively good results.

**An ST connector and
mechanical splicing joint**

Fibers are mechanically aligned, in reference to their surfaces and (usually) epoxied together. The performance cannot be as good as fusion splicing, but it may come very close to it. More importantly, the equipment used to perform the mechanical splicing is far less expensive.

Losses in a good mechanical splicing range between 0.1 and 0.4 dB.

The mechanical splicing is based on two principles:

    - V groove

    - Axis alignment

Both of these are shown on the diagrams on the right.

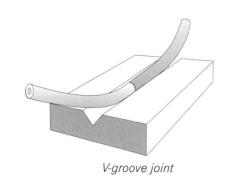

V-groove joint

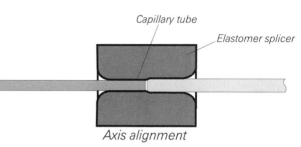

Capillary tube

Elastomer splicer

Axis alignment

Mechanical splicing

For a good connection, the fiber optics cable needs a good termination, which is still the hardest part of a fiber optics installation. It needs high precision and patience and a little bit of practice. Anyone can learn to terminate a fiber cable and in cases where they have no such skills, installers can hire specialized people who supply the terminals, terminate the cable and test it. The latter is the most preferred arrangement in the majority of CCTV fiber optics installations.

Fiber optics multiplexers

These multiplexers are different to the VCR multiplexers described earlier. **Fiber optics multiplexers combine more signals into one, in order to use only a single fiber cable to simultaneously transmit several live signals**. They are especially practical in systems with an insufficient number of cables (relative to the number of cameras).

There are a few different types of fiber multiplexers. The simplest and most affordable multiplexing for fiber optics transmission is by use of **wavelength division multiplexing** (WDM) couplers. These are couplers that transmit optical signals from two or more sources, operating at different wavelengths,

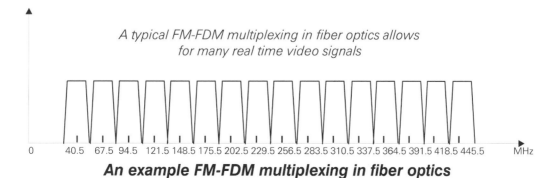

A typical FM-FDM multiplexing in fiber optics allows for many real time video signals

0   40.5 67.5 94.5 121.5 148.5 175.5 202.5 229.5 256.5 283.5 310.5 337.5 364.5 391.5 418.5 445.5   MHz

An example FM-FDM multiplexing in fiber optics

over the same fiber. This is possible since **light rays of different wavelengths do not interfere with each other**. Thus, the capacity of the fiber cable can be increased and if necessary, bidirectional operation over a single fiber can be achieved.

Frequency-modulated frequency division multiplexing (FM-FDM) is a reasonably economical design with acceptable immunity to noise and distortions, good linearity and moderately complex circuitry. There are a few brands on the market that produce FM-FDM multiplexers for CCTV applications. They are made with 4, 8 or 16 channels.

Amplitude vestigial sideband modulation, frequency division multiplexing (AVSB-FDM) is another design, perhaps too expensive for CCTV, but very attractive for CATV, where with high-quality optoelectronics up to 80 channels per fiber are possible.

Fully digital **pulse code modulation, time division multiplexing** (PCM-TDM) is another expensive type of multiplexing, but of digitized signals, which may become attractive as digital video gets more accepted in CCTV.

Combinations of these methods are also possible.

In CCTV we would most often use the FM-FDM for more signals over a single fiber. The WDM type of multiplexing is particularly useful for PTZ, or keyboard control with matrix switchers. Video signals are sent via separate fibers (one fiber per camera), but only one fiber uses WDM to send control data in the opposite direction.

Even though the fiber optics multiplexing is becoming more affordable it should be noted that in the planning stage of fiber installation it is still recommended that at least one spare fiber is run in addition to the one intended for use.

Fiber optics cables

The fiber optics itself is very small in size. The external diameter, as used in CCTV and security in general, is only 125 μm (1 μm = 10^{-6} m). Fiberglass, as a material, is relatively strong, but can easily be broken when bent to below a certain minimum radius. Therefore, the aim of the cabling is to provide adequate mechanical protection and impact and crush resistance to preserve minimum bending radius as well as to provide easy handling for installation and service and to ensure that the transmission properties remain stable throughout the life of the system.

The overall design may vary greatly and depends on the

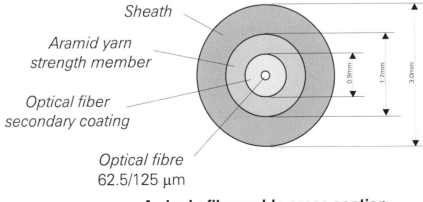

A single-fiber cable cross section

application (underwater, underground, in the air, in conduit), the number of channels required and similar. Invariably, it features some form of tensile strength member and a tough outer sheath to provide the necessary mechanical and environmental protection.

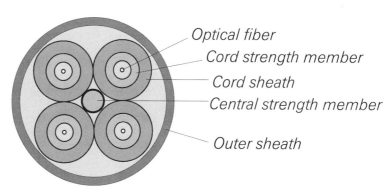

A four-fiber cable with a strength member

Fiber optics cables have various designs, like a simple single fiber, loose tube (fiber inserted into a tube), slotted core (or open channel), ribbon, tight buffer.

We will discuss a few that are the most commonly used in CCTV.

Single-fiber and dual-fiber cables usually employ a fibrous strength member (aramid yarn) laid around the secondary coated fiber. This is further protected by a plastic outer sheath.

Multi-fiber cables are made in a variety of configurations.

The simplest involves grouping a number of single fiber cables with a central strength member within the outer jacket. The central strength member can be high tensile steel wire, or a fiberglass reinforced plastic rod. Cables with this design are available with two to twelve or more communication fibers. When the plastic rod is applied to the central strength member, it becomes a **metal-free** optical fiber cable. Constructed entirely from polymeric material and glass, these cables are intended for use in installations within buildings. They are suitable for many applications including CCTV, security, computer links, instrumentation, etc. These heavy-duty cables are made extremely rugged to facilitate pulling through ducts.

Loose tube cables are designed as a good alternative to the single core and slotted cables. The optical fibers are protected by water-blocking gel-filled polyester tubes. This type of multi-fiber cable is designed for direct burial or duct installation in long-haul applications. It can be air pressurized or gel-filled for waterblocking.

There are some other configurations manufactured with **slotted polyethylene core profiles** to accommodate larger

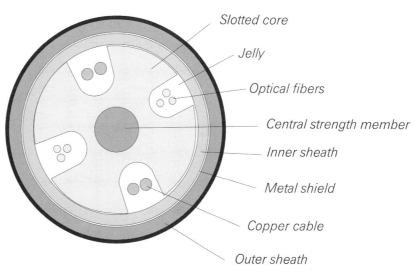

Composite optic/metallic cable

numbers of fibers. This type is also designed for direct burial or duct installation in long-haul applications. It can be air pressurized or gel filled for water blocking.

Finally, another type of cable is the **composite optic/metallic** cable. These cables are made up of a combination of optical fibers and insulated copper wire and are designed for both indoor and

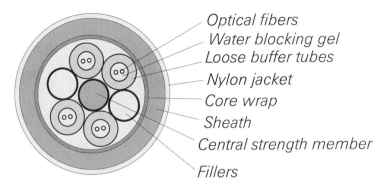

A typical fiber cable with a strength member and fillers

outdoor use. These cables can be fully filled with a water-blocking compound to protect the fibers from moisture in underground installations, for example.

Since the fiber cable is much lighter than other cables, the installations are generally easier compared to an electrical cable of the same diameter.

The protection they have will allow fiber cables to be treated in much the same way as electrical cables. However, care should be taken to ensure that the manufacturer's **recommended maximum tensile and crushing force** are not exceeded.

Within a given optical cable, tension is carried by the strength members, usually fiber-reinforced plastic, steel, kevlar or a combination, that protect the comparatively fragile glass fibers. If the cable tension exceeds the manufacturer's ratings, permanent damage to the fibers can result.

The rating to be observed, as far as installation tension is concerned, is the **maximum installation tension**, expressed in Newtons or kilo-Newtons (N or kN). A typical cable has a tension rating of around 1000 N (1 kN). To get an idea of what a Newton feels like, consider that 9.8 N of tension is created on a cable hanging vertically and supporting a mass of 1 kg. In addition, manufacturers sometimes specify a maximum long-term tension. This is typically less than half of the maximum installation tension.

As with coaxial cables, optical fiber cables must not be bent to a tighter curve than their rated **minimum bending radius**. In this case, the reason is not the electrical impedance change, but rather **preventing the fiber from breaking and preserving the total angle of reflection**. The minimum bending radius varies greatly for various cable constructions and may even be specified at different values, depending on the presence of various levels of tension in the cable. Exceeding the bending radius specification will place undue stress on the fibers and may even damage the stiff strength members.

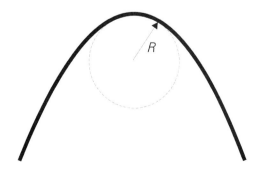

Minimum bending radius

Whenever a cable is being handled or installed, it is most important to keep the curves as smooth as possible.

Often, during an installation, the cable is subject to crush stresses such as being walked on or, even worse, driven over.

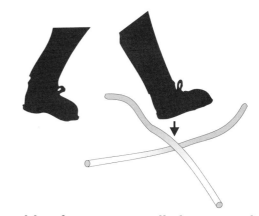

Although great care should be taken to avoid such stresses, the cable is able to absorb such forces up to its rated **crush resistance** value. Crush resistance is expressed in N/m or kN/m of cable length. For example, a cable with a specified crush resistance of 10 kN/m can withstand a load of 1000 kg spread across

Crushing force can easily be exceeded

a full 1 m of cable length (10 Newtons is approximately the force that results from a 1 kg mass). If we consider a size 9 boot (European 42) to be 100 mm wide, then the cable will support a construction worker who weighs 100 kg standing on one foot squarely on the cable. However, a vehicle driving over this cable may exceed the crush resistance spec and probably damage the cable.

Be careful if a cable has one loop crossing over another, because then the forces on the cable due to, say, a footstep right on the crossover will be **greatly magnified because of the smaller contact area**. Likewise in a crowded duct, a cable can be crushed at localized stress points even though the weight on it may not seem excessive.

Optical cable is usually wound onto wooden drums with some form of heavy plastic protective layer or wooden cleats around the circumference of the drums. When handling a cable drum, due consideration should be given to the mass of the drum. The most vulnerable parts of a cable drum are the outer layers of the cable. This is especially the case when the cable drums are vertically interleaved with each other. Then damage due to local crushing should be of concern. To alleviate such problems, the drums should be stacked either horizontally or, if vertically, with their rims touching. Do not allow the drums to become interlocked. Also, when lifting drums, with a forklift, for example, do not apply force to the cable surface. Instead, lift at the rims or through the center axis.

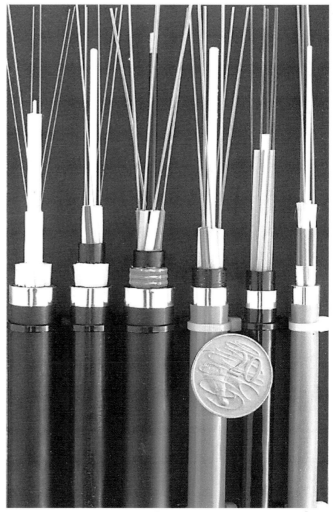

Various types of multi-fiber cables

Installation techniques

Prior to installation, the cable drums should be checked for any sign of damage or mishandling. The outer layer of a cable should be carefully examined to reveal any signs of scratching or denting. Should a drum be suspected of having incurred damage, then it should be marked and put aside. For shorter lengths (i.e., <2 km) a simple continuity check can be made of the whole fiber using a penlight as a light source. A fiber cable, even though used with infrared wavelengths, transmits normal light just as well. This is useful in finding out if there are serious breaks in the cable. Continuity of the fiber can be checked by using a penlight.

The following precautions and techniques are very similar to what was said earlier for coaxial cable installations, but since it is very important we will go through it again.

Before cable laying commences, the route should be inspected for possible problems such as feed-through, sharp corners, clogged ducts and the like. Once a viable route has been established, the cable lengths must be arranged so that should any splices occur, they will do so at accessible positions.

At the location of a splice it is important to leave an adequate overlap of the cables so that sufficient material is available for the splicing operation. Generally, the overlap required is about 5 m when the splice is of the in-line type. A length of about 2.5 m is required where the cable leaves the duct and is spliced.

Note that whenever a cable end is exposed it must be fitted with a watertight end cap. Any loose cable should be placed to avoid bending stress or damage from passing traffic. At either end of the cable run, special lengths are often left depending on the configuration planned.

Foremost consideration, when burying a cable, is the prevention of damage due to excessive local points loading. Such loading occurs when backfill material is poured onto or an uneven trench profile digs into the cable, thus either puncturing the outer sheath or locally crushing the cable. The damage may become immediately obvious or it may take some time to show itself. Whichever, the cost of digging up the cable and repairing it makes the expenditure of extra effort during laying well worthwhile.

When laying cables in trenches, a number of precautions must be taken to avoid damage to the cable or a reduction in cable life expectancy.

The main protection against cable damage is laying the cable on a bed of sand approximately 50-150 mm deep and backfilling with another 50-150 mm of sand. Due care needs to be taken in the digging of the trench so that the bottom of the trench is fairly even and free of protrusions. Likewise, when backfilling, do not allow rocky soil to fall onto the sand because it may put a rock through the cable.

Trench depth is dependent upon the type of ground being traversed as well as the load that is expected to be applied to the ground above the cable. A cable in solid rock may need a trench of only 300 mm or so, whereas a trench crossing a road in soft soil should be taken down to about 1 m. A general-purpose trench in undemanding situations, should be 400-600 mm deep with 100-300 mm total sand bedding.

The most straightforward technique is to lay the cable directly from the drum into a trench or onto a cable tray. For very long cable runs, the drum is supported on a vehicle and allowed to turn freely on its axis, or it can be held and rested on a metal axis. As the vehicle (or person) advances, the cable is wound off the drum straight to its resting place. Avoid excessive speed and ensure that the cable can be temporarily tied down at regular intervals prior to its final securing.

Placing an optical cable on a cable tray is not particularly different from doing so with conventional cables of a similar diameter. The main points to observe are, again, minimum bending radius and crush resistance.

The minimum bending radius must be observed even when the cable tray does not facilitate this. The tendency to keep it neat and bend the optical cable to match other cables on the tray must be avoided.

Crush loading on cable trays can become a critical factor, where the optical cable is led across a sharp protrusion or crossed over another cable. The optical cable can then be heavily loaded by further cables being placed on top of it or personnel walking on the tray. Keep the cable as flat as possible and avoid local stress points.

The pulling of optical cables through ducts is no different from conventional cabling. At all times use only the amount of force required but stay below the manufacturer's ratings.

The types of hauling eyes and cable clamps normally used are generally satisfactory, but remember that the strength members, not the outer sheath, must take the load.

If a particular duct requires a lubricant, then it is best to obtain a recommendation from the cable manufacturer. Talcum powder and bean bag polystyrene beans can also be quite useful in reducing friction.

In some conditions the cable may already be terminated with connectors. These must be heavily protected while drawing the cable. The connectors themselves must not be damaged or contaminated and the cable must not experience any undue stress around the connectors or their protective sheathing.

Once the cable is installed it is often necessary to tie it down. On a cable tray, the cable can be held down simply with nylon ties. Take particular care to anchor the cable runs in areas of likely creep. On structures that are unsuited to cable ties, some form of saddle clamp is recommended. Care is required in the choice and use of such devices so that the cable crush resistance is not exceeded and that the outer jacket is not punctured by sharp edges. Clips with molded plastic protective layers are preferred and only one clip should be used for each cable. Between the secured points of a cable it is wise to allow a little slack rather than to leave a tightly stretched length that may respond poorly to temperature variations or vibration.

Fiber optics receiver modules

If the cable is in some way damaged during installation, then leave enough extra cable length around the damaged area so that an additional splice can be inserted.

The conclusion is that **installation of fiber cables is not greatly different from conventional cables, and provided a few basic concepts are observed, the installation should be trouble free.**

Fiber-optic link analysis

Now that we have learned the individual components of a fiber optics system, i.e., the sources, cables, detectors and installation techniques, we may use this in a complete system. But before the installation, we first have to do a link analysis, which shows how much signal loss or gain occurs in each stage of the system. This type of analysis can be done with other transmission media, but it is especially important with fiber optics because the power levels we are handling are very small. They are sufficient to go over many kilometers, but can easily be lost if we don't take care of the microscopic connections and couplings.

The goal of the link analysis is to determine the signal strength at each point in the overall system and to calculate if the power at the receiver (the detector) are sufficient for acceptable performance. If it is not, each stage is examined and some are upgraded (usually to a higher cost), or guaranteed performance specifications (distance, speed, errors) are reduced.

For fiber optics systems, the link analysis should also include unavoidable variations in performance that occur with temperature as a result of component aging and from manufacturing tolerance differences between two nearly identical devices. In this respect, fiber optics systems need more careful study than all-electronic systems as there is greater device-to-device variation, together with larger performance changes due to time and temperature.

As a practical example, the diagram on the next page shows a basic point-by-point fiber optics system, which consists of an electrical data input signal, a source driver, an optical source, a 1-km optical fiber with realistic maximum attenuation of 4 dB/km, an optical detector and the receiver electronics.

We have assumed that the system is handling digital signals, as is the case with PTZ control, but the logic will be very similar when analog signal budgeting is calculated.

The calculation begins with the optical output power of the source (–12 dBm in this case) and ends with the power that is seen by the detector.

This analysis looks at each stage in the system and shows both the best and worst case power loss (or gain) for each link as a result of various factors, such as coupling losses, path losses, normal parts tolerance (best and worst for a specific model), temperature and time.

The analysis also allows for an additional 5-dB signal loss that will occur if any repairs or splices are made over the life of the system.

The conclusion of the example is that the received optical power, for a signal to be recognized, can be anywhere between +7 dB (in the best case) and –23 dB (in the worst case) relative to the nominal source value. Technically, +7 dB would mean amplification, which is not really what we have, but rather it refers to the possible tolerance variations of the components. Therefore, the receiving detector must handle a dynamic range of optical signals from –5 dBm (–12 dBm + 7 dB = –5 dBm) to –35 dBm (–12 dBm – 23 dB = –35 dBm), representing a binary 1. Of course, when the source is dark (no light, which means binary 0), the received signal is also virtually zero (except for the system noise).

It is understandable that a digital signal can go further in distance, using the same electronics and fiber cable, than an analog video signal, simply because of the big error margins digital signals have. Nevertheless, a similar analysis can be performed with analog signals. If, however, we are not prepared

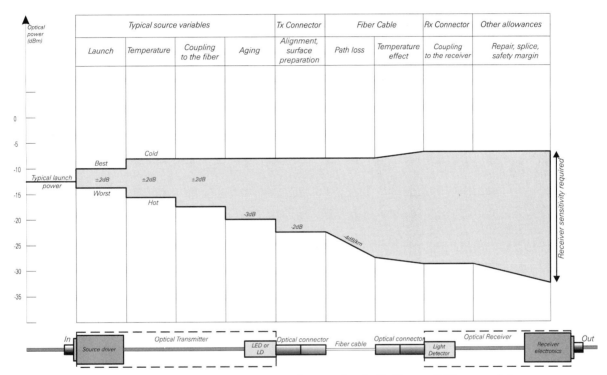

Link analysis is very important prior to installation of fiber cables

or don't know how to, we can still get an answer to the basic question Will it work? Unfortunately, the answer can only be obtained once the fiber is installed. To do so we need an instrument that measures cable continuity as well as attenuation. This is the optical time domain reflectometer.

OTDR

An **optical time domain reflectometer** (OTDR) is an instrument that can test a fiber cable after it has been installed, to determine the eventual breaks, attenuation and quality of termination.

The OTDR sends a light pulse into one end of the optical fiber and detects the returned light energy versus time, which corresponds directly to the distance of light travelled.

It requires connection to only one end of the cable and it actually shows the obvious discontinuity in the optical path, such as splices, breaks and connectors.

It uses the physical phenomenon known as **Rayleigh backscattering**, which occurs within the fiber, to show the signal attenuation along the fiber's length. As a light wave travels through the fiber, a very small amount of incident light in the cable is reflected and refracted back to the source by the atomic structure and impurities within the optical fiber. This is then measured and shown visually on a screen and/or printed out on a piece of paper as evidence of the particular installation. Eventual breaks in a fiber cable are found most easily with an OTDR. Being an expensive instrument, an OTDR is usually hired for a fiber optics installation evaluation or used by the specialized people that terminate the cable.

Photo courtesy of 3M

An Optical Time Domain Reflectometer

10. Auxiliary Equipment in CCTV

There are many items in CCTV that can be classified as auxiliaries. Some of them are simple to understand and use; others are very sophisticated and complex. We'll start from the very popular moving mechanism, usually called **pan and tilt head**.

Pan and tilt heads

When quoting or designing a CCTV system, the first question to ask is how many and what type of cameras: fixed or pan and tilt?

Fixed cameras, as the name suggests, are cameras installed on fixed brackets, using fixed focal length lenses and looking in the one direction without change.

The alternative to fixed are moving (or pan and tilt) cameras. They are placed on some kind of moving platform, usually employing a zoom lens, so the whole set can pan and tilt in virtually all directions and can be zoomed and focused at various distances.

In CCTV terminology, this type of camera is usually referred to as a "**PTZ camera.**" Perhaps a more appropriate term would be "PTZF camera," referring to Pan/Tilt/Zoom/Focus, or even more precisely in the last few years, a "PTZFI" for an additional iris control. "PTZ camera" is, however, more popularly accepted, and we will use the same abbreviation for a camera that, apart from pan, tilt and zoom functions, might have focus or even iris remote control.

A typical outdoor pan/tilt head

A typical P/T head, as shown on the picture, has a side platform for the load (a camera with a zoom lens in a housing). There are pan and tilt heads that have an overhead platform instead. The difference between the two is the load rating that each can have, which, depends on the load's center of gravity. This center is lower for side platform pan and tilt heads, meaning of the two types of heads, with the same size motors and torque, the side platform has a better load rating. This should not be taken as a conclusion that the overhead platform P/T heads are of inferior quality, but it is only an observation of the load rating, which in the last few years is not as critical because camera and lens sizes, together with housings, are getting smaller.

On the basis of the application, there are two major subgroups of P/T heads:

- Outdoor and

- Indoor.

Outdoor P/T heads fall into one of the three categories:

- Heavy duty (for loads of over 35 kg),

- Medium duty (for loads between 10 and 35 kg) and

- Light duty (for loads of up to 10 kg).

Custom-made PT bracket

With the recent camera size and weight reductions, together with the miniaturization of zoom lenses and housings, it is very unlikely that you will need a heavy-duty P/T head these days. A medium-duty load rating will suffice in the majority of applications.

The outdoor P/T heads are weatherproof, heavier and more robust. The reason for this is that they need to carry heavier housings and quite often additional devices such as wash/wipe assemblies and/or infrared lights.

Indoor P/T heads, as the name suggests, should only be used in premises protected from external elements, especially rain, wind and snow. Indoor P/T heads are usually smaller and lighter and in most cases they fall into the light-duty load category, i.e., they can handle loads of no more than a few kilograms. Because of this, indoor pan and tilt heads are often made of plastic molding and have a more aesthetic appearance than the outdoor ones.

An outdoor PTZ camera and a PTZ driver on a pole

In most cases, a typical P/T head is driven by 24 V AC synchronous motors. Mains voltage P/T heads are also available (220/240 V AC or 110 V AC), but the 24 V AC is more popular because of the safety factor (voltages less than 50 V AC are not fatal to the human body) and it is more universal, irrespective of whether you are working on a European, American or Australian CCTV system. Most manufacturers have a 24 V AC version of all P/T site drivers.

Pan and tilt domes

Other divisions of pan and tilt heads, on the basis of physical appearance, are also possible. In the last few years, **pan and tilt domes** have become more popular. They work in the same way as the heads, only **inside the domes they usually have both, the moving mechanism (P/T head) and the control electronics**. They are usually enclosed in a transparent or semitransparent dome, so they make an acceptable appearance in aesthetically demanding interiors or exteriors. Again, thanks to camera and lens size reductions, P/T domes are getting smaller in diameter. A few years ago, pan and tilt domes up to 1 m in diameter were not rare, while today most of them are between 300 and 400 mm.

One of the biggest problems with P/T domes is the optical precision of the dome. It is very hard to get no distortions at all, especially with heat-blown domes. Much better precision is achieved with injection

Photo courtesy of Pelco

A typical PTZ dome with built-in camera, auto focus zoom lens, pan/tilt mechanism and site driver

molded domes, which are more expensive. Also, thicker domes cause more distortion, especially when the lens is zooming. So the best optical quality is achieved with thin and injection moulded domes.

A lot of manufacturers, instead of going to the trouble of producing optically non-distorting domes, concentrate the optical precision on a thin vertical strip through which the camera can see and freely tilt up and down. The panning movement revolves the camera and the dome. Although a clever solution, this can be mechanically troublesome and a limiting factor for faster movements.

Let's also mention that domes can be transparent or neutral color tinted. Transparent domes usually have an inner mask, with an optical slot in front of the lens, while the rest of the mask is a non-transparent

**An outdoor
pan/tilt dome**

PTZ dome camera in Sydney

black plastic. By keeping the interior dark (black zoom lenses and camera bodies), they offer a very discrete and concealed surveillance. Very often it is impossible to judge where the camera is pointing, which is one of the very important features of dome cameras.

Tinted domes usually have no mask and so the whole dome is transparent but tinted. It is important in such cases to know the F-stop attenuation of the tinting to compensate for the light. A typical attenuation is around one F-stop, which means 50% light attenuation. With today's CCD cameras this does not present any threat to the picture quality. The camera and zoom lens colors are more critical with this type of dome, so if they appear too obtrusive from the outside a careful black matt spray can minimize this. Utmost care should be taken, though, to protect the lens, CCD chip and connectors from the paint.

Preset positioning P/T heads

Finally, another subgroup of P/T heads look the same as all the others but are fitted with **preset potentiometers**. They are usually referred to as **P/T heads with PP pots**.

The potentiometers are built in the head itself, mechanically coupled with each of the motors. Their value is typically 1 kΩ or 5 kΩ and they are connected to the site driver electronics (discussed in the next chapter). A low voltage (typically 5 V DC) is applied across the pots and the site driver electronics read the voltage drop over its center tap, depending on the pan or tilt position, thus allowing the site driver to remember the particular position, which is later recalled by either manual command or automatic alarm response.

Basically, when a site driver gets an instruction to go to a preset position, it forces the pan and tilt motors to move (the same applies to zoom and focus) until the preset potentiometers reach the preset value. So, if a certain door is protected, for example, by using a simple reed switch we can force a camera to automatically turn in that direction, zooming and focusing on the previously stored view of the door.

The number of preset positions a PTZ site can store depends on the design itself, but the most common numbers are 8, 10, 16 or 32.

A very important question is "How precisely can the preset positions be repeatedly recalled?" This is defined by the mechanics, electronics and by the software and hardware design. The precision of preset positioning is especially important with the very fast pan and tilt units. An error of only a couple of degrees may not be noticed when a zoom lens is fully zoomed out, but it will make a big difference when it is fully zoomed in.

When ordering a pan and tilt head, you must specify that you want preset positioning. A pan and tilthead with preset potentiometers looks the same as an ordinary non-preset P/T head, because the pots are fitted inside the unit.

Almost all PTZ domes of the newer design have preset positioning

PTZ Site drivers

A very easy way of controlling a 24 V AC pan and tilt head is by simply applying 24 V to one of the motors. This means pan and tilt control can be achieved by having voltage applied to a hard-wired connection (for each of the four movement directions) relative to a common wire. So, **a total of five wires will give us full control over a typical pan and tilt head. For zoom and focus control as well, another three wires are required** (one for zoom, positive and

Photo courtesy of Pelco

A hard-wired PTZ controller

negative voltage, one for focus and one common). This gives us **a total of eight wires that would be required for a so-called Hard-wired PTZ controller.** They are the cheapest way of controlling single PTZ camera assemblies but are impractical for long distance control of over a couple of hundred meters.

In the majority of CCTV systems, though, we use digital control, which only requires a twisted pair cable via which a matrix switcher can talk to a number of PTZ devices at the same time. These devices are often called **PTZ site drivers**, **PTZ decoders** or **PTZ receiver drivers**. They are electronic boxes (discussed with video matrix switchers) that receive and decode the instructions of the control keyboard for the camera's movements: pan, tilt, zoom and focus (and sometimes iris as well).

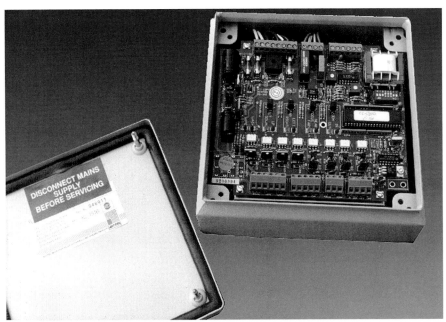

A typical PTZ site driver (receiver)

As mentioned earlier, **there is unfortunately no standard among manufacturers of the control encoding schemes and protocols, which means the PTZ site driver of one manufacturer cannot be used with a matrix switcher of another.**

Depending on the site driver design, other functions might also be controllable, such as wash and wipe, turning auxiliary devices on and off and similar. PTZ drivers can also deliver power for the camera, either 12 V DC or 24 V AC.

The P/T heads' movement speed, when driven by 24 V AC synchronous motors (which is most often the case), depends on the mains frequency, the load on the head and the gearing mechanism. Typical panning speeds are 9°/s and tilting 6°/s. This is closely related to the torque required to move a certain load, which in most cases exceeds 5 kg (that is: camera + zoom lens + housing). Some designs can reach a faster speed of around 15°/s pan because of camera/lens weight reductions and different gear ratios. **Most AC-driven P/T heads, which are driven by synchronous motors, have fixed speeds** because they depend on the mains frequency.

There are some advanced AC pan and tilt head site drivers where an artificial frequency, lower and higher than the mains', is produced for better control of the heads. A slower speed is used for finer control (when the zoom lens is fully zoomed in) and a faster speed for quicker response to emergency situations. The control keyboard determines the speed it should apply on the basis of the amount of time the joystick is kept pressed in any direction.

Even faster speeds can be achieved with DC-driven stepper motors and specially designed PTZ site

PTZ site drivers are integrated into most PTZ domes

drivers. Over the last few years, P/T heads (more so, P/T domes) have become much faster, exceeding 100°/s.

Producing such fast P/T assemblies brings a few problems to attention: the camera moves so quickly that an appropriate manual control is impossible, or at least impractical and the mechanical construction and durability are even more critical because of increased forces of inertia. When such a speed is magnified by the zoom lens magnification factor, we actually see already fast movement even faster.

So, a novel approach to the PTZ control is now required. Such solutions can be seen in some advanced designs, achieving speeds of over 300°/s with highly accurate movement. This is achieved by combining great electronic and mechanical precision. Details like reducing the pan and tilt speed when the lens is zoomed in and increasing it when the lens is zoomed out, or having the very fast preset position speed of 300°/s drop down to a manageable 45°/s when manual control is required, make the difference between a fast and a fast-and-user-friendly system.

Larger pan/tilt domes accommodate a separate camera/lens combination

A preset operation is only possible with a PTZ site driver equipped with PP electronics. Clearly, the P/T head and the zoom lens should both have preset potentiometers built in.

The number of wires required between the site driver and the PTZ head is as follows: 5 wires are required for the basic pan and tilt functions as described earlier (pan left, pan right, tilt up, tilt down and common), 4 wires for pan and tilt preset positioning (positive pot supply, negative pot supply, pan feedback and tilt feedback), 3 wires for the zoom and focus functions (sometimes 4 are required, depending on the zoom lens) and 4 wires for the zoom and focus preset positioning. This makes a **total of 16 wires**. The thickness of the preset wires and the zoom and focus wires is not critical as we have very low current for these functions, but the pan and tilt wires need to be considered carefully because they depend on the pan and tilt motors' requirements.

Let's not forget to mention that a PTZ site driver is usually installed next to the camera. There are two main reasons for this: practicality (long runs of a 16-core

Ceiling-mount dome camera

cable are not needed) and maintenance (one needs to see what the camera P/T head does when certain instructions are sent to the site driver).

However, if the situation demands, the site driver can be up to a couple of hundred meters away from the camera itself.

Camera housings

In order to protect the cameras from environmental influences and/or conceal their viewing direction, we use camera housings.

Camera housings can be very simple and straightforward to install and use, but equally they can affect the picture quality and camera lifetime if they are not well protected from rain, snow, dust and wind or if they are of poor quality.

They are available in all shapes and sizes, depending on the camera application and length. Earlier, tube cameras and zoom lenses were much bigger, calling for housings of as much as 1 m in length and over 10 kg in weight. Nowadays, CCD cameras are getting smaller and so are zoom lenses. As a consequence, housings are becoming smaller too.

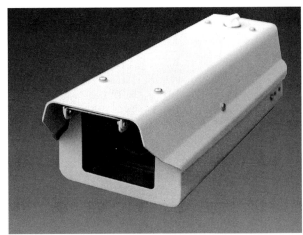

A typical outdoor camera housing

A lot of attention in the last few years has been paid to the aesthetics and functionality of the housings, like easy access for maintenance, concealed cable entries and similar.

With camera size reductions, these days tinted domes are used instead of housings, offering much better blending with the interior and exterior.

*Corner-mount
vandal-resistant housing*

The glass of a housing is often considered as unimportant, but optical distortions and certain spectral attenuation might be present if the glass is unsuitable. Another very important factor is the toughness of the glass for camera protection in demanding environments. The optical precision and uniformity are even more critical when domes are used because the optical precision and glass (plastic) distortions are more apparent. Tinted domes are very often used to conceal the camera's viewing direction. For tinted domes, light attenuation has to be taken into account. This is usually in the range of one F-stop, which is equal to half the light without the dome.

A lot of housings have provision for heaters and fans. Heaters might be required in areas where a lot of moisture, ice or snow is expected. Usually about 10 W of electrical energy is sufficient to produce enough heat for a standard housing interior. The heaters can work on 12 V DC, 24 V AC, or even mains voltage. Check with the supplier before connecting. No damage will occur if a 240 V (or even 110 V) heater is connected to 24 V (however, sufficient heat will not be produced), but the opposite is not recommended. Also, avoid primitive improvisations without any calculations, such as, for example, connecting two 110 V heaters in series to replace a single 240 V heater (110 + 110 = 220). The little bit of difference (240 V instead of 220 V) is enough to produce excessive heat and cause a quicker burning of the heater and even possibly cause a fire.

In case a heater is required for an already installed housing, it is relatively easy to simulate one with a resistor of 30~50 Ω and 20 W power rating (for 24 V AC). As a circuit break element, an N/C thermostat, with a low on temperature, can be used. Don't forget, though, that the camera, having a power rating of a couple of watts, acts as a heater and if the housing is small and well sealed, this should create sufficient heat to dry the moisture inside. For snowy areas, however, a proper heater is needed, mounted close to the housing glass.

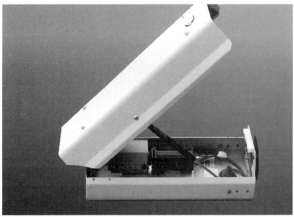

Access to the camera is an important consideration for the type of housing

Fans should be used in areas with very high temperatures and sometimes they can be combined with heaters. The voltage required for the fan to work can also be DC or AC, but be sure to use good quality fans, as most of the DC fans will sooner or later produce sparks from the brushes when rotating, which will interfere with the video signal.

So heaters and fans are an extra obligation, but if you have to have them, make sure you provide them with the correct and sufficient power. They are usually set to work automatically with a rise or fall in temperature, i.e., there is no need for manual control.

Photo courtesy of Pelco

Special liquid-cooled housing for up to 1300°C

Special housings are required if a **wash and wipe** assembly is to be added to the PTZ camera. They are special because of the matching required between the wipe mechanism and the housing window. It should be pointed out that when the wash/wipe assembly is used, the PTZ driver needs to have output controls for these functions as well. They might be 24 V, 220~240 V or 110 V AC. Another responsibility when using washers is to make sure that the washer bottle is always filled with a sufficient amount of clean water.

Housings and boxes (such as PTZ site drivers) that are exposed to environmental influences are rated

Meaning of IP ratings

IP	First number: *Protection against solid objects*	IP	Second number: *Protection against liquids*	IP	Third number: *Protection against mechanical impacts*
0	No protection of the electrical equipment	0	No protection of the electrical equipment	0	No protection of the electrical equipment
1	Protected against solid objects up to 50mm, e.g., accidental touch by hands	1	Protected against vertical falling drops of water	1	15cm 150g Impact 0.225 Joules
2	Protected against solid objects over to 12mm, e.g., fingers	2	Protected against direct sprays of water up to 15° from the vertical	2	15cm 250g Impact 0.375 Joules
3	Protected against solid objects over 2.5mm (tools, wires)	3	Protected against direct sprays of water up to 60° from the vertical	3	20cm 250g Impact 0.50 Joules
4	Protected against solid objects over 1mm (tools, wires, small wires)	4	Protected against water sprayed from all directions – limited ingress permitted	4	N / U
5	Protected against dust-limited ingress (no harmful deposit)	5	Protected against low pressure jets of water from all directions – limited ingress permitted.	5	40cm 500g Impact 2 Joules
6	Totally protected against dust	6	Protected against strong jets of water, e.g., for use on shipdecks – limited ingress permitted	6	N / U
		7	15cm - 1m Protected against the effects of immersion between 15cm and 1m	7	40cm 1500g Impact 6 Joules
		8	Protected against long periods of immersion under pressure	8	N / U
				9	40cm 5kg Impact 20 Joules

IP Ratings for protection from dust, water and impact of electrical equipment for voltages of up to 1000 V AC and 1200 V DC, as per RS data.

with the IP numbers. These numbers indicate to what degree of shock, dust and water aggression the box is resistant.

Most camera housings are well protected from the environment, but in special system designs, even better protection might be required. **Vandal-proof housings** are required in systems where human or vehicle intervention is predicted, so a special, toughened (usually lexan) glass needs to be used, together with special locking screws. Tamper switches may also be added for extra security. In cases like that, the tamper alarm has to come back to the control center, usually through the PTZ driver, providing it has such a facility.

And last, **bullet-proof**, **explosion-proof** and **underwater housings** are also available, but they are very rare, specially built and very expensive. Because of this, we will not dedicate any space to them in this book, but should you need more details contact your local supplier.

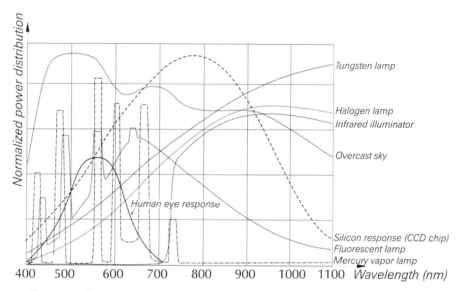

Spectral energy dissipation of various light sources

Lighting in CCTV

Most of the CCTV systems with outdoor cameras use both day and night light sources for better viewing. Systems for indoor applications use, obviously, indoor (artificial) light sources, although some may mix with daylight, like in situations where sunlight penetrates through a window.

The sun is our daylight source, and as mentioned earlier, the light intensity can vary from as low as 100 lx at sunset to 100,000 lx at noon. The color temperature of sunlight can also vary, depending on the sun's altitude and the atmospheric conditions, like clouds, rain, fog, etc. This might not be critical for B/W cameras, but a color system will reflect these variations.

Artificial light sources fall into three main groups, according to their spectral power content:

1. The first group consists of sources that emit **radiation by incandescence**, like candles, tungsten electric lamps, halogen lamps and similar.

2. The second group consists of sources that emit radiant energy as a result of an **electrical discharge through a gas or vapor**, such as neon lamps and sodium and mercury vapor lamps.

3. The third group consists of **fluorescent tubes**, in which a gas discharge emits visible or ultraviolet radiation within the tube and this causes phosphors on the inside surface of the tube to glow with their own spectrum.

The light sources of the first group produce a **smooth and continuous light spectrum** as per the Max Planck formula, similar to the black body radiation law. These light sources are very suitable for B/W cameras because of the similarity in the spectrums, especially on the left side of the CCD chip spectral response.

The second group of light sources produce almost discrete components of particular wavelengths, depending on the gas type.

The third group has a more continuous spectrum than the second one, but it still has components of significant levels (at particular wavelengths only), again, depending on the type of gas and phosphor used.

The last two groups are very tricky for color cameras. Special attention should be paid to the color temperature and white balance capability of the cameras used with such lights.

Infrared lights

In situations where events need to be monitored at night, B/W cameras can be used in conjunction with infrared illuminator(s). Infrared light is used because B/W CCD cameras have very good sensitivity in and near the infrared region. These are the wavelengths longer than 700 nm. The human eye can see, as mentioned at the beginning of this book, up to 780 nm, with the sensitivity above 700 nm being very weak, so in general we say that the human eye only sees up to 700 nm.

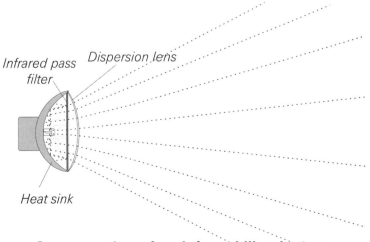

Cross section of an infrared illuminator

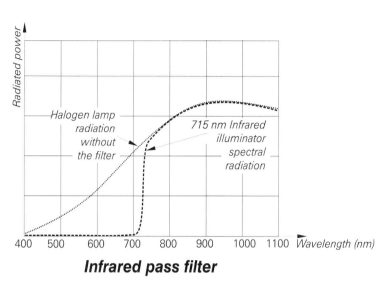

Infrared pass filter

Monochrome CCD chips see better in the infrared portion of the spectrum than the human eye. The reason for this is the nature of the photo effect itself (longer wavelength photons penetrate the CCD structure more deeply). The infrared response is especially high with B/W CCD chips without an infrared cut filter.

A few infrared light wavelengths are common to CCTV infrared viewing. Which one is to be used and in what case depends first on the camera's spectral sensitivity (various chip manufacturers have different spectral sensitivity chips) and, second, on the purpose of the system.

The two typical infrared wavelengths used with **halogen lamp illuminators** are: one starting from around 715 nm and the other from around 830 nm.

If the idea is to have infrared lights that will be visible to the public, the 715-nm wavelength is the better choice. If night-time hidden surveillance is wanted, the 830-nm wavelength (which is invisible to the human eye) should be used.

The halogen lamp infrareds come in two versions: 300 W and 500 W. The principle of operation is very simple: a halogen lamp produces light (with a similar spectrum as the black body radiation), which then goes through an **optical high pass filter**, blocking the wavelengths shorter than 715 nm (or 830 nm). This is why we say wavelengths **starting** from 715 nm or **starting** from 830 nm. The infrared radiation is **not one frequency only but a continuous spectrum starting from the nominated wavelength.**

The energy contained in the wavelengths that do not pass the filter is reflected back and accumulated inside the infrared illuminator. There are heat sinks on the IR light itself that help cool down the unit, but still, the biggest reason for the short MTBF (1000~2000 hr) of the halogen lamp is the excessive heat trapped inside the IR light.

The same description applies to the 830-nm illuminators, only in this case we have infrared frequencies invisible to the human eye (as mentioned earlier, 715 nm is still visible to many).

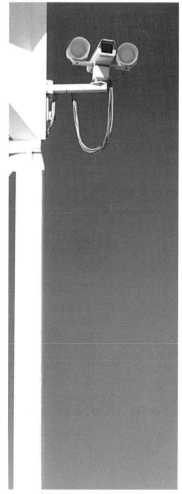

**IR illuminators
usually go in pairs**

There is a certain danger in such infrared illuminators, especially for the installers and maintenance people. The reason for this is that the human eye's iris stays open since it doesn't see any light, and blindness could result. This would happen only when very close to the illuminator at night, which is when the human eye's iris is fully opened.

The IR photo cell, being active at night, turns the light on.

The best way to check that the IR works is to feel the temperature radiation with your hand, human skin senses heat very well. Remember, heat is nothing else but infrared radiation.

A solid state IR

The infrared illuminators are mains operated and photo cells are used to turn them on when daylight falls below a certain level.

Both types of halogen infrared illuminators mentioned come with various types of dispersion lenses and it is desirable to know what angle of coverage is best for a situation. If the infrared beam is concentrated to a narrow angle, the camera can see farther, provided a corresponding narrow angle lens is used (or a zoom lens zoomed in).

Halogen lamp infrared lights offer the best illumination possible for a B/W CCD chip, but their short life-span has initiated new technologies, one of which is the concept of **solid-state infrared LEDs** (LED = light emitting diode) mounted in the form of a matrix. This type of infrared is made with high-luminosity infrared LEDs, which have a much higher efficiency than standard diodes and radiate a considerable amount of light. Such infrared lights come with a few different power ratings: 7 W, 15 W and 50 W. They are not as powerful as the halogen ones, but the main advantage is their MTBF of over 100,000 hr (20~30 years of continuous night operation).

How far you can see with such infrareds depends, again, on the camera in use and its spectral characteristics. It is always advisable to conduct a site test at night for best understanding of distances.

The angle of dispersion is limited to the LED's angle of radiation, which usually ranges between about 30° and 40°, if no additional optics are placed in front of the LED matrix.

Another type of IR used in applications, is an **infrared LASER diode** (LASER = light amplification by stimulated emission of radiation). Perhaps not as powerful as the LEDs, but with a laser source the wavelength is very clean and coherent. A typical LASER diode radiates light in a very narrow angle, so a little lens is used to disperse the beam (usually up to about 30°). Lasers use very little power. They concentrate coherent light into one beam, but their MTBF is shorter than the LED's and it usually goes up to about 10,000 hr (approximately 2~3 years of continuous night operation). The major advantages of the LASER infrared light are its very low current consumption and its small size.

We need not mention that **color cameras cannot see infrared light** due to the spectrum filtering of their infrared cut filter. There are, however, camera manufacturers that have come up with some innovative ideas of using a color CCD chip setup for day viewing and at night converting the same chip to monochrome by removing the infrared cut filter.

Others use a simpler method, which is to place two chips (one color and the other B/W) in the one camera body, where the light is split by a semitransparent mirror.

A ground loop corrector

Ground loop correctors

Quite often, even if all precautions have been taken during installation, problems of a specific nature may occur: **ground loops**.

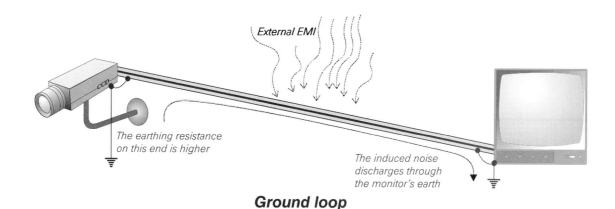

External EMI

The earthing resistance on this end is higher

The induced noise discharges through the monitor's earth

Ground loop

Ground loops are an unwanted phenomenon caused by the ground potential difference between two distant points. It is usually the difference between the camera and the monitor point, but it could also be between a camera and a switcher, or two cameras, especially if they are daisy-chained for synchronization purposes. The picture appears wavy and distorted. Small ground loops may not be noticeable at all, but substantial ones are very disturbing for the viewers. When this is the case, the only solution is to galvanically isolate the two sides. This is usually done with a video **isolation transformer**, sometimes called a **ground loop corrector** or even a **hum bug unit**.

Ground loops can be eliminated, or at least minimized, by using monitors or processing equipment with **DC restoration**. The DC restoration is performed by the input stage of a device that has DC restoration, where the "wavy" video signal is sampled at the sync pedestals so as to regenerate a "straight" DC level video signal. This in effect eliminates low frequency induction, which is the most common ground loop artefact. One better solution, though more expensive, is the use of a fiber optics cable instead of a coaxial, at least between the distant camera(s) and the monitor end.

Photo courtesy of Furse

Lightning protectors

Lightning protection

Lightning is a natural phenomenon about which there is not much we can do. PTZ sites are particularly vulnerable, because they have video, power and control cables concentrated in the one area. **A good and proper earthing is strongly recommended** in areas where intensive lightning occurs and of course surge arresters (also known as spark or lightning arresters) should be put inside all the system channels (control, video, etc.). Most good PTZ site drivers have **spark arresters** built in at the data input terminals and/or galvanic isolation through the communication transformers.

Spark arresters are special devices made of two electrodes, which are connected to the two ends of a broken cable, housed in a special gas tube that allows excessive voltage induced by lightning to discharge through it. They are helpful, but they do not offer 100% protection.

An important thing to consider about lightning is that it is dangerous not only when it directly hits the camera or cable but also when it strikes within close range. The probability of having a direct lightning hit is close to zero. The more likely situation is that lightning will strike close by (within a couple of hundred meters of the camera). The induction produced by such a discharge is sufficient to cause irrepairable damage. Lightning measuring over 10,000,000 V and 1,000,000 A is possible; imagine the induction it can create.

Again, as with the ground loops, the best protection from lightning is using a fiber optics cable; with no metal connection, no induction is possible.

In-line video amplifiers/equalizers

When coaxial cables are used for video transmission of distances longer than what is recommended for the particular coax, **in-line amplifiers** (sometimes called **video equalizers** or **cable compensators**) are used.

The role of an in-line amplifier/equalizer is very straightforward: **it amplifies and equalizes the video signal**, so by the time it gets to the monitor end it is restored, more or less, to the levels it should be when a camera is connected to a monitor directly next to it.

If no amplifier is used on long runs, the total cable resistance and capacitance rise to the values where they affect the video signal considerably, both in level and bandwidth. When using a couple of hundred meters of coaxial cable (RG-59), the video signal level can drop from the normal 1 V_{pp} to 0.2 or 0.3 V_{pp}. Such levels become unrecognizable to the monitor (or VCR). As a result, the contrast is very poor, the syncs are low, and the picture starts breaking and rolling. In addition, the higher frequencies are attenuated much more

Video equalizer/amplifier

than the lower ones, which is reflected in the loss of fine details in the video signal. From fundamental electronics it is known that higher frequencies are always attenuated more due to various effects such as the skin-effect or impedance-frequency relation, just to name a few.

This is why equalization of the video signal spectrum is necessary and not only the amplification of it.

Obviously, with every amplification stage the noise is also amplified. That is why there are certain guidelines, with each in-line amplifier/equalizer, that need to be followed. Theoretically it would be best if the amplifier/equalizer is inserted in the middle of the long cable run, where the signal is still

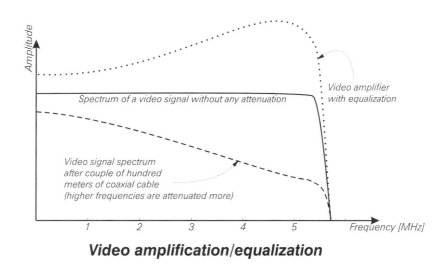

Video amplification/equalization

considerably high relative to the noise level. However, the middle of the cable is not a very practical place, mainly because it requires power and mounting somewhere in the field or under the ground.

This is why most manufacturers suggest one of the two other alternatives.

The first and most common, is to install the in-line amplifier at the camera end, often in the camera housing itself. In such a case, we actually do a **pre-amplification and pre-equalization**, where the video signal is boosted up and equalized to unnatural levels, so by the time it gets to the receiving end (the distance should be roughly known), it drops down to $1V_{pp}$.

The second installation alternative is at the monitor end, where more noise will accumulate along the length, but the amplification can be controlled better and needs to be brought up from a couple of hundreds millivolts to a standard $1 V_{pp}$. This might be more practical in installations where there is no access to the camera itself.

In both of the above alternatives, there is usually a potentiometer available at the front of the unit, with calibrated positions for the cable length to be compensated. In any case, it is of great importance to know the cable length being compensated for.

A number of in-line amplifiers can be used in series, i.e., if 300 m of RG-59/U is the maximum recommended length for a B/W signal, 1 km can be reached by using two amplifiers (some manufacturers may suggest only one for runs longer than a kilometer), or maybe even three. Don't forget though, **the noise cannot be avoided and it always accumulates**.

Photo courtesy of Pelco
Video distribution amplifier

Furthermore, the risk of ground loops, lightning and other inductions, with more (two or three) in-line amplifiers will be even greater.

Again, the best suggestion is, if you know in advance your installation has to go over half a kilometer to use fiber optics. Many would suggest an RG-11/U coaxial cable instead, where a single run, without an amplifier, can go up to 600-700 m, but the cost of fiber optics these days is comparable to, if not lower than the RG-11/U. We have already covered the many advantages fiber offers.

Video distribution amplifiers (VDAs)

Very often, a video signal has to be taken to a couple of different users: a switcher, a monitor and another switcher or quad, for example. This may not be possible with all of these units, because not all of them have the looping video inputs. Looping BNCs are most common on monitors. Usually, there is a switch near the BNCs, indicated with "75 Ω" and "High" positions. This is a so-called **passive input impedance matching**. If you want to go to another device, a monitor, for example, the procedure would be to switch the first monitor to **High Impedance** and loop the coaxial cable to the second monitor, where the impedance setting should be at 75 Ω.

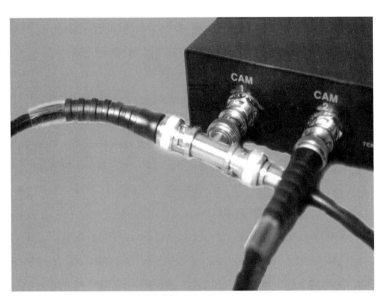

BNC T-piece

This is important, as we discussed earlier, because a **camera is a 75-Ω source and it has to see 75 Ω at the end of the line** to have a correct video transmission with 100% energy transfer, i.e., no reflections.

Now picture a situation, very common in CCTV, where a customer wants to have two switchers at two different locations, switching the same cameras, but independently from each other. This can easily be solved by using two video switchers, one looping and the other terminating, where we can use the same logic as with the monitors.

In practice, though, simple and cheap switchers are usually made with just one BNC per video input, which means that they are **terminating inputs**, i.e., with 75-Ω input impedance and looping.

It would be wrong to use BNC T adaptors to loop from one switcher to another, as many installers do. This is incorrect because then we will have two 75-Ω terminations per channel, so the video cameras will see incorrect impedance, causing partial reflection of the signals, in which case the reproduction will be with double imaging and incorrect dynamics.

The solution for these sorts of cases is the use of **video distribution amplifiers (VDA)**. They do exactly what the name suggests – they distribute one video input to more outputs, preserving the necessary impedance matching. This is achieved with the use of some transistors or op-amp stages. Because active electronics is used (where power needs to be brought to the circuit), this is called **active impedance matching**.

A typical VDA usually has one input and four outputs, but models with six, eight or more outputs are available as well. One VDA is necessary for each video signal, even if not all four outputs are used.

Video matrix switchers use the same concept as the VDAs when distributing a single video signal to many output channels. In such a case there is a limit to the number of VDA stages that can be used in bigger matrix systems. This is due to the fact that every new stage injects a certain amount of noise, which with analog signals cannot be avoided.

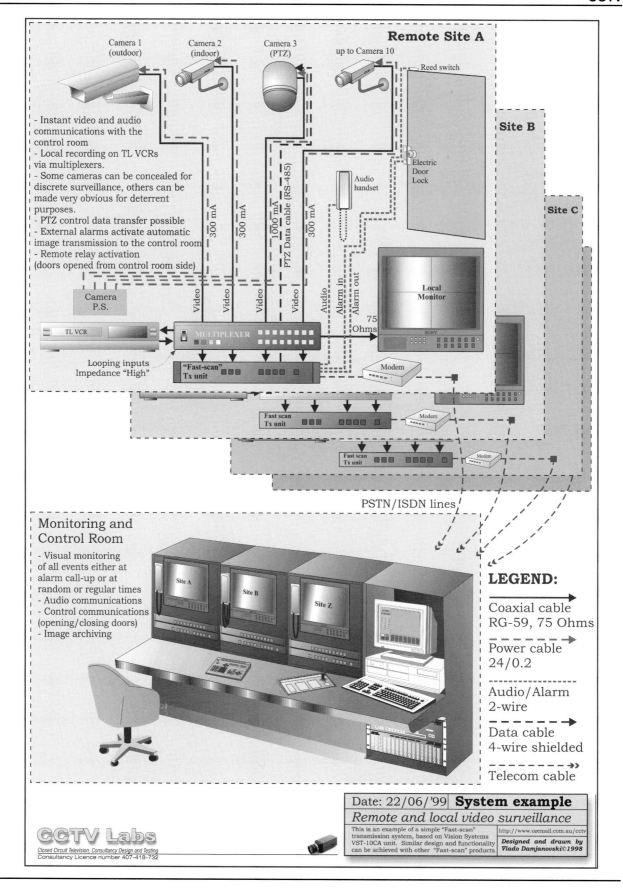

Remote Site A

Camera 1 (outdoor) Camera 2 (indoor) Camera 3 (PTZ) up to Camera 10

Reed switch

Site B

Site C

- Instant video and audio communications with the control room
- Local recording on TL VCRs via multiplexers.
- Some cameras can be concealed for discrete surveillance, others can be made very obvious for deterrent purposes.
- PTZ control data transfer possible
- External alarms activate automatic image transmission to the control room
- Remote relay activation (doors opened from control room side)

Electric Door Lock

Audio handset

300 mA 300 mA 1000 mA PTZ Data cable (RS-485) 300 mA

Local Monitor

SONY

75 Ohms

Camera P.S.

Video Video Video Video Audio Alarm in Alarm out

TL VCR

MULTIPLEXER

Looping inputs Impedance "High"

"Fast-scan" Tx unit

Modem

Fast scan Tx unit

Modem

Fast scan Tx unit

Modem

PSTN/ISDN lines

Monitoring and Control Room

- Visual monitoring of all events either at alarm call-up or at random or regular times
- Audio communications
- Control communications (opening/closing doors)
- Image archiving

Site A Site B Site Z

LEGEND:

Coaxial cable RG-59, 75 Ohms

Power cable 24/0.2

Audio/Alarm 2-wire

Data cable 4-wire shielded

Telecom cable

CCTV Labs
Closed Circuit Television, Consultancy Design and Testing
Consultancy Licence number 407-418-732

Date: 22/06/'99 | **System example**

Remote and local video surveillance

This is an example of a simple "Fast-scan" transmission system, based on Vision Systems VST-10CA unit. Similar design and functionality can be achieved with other "Fast-scan" products.

http://www.ozemail.com.au/cctv

Designed and drawn by Vlado Damjanovski©1998

11. CCTV System Design

Designing a CCTV system is a very complex task. We need to have at least the basic knowledge of all the stages in a system, as well as its components, in order to do this. But more importantly, prior to designing the system, we need to know what the customer expects from it.

Understanding the customers' requirements

The first and most important thing before commencing the design is to **know and understand the customer's requirements**. The customers could be technically oriented people and many understand CCTV as good as you do, but most often they would not be aware of the latest technical developments and capabilities of each of the components.

The most important thing to understand is the general concept of the surveillance the customer wants: constant monitoring of cameras and activities undertaken by 24-hour security personnel, or perhaps just an unattended operation (usually with constant recording), or maybe a mixture of the two. Once you understand their general requirements it might be a good idea to explain to them what is achievable with the equipment you would be suggesting. This is reasonably easy to accomplish with smaller and simpler systems, but once they grow to a size of more than 10 cameras some of which could be PTZs, a few monitors, more than one control point, a number of alarms, VCRs, etc.– things will get tougher.

There are many unknown variables which need to be considered: What happens if a number of alarms go off simultaneously? Which monitor should display the alarms? Will the alarms be recorded if the VCR(s) is/are playing back? What is the level of priority for each operator? and so on.

Those are the variables that define the system complexity and like in mathematics, in order to solve a system with more variables, one needs to know more parameters. They can be specified by the customer, but only after the customer has understood the technical capabilities of the equipment.

Understandably, it is imperative for you, as a CCTV expert, to know the components, hardware and software you would be offering and achieve what is required in the best possible way.

You would create a favorable impression in the customer's mind, if at the end, you give him or her as much as, or even more than, what you have promised. But you would certainly prove unsatisfactory if you don't. Remember that if the customer is fully satisfied the first time, chances are he or she will come back to do business with you again.

To put it simply: Don't claim the system will do this and that, if you are not certain and make sure your system delivers what you say it will.

Talking and listening to customers are very important

So, without any doubt, to design a good, functional system, one has to know the components used, their benefits and limitations, how they interconnect and how the customer wants them to be used.

The first few parts are assumed to be fulfilled, since you wouldn't be doing that job unless you know a few things about CCTV. The last one, i.e., what the customer wants, can be determined during the first phone call or meeting.

Sydney's Star City Casino CCTV control console

Usually, the next thing to do is a site inspection. Here is a short list of questions you should ask your customer prior to designing the system and before or during the site inspection:

- What is the main purpose of the CCTV system?

If it is a deterrent, you need to plan for cameras and monitors that will be displayed to the public. If it is a concealed surveillance, you will need to pay special attention to the camera type and size, its protection, concealed cabling and similar, as well as when it is supposed to be installed (after hours perhaps).

- Who will be the operator(s)?

If a dedicated 24-hr guard is going to use the system, the alarm response needs to be different to when an unattended, or a partially attended system operation is expected.

- Will it be a monochrome or color system?

This will dictate the price, as well as the minimum illumination response. Consequently, the lighting in the area needs to be looked at. A color picture will give more details about the observed events, but if the intention is to see images in very low light levels, or with infrared lights, there is no other alternative but B/W cameras (unless the customer is prepared to pay for some of the new cameras available on the market that switch between color and monochrome operation).

The price of a color system is dictated not only by the cameras, but also by the monitors, multiplexers and/or quads (if any). Needless to say, sequential or matrix switchers, as well as time lapse VCRs are the same for both B/W and color.

- How many cameras are to be used?

A small system with up to half a dozen cameras can be easily handled by a switcher or multiplexer, but bigger systems usually need a matrix switcher or a larger number of switchers and multiplexers.

 - How many of the cameras will be fixed focal length and how many PTZ?

There is a big difference in price between the two, because if a PTZ camera is used instead of a fixed one, the extra cost is in the zoom lens (as opposed to the fixed one), the pan and tilt head or dome, the site driver and the control keyboard to control it. But, the advantages your customer will get having a PTZ camera will be quadrupled. If on top of this, preset positioning PTZ cameras are used, the system flexibility and efficiency will be too great to be compared with the fixed camera system. A system with only one PTZ camera and half a dozen fixed ones is a choice that may require a matrix switcher for control and will increase the price dramatically (compared to a system with only fixed cameras). Alternatively, single PTZ camera control can be achieved via a special single-camera digital or hard-wired controller but they would also increase the price considerably. So, if a PTZ camera is required, it would be more economical to have more than one PTZ camera.

- How many monitors and control keyboards are required?

If it is a small system, one monitor and keyboard is the logical proposal, but once you get more operators and/or channels to control and view simultaneously, it becomes harder to plan a practical

A well-designed control console

and efficient system. Then, an inspection of the control room is necessary in order to plan the equipment layout and interconnection.

- Will the system be used for live monitoring (which will require an instant response to alarms), or perhaps recording of the signals for later review and verification?

This is the question which will define whether you need to use VCR(s) with multiplexer(s). If you have a matrix switcher, you will still need a multiplexer or two in addition. Have in mind that the time lapse mode you are going to use depends on how often the tapes can be changed and this defines the update rate of each camera recorded. Choose, whenever possible, a pair of 9-way (or 8-way) multiplexers instead of one 16-way, if you want to minimize the delay time in the recording rate update.

- What transmission media can be used on the premises?

Usually a coaxial cable is taken as an unwritten rule and installation should be planned accordingly. Sometimes, however, there is no choice but to use a wireless microwave or even a fiber optics transmission, which will add quite a bit to the total price. If the premises are subject to regular lightning activity, you'd better propose fiber optics from the beginning and explain to the customer the savings in the long run. So, you have to find out more about the environment in which the system is going, what is physically possible and what is not and then plan an adequate video and data transmission media.

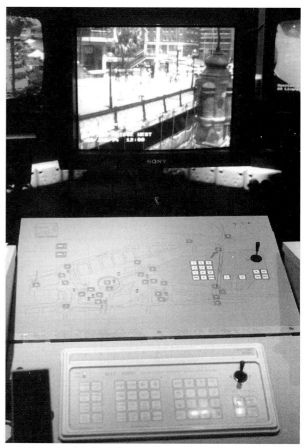

- Lastly and probably the most important thing to find out, if possible, is what sort of budget is planned for such a CCTV system.

This question will define and clarify some of the previous queries and will force you to narrow down either the type of equipment, the number of cameras or how the system is expected to work. Although this is one of the most important factors, it should not force you to downgrade the system to something which you know will not operate satisfactorily.

If the budget cannot allow for the desired system, it is still good to go back to the customer with a system proposal that you are convinced will work as per his or her requirements (even if it is over budget) and another one designed within the budget with as many features as the budget will allow for.

A mimic keyboard can improve the response time considerably

This will usually force you to narrow down the number of cameras, or change some from PTZ to fixed.

The strongest argument you should put forward when suggesting your design is that a CCTV system should be a **secure one** that can only be the case if it is done properly. Thus by having a well-designed system, bigger savings will be made in the long run.

By presenting a fair and detailed explanation of how **you think the system should work**, the customer will usually accept the proposal.

Site inspections

After the initial conversation with the customer and assuming you have a reasonably good idea of what is desired, you have to make a site inspection where you would usually collect the following information:

- Cameras: type, i.e., B/W or color, fixed or PTZ, resolution, etc.

- Lenses: angles of view, zoom magnification ratio for zoom lenses (12.5-75 mm, 8-80 mm, etc.).

- Camera protection: housing type (standard, weatherproof, dome, discrete, etc.), mounting.

- Light: levels, light sources in use (especially when color cameras are to be used), east/west viewing direction. Visualize the sun's position during various days of the year, both summer and winter. This will be very important for overall picture quality.

- Video receiving equipment: location, control room area, physical space and the console.

- Monitors: resolution, size, position, mounting, etc.

- Power supply: type, size (always consider more amperes than what are required). Is there a need for an uninterruptable power supply (UPS)? (VA rating in that case).

- If pan/tilt heads are to be used: type, size, load rating, control (two wire – digital or multi-core). Is there a need for preset positioning (**highly recommended** for bigger systems)? Where are they going to be mounted, what type of brackets?

- Make a rough sketch of the area, with the approximate initial suggestions for the camera positions. Take into account, as much as possible,

When making site inspections you can see the sunlight effects

the installer's point of view. A small change in the camera's position which will not affect the camera's performance, can save a lot of time and hassle for the installer and in the end, money for the customer. An unwritten golden rule for a good picture is to try and keep the camera from directly facing light.

- Put down the reference names of areas where the customer wants (or where you have suggested) the cameras to be installed. Also write down the reference names of areas to be monitored, as you will need them in your documentation as reference points. Be alert for obvious "no-nos" (in respect to installation), even if the customer wishes something to be done. Sometimes small changes may result in high installation costs or technical difficulties which would be impossible to solve. It is always easier to deter him or her from that in the initial stage by explaining why, rather than having to do so later in the course of installation, where additional costs will be unavoidable.

Designing and quoting a CCTV system

With all of the above information, plus the product knowledge (which **needs constant updating**), you need to sit down and think.

Designing a system, like designing anything new, is a form of art. Like with many artists, your work may not be rewarded immediately, or it may not be accepted for some reason. But think positively and concentrate as if that is to be the best system you can propose. With a little bit of luck you may really make it the best and tomorrow you can proudly show it to your colleagues and customers.

Different people will use different methods when designing a system. There is, however, an easy and logical beginning.

Always start with a hand drawing of what you think the system should feature. Draw the monitors, cameras, housings, interconnecting cables, power supplies, etc. While drawing you will see the physical interconnection and component requirements. Then you won't omit any of the little things which can sometimes be forgotten, like camera brackets, types of cable used, cable length, etc. Making even a rough hand sketch will bring you to some corrections, improvements or perhaps further inquiries to the customer. You may have, for example, forgotten to check what the maximum distance for the PTZ control is, or how far the operators are to be from the central video processing equipment, power cable distances and voltage drops and so on.

Once you've made the final hand drawing, you then know what equipment is required and this is the point where you can **make a listing of the proposed equipment**. Then, perhaps, you will come to the stage of matching camera/lens combinations. Make sure that they will fit in the housings or domes you intend to use. This is another chance to glance through the supplier's specifications booklet. Don't forget to take into account some trivial things which may make installation difficult, like the coaxial cable space behind the camera (remember, it is always good to have at least 50 mm for BNC terminations), the focusing movement of a zoom lens (as mentioned earlier in the chapter on zoom lenses, in a lot of zoom lenses focusing near makes the front optical element protrude for an additional couple of millimeters), etc.

The next stage is **pricing the equipment** – costs, sales tax and duty, installation costs, profit margins and the most important of all (especially for the customer) the **total price**.

Don't forget to **include commissioning costs** in there, although a lot of people break that up and show the commissioning figure separately. This is more of a practical nature, since the commissioning cost may vary considerably and it could take longer or shorter than planned. General practical experience shows that it will always take at least three times longer than planned. Also, in the commissioning fees, time should be allocated for the CCTV **operator's training**.

After this has been finished, you need to make a **final and more accurate drawing** of the system you are proposing. This can be hand drawn, but most CCTV designers these days use computers and CAD programs. It is easier and quicker (once you get used to it) and it looks better.

Also, the hand calculated price needs to be written in **a quotation form, with a basic explanation of how the system will work and what it will achieve**. It is important for this to be written in a concise and simple form, yet precise, because quotations and proposals (besides being read by security managers and technical people) are also read by nontechnical people such as purchasing officers, accountants and alike. Often, spreadsheet programs are used for the purpose of precise calculation and this is another chance to double-check the equipment listing with your drawing and make sure nothing has been left out.

As with any quotation, it is more professional to **have a set of brochures enclosed** for the components you are proposing.

In the quotation, you should not forget to include your company's **terms and conditions of sale** which will protect your legal position.

If the quotation is a response to a **tender** invitation, you will most likely need to submit a **statement of compliance**. This is where you confirm whether your equipment complies or doesn't comply with the tender requirements. This is where you also have to highlight eventual extra benefits and features your equipment offers. In the tender, you may also be asked to commit yourself to the progress of the work and supply and liabilities and insurance, in which case you will need a little bit of help from your accountant and/or legal advisor.

A spreadsheet program can help a lot in preparing a precise CCTV Quotation

A lot of specialized companies only design and supply CCTV equipment, in which case you will need to get a quote from a specialized installer, who, understandably, will need to inspect the site. It is a good practice, at the end, to have all the text, drawings and brochures bound in a single document, in a few copies, so as to be practical and efficient for reviewing and discussions.

Installation considerations

If you are a CCTV system designer you do not have to worry about how certain cables will be pulled through a ceiling, raisers or camera pole mounting; that is the installer's job. But it would be very helpful and will save a lot of money, if you have some knowledge in that area. If nothing else, it is a good practice, before you prepare the final quotation, to take your preferred installer on site, so that you can take into account his or her comments and suggestions of how the practical installation should be carried out.

Firstly, the most important thing to consider is the type of cable to be used for video, power and data transmission, their distances and protection from mechanical damage, electromagnetic radiation, ultraviolet protection, rain, salty air and similar. For this purpose it is handy to know the surrounding area. This might be especially important if you have powerful electrical machinery next door, which consumes a lot of current and could possibly affect the video and control signals.

Powerful electric motors which start and stop often may produce a very strong electromagnetic field and even affect the phase stability of the mains. This in turn will affect the camera synchronization (if line-locked cameras are used) as well as monitor's picture display.

For example, there might be a radio antenna installed in the vicinity, whose radiation harmonics may influence the high frequency signals your CCTV system uses.

Mounting considerations are also important at both the camera and monitor end. If poles are to be installed, not only is the height important, but also the elasticity of the poles. Namely, steel poles are much more elastic than concrete poles.

If a PTZ camera is installed, the zoom lens magnification factor will also magnify the pole's movement which could result from wind, or vibrations from the pan/tilt head movement itself. This magnification factor is the same as the optical magnification (i.e., **a zoom lens, when fully zoomed in, may magnify a 1**

Strapping a bracket around a concrete column

mm movement of the camera due to wind, to a 1 m variation at the object plane).

The shape of the pole is also very important, i.e., hexagonal poles are less elastic than round ones of the same height and diameter.

The same logic applies to camera and pan/tilt head mounting brackets. A very cheap bracket of a bad design can cause an unstable and oscillating picture from even the best camera.

If the system needs to be installed in a prestigious hotel or shopping center, the aesthetics would be an additional factor to determine the type of brackets and mounting. It is especially important then not to have any cables hanging.

The monitoring end demands attention to all aspects, it needs to be: durable (people will be working with the equipment day and night), or aesthetical (it should look good) and practical (easy to see pictures, without getting tired of too much noise and flashing screens).

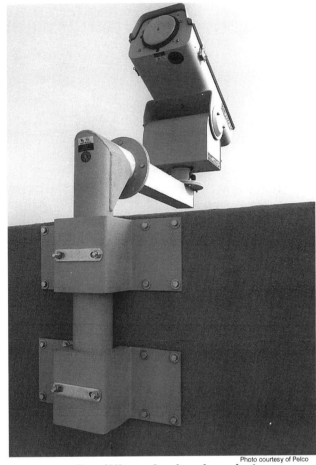

Photo courtesy of Pelco

Pan/tilt swinging bracket

Since all of the cables used in a system wind up at the monitoring end and in most cases this is the same room where the equipment is located, special attention needs to be paid to cable arrangement and protection.

Often, cables lying around on the floor for a few days (during the installation) are subject to people walking on them, which is enough weight to damage the cable characteristics, especially the coaxial cable impedance (remember, the impedance depends on the physical relation between the center core, the insulation and the shield). If a bigger system is in question, it is always a better idea to propose a raised floor, where all the cables are installed freely below the raised floor.

Sometimes, if a raised floor is not possible, many cables can be run over a false ceiling. In such cases special care should be taken for securing the cables as they could become very heavy when bundled together.

A hexagonal metal pole is stiffer than a circular

Larger installations may want a patch panel for the video signals. This is usually housed in a 19" rack cabinet and its purpose is to break the cables with special coax link connectors so as to be able to reroute them in case of a problem or testing.

Many installers don't get into the habit of marking the cables properly. Most of them would know all of the cables at the time of installation, but two days later they can easily forget them. Cable marking is especially critical with larger and more complex systems.

Insist on proper and permanent cable markings as per your drawings. There are plenty of special cable-marking systems on the market. In addition, listing of all the numbers used on the cables should be prepared and added to the system drawings.

Remember, good installers differ from bad ones in the way they terminate, run, arrange and mark the cables, as well as in documenting their work.

Hinged PTZ camera pole makes servicing easier

A large cable installation can be a creative challenge

Drawings

There is no standard for drawing CCTV system block diagrams, as there is in electronics or architecture. Any clear drawing should be acceptable as long as you have clearly shown the equipment used, i.e., cameras, monitors, VCRs and similar and their interconnection.

Many people use technical drawing aids, such as CAD programs, or other PC or Mac-based drawing packages. Depending on the system size, it might be necessary to have two different types of drawings: one of a CCTV block diagram showing the CCTV components' interconnection and cabling requirements, while the other could be a site layout with the camera positions and coverage area. In smaller installations, just a block diagram may be sufficient.

The CCTV block diagram needs to show the system in its completeness, how the components are interconnected, which part goes where and what type of cable is used and where it is used.

If the site layout drawing is well prepared, it can later be used as a reference by the installer, as well as by your customer and yourself when reviewing camera locations, reference names and discussing eventual changes.

When the CCTV system is installed and the job is finished, drawings may need small alterations, depending on the changes made during the installation. After the installation, the drawings are usually

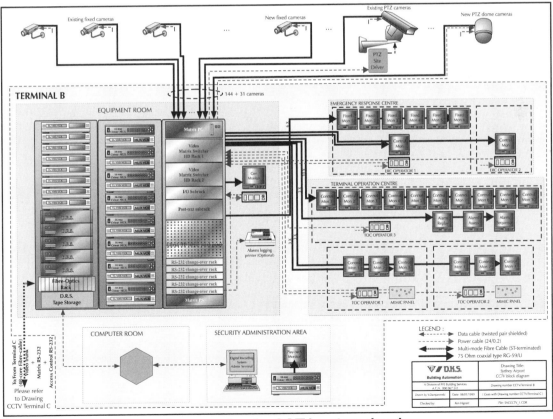

An example of a CCTV system drawing

enclosed with the final documentation, which should also include manuals, brochures and other relevant documentation.

Commissioning

Commissioning is the last and most important procedure in a CCTV system design before handing it over to the customer. It involves great knowledge and understanding of both the customer's requirements and the system's possibilities. Quite often, CCTV equipment programming and setup are also part of this. This includes video matrix switcher programming, time lapse VCR programming, camera setup and so on.

Commissioning is usually conducted in close cooperation with the customer's system manager and/or operator(s), since a lot of settings and details are made to suit the environment they are to work in.

The following is a typical list of what is usually checked when commissioning:

- All wiring is correctly terminated.

- Supply voltage is correct to all appropriate parts of the system.

- Camera type and lens fitted are correct for each position.

- Operation of auto irises under various light levels is satisfactory.

- VCRs record in the most efficient time lapse mode (especially when multiplexed cameras are being recorded).

Commissioning may also include various measurements

- All system controls are properly functioning (pan/tilt, zoom, focus, etc.)

- Correct setting of all pan and tilt limits.

- Correct preset positioning, if such cameras are used.

- Satisfactory level of supplementary lighting.

- Ensure that the system continues to work when the mains supply is disconnected and check how long it does (if UPS is used).

Commissioning larger systems may take a bit longer than the smaller ones. This is an evolution from the system on paper to the real thing, where a lot of small and unplanned things may come up because of new variations in the system concept. Customers, or users, can suggest the way they want things to be done, only when they see the initial system appearance. So clearly, commissioning in such cases may take up to a few days.

Training and manuals

After the initial setup, programming and commissioning is finished, the operators, or system users, will need some form of training.

For smaller systems this is fairly straightforward and simple. Just a verbal explanation may be sufficient, although every customer deserves a written user's manual. This can be as simple as a laminated sheet of paper with clearly written instructions.

Understandably, every piece of equipment should come with its own User's Manual, be it a time lapse VCR, a camera, or a switcher, but they have to be put together in a system with all their interconnections and this is what has to be shown to the customer. Every detail should be covered, especially alarm response and the system's handling in such cases. This is, perhaps, the most important piece of info rmation to the operators.

User manuals and equipment documentation are very important to the customer

For larger systems, it is a good idea to bind all the component manuals, together with the system drawings, wiring details and operator's instructions, in a separate folder or a binder. Naturally, for systems of a larger size, training can be a more complex task. It may even require some special presentation with slides and drawings so as to cover all the major aspects.

Good systems are recognized not only by their functionality but also by their documentation.

Handing over

When all is finished and the customer is comfortable with what he or she is getting, it is time to hand over the system. This is an official acceptance of the system as demonstrated and is usually backed by the signing of appropriate documents.

It is at this point in time that the job can be considered finished and the warranty begins to be effective. From now on, the customer takes over the responsibility for the system's integrity and operation.

If customers are happy with the job, they usually write an official note of thanks. This may be used later, together with your other similar letters, as a reference for future customers.

A fully installed system in a 19" racking cabinet

Preventative maintenance

Irrespective of the system's use, the equipment gets old, dirty and faults may develop due to various factors. It is of benefit to the customer if you suggest preventative maintenance of the system after the warranty expires.

Preventative maintenance

This should be conducted by appropriately qualified persons and most often it is the installer that can perform this task successfully. However, a third party can also do this provided the documentation gives sufficient details about the system's construction and interconnection.

The system should be inspected at least twice a year, or in accordance with the manufacturer's recommendations and depending on the environmental aggressiveness. Where applicable, the inspection should be carried out in conjunction with a checklist, or equipment schedule and should include inspections for loosened or corroded brackets, fixing and cleaning of the housings or domes, monitor screens, VCR heads, improving back-focus on some cameras, etc.

Larger systems, that include intelligent video matrix switchers, may require reprogramming of some functions, depending on the customer's suggestions.

12. The CCTV Test Chart

In order to help you determine your camera resolution, as well as check other video details, I have designed the special test chart that appears on the back cover of this book.

I have tried to make it as accurate and informative as possible and although it can be used in the broadcast applications it should not be taken as a substitute for the various broadcast test charts. It should be used for CCTV applications only and as a guide in comparing different equipment and/or transmission media.

This test chart has been updated with some new features compared to the chart in the previous edition. This addition refers primarily to the white lines which will allow you to check whether you can recognize a person at a certain distance. This procedure is based on the recommendations of **VBG (Verwaltungs-Berufsgenossenschaft)**: Installationshinweise für Optische Raumüberwachungs-anlagen (ORÜA) SP 9.7/5.

With this chart you can check a lot of other details of a video signal, primarily the resolution, but also bandwidth, monitor linearity, gamma, color reproduction, impedance matching, and reflection.

Before you start testing

For the best quality picture reproduction of your camera you first have to select a very good lens (that has much better resolution than the CCD chip itself). In order to be able to control the optical resolution of the lens, the best choice would be a fixed focal length manual iris lens.

Shorter focal lengths, showing angles of view wider than 30°, should usually be avoided because of the spherical image distortion they may introduce. A good choice for 1/2" CCD cameras would be an 8 mm, 12 mm, 16 mm, or 25 mm lens. For 1/3" CCD cameras a good choice would be when 6 mm, 8 mm, 12 mm or 16 mm lens is used.

Monitor with underscan feature

Standard monitors are usually overscanning

The longer focal length will force you to position the camera further away from the test chart. For this purpose it is recommended that you get a photographic tripod for the camera.

Next, you must use a high resolution monitor with an underscan feature. Most standard CCTV monitors don't have this feature.

When testing camera resolution the best choice would be a high quality monochrome (B/W) monitor since their resolution reaches 1000 TV lines in the center.

Color monitors are acceptable only if they are of broadcast, or near-broadcast, quality. To qualify for this, a monitor should have at least 500 TV lines of horizontal resolution. Understandably, B/W cameras having over 500 TV lines of horizontal resolution cannot have their resolution tested with such a monitor, but the majority of color cameras (which have up to 480 TV lines) should be OK for testing with such a monitor.

Setup procedure

Position the chart horizontally and perpendicular to the optical axis of the lens (see the diagram on the next page). The camera has to see a full image of the chart **exactly** to the yellow triangular arrows. To see this you must switch the monitor to the underscan position so you can see 100% of the image.

If you do not have a monitor with an underscanning feature the dotted line around the perimeter of the chart indicates 10% narrower view, which might be close to what a normal overscanning monitor would show. This is, however, not precise for checking resolution. So, if you only have a standard monitor, the following little trick might substitute the expensive underscanning monitor:

Position the camera with its tripod as closely to displaying the full image as possible. Set the vertical hold on the monitor in such a position to view the vertical blanking sync signal (the horizontal black bar in between TV fields). You should be able to set the V-hold button to such a position to have a steady horizontal bar somewhere in the middle of the screen. Then, try to adjust the camera with its tripod and/or lens so you can see both the top and bottom positional triangles on the test chart touching the edge of the black vertical blanking bar. Once you

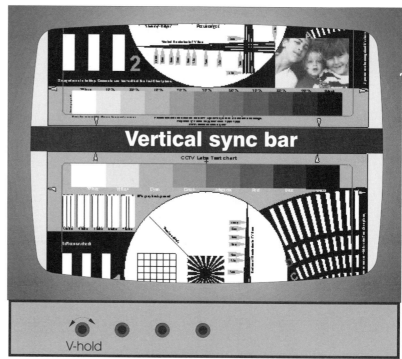

Setting 100% of the camera's view with an ordinary monitor

adjust the vertical camera position it is easy to adjust the horizontal so the test chart picture is in the middle of the monitor screen. Then and only then, can you read precise data from the test chart.

Illuminate the chart with two diffused tungsten lights (approximately 60 W each) on either side to avoid light reflection off the chart. It would be an advantage to have these two lights controlled by a light dimmer, because then, you can also test the camera's minimum illumination. Naturally, if this needs to be tested, this whole operation would need to be conducted in a room without any additional light. Also, if you want to check the low light level performance of your camera you would need to obtain a precise lux-meter.

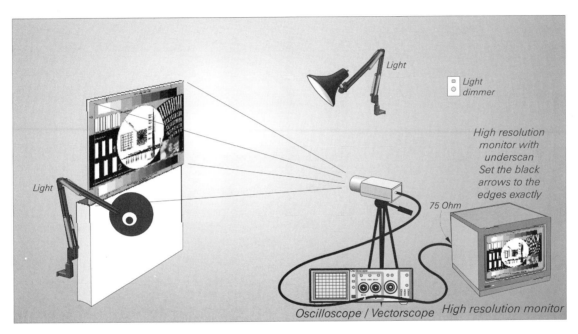

Setting up a CCTV chart test bench

Position the camera on a tripod, or a fixed bracket, at a distance which will allow you to see a sharp image of the full test chart. Make sure the arrows' tips touch the underscanned picture edge or the black vertical sync bar, if you are using the alternative method described above.

Set the lens' iris to the middle position (F/5.6 or F/8) as this is the best optical resolution in most lenses and then adjust the light dimmer to get a full dynamic range video signal. In order to see this, an oscilloscope will be necessary. Don't forget to switch off all the video processing circuits in the camera you are testing, i.e., AGC, CCD-iris, BLC.

Make sure that all the impedances are matched, i.e., the camera sees 75 Ohms at the end of the coaxial line.

What you can test

To check the **camera resolution** (either vertical or horizontal) you have to determine the point at which the four sharp triangular lines inside the circle converge into three. That is the point where the resolution limits can be read off the chart. For a more precise reading of the horizontal resolution, as per the broadcast definition, you would need an oscilloscope with a line selection feature.

If you want to check the **video bandwidth** of the signal, read the megahertz number next to the finest group of lines where black and white lines are distinguishable.

The small concentric lines in the center square of the test chart can be used for easy **focusing** and/or **back-focus adjustments**. Prior to doing this, you should check the exact distance between the camera and the test chart. In most cases, the distance should

Line-selective oscilloscope is required for accurate resolution measurement

be measured to the plane where the CCD chip resides. Some lenses though, may have the indicator of the distance referring to the front part of the lens.

Setting up the test bench with an A3 size test chart

The circle reproduction below will show you the **linearity** of your monitor only, since CCD cameras have no geometrical distortion by design. Sometimes, linearity can be more easily checked by measuring the vertical and horizontal length of the 6 × 6 squares, left of the focus square.

The wide black and white bars on the left-hand side have twofold function. Firstly, they will show you if your impedances are matched properly or if you have **signal reflection**, i.e., if you have a spillage of the white into the black area (and the other way around), which is a sign of reflections from the end of the line. The same can be used to test long cable run quality, VCR playback and other transmission or reproduction media. Secondly, you can determine whether your camera/lens combination gives sufficient details to **recognize human activity**, such as intrusion or holdup. For this reason you must position the camera at such a distance to see 3 m width at the test chart plane. If you can distinguish the bars, then your camera/lens combination is good for recognizing activity. Obviously, reading bars at number 1 is better than number 2. Use one of the formulas described under the focal length section to find out the distance you have to go to with the lens you have.

The white tilted bars on the right-hand side have a similar purpose as the thicker ones on the left-hand side. If you recognize the lines near the green letter C, or even better B and A when the camera is at a distance to see 1 m width at the chart, then you can **recognize a person** at such a distance. A is better than B, which is better than C. Again, to find out at what distance you need to position the camera so as to see 1 meter width, use the same formula mentioned earlier. This test can be very useful to find out if your camera/lens combination gives sufficient details. Such measurement is even more informative

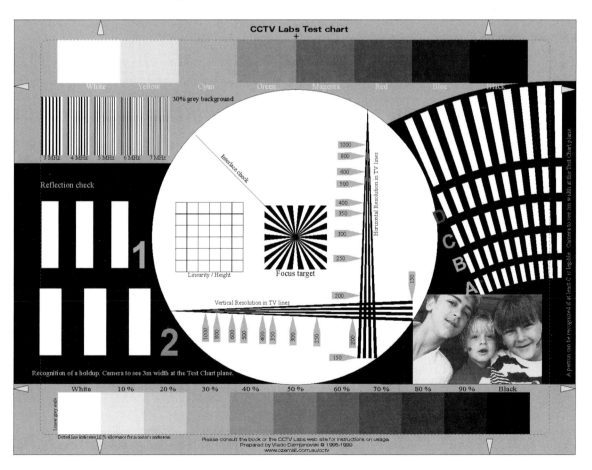

in determining the playback quality of a digital video recorder since there is no objective method of determining compression/decompression quality in CCTV.

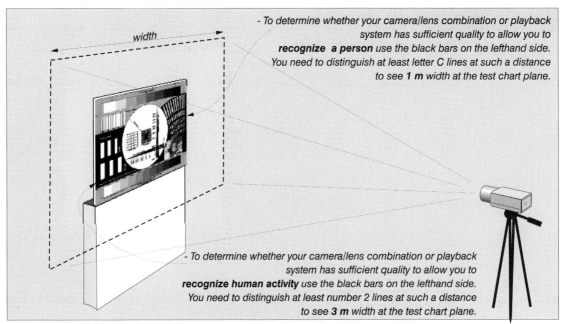

The CCTV test chart can be used to evaluate practical quality of a system

The color picture of the three kids will give you a good indication of the color of human flesh, so if you are using a color camera you can check the light source color temperature and the **automatic white balance** of the camera, if any. Have in mind in that case to take into account the color temperature of your light source, which, in the case of tungsten globes, is 2800° K.

For an even more accurate color test of your camera, use the color scale on the top of the chart, which are printed colors matching the **color bars** produced by a typical broadcast **test generator**. If you have a vectorscope you can check the color output on one of the lines scanning the color bar. Like with any color reproduction system, the color temperature of the source is very important and in most cases it should be a daylight source.

The gray background is set to be exactly 30% gray, which, together with the **gray scale** at the bottom, can be used to check the gamma setting of the camera/monitor. This gray scale is a linear one, as opposed to some logarithmic scales you may find. The reason for choosing a linear scale is the fact that the majority of today's cameras are with linear response and this makes it easy to adjust various levels on an oscilloscope. The gray scale can also be used to set up the optimum **contrast/brightness of a monitor**.

To have the best possible picture setting on a monitor follow these steps:

- Set the camera to 1 Vpp video signal, while viewing the full image of the CCTV Labs test chart.
- Set the monitor contrast pot in the middle position.
- Set the brightness pot to see all steps of the gray scale. While doing this, readjust the contrast pot if necessary.
- Observe and note the light conditions in the room while setting this up, as this dictates the contrast/brightness setting combination.
- Always use minimum amount of light in the monitor room so that you can set the monitor brightness pot at the lowest position. When this is the case, the sharpness of the electron beam of the monitor's CRT is maximum since it uses less electrons. The monitor picture is then, not only sharper, but the lifetime expectancy of the phosphor would be prolonged.

And just to repeat what I have said at the very beginning of this book, for the more dedicated CCTV technicians such a test chart is also available on A3 format, foam framed and printed on non-reflective chemical proof paper with long duration and stable colors.

For latest updates and instructions on various measurements please visit the CCTV Labs web site regularly at **www.cctvlabs.com**.

defines both the parallel and serial connector pinouts, as well as the blanking, sync and multiplexing schemes used in both parallel and serial interfaces.

CCTV. Closed Circuit Television - a Television system intended for only a limited number of viewers, as opposed to Broadcast TV.

CCTV camera. A unit containing an imaging device which produces a video signal in the basic bandwidth.

CCTV installation. A CCTV system, or an associated group of systems, together with all necessary hardware, auxiliary lighting, etc., located at the protected site.

CCTV system. An arrangement comprising of a camera and lens with all ancillary equipment required for the surveillance of a specific protected area.

CCVE. Stands for Closed Circuit Video Equipment, an alternative acronym for CCTV.

CD. Compact Disk. A standard of media as proposed by Philips and Sony, where music and data are stored in digital format.

CD-ROM. Compact Disk Read Only Memory. The total capacity of a CD-ROM when storing data is 640 MB.

CDS. Correlated Double Sampling. A technique used in the design of some CCD cameras that reduces the video signal noise generated by the chip.

CFA. Color Filter Array is a set of optica

Appendix A: Common Terms Used in CCTV

Aberration. A term from optics that refers to anything affecting the fidelity of the image in regards to the original scene.

AC. Alternating current.

Activity detection. Refers to a method built into some multiplexers for detecting movement within the camera's field of view (connected to the multiplexer), which is then used to improve camera recording update rate.

AC/DC. Alternating current/direct current.

A/D (or AD). Refers to analog to digital conversion.

ADC. Analog to digital conversion. This is usually the very first stage of an electronic device that processes signals into digital format. The signal can be video, audio, control output and similar.

AGC. Automatic gain control. A section in an electronic circuit that has feedback and regulates a certain voltage level to fall within predetermined margins.

ALC. Automatic light control. A part of the electronics of an automatic iris lens that has a function similar to backlight compensation in photography.

Aliasing. An occurrence of sampled data interference. This can occur in CCD image projection of high spatial frequencies and is also known as Moiré patterning. It can be minimized by a technique known as optical low pass filtering.

Alphanumeric video generator (also text inserter). A device for providing additional information, normally superimposed on the picture being displayed; this can range from one or two characters to full-screen alphanumeric text. Such generators use the incoming video signal sync pulses as a reference point for the text insertion position, which means if the video signal is of poor quality, the text stability will also be of poor quality.

Amplitude. The maximum value of a varying waveform.

Analog signal. Representation of data by continuously varying quantities. An analog electrical signal has a different value of volts or amperes for electrical representation of the original excitement (sound, light) within the dynamic range of the system.

ANSI. American National Standards Institute.

Anti-aliasing. A procedure employed to eliminate or reduce (by smoothing and filtering) the aliasing effects.

Aperture. The opening of a lens that controls the amount of light reaching the surface of the pickup device. The size of the aperture is controlled by the iris adjustment. By increasing the F-stop number (F/1.4, F/1.8, F/2.8, etc.) less light is permitted to pass to the pickup device.

Apostilb. A photometric unit for measuring luminance where, instead of candelas, lumens are used to measure the luminous flux of a source.

Archive. Long-term off-line storage. In digital systems, pictures are generally archived onto some form of hard disk, magnetic tape, floppy disk or DAT cartridge.

Artifacts. Undesirable elements or defects in a video picture. These may occur naturally in the video process and must be eliminated in order to achieve a high-quality picture. The most common are cross-color and cross-luminance.

ASCII. American Standard Code for Information Interchange. A 128-character set that includes the uppercase and lowercase English alphabet, numerals, special symbols and 32 control codes. A 7-bit binary number represents each character. Therefore, one ASCII-encoded character can be stored in one byte of computer memory.

Aspect ratio. This is the ratio between the width and height of a television or cinema picture display. The present aspect ratio of the television screen is 4:3, which means four units wide by three units high. Such aspect ratio was elected in the early days of television, when the majority of movies were of the same format. The new, high-definition television format proposes a 16:9 aspect ratio.

Aspherical lens. A lens that has an aspherical surface. It is harder and more expensive to manufacture, but it offers certain advantages over a normal spherical lens.

Astigmatism. The uneven foreground and background blur that is in an image.

Asynchronous. Lacking synchronization. In video, a signal is asynchronous when its timing differs from that of the system reference signal. A foreign video signal is asynchronous before a local frame synchronizer treats it.

ATM. Asynchronous transfer mode. A transporting and switching method in which information does not occur periodically with respect to some reference such as a frame pattern.

Attenuator. A circuit that provides reduction of the amplitude of an electrical signal without introducing appreciable phase or frequency distortion.

ATSC. Advanced Television System Committee (think of it as a modern NTSC). An American committee involved in creating the high-definition television standards.

Attenuation. The decrease in magnitude of a wave, or a signal, as it travels through a medium or an electric system. It is measured in decibels (dB).

Auto iris (AI). An automatic method of varying the size of a lens aperture in response to changes in scene illumination.

AWG. American wire gauge. A wire diameter specification based on the American standard. The smaller the AWG number, the larger the wire diameter (see the reference table in the Camera Power Supply section).

Back-focus. A procedure of adjusting the physical position of the CCD-chip/lens to achieve the correct focus for all focal length settings (especially critical with zoom lenses).

Back porch. 1. The portion of a video signal that occurs during blanking from the end of horizontal sync to the beginning of active video. 2. The blanking signal portion that lies between the trailing edge of a horizontal sync pulse and the trailing edge of the corresponding blanking pulse. Color burst is located on the back porch.

Balanced signal. In CCTV this refers to a type of video signal transmission through a twisted pair cable. It is called balanced because the signal travels through both wires, thus being equally exposed to the external interference, so by the time the signal gets to the receiving end, the noise will be cancelled out at the input of a differential buffer stage.

Balun. This is a device used to match or transform an unbalanced coaxial cable to a balanced twisted pair system.

Bandwidth. The complete range of frequencies over which a circuit or electronic system can function with minimal signal loss, usually measured to the point of less than 3 dB. In PAL systems the bandwidth limits the maximum visible frequency to 5.5 MHz, in NTSC to 4.2 MHz. The ITU 601 luminance channel sampling frequency of 13.5 MHz was chosen to permit faithful digital representation of the PAL and NTSC luminance bandwidths without aliasing.

Baseband. The frequency band occupied by the aggregate of the signals used to modulate a carrier before they combine with the carrier in the modulation process. In CCTV the majority of signals are in the baseband.

Baud. Data rate, named after Maurice Emile Baud, which generally is equal to 1 bit/s. Baud is equivalent to bits per second in cases where each signal event represents exactly 1 bit. Typically, the baud settings of two devices must match if the devices are to communicate with one another.

BER. Bit error rate. The ratio of received bits that are in error relative to the total number of bits received, used as a measure of noise induced distortion in a digital bit stream. BER is expressed as a power of 10. For example, a 1 bit error in 1 million bits is a BER of 10^{-6}.

Betamax. Sony's domestic video recording format, a competitor of VHS.

Bias. Current or voltage applied to a circuit to set a reference operating level for proper circuit performance, such as the high-frequency bias current applied to an audio recording head to improve linear performance and reduce distortion.

Binary. A base 2 numbering system using the two digits 0 and 1 (as opposed to ten digits [0-9] in the decimal system). In computer systems, the binary digits are represented by two different voltages or currents, one corresponding to zero and another corresponding to one. All computer programs are executed in binary form.

Bipolar. A signal containing both positive-going and negative-going amplitude. May also contain a zero amplitude state.

B-ISDN. Broadband Integrated Services Digital Network. An improved ISDN, composed of an intelligent combination of more ISDN channels into one that can transmit more data per second.

Bit. A contraction of binary digit. Elementary digital information that can only be 0 or 1. The smallest part of information in a binary notation system. A bit is a single 1 or 0. A group of bits, such as 8 bits or 16 bits, compose a byte. The number of bits in a byte depends on the processing system being used. Typical byte sizes are 8, 16 and 32.

Bitmap (BMP). A pixel-by-pixel description of an image. Each pixel is a separate element. Also a computer file format.

Bit rate. Bps = Bytes per second, bps = bits per second. The digital equivalent of bandwidth, bit rate is measured in bits per second. It is used to express the rate at which the compressed bitstream is transmitted. The higher the bit rate, the more information that can be carried.

Blackburst (color-black). A composite color video signal. The signal has composite sync, reference burst and a black video signal, which is usually at a level of 7.5 IRE (50 mV) above the blanking level.

Black level. A part of the video signal, close to the sync level, but slightly above it (usually 20 mV - 50 mV) in order to be distinguished from the blanking level. It electronically represents the black part of an image, whereas the white part is equivalent to 0.7 V from the sync level.

Blanking level. The beginning of the video signal information in the signal's waveform. It resides at a reference point taken as 0 V, which is 300 mV above the lowest part of the sync pulses. Also known as pedestal, the level of a video signal that separates the range that contains the picture information from the range that contains the synchronizing information.

Blooming. The defocusing of regions of a picture where brightness is excessive.

BNC. BNC stands for Bayonet-Neil-Concelman connector, and it is the most popular connector in CCTV and broadcast TV for transmitting a basic bandwidth video signal over a coaxial cable.

B-picture. Bidirectionally predictive coded picture; an MPEG term for a picture that is coded using motion-compensated prediction from a past and/or future reference picture.

Braid. A group of textile or metallic filaments interwoven to form a tubular structure that may be applied over one or more wires or flattened to form a strap.

Brightness. In NTSC and PAL video signals, the brightness information at any particular instant in a picture is conveyed by the corresponding instantaneous DC level of active video. Brightness control is an adjustment of setup (black level, black reference).

Burst (color burst). Seven to nine cycles (NTSC) or ten cycles (PAL) of sub-carrier placed near the end of horizontal blanking to serve as the phase (color) reference for the modulated color sub-carrier. Burst serves as the reference for establishing the picture color.

Bus. In computer architecture, a path over which information travels internally among various components of a system and is available to each of the components.

Byte. A digital word made of 8 bits (zeros and ones).

Cable equalization. The process of altering the frequency response of a video amplifier to compensate for high-frequency losses in coaxial cable.

CAD. Computer-aided design. This usually refers to a design of system that uses computer specialized software.

Candela [cd]. A unit for measuring luminous intensity. One candela is approximately equal to the amount of **light energy** generated by an ordinary candle. Since 1948 a more precise definition of a candela has become: "the luminous intensity of a black body heated up to a temperature at which platinum converges from a liquid state to a solid."

CATV. Community antenna television.

C-band. A range of microwave frequencies, 3.7~4.2 GHz, commonly used for satellite communications.

CCD. Charge-coupled device. The new age imaging device, replacing the old tubes. When first invented in the 1970s, it was initially intended to be used as a memory device. Most often used in cameras, but also in telecine, fax machines, scanners, etc.

CCD aperture. The proportion of the total area of a CCD chip that is photosensitive.

CCIR. Committée Consultatif International des Radiocommuniqué or, in English, Consultative Committee for International Radio, which is the European standardization body that has set the standards for television in Europe. It was initially monochrome; therefore, today the term CCIR is usually used to refer to monochrome cameras that are used in PAL countries.

CCIR 601. An international standard (renamed ITU 601) for component digital television that was derived from the SMPTE RP1 25 and EBU 3246E standards. ITU 601 defines the sampling systems, matrix values and filter characteristics for Y, Cr, Cb and RGB component digital television. It establishes a 4:2:2 sampling scheme at 13.5 MHz for the luminance channel and 6.75 MHz for the chrominance channels with eight-bit digitizing for each channel. These sample frequencies were chosen because they work for both 525-line 60 Hz and 625-line 50 Hz component video systems. The term 4:2:2 refers to the ratio of the number of luminance channel samples to the number of chrominance channel samples; for every four luminance samples, the chrominance channels are each sampled twice. The Dl digital videotape format conforms to ITU 601.

CCIR 656. The international standard (renamed ITU 601) defining the electrical and mechanical interfaces for digital television equipment operating according to the ITU 601 standard. ITU 656 defines both the parallel and serial connector pinouts, as well as the blanking, sync and multiplexing schemes used in both parallel and serial interfaces.

CCTV. Closed circuit television. A television system intended for only a limited number of viewers, as opposed to broadcast TV.

CCTV camera. A unit containing an imaging device that produces a video signal in the basic bandwidth.

CCTV installation. A CCTV system, or an associated group of systems, together with all necessary hardware, auxiliary lighting, etc., located at the protected site.

CCTV system. An arrangement comprising of a camera and lens with all ancillary equipment required for the surveillance of a specific protected area.

CCVE. Stands for closed circuit video equipment. An alternative acronym for CCTV.

CD. Compact disc. A standard of media as proposed by Philips and Sony, where music and data are stored in digital format.

CD-ROM. Compact disc read only memory. The total capacity of a CD-ROM when storing data is 640 MB.

CDS. Correlated double sampling. A technique used in the design of some CCD cameras that reduces the video signal noise generated by the chip.

CFA. Color filter array. A set of optical pixel filters used in single-chip color CCD cameras to produce the color components of a video signal.

Chip. An integrated circuit in which all the components are micro-fabricated on a tiny piece of silicon or similar material.

Chroma crawl. An artifact of encoded video, also known as dot crawl or cross-luminance, Occurs in the video picture around the edges of highly saturated colors as a continuous series of crawling dots and is a result of color information being confused as luminance information by the decoder circuits.

Chroma gain (chroma, color, saturation). In video, the gain of an amplifier as it pertains to the intensity of colors in the active picture.

Chroma key (color key). A video key effect in which one video signal is inserted in place of areas of a particular color in another video signal.

Chrominance. The color information of a color video signal.

Chrominance-to-luminance intermodulation (crosstalk, cross-modulation). An undesirable change in luminance amplitude caused by superimposition of some chrominance information on the luminance signal. Appears in a TV picture as unwarranted brightness variations caused by changes in color saturation levels.

CIE. Commission Internationale de l'Eclairagé. This is the International Committee for Light, established in 1965. It defines and recommends light units.

Clamping (DC). The circuit or process that restores the DC component of a signal. A video clamp circuit, usually triggered by horizontal synchronizing pulses, re-establishes a fixed DC reference level for the video signal. A major benefit of a clamp is the removal of low-frequency interference, especially power line hum.

Cladding. The outer part of a fiber optics cable, which is also a fiber but with a smaller material density than the center core. It enables a total reflection effect so that the light transmitted through the internal core stays inside.

Clipping level. An electronic limit to avoid overdriving the video portion of the television signal.

C-mount. The first standard for CCTV lens screw mounting. It is defined with the thread of 1" (2.54 mm) in diameter and 32 threads/inch, and the back flange-to-CCD distance of 17.526 mm (0.69"). The C-mount description applies to both lenses and cameras. C-mount lenses can be put on both C-mount and CS-mount cameras, only in the latter case an adaptor is required.

CMYK. A color encoding system used by printers in which colors are expressed by the "subtractive primaries" (cyan, magenta and yellow) plus black (called K). The black layer is added to give increased contrast and range on printing presses.

Coaxial cable. The most common type of cable used for copper transmission of video signals. It has a coaxial cross-section, where the center core is the signal conductor, while the outer shield protects it from external electromagnetic interference.

CODEC. Code/Decode. An encoder plus a decoder is an electronic device that compresses and decompresses digital signals. CODECs usually perform A/D and D/A conversion.

Color bars. A pattern generated by a video test generator, consisting of eight equal width color bars. Colors are white (75%), black (7.5% setup level), 75% saturated pure colors red, green and blue, and 75% saturated hues of yellow, cyan and magenta (mixtures of two colors in 1:1 ratio without third color).

Color carrier. The sub-frequency in a color video signal (4.43 MHz for PAL) that is modulated with the color information. The color carrier frequency is chosen so its spectrum interleaves with the luminance spectrum with minimum interference.

Color difference signal. A video color signal created by subtracting luminance and/or color information from one of the primary color signals (red, green or blue). In the Betacam color difference format, for example, the luminance (Y) and color difference components (R–Y and B–Y) are derived as follows:

$$Y = 0.3 \text{ Red} + 0.59 \text{ Green} + 0.11 \text{ Blue}$$

$$R–Y = 0.7 \text{ Red} – 0.59 \text{ Green} – 0.11 \text{ Blue}$$

$$B–Y = 0.89 \text{ Blue} – 0.59 \text{ Green} – 0.3 \text{ Red}$$

The G-V color difference signal is not created because it can be reconstructed from the other three signals. Other color difference conventions include SMPTE, EBU-N1 0 and MII. Color difference signals should not be referred to as component video signals. That term is reserved for the RGB color components. In informal usage, the term "component video" is often used to mean color difference signals.

Color field. In the NTSC system, the color sub-carrier is phase-locked to the line sync so that on each consecutive line, sub-carrier phase is changed 180° with respect to the sync pulses. In the PAL system, color subcarrier phase moves 90° every frame. In NTSC this creates four different field types, while in PAL there are eight. In order to make clean edits, alignment of color field sequences from different sources is crucial.

Color frame. In color television, four (NTSC) or eight (PAL) properly sequenced color fields compose one color frame.

Color phase. The timing relationship in a video signal that is measured in degrees and keeps the hue of a color signal correct.

Color sub-carrier. The 3.58 MHz signal that carries color information. This signal is superimposed on the luminance level. Amplitude of the color sub-carrier represents saturation and phase angle represents hue.

Color temperature. Indicates the hue of the color. It is derived from photography where the spectrum of colors is based upon a comparison of the hues produced when a black body (as in physics) is heated from red through yellow to blue, which is the hottest. Color temperature measurements are expressed in Kelvin.

Comb filter. An electrical filter circuit that passes a series of frequencies and rejects the frequencies in between, producing a frequency response similar to the teeth of a comb. Used on encoded video to select the chrominance signal and reject the luminance signal, thereby reducing cross-chrominance artifacts or conversely, to select the luminance signal and reject the chrominance signal, thereby reducing cross-luminance artifacts. Introduced in the S-VHS concept for a better luminance resolution.

Composite sync. A signal consisting of horizontal sync pulses, vertical sync pulses and equalizing pulses only, with a no-signal reference level.

Composite video signal. A signal in which the luminance and chrominance information has been combined using one of the coding standards NTSC, PAL, SECAM, etc.

Concave lens. A lens that has negative focal length, i.e., the focus is virtual and it reduces the objects.

Contrast. A common term used in reference to the video picture dynamic range, i.e., the difference between the darkest and the brightest parts of an image.

Convex lens. A convex lens has a positive focal length, i.e., the focus is real. It is usually called magnifying glass, since it magnifies the objects.

CPU. Central processing unit. A common term used in computers.

CRO. Cathode ray oscilloscope (see Oscilloscope).

Crosstalk. A type of interference or undesired transmission of signals from one circuit into another circuit in the same system. Usually caused by unintentional capacitance (AC coupling).

CS-Mount. A newer standard for lens mounting. It uses the same physical thread as the C-mount, but the back flange-to-CCD distance is reduced to 12.5 mm in order to have the lenses made smaller, more compact and less expensive. CS-mount lenses can only be used on CS-mount cameras.

CS-to-C-mount adaptor. An adaptor used to convert a CS-mount camera to C-mount to accomodate a C-mount lens. It looks like a ring 5 mm thick, with a male thread on one side and a female on the other, with 1" diameter and 32 threads/inch. It usually comes packaged with the newer type (CS-mount) of cameras.

CVBS. Composite video bar signal. In broadcast television this refers to the video signal, including the color information and syncs.

D/A (also DA). Opposite to A/D, i.e., digital to analog conversion.

Dark current. Leakage signal from a CCD sensor in the absence of incident light.

Dark noise. Noise caused by the random (quantum) nature of the dark current.

DAT (digital audio tape). A system developed initially for recording and playback of digitized audio signals, maintaining signal quality equal to that of a CD. Recent developments in hardware and software might lead to a similar inexpensive system for video archiving, recording and playback.

dB. Decibel. A logarithmic ratio of two signals or values, usually refers to power, but also voltage and current. When power is calculated the logarithm is multiplied by 10, while for current and voltage by 20.

DBS. Direct broadcast satellite. Broadcasting from a satellite directly to a consumer user, usually using a small aperture antenna.

DC. Direct current. Current that flows in only one direction, as opposed to AC.

DCT. Discrete cosine transform. Mathematical algorithm used to generate frequency representations of a block of video pixels. The DCT is an invertible, discrete orthogonal transformation between time and frequency domain. It can be either forward discrete cosine transform (FDCT) or inverse discrete cosine transform (IDCT).

Decoder. A device used to recover the component signals from a composite (encoded) source.

Degauss. To demagnetize.

Delay line. An artificial or real transmission line or equivalent device designed to delay a wave or signal for a specific length of time.

Demodulator. A device that strips the video and audio signals from the carrier frequency.

Depth of field. The area in front of and behind the object in focus that appears sharp on the screen. The depth of field increases with the decrease of the focal length, i.e., the shorter the focal length the wider the depth of field. The depth of field is always wider behind the objects in focus.

Dielectric. An insulating (nonconductive) material.

Differential gain. A change in sub-carrier amplitude of a video signal caused by a change in luminance level of the signal. The resulting TV picture will show a change in color saturation caused by a simultaneous change in picture brightness.

Differential phase. A change in the sub-carrier phase of a video signal caused by a change in the luminance level of the signal. The hue of colors in a scene change with the brightness of the scene.

Digital disc recorder. A system that allows recording of video images on a digital disc.

Digital signal. An electronic signal where every different value from the real-life excitation (sound, light) has a different value of binary combinations (words) that represent the analog signal.

DIN. Deutsche Industrie-Normen. Germany's standard.

Disk. A flat circular plate, coated with a magnetic material, on which data may be stored by selective magnetization of portions of the surface. May be a flexible, floppy disk or rigid hard disk. It could also be a plastic compact disc (CD) or digital video disk (DVD).

Distortion. Nonproportional representation of an original.

DMD. Digital micro-mirror device. A new video projection technology that uses chips with a large number of miniature mirrors, whose projection angle can be controlled with digital precision.

DOS. Disk operating system. A software package that makes a computer work with its hardware devices such as hard drive, floppy drive, screen, keyboard, etc.

Dot pitch. The distance in millimeters between individual dots on a monitor screen. The smaller the dot pitch the better, since it allows for more dots to be displayed and better resolution. The dot pitch defines the resolution of a monitor. A high-resolution CCTV or computer monitor would have a dot pitch of less than 0.3 mm.

Drop-frame time code. SMPTE time code format that continuously counts 30 frames per second, but drops two frames from the count every minute except for every tenth minute (drops 108 frames every hour) to maintain synchronization of time code with clock time. This is necessary because the actual frame rate of NTSC video is 29.94 frames per second rather than an even 30 frames.

DSP. Digital signal processing. It usually refers to the electronic circuit section of a device capable of processing digital signals.

Dubbing. Transcribing from one recording medium to another.

Duplex. A communication system that carries information in both direction is called a duplex system. In CCTV, duplex is often used to describe the type of multiplexer that can perform two functions simultaneously, recording in multiplex mode and playback in multiplex mode. It can also refer to duplex communication between a matrix switcher and a PTZ site driver, for example.

DV-Mini. Mini digital video. A new format for audio and video recording on small camcorders, adopted by the majority of camcorder manufacturers. Video and sound are recorded in a digital format on a small cassette (66×48×12 mm), superseding S-VHS and Hi 8 quality.

D-VHS. A new standard proposed by JVC for recording digital signals on a VHS video recorder.

Dynamic range. The difference between the smallest amount and the largest amount that a system can represent.

EBU. European Broadcasting Union.

EIA. Electronics Industry Association, which has recommended the television standard used in the U.S., Canada and Japan, based on 525 lines interlaced scanning. Formerly known as RMA or RETMA.

Encoder. A device that superimposes electronic signal information on other electronic signals.

Encryption. The rearrangement of the bit stream of a previously digitally encoded signal in a systematic fashion to make the information unrecognizable until restored on receipt of the necessary authorization key. This technique is used for securing information transmitted over a communication channel with the intent of excluding all other than authorized receivers from interpreting the message. Can be used for voice, video and other communications signals.

ENG camera. Electronic News Gathering camera. Refers to CCD cameras in the broadcast industry.

EPROM. Erasable and programmable read only memory. An electronic chip used in many different security products that stores software instructions for performing various operations.

Equalizer. Equipment designed to compensate for loss and delay frequency effects within a system. A component or circuit that allows for the adjustment of a signal across a given band.

Ethernet. A local area network used for connecting computers, printers, workstations, terminals, etc. within the same building. Ethernet operates over twisted wire and coaxial cable at speeds up to 10 Mbps. Ethernet specifies a CSMA/CD (carrier sense multiple access with collision detection). CSMA/CD is a technique of sharing a common medium (wire, coaxial cable) among several devices.

External synchronization. A means of ensuring that all equipment is synchronized to the one source.

FCC. Federal Communications Commission (U.S.).

FFT. Fast Fourier Transformation.

Fiber optics. A technology designed to transmit signals in the form of pulses of light. Fiber optic cable is noted for its properties of electrical isolation and resistance to electrostatic and electromagnetic interference.

Field. Refers to one-half of the TV frame that is composed of either all odd or even lines. In CCIR systems each field is composed of $625/2 = 312.5$ lines, in EIA systems $525/2 = 262.5$ lines. There are 50 fields/second in CCIR/PAL, and 60 in the EIA/NTSC TV system.

Film recorder. A device for converting digital data into film output. Continuous tone recorders produce color photographs as transparencies, prints or negatives.

Fixed focal length lens. A lens with a predetermined fixed focal length, a focusing control and a choice of iris functions.

Flash memory. Nonvolatile, digital storage. Flash memory has slower access than SRAM or DRAM.

Flicker. An annoying picture distortion, mainly related to vertical syncs and video fields display. Some flicker normally exists due to interlacing; more apparent in 50 Hz systems (PAL). Flicker shows also when static images are displayed on the screen such as computer-generated text transferred to video. Poor digital image treatment, found in low-quality system converters (going from PAL to NTSC and vice versa), creates an annoying flicker on the screen. There are several electronic methods to minimize flicker.

F-number. In lenses with adjustable irises, the maximum iris opening is expressed as a ratio (focal length of the lens)/(maximum diameter of aperture). This maximum iris will be engraved on the front ring of the lens.

Focal length. The distance between the optical center of a lens and the principal convergent focus point.

Focusing control. A means of adjusting the lens to allow objects at various distances from the camera to be sharply defined.

Foot-candela. An illumination light unit used mostly in American CCTV terminology. It equals ten times (more precisely, 9.29) of the illumination value in luxes.

Fourier Transformation. Mathematical transformation of time domain functions into frequency domain.

Frame. (See also Field). Refers to a composition of lines that make one TV frame. In CCIR/PAL TV system one frame is composed of 625 lines, while in EIA/NTSC TV system of 525 lines. There are 25 frames/second in the CCIR/PAL and 30 in the EIA/NTSC TV system.

Frame store. An electronic device that digitizes a TV frame (or TV field) of a video signal and stores it in memory. Multiplexers, fast scan transmitters, Quad compressors and even some of the latest color cameras have built-in framestores.

Frame switcher. Another name for a simple multiplexer, which can record multiple cameras on a single VCR (and play back any camera in full screen) but does not have a mosaic image display.

Frame synchronizer. A digital buffer that, by storage and comparison of sync information to a reference and timed release of video signals, can continuously adjust the signal for any timing errors.

Frame transfer (FT). Refers to one of the three principles of charge transfer in CCD chips. The other two are interline and frame-interline transfer.

Frame-interline transfer (FIT). Refers to one of the few principles of charge transfer in CCD chips. The other two are interline and frame transfer.

Frequency. The number of complete cycles of a periodic waveform that occur in a given length of time. Usually specified in cycles per second (Hertz).

Frequency modulation (FM). Modulation of a sine wave or carrier by varying its frequency in accordance with amplitude variations of the modulating signal.

Front porch. The blanking signal portion that lies between the end of the active picture information and the leading edge of horizontal sync.

Gain. Any increase or decrease in strength of an electrical signal. Gain is measured in terms of decibels or number of times of magnification.

Gamma. A correction of the linear response of a camera in order to compensate for the monitor phosphor screen nonlinear response. It is measured with the exponential value of the curve describing the non-linearity. A typical monochrome monitor's gamma is 2.2, and a camera needs to be set to the inverse value of 2.2 (which is 0.45) for the overall system to respond linearly (i.e., unity).

Gamut. The range of voltages allowed for a video signal, or a component of a video signal. Signal voltages outside of the range (i.e., exceeding the gamut) may lead to clipping, crosstalk or other distortions.

Gen-lock. A way of locking the video signal of a camera to an external generator of synchronization pulses.

GHz. GigaHertz. One billion cycles per second.

GB. Gigabyte. Unit of computer memory consisting of about one thousand million bytes (a thousand megabytes). Actual value is 1,073,741,824 bytes.

GND. Ground (electrical).

Gray scale. A series of tones that range from true black to true white, usually expressed in 10 steps.

Ground loop. An unwanted interference in the copper electrical signal transmissions with shielded cable, which is a result of ground currents when the system has more than one ground. For example, in CCTV, when we have a different earthing resistance at the camera, and the switcher or monitor end. The induced electrical noise generated by the surrounding electrical equipment (including mains) does not discharge equally through the two earthings (since they are different) and the induced noise shows up on the monitors as interference.

GUI. Graphical user interface.

HAD. Hole accumulated diode. A type of CCD sensor with a layer designed to accumulate holes (in the electronic sense), thus reducing noise level.

HDD. Hard disk drive. A magnetic medium for storing digital information on most computers and electronic equipment that process digital data.

HDDTV. High definition digital television. The upcoming standard of broadcast television with extremely high resolution and aspect ratio of 16:9. It is an advancement from the analog high definition, already used experimentally in Japan and Europe. The picture resolution is nearly 2000×1000 pixels, and uses the MPEG-2 standard.

HDTV. High-definition television. It usually refers to the analog version of the HDDTV. The SMPTE in the US and ETA in Japan have proposed a HDTV product standard: 1125 lines at 60 Hz field rate 2:1 interlace; 16:9 aspect ratio; 30 MHz RGB and luminance bandwidth.

Headend. The electronic equipment located at the start of a cable television system, usually including antennas, earth stations, preamplifiers, frequency converters, demodulators, modulators and related equipment.

Helical scan. A method of recording video information on a tape, most commonly used in home and professional VCRs.

Horizontal drive (also Horizontal sync). This signal is derived by dividing sub-carrier by 227.5 and then doing some pulse shaping. The signal is used by monitors and cameras to determine the start of each horizontal line.

Horizontal resolution. Chrominance and luminance resolution (detail) expressed horizontally across a picture tube. This is usually expressed as a number of black to white transitions or lines that can be differentiated. Limited by the bandwidth of the video signal or equipment.

Herringbone. Patterning caused by driving a color-modulated composite video signal (PAL or NTSC) into a monochrome monitor.

Horizontal retrace. At the end of each horizontal line of video, a brief period when the scanning beam returns to the other side of the screen to start a new line.

Horizontal sync pulse. The synchronizing pulse at the end of each video line that determines the start of horizontal retrace.

Hertz. An unit that measures the number of certain oscillations per second.

Housings, environmental. Usually refers to cameras' and lenses containers and associated accessories, such as heaters, washers and wipers, to meet specific environmental conditions.

HS. Horizontal sync.

Hue (tint, phase, chroma phase). One of the characteristics that distinguishes one color from another. Hue defines color on the basis of its position in the spectrum, i.e., whether red, blue, green or yellow, etc. Hue is one of the three characteristics of television color: see also Saturation and Luminance. In NTSC and PAL video signals, the hue information at any particular point in the picture is conveyed by the corresponding instantaneous phase of the active video sub-carrier.

Hum. A term used to describe an unwanted induction of mains frequency.

Hum bug. Another name for a ground loop corrector.

Hyper-HAD. An improved version of the CCD HAD technology, utilizing on-chip micro-lens technology to provide increased sensitivity without increasing the pixel size.

IDE. Interface device electronics. Software and hardware communication standard for interconnecting peripheral devices to a computer.

I/O. Input/Output.

I/P. Input. A signal applied to a piece of electric apparatus or the terminals on the apparatus to which a signal or power is applied.

I^2R. Formula for power in watts (W), where I is current in amperes (A), R is resistance in ohms (Ω).

IEC. International Electrotechnical Commission (also CEI).

Imaging device. A vacuum tube or solid-state device in which the vacuum tube light-sensitive face plate or solid-state light-sensitive array provides an electronic signal from which an image can be created.

Impedance. A property of all metallic and electrical conductors that describes the total opposition to current flow in an electrical circuit. Resistance, inductance, capacitance and conductance have various influences on the impedance, depending on frequency, dielectric material around conductors, physical relationship between conductors and external factors. Impedance is often referred to with the letter Z. It is measured in ohms, whose symbol is the Greek letter omega, Ω.

Input. Same as I/P.

Inserter (also alphanumeric video generator). A device for providing additional information, normally superimposed on the picture being displayed; this can range from one or two characters to full-screen alphanumeric text. Usually, such generators use the incoming video signal sync pulses as a reference point for the text insertion position, which means if the video signal is of poor quality, the text stability will also be of poor quality.

Interference. Disturbances of an electrical or electromagnetic nature that introduce undesirable responses in other electronic equipment.

Interlaced scanning. A technique of combining two television fields in order to produce a full frame. The two fields are composed of only odd and only even lines, which are displayed one after the other but with the physical position of all the lines interleaving each other, hence interlace. This type of television picture creation was proposed in the early days of television to have a minimum amount of information yet achieve flickerless motion.

Interline transfer. This refers to one of the three principles of charge transferring in CCD chips. The other two are frame transfer and frame-interline transfer.

IP. Index of protection. A numbering system that describes the quality of protection of an enclosure from outside influences, such as moisture, dust and impact.

IRE. Institute of Radio Engineers. Units of measurement dividing the area from the bottom of sync to peak white level into 140 equal units. 140 IRE equals $1V_{pp}$. The range of active video is 100 IRE.

IR light. Infrared light, invisible to the human eye. It usually refers to wavelengths longer than 700 nm. Monochrome (B/W) cameras have extremely high sensitivity in the infrared region of the light spectrum.

Iris. A means of controlling the size of a lens aperture and therefore the amount of light passing through the lens.

ISDN. Integrated Services Digital Network. The newer generation telephone network, which uses 64 kbps speed of transmission (being a digital network, the signal bandwidth is not expressed in kHz, but rather with a transmission speed). This is much faster than a normal PSTN telephone line. To use the ISDN network you have to talk to your communications provider, but in general a special set of interface units (like modems) are required.

ISO. International Standardization Organization.

ITU. International Telecommunications Union (also UIT).

JPEG. Joint Photographic Experts Group. A group that has recommended a compression algorithm for still digital images that can compress with ratios of over 10:1. Also the name of the format itself.

kb/s. Kilobits per second. Thousand bits per second. Also written as kbps.

Kelvin. One of the basic physical units of measurement for temperature. The scale is the same as the Celcius, but the 0°K starts from -273°C. Also the unit of measurement of the temperature of light is expressed in Kelvins or K. In color recording, light temperature affects the color values of the lights and the scene that they illuminate.

K factor. A specification rating method that gives a higher factor to video disturbances that cause the most observable picture degradation.

kHz. Kilohertz. Thousand Hertz.

Kilobaud. A unit of measurement of data transmission speed equalling 1000 baud.

Kilobyte. 1024 bytes.

Lambertian source or surface. A surface is called a Lambert radiator or reflector (depending whether the surface is a primary or a secondary source of light) if it is a perfectly diffusing surface.

LAN. Local Area Network. A short distance data communications network (typically within a building or campus) used to link together computers and peripheral devices (such as printers, CD ROMs and modems) under some form of standard control.

Laser. Light amplification by stimulated emission of radiation. A laser produces a very strong and coherent light of a single frequency.

LED. Light emitting diode. A semiconductor that produces light when a certain low voltage is applied to it in one direction.

Lens. An optical device for focusing a desired scene onto the imaging device in a CCTV camera.

Level. When relating to a video signal it refers to the video level in volts. In CCTV optics, it refers to the auto iris level setting of the electronics that processes the video signal in order to open or close the iris.

Line-locked. In CCTV, this usually refers to multiple cameras being powered by a common alternative current (AC) source (either 24 V AC, 110 V AC or 240 V AC) and consequently have field frequencies locked to the same AC source frequency (50 Hz in CCIR systems and 60 Hz in EIA systems).

Liquid crystal display (LCD). A screen for displaying text/graphics based on a technology called liquid crystal, where minute currents change the reflectiveness or transparency of the screen. The advantages of LCD screens are very small power consumption (can be easily battery driven) and low price of mass-produced units. The disadvantages are narrow viewing angle, slow response (a bit too slow to be used for video), invisibility in the dark unless the display is back lighted, and difficulties displaying true colors with color LCD displays.

Lumen [lm]. A light intensity produced by the luminosity of 1 candela in one radian of a solid angle.

Luminance. Refers to the video signal information about the scene brightness. The measurable, luminous intensity of a video signal. Differentiated from brightness in that the latter is nonmeasurable and sensory. The color video picture information contains two components, luminance (brightness and contrast) and chrominance (hue and saturation). The photometric quantity of light radiation.

LUT. Look-up table. A cross-reference table in the computer memory that transforms raw information from the scanner or computer and corrects values to compensate for weakness in equipment or for differences in emulsion types.

Lux [lx]. Light unit for measuring illumination. It is defined as the illumination of a surface when luminous flux of 1 lumen falls on an area of 1 m^2. It is also known as lumen per square meter or meter-candelas.

MAC. Multiplexed analog components. A system in which the components are time multiplexed into one channel using time domain techniques, i.e., the components are kept separate by being sent at different times through the same channel. There are many different MAC formats and standards

Manual iris. A manual method of varying the size of a lens's aperture.

Matrix. A logical network configured in a rectangular array of intersections of input/output channels.

Matrix switcher. A device for switching more than one camera, VCR, video printer and similar, to more than one monitor, VCR, video printer and similar. Much more complex and more powerful than video switchers.

MATV. Master antenna television.

MB. Megabyte. Unit of measurement for computer memory consisting of approximately one million bytes. Actual value is 1,048,576 bytes. Kilobyte × Kilobyte = Megabyte.

MB/s. Megabytes per second. Million bytes per second or 8 million hits per second. Also written as MBps.

Mb/s. Megabits per second. Million bits per second. Also written as Mbps.

MHz. Megahertz. One million hertz.

Microwave. One definition refers to the portion of the electromagnetic spectrum that ranges between 300 MHz and 3000 GHz. The other definition is when referring to the transmission media where microwave links are used. Frequencies in microwave transmission are usually between 1 GHz and 12 GHz.

MOD. Minimum object distance. Feature of a fixed or a zoom lens that indicates the closest distance an object can be from the lens's image plane, expressed in meters. Zoom lenses have MOD of around 1 m, while fixed lenses usually much less, depending on the focal length.

Modem. This popular term is made up of two words: modulate and demodulate. The function of a modem is to connect a device (usually computer) via a telephone line to another device with a modem.

Modulation. The process by which some characteristic (i.e., amplitude, phase) of one RF wave is varied in accordance with another wave (message signal).

Moiré pattern. An unwanted effect that appears in the video picture when a high-frequency pattern is looked at with a CCD camera that has a pixel pattern close (but lower) to the object pattern.

Monochrome. Black-and-white video. A video signal that represents the brightness values (luminance) in the picture, but not the color values (chrominance).

MPEG. Motion Picture Experts Group. An ISO group of experts that has recommended manipulation of digital motion images. Today there are a couple of MPEG recommendations, of which the most well-known are MPEG-1 and MPEG-2. The latter one is widely accepted for high definition digital television, as well as multimedia presentation.

MPEG-1. Standard for compressing progressive scanned images with audio. Bit rate is from 1.5 Mbps up to 3.5 Mbps.

MPEG-2. The standard for compression of progressive scanned and interlaced video signals with high quality audio over a large range of compression rates with a range of bit rates from 1.5 to 100 Mbps. Accepted as a HDTV and DVD standard of video/audio encoding.

Noise. An unwanted signal produced by all electrical circuits working above the absolute zero. Noise cannot be eliminated but only minimized.

Non-drop frame time code. SMPTE time code format that continuously counts a full 30 frames per second. Because NTSC video does not operate at exactly 30 frames per second, non-drop-frame time code will count 108 more frames in one hour than actually occur in the NTSC video in one hour. The result is incorrect synchronization of time code with clock time. Drop-frame time code solves this problem by skipping or dropping 2 frame numbers per minute, except at the tens of the minute count.

Noninterlaced. The process of scanning whereby every line in the picture is scanned during the vertical sweep.

NTSC. National Television System Committee. American committee that set the standards for color television as used today in the U.S., Canada, Japan and parts of South America. NTSC television uses a 3.57945 MHz sub-carrier whose phase varies with the instantaneous hue of the televised color and whose amplitude varies with the instantaneous saturation of the color. NTSC employs 525 lines per frame and 59.94 fields per second.

Numerical aperture. A number that defines the light-gathering ability of a specific fiber. The numerical aperture is equal to the sine of the maximum acceptance angle.

O/P. Output.

Objective. The very first optical element at the front of a lens.

Ocular. The very last optical element at the back of a lens (the one closer to the CCD chip).

Ohm. The unit of resistance. The electrical resistance between two points of a conductor where a constant difference of potential of 1 V applied between these points produces in the conductor a current of 1 A, the conductor not being the source of any electromotive force.

Oscilloscope (also CRO, from cathode ray oscilloscope). An electronic device that can measure the signal changes versus time. A must for any CCTV technician.

Overscan. A video monitor condition in which the raster extends slightly beyond the physical edges of the CRT screen, cutting off the outer edges of the picture.

Output impedance. The impedance a device presents to its load. The impedance measured at the output terminals of a transducer with the load disconnected and all impressed driving forces taken as zero.

PAL. Phase alternating line. Describes the color phase change in a PAL color signal. PAL is a European color TV system featuring 625 lines per frame, 50 fields per second and a 4.43361875-MHz sub-carrier. Used mainly in Europe, China, Malaysia, Australia, New Zealand, the Middle East and parts of Africa. PAL-M is a Brazilian color TV system with phase alternation by line, but using 525 lines per frame, 60 fields per second and a 3.57561149-MHz sub-carrier.

Pan and tilt head (P/T head). A motorized unit permitting vertical and horizontal positioning of a camera and lens combination. Usually 24 V AC motors are used in such P/T heads, but also 110 VAC, i.e., 240 VAC units can be ordered.

Pan unit. A motorized unit permitting horizontal positioning of a camera.

Peak-to-peak (pp). The amplitude (voltage) difference between the most positive and the most negative excursions (peaks) of an electrical signal.

Pedestal. In the video waveform, the signal level corresponding to black. Also called setup.

Phot. A photometric light unit for very strong illumination levels. One phot is equal to 10,000 luxes.

Photodiode. A type of semiconductor device in which a PN junction diode acts as a photosensor.

Photo-effect. Also known as photoelectric-effect. This refers to a phenomenon of ejection of electrons from a metal whose surface is exposed to light.

Photon. A representative of the quantum nature of light. It is considered as the smallest unit of light.

Photopic vision. The range of light intensities, from 10^5 lux down to nearly 10^{-2} lux, detectable by the human eye.

Pinhole lens. A fixed focal length lens, for viewing through a very small aperture, used in discrete surveillance situations. The lens normally has no focusing control but offers a choice of iris functions.

Pixel. Derived from picture element. Usually refers to the CCD chip unit picture cell. It consists of a photosensor plus its associated control gates.

Phase-locked loop (PLL). A circuit containing an oscillator whose output phase or frequency locks onto and tracks the phase or frequency of a reference input signal. To produce the locked condition, the circuit detects any phase difference between the two signals and generates a correction voltage that is applied to the oscillator to adjust its phase or frequency.

Photo multiplier. A highly light-sensitive device. Advantages are its fast response, good signal-to-noise ratio and wide dynamic range. Disadvantages are fragility (vacuum tube), high voltage and sensitivity to interference.

Pixel or picture element. The smallest visual unit that is handled in a raster file, generally a single cell in a grid of numbers describing an image.

Plumbicon. Thermionic vacuum tube developed by Philips, using a lead oxide photoconductive layer. It represented the ultimate imaging device until the introduction of CCD chips.

Polarizing filter. An optical filter that transmits light in only one direction (perpendicular to the light path) out of 360° possible. The effect is such that it can eliminate some unwanted bright areas or reflections, such as when looking through a glass window. In photography, polarizing filters are used very often to darken a blue sky.

POTS. Plain old telephone service. The telephone service in common use throughout the world today. Also known as PSTN.

P-picture. Prediction-coded picture. An MPEG term to describe a picture that is coded using motion-compensated prediction from the past reference picture.

Preset positioning. A function of a pan and tilt unit, including the zoom lens, where a number of certain viewing positions can be stored in the system's memory (usually this is in the PTZ site driver) and recalled when required, either upon an alarm trigger, programmed or manual recall.

Primary colors. A small group of colors that, when combined, can produce a broad spectrum of other colors. In television, red, green and blue are the primary colors from which all other colors in the picture are derived.

Principal point. One of the two points that each lens has along the optical axis. The principal point closer to the imaging device (CCD chip in our case) is used as a reference point when measuring the focal length of a lens.

PROM. Programmable read only memory. A ROM that can be programmed by the equipment manufacturer (rather than the PROM manufacturer).

Protocol. A specific set of rules, procedures or conventions relating to format and timing of data transmission between two devices. A standard procedure that two data devices must accept and use to be able to understand each other. The protocols for data communications cover such things as framing, error handling, transparency and line control.

PSTN. Public switched telephone network. Usually refers to the plain old telephone service, also known as POTS.

PTZ camera. Pan, tilt and zoom camera.

PTZ site driver (or receiver or decoder). An electronic device, usually a part of a video matrix switcher, which receives digital, encoded control signals in order to operate pan, tilt, zoom and focus functions.

Pulse. A current or voltage that changes abruptly from one value to another and back to the original value in a finite length of time. Used to describe one particular variation in a series of wave motions.

QAM. Quadrature amplitude modulation. Method for modulating two carriers. The carriers can be analog or digital.

Quad compressor (also split screen unit). Equipment that simultaneously displays parts or more than one image on a single monitor. It usually refers to four quadrants display.

Radio frequency (RF). A term used to describe incoming radio signals to a receiver or outgoing signals from a radio transmitter (above 150 Hz). Even though they are not properly radio signals, TV signals are included in this category.

RAID. Redundant arrays of independent disks. This a technology of connecting a number of hard drives into one mass storage device, which can be used, among other things, for digital recording of video images.

RAM. Random access memory. Electronic chips, usually known as memory, holding digital information while there is power applied to it. Its capacity is measured in kilobytes. This is the computer's work area.

Random interlace. In a camera, a free-running horizontal sync as opposed to a 2:1 interlace type that has the sync locked and therefore has both fields in a frame interlocked together accurately.

Registration. An adjustment associated with color sets and projection TVs to ensure that the electron beams of the three primary colors of the phosphor screen are hitting the proper color dots/stripes.

Resolution. A measure of the ability of a camera or television system to reproduce detail. The number of picture elements that can be reproduced with good definition.

Retrace. The return of the electron beam in a CRT to the starting point after scanning. During retrace, the beam is typically turned off. All of the sync information is placed in this invisible portion of the video signal. May refer to retrace after each horizontal line or after each vertical scan (field).

Remote control. A transmitting and receiving of signals for controlling remote devices such as pan and tilt units, lens functions, wash and wipe control and similar.

RETMA. Former name of the EIA association. Some older video test charts carry the name RETMA Chart.

RF signal. Radio frequency signal that belongs to the region up to 300 GHz.

RG-11. A video coaxial cable with 75-Ω impedance and much thicker diameter than the popular RG-59 (of approximately 12 mm). With RG-11 much longer distances can be achieved (at least twice the RG-59), but it is more expensive and harder to work with.

RG-58. A coaxial cable designed with 50-Ω impedance; therefore, not suitable for CCTV. Very similar to RG-59, only slightly thinner.

RG-59. A type of coaxial cable that is most common in use in small to medium-size CCTV systems. It is designed with an impedance of 75-Ω. It has an outer diameter of around 6 mm and it is a good compromise between maximum distances achievable (up to 300 m for monochrome signal and 250 m for color) and good transmission.

Rise time. The time taken for a signal to make a transition from one state to another; usually measured between the 10% and 90% completion points of the transition. Shorter or faster rise times require more bandwidth in a transmission channel.

RMS. Root Mean Square. A measure of effective (as opposed to peak) voltage of an AC waveform. For a sine wave it is 0.707 times the peak voltage. For any periodic waveform, it is the square root of the average of the squares of the values through one cycle.

ROM. Read only memory. An electronic chip, containing digital information that does not disappear when power is turned off.

Routing switcher. An electronic device that routes a user-supplied signal (audio, video, etc.) from any input to any user-selected output. This is a broadcast term for matrix switchers, as we know them in CCTV.

RS-125. A SMPTE parallel component digital video standard.

RS-170. A document prepared by the Electronics Industries Association describing recommended practices for NTSC color television signals in the United States.

RS-232. A format of digital communication where only two wires are required. It is also known as a serial data communication. The RS-232 standard defines a scheme for asynchronous communications, but it does not define how the data should be represented by the bits, i.e., it does not define the overall message format and protocol. It is very often used in CCTV communications between keyboards and matrix switchers or between matrix switchers and PTZ site drivers. The advantage of RS-232 over others is its simplicity and use of only two wires.

RS-422. This is an advanced format of digital communication when compared to RS-232. The basic difference is in the need for four wires instead of two as the communications is not single-ended as with RS-232, but differential. In simple terms, the signal transmitted is read at the receiving end as the difference between the two wires without common earth. So if there is noise induced along the line, it will be cancelled out. The RS-422 can drive lines of over a kilometer in length and distribute data to up to 10 receivers.

RS-485. This is an advanced format of digital communications compared to RS-422. The major improvement is in the number of receivers that can be driven with this format, and this is up to 32.

Saturation (in color). The intensity of the colors in the active picture. The degree by which the eye perceives a color as departing from a gray or white scale of the same brightness. A 100% saturated color does not contain any white; adding white reduces saturation. In NTSC and PAL video signals, the color saturation at any particular instant in the picture is conveyed by the corresponding instantaneous amplitude of the active video sub-carrier.

Scanning. The rapid movement of the electron beam in the CRT of a monitor or television receiver. It is formatted line-for-line across the photo-sensitive surface to produce or reproduce the video picture. When referred to a PTZ camera, it is the panning or the horizontal camera motion.

Scanner. When referring to a CCTV device it is the pan only head. When referring to an imaging device it is the device with CCD chip that scans documents and images.

Scene illumination. The average light level incident upon a protected area. Normally measured for the visible spectrum with a light meter having a spectral response corresponding closely to that of the human eye and is quoted in lux.

Scotopic vision. Illumination levels below 10^{-2} lux, thus invisible to the human eye.

SCSI. Small computer systems interface. A computer standard that defines the software and hardware methods of connecting more external devices to a computer bus.

SECAM. Sequential Couleur Avec Memoire, sequential color with memory. A color television system with 625 lines per frame (used to be 819) and 50 fields per second developed by France and the former U.S.S.R. Color difference information is transmitted sequentially on alternate lines as an FM signal.

Serial data. Time-sequential transmission of data along a single wire. In CCTV, the most common method of communicating between keyboards and the matrix switcher and also controlling PTZ cameras.

Serial interface. A digital communications interface in which data are transmitted and received sequentially along a single wire or pair of wires. Common serial interface standards are RS-232 and RS-422.

Serial port. A computer I/O (input/output) port through which the computer communicates with the external world. The standard serial port is RS-232 based and allows bidirectional communication on a relatively simple wire connection as data flow serially.

Sidebands. The frequency bands on both sides of a carrier within which the energy produced by the process of modulation is carried.

Signal-to-Noise ratio (S/N). An S/N ratio can be given for the luminance signal, chrominance signal and audio signal. The S/N ratio is the ratio of noise to actual total signal, and it shows how much higher the signal level is than the level of noise. It is expressed in decibels (dB), and the bigger the value is, the crisper and clearer the picture and sound will be during playback. An S/N ratio is calculated with the logarithm of the normal signal and the noise RMS value.

Silicon. The material of which modern semiconductor devices are made.

Simplex. In general, it refers to a communications system that can transmit information in one direction only. In CCTV, simplex is used to describe a method of multiplexer operation where only one function can be performed at a time, e.g., either recording or playback individually.

Single-mode fiber. An optical glass fiber that consists of a core of very small diameter. A typical single-mode fiber used in CCTV has a 9 μm core and a 125 μm outer diameter. Single-mode fiber has less attenuation and therefore transmits signals at longer distances (up to 70 km). Such fibers are normally used only with laser sources because of their very small acceptance cone.

Skin effect. The tendency of alternating current to travel only on the surface of a conductor as its frequency increases.

Slow scan. The transmission of a series of frozen images by means of analog or digital signals over limited bandwidth media, usually telephone.

Smear. An unwanted side effect of vertical charge transfer in a CCD chip. It shows vertical bright stripes in places of the image where there are very bright areas. In better cameras smear is minimized to almost undetectable levels.

SMPTE. Society of Motion Picture and Television Engineers.

SMPTE time code. In video editing, time code that conforms to SMPTE standards. It consists of an 8-digit number specifying hours: minutes: seconds: frames. Each number identifies one frame on a videotape. SMPTE time code may be of either the drop-frame or non-drop-frame type.

Snow. Random noise on the display screen, often resulting from dirty heads or weak broadcast video reception.

S/N ratio. See Signal-to-noise ratio.

Spectrum. In electromagnetics, spectrum refers to the description of a signal's amplitude versus its frequency components. In optics, spectrum refers to the light frequencies composing the white light which can be seen as rainbow colors.

Spectrum analyzer. An electronic device that can show the spectrum of an electric signal.

SPG. Sync pulse generator. A source of synchronization pulses.

Split-screen unit (quad compressor). Equipment that simultaneously displays parts or more than one image on a single monitor. It usually refers to four quadrants' display.

Staircase (in television). Same as color bars. A pattern generated by the TV generator, consisting of equal width luminance steps of 0, +20, +40, +60, +80, and +100 IRE units and a constant amplitude chroma signal at color burst phase. Chroma amplitude is selectable at 20 IRE units (low stairs) or 40 IRE units (high stairs). The staircase pattern is useful for checking linearity of luminance and chroma gain, differential gain and differential phase.

Start bit. A bit preceding the group of bits representing a character used to signal the arrival of the character in asynchronous transmission.

Sub-carrier (SC). Also known as SC: 3.58 MHz for NTSC, 4.43 MHz for PAL. These are the basic signals in all NTSC and PAL sync signals. It is a continuous sine wave, usually generated and distributed at 2 V in amplitude, and having a frequency of 3.579545 MHz (NTSC) and 4.43361875 MHz (PAL). Sub-carrier is usually divided down from a primary crystal running at 14.318180 MHz, for example, in NTSC, and that divided by 4 is 3.579545. Similar with PAL. All other synchronizing signals are directly divided down from sub-carrier.

S-VHS. Super VHS format in video recording. A newer standard proposed by JVC, preserving the downwards compatibility with the VHS format. It offers much better horizontal resolution up to 400 TV lines. This is mainly due to the color separation techniques, high-quality video heads and better tapes. S-VHS is usually associated with Y/C separated signals.

Sync. Short for synchronization pulse.

Sync generator (sync pulse generator, SPG). Device that generates synchronizing pulses needed by video source equipment to provide proper equipment video signal timing. Pulses typically produced by a sync generator could be sub-carrier, burst flag, sync, blanking, H and V drives and color black. Most commonly used in CCTV are H and V drives.

T1. A digital transmission link with a capacity of 1.544 Mbps. T1 uses two pairs of normal twisted wires. T1 lines are used for connecting networks across remote distances. Bridges and routers are used to connect LANs over T1 networks.

T1 channels. In North America, a digital transmission channel carrying data at a rate of 1.544 million bits per second. In Europe, a digital transmission channel carrying data at a rate of 2.048 million bits per second. AT&T term for a digital carrier facility used to transmit a DS-1 formatted digital signal at 1.544 Mbps.

T3 channels. In North America, a digital channel that communicates at 45.304 Mbps commonly referred to by its service designation of DS-3.

TBC. Time base correction. Synchronization of various signals inside a device such as a multiplexer or a time base corrector.

TDG. Time and date generator.

TDM. Time division multiplex. A time-sharing of a transmission channel by assigning each user a dedicated segment of each transmission cycle.

Tearing. A lateral displacement of the video lines due to sync instability. It appears as though parts of the images have been torn away.

Teleconferencing. Electronically linked meeting conducted among groups in separate geographic locations.

Telemetry. Remote controlling system of, usually, digital encoded data, intended to control pan, tilt, zoom, focus, preset positions, wash, wipe and similar. Being digital, it is usually sent via twisted pair cable or coaxial cable together with the video signal.

Termination. This usually refers to the physical act of terminating a cable with a special connector, which for coaxial cable is usually BNC. For fiber optic cable this is the ST connector. It can also refer to the impedance matching when electrical transmission is in use. This is especially important for high frequency signals, such as the video signal, where the characteristic impedance is accepted to be 75 Ω.

TFT. Thin-film-transistor. This technology is used mainly for manufacturing flat computer and video screens that are superior to the classic LCD screens. Color quality, fast response time and resolution are excellent for video.

Time lapse VCR (TL VCR). A video recorder, most often in VHS format, that can prolong the video recording on a single tape up to 960 hours (this refers to a 180 min tape). This type of VCR is often used in CCTV systems. The principle of operation is very simple – instead of having the video tape travel at a constant speed of 2.275 cm/s (which is the case with the domestic models of VHS VCRs), it moves with discrete steps that can be controlled. Time Lapse VCRs have a number of other special functions very useful in CCTV, such as external alarm trigger, time and date superimposed on the video signal, alarm search and so on.

Time lapse video recording. The intermittent recording of video signals at intervals to extend the recording time of the recording medium. It is usually measured in reference to a 3-hr (180-min) tape.

Time multiplexing. The technique of recording several cameras onto one time lapse VCR by sequentially sending camera pictures with a timed interval delay to match the time lapse mode selected on the recorder.

T-pulse to bar. A term relating to frequency response of video equipment. A video signal containing equal amplitude T-pulse and bar portions is passed through the equipment and the relative amplitudes of the T-pulse and bar are measured at the output. A loss of response is indicated when one portion of the signal is lower in amplitude than the other.

Tracking. The angle and speed at which the tape passes the video heads.

Transcoder. A device that converts one form of encoded video to another, e.g., to convert NTSC video to PAL. Sometimes mistakenly used to mean translator.

Transducer. A device that converts one form of energy into another. For example, in fiber optics, a device that converts light signals into electrical signals.

Translator. A device used to convert one component set to another, e.g., to convert Y, R-Y, B-Y signals to RGB signals.

Transponder. The electronics of a satellite that receives an uplinked signal from the earth, amplifies it, converts it to a different frequency and returns it to the earth.

TTL. Transistor-transistor logic. A term used in digital electronics mainly to describe the ability of a device or circuit to be connected directly to the input or output of digital equipment. Such compatibility eliminates the need for interfacing circuitry. TTL signals are usually limited to two states, low and high, and are thus much more limited than analog signals. Also stands for thru-the-lens viewing or color measuring.

Twisted-pair. A cable composed of two small insulated conductors twisted together. Since both wires have nearly equal exposure to any interference, the differential noise is slight.

UHF signal. Ultra high frequency signal. In television it is defined to belong in the radio spectrum between 470 MHz and 850 MHz.

Unbalanced signal. In CCTV, this refers to a type of video signal transmission through a coaxial cable. It is called unbalanced because the signal travels through the center core only, while the cable shield is used for equating the two voltage potentials between the coaxial cable ends.

Underscan. Decreases raster size H and V so that all four edges of the picture are visible on the monitor.

UPS. Uninterruptible power supply. These are power supplies used in the majority of high security systems, whose purpose is to back up the system for at least 10 minutes without mains power. The duration of this depends on the size of the UPS, usually expressed in VA, and the current consumption of the system itself.

UTP. Unshielded twisted pair. A cable medium with one or more pairs of twisted insulated copper conductors bound in a single sheath. Now the most common method of bringing telephone and data to the desktop.

Variable bit rate. Operation where the bit rate varies with time during the decoding of a compressed bit stream.

VDA. See video distribution amplifier.

Vectorscope. An instrument similar to an oscilloscope, that is used to check and/or align amplitude and phase of the three color signals (RGB).

Velocity of propagation. Speed of signal transmission. In free space, electromagnetic waves travel at the speed of light. In coaxial cables, this speed is reduced by the dielectric material. Commonly expressed as percentage of the speed in free space.

Vertical interval. The portion of the video signal that occurs between the end of one field and the beginning of the next. During this time, the electron beams in the monitors are turned off (invisible) so that they can return from the bottom of the screen to the top to begin another scan.

Vertical interval switcher. A sequential or matrix switcher that switches from one camera to another exactly in the vertical interval, thus producing roll-free switching. This is possible only if the various camera sources are synchronized.

Vertical resolution. Chrominance and luminance detail expressed vertically in the picture tube. Limited by the number of scan lines.

Vertical retrace. The return of the electron beam to the top of a television picture tube screen or a camera pickup device target at the completion of the field scan.

Vertical shift register. The mechanism in CCD technology whereby charge is read out from the photosensors of an interline transfer or frame interline transfer sensor.

Vertical sync pulse. A portion of the vertical blanking interval that is made up of blanking level. Synchronizes vertical scan of television receiver to composite video signal. Starts each frame at same vertical position.

Vestigial sideband transmission. A system of transmission wherein the sideband on one side of the carrier is transmitted only in part.

VGA. Video graphics array.

Video bandwidth. The highest signal frequency that a specific video signal can reach. The higher the video bandwidth, the better the quality of the picture. A video recorder that can produce a very broad video bandwidth generates a very detailed, high-quality picture on the screen. Video bandwidths used in studio work vary between 3 and 12 MHz.

Video distribution amplifier (VDA). A special amplifier for strengthening the video signal so that it can be supplied to a number of video monitors at the same time.

Video equalization corrector (video equalizer). A device that corrects for unequal frequency losses and/or phase errors in the transmission of a video signal.

Video framestore. A device that enables digital storage of one or more images for steady display on a video monitor.

Video gain. The range of light-to-dark values of the image that are proportional to the voltage difference between the black and white voltage levels of the video signal. Expressed on the waveform monitor by the voltage level of the whitest whites in the active picture signal. Video gain is related to the contrast of the video image.

Video in-line amplifier. A device providing amplification of a video signal.

Video matrix switcher (VMS). A device for switching more than one camera, VCR, video printer and similar to more than one monitor, VCR, video printer and similar. Much more complex and more powerful than video switchers.

Video monitor. A device for converting a video signal into an image.

Video printer. A device for converting a video signal to a hard copy printout. It could be a monochrome (B/W) or color. They come in different format sizes. Special paper is needed.

Video signal. An electrical signal containing all of the elements of the image produced by a camera or any other source of video information.

Video switcher. A device for switching more than one camera to one or more monitors manually, automatically or upon receipt of an alarm condition.

VITS. Video insertion test signals. Specially shaped electronic signals inserted in the invisible lines (in the case of PAL, lines 17, 18, 330 and 331) that determine the quality of reception.

Video wall. A video wall is a large screen made up of several monitors placed close to one another, so when viewed from a distance, they form a large video screen or wall.

VOD. Video on Demand. A service that allows users to view whatever program they want whenever they want it with VCR-like control capability such as pause, fast forward and rewind.

VHF. Very high frequency. A signal encompassing frequencies between 30 and 300 MHz. In television, VHF band I uses frequencies between 45 MHz and 67 MHz, and between 180 MHz and 215 MHz for Band III. Band II is reserved for FM radio from 88 MHz to 108 MHz.

VHS. Video home system. As proposed by JVC, a video recording format used most often in homes but also in CCTV. Its limitations include the speed of recording, the magnetic tapes used and the color separation technique. Most of the CCTV equipment today supersedes VHS resolution.

VLF. Very low frequency. Refers to the frequencies in the band between 10 and 30 kHz.

VMD. Video motion detector. A detection device generating an alarm condition in response to a change in the video signal, usually motion, but it can also be change in light. Very practical in CCTV as the VMD analyzes exactly what the camera sees, i.e., there are no blind spots.

VR. Virtual Reality. Computer-generated images and audio that are experienced through high-tech display and sensor systems and whose imagery is under the control of a viewer.

VS. Vertical sync.

WAN. Wide area network.

Waveform monitor. Oscilloscope used to display the video waveform.

Wavelet. A particular type of video compression that is especially suitable for CCTV. Offers higher compression ratio with equal or better quality to JPEG.

White balance. An electronic process used in video cameras to retain true colors. It is performed electronically on the basis of a white object in the picture.

White level. This part of the video signal electronically represents the white part of an image. It resides at 0.7 V from the blanking level, whereas the black part is taken as 0 V.

Wow and flutter. Wow refers to low frequency variations in pitch while flutter refers to high-frequency variations in pitch caused by variations in the tape-to-head speed of a tape machine.

W-VHS. A new wide-VHS standard proposed by JVC, featuring a high resolution format and an aspect ratio of 16:9.

Y/C. A video format found in Super-VHS video recorders. Luminance is marked with Y and is produced separate to the C, which stands for chrominance. Thus, an S-VHS output Y/C requires two coaxial cables for a perfect output.

Y, R-Y, B-Y. The general set of component video signals used in the PAL system as well as for some encoder and most decoder applications in NTSC systems; Y is the luminance signal, R-Y is the first color difference signal and B-Y is the second color difference signal.

Y, U, V. Luminance and color difference components for PAL systems; Y, B-Y, R-Y with new names; the derivation from RGB is identical.

Z. In electronics and television this is usually a code for impedance.

Zoom lens. A camera lens that can vary the focal length while keeping the object in focus, giving an impression of coming closer to or going away from an object. It is usually controlled by a keyboard with buttons that are marked zoom-in and zoom-out.

Zoom ratio. A mathematical expression of the two extremes of focal length available on a particular zoom lens.

Appendix B: Bibliography

- **A Broadcasting Engineer's Vade Mecum**, an IBA Technical Review

- **Advanced Imaging** magazines, 1995~1999, Cygnus Publishing Inc.

- **CCD Cameras,** Thesis 1982, by Vlado Damjanovski

- **CCD Data Book,** Loral Fairchild, 1994/1995, Loral Fairchild Imaging Sensors

- **CCD Data Book**, Thomson composants militaires at spatiaux, 1988, Thomson-CSF Silicon Division

- **CCD Image Sensors,** DALSA Inc., 1992

- **CCTV Standards by NACOSS**

- **CCVE Catalogues,** Panasonic, 1995~1999

- **Charge -Coupled Devices,** by D.F. Barbe

- **Charge Coupled Imaging Devices,** IEEE Trans., by G.F. Amelio, W.J. Bertram and M.F. Tompsett

- **Elbex literature on EXYZ matrix switcher,** 1998

- **Electronic Communication Systems**, by William Schweber, 1991, Prentice Hall

- **EWW** magazines, 1992~1996

- **Fiber Optics in Local Area Networks,** by John Wise, Course organized by Optical Systems Design

- **Fiber-Optics in Security**, by Vlado Damjanovski, One-day Seminars organized by STAM

- **Image Processing Europe** magazines, 1995~1999, PennWell

- **In-depth Technical review and fault finding,** by Vlado Damjanovski, Two-day Seminars organized by STAM

- **Light and Color Principles**, an IBA Technical Review

- **Osnovi Televizijske Tehnike**, by Branislav Nastic, 1977, Naucna knjiga, Beograd

- **Pacific Communications CCTV Systems catalogue**, 1999

- **Pelco Product Specification Book**, 1995~1998

- **Physics for Scientists and Engineers**, by Raymond Serway, 1992, Saunders College Publishing

- **Plettac electronic various technical bulletins and brochures**, 1998

- **Predavanja po Televizija**, by Prof. Dr. Ljupco Panovski, 1979~1981, ETF Skopje

- **Solid State Imaging,** by D.F. Barbe & S.B. Campana

- **Television measurements in PAL systems,** by Margaret Craig, 1991, Tektronix

- **Television measurements in NTSC systems,** by Margaret Craig, 1994, Tektronix

- **The Art of Electronics**, by Paul Horowitz and Winfield Hill, 1989, Cambridge University Press

- **TV Optics II,** Shigeru Oshima, 1991, Broadcast Equipment Group, Canon Inc.

- **Video Equipment Catalogue,** 1998, Sony

- **VBG (Verwaltungs-Berufsgenossenschaft)**: Installationshinweise für Optische Raumüberwachungs-anlagen (ORÜA) SP 9.7/5

- **Various CCTV and video related web sites**

Appendix C: CCTV Manufacturers and Their Major Distributors Listing

On the following pages you will find a worldwide listing of major CCTV manufacturers and their major distributors. Also a listing of some important security and CCTV exhibitions is enclosed.

This information was available to me at the time of preparation of this edition. I have tried to have accurate information about their range of products, addresses and web sites or e-mails.

Most of these details were provided by the companies themselves by answering a form forwarded to them prior to publishing this material.

I am aware, however, that errors are possible and addresses might have small inaccuracies. Also addresses may change.

I do apologize for any inconvenience if some information is found to be inaccurate.

I encourage your feedback with suggestions, corrections or new companies and their details.

The most up-to-date listing with the appropriate web links will be available on our web site, which you can always find when searching under **CCTV Labs**.

At the present moment this address is **www.ozemail.com.au/cctv**.

Thank you for your understanding and I hope you do find this listing helpful.

The authorThe most up-to-date listing with the appropriate web links will be available on our web site, which you can always find when searching under **CCTV Labs**.

At the present moment this address is **www.ozemail.com.au/cctv**.

Thank you for your understanding and I hope you do find this listing helpful.

The author

Sydney

April, 1999

Company Name	CCTV Products manufactured	Address	International Telephone	Fax	Web/E-mail
Ademco	Covert surveillance, wireless video transmission, cameras, VCR's, monitors	PO Box 642057, Los Angeles, CA 90064. USA	1 310 821 6770	1 310 821 6690	www.ademco.com
Ademco Australia	Distributors of covert surveillance, wireless video transmission, cameras, VCR's, monitors	5/24-28 River Road West, Parramatta, NSW 2150, AUSTRALIA	61 2 98429366	61 2 98939480	
Advanced Electronics Group	Covert surveillance, wireless video transmission, cameras, VCR's, monitors	PO Box 642057, Los Angeles, CA 90064, USA	1 310 821 6770	1 310 821 6690	www.aegi.com
Advanced Technology Video	Switchers, quads, multiplexers	14842 NE 95th Street, Redmond WA 98052, USA	1 425 885 7000	1 425 881 7014	www.atvideo.com
Allguard	Distributors of Fiber Options equipment, wireless, microwave links, twisted pair video transmission	Units 5-6, 134-136 Pascoe Vale Rd, Moonee Ponds, 3039, AUSTRALIA	61 3 93709192	61 3 93709936	www.allguard.com.au
Allthings Sales & Service	Distributor of cameras, multiplexers, digital switchers, lenses	PO Box 25, Westminster WA 6061, AUSTRALIA	61 8 9349 9413	61 8 9344 5905	www.allthings.com.au
Alpha Systems	Digital video recording, fast-scan video transmission, video software	17712 Mitchell North, Irvine, California 92614, USA	1 949 6220688	1 949 2520887	www.aslrwp.com
Altron Communications Equipment	Columns, towers, poles, brackets	Plot 20, Heol Parc Mawr Business Park Cross Hands, Llanelli, Carms SA14 6RE, UK	44 1269 831 431	44 1269 845 348	
Altronix Corp	Specialized camera power supplies	140, 58 St. Brooklyn NY 11218. USA	1 718 567 8181	1 718 567 9056	www.altronix.com
American Fibertek	Fiber optics products	27 Worlds Fair Drive, Somerset, NJ 08873-1353, USA	1 732 3020660	1 732 3020667	www.americanfibertek.com
Anicom	Cables and wires	6133 N. River Road, Suite 1000, Rosemont, IL 60018, USA	1 847 5188700	1 847 5188777	www.anicomm.com
AVE	Cash register interfaces, ATM interfaces, multiplexers, cameras, mobile VCR's	1617 E. Richey Road, Houston, Texas 77073, USA	1 281 4432300	1 281 4438915	www.americanvideoequipment.com
AVE UK	Distributors of cash register interfaces, ATM interfaces, multiplexers, cameras, mobile VCR's	UNIT 8 Leeside Business Centre 156 Millmarsh Lane - Brimsdown Enfield Middlesex, UK	44 181 8059323	44 181 4430889	www.multiview.net
Baxall	Cameras, multiplexers, switchers, PTZ controllers and drivers	Horsfield Way, Bredbury Park Industrial Estate, Stockport SK6 2SU, UK	44 161 14066611	44 161 4068988	www.baxall.com
Beard & Fitch LTD	CCTV test target	Unit 1, Grammond Parkm Lovet Rd Harlow, Essex CM17 OED, UK	44 1279 425 358	44 1279 425 187	100350.2512@compuserve.com
Belden	Coaxial cables, multi-core cables	P.O. Box 1980, Richmond, IN 47375, USA	1 765 9835200	1 765 9835294	www.belden.com
Canon Australia	CCTV lenses, modular cameras, video printers	Thomas Holt Drive, North Ryde, NSW 2113, AUSTRALIA	61 2 9805-2695	61 2 98052444	
Canon USA	CCTV lenses, modular cameras, video printers	400 Sylvan Ave. - Englewood Cliffs NJ 07632, USA	1 201 816 2900	1 201 816 2909	pbreheny@cusa.canon.com
Carol Products Co.	Covert surveillance systems	1750 Brielle Ave, Ocean NJ 07712, USA	1 732 918 0800	1 732 918 9051	www.carolproducts.com

Company Name	CCTV Products manufactured	Address	International Telephone	Fax	Web/E-mail
CCTV Labs	Book "CCTV", CCTV Labs Test Chart	5 Aspinall Avenue, Minchinbury, NSW 2770, AUSTRALIA	61 2 9832 3008	61 2 9677 0248	www.ozemail.com.au/cctv
Channel Ten Security Imports	Distributors of a full range of CCTV products	PO Box 11-507, Ellerslie, Auckland, NEW ZEALAND	64 9 262 0535	64 9 262 0435	www.channelten.co.nz
Coherent Communications	Wireless video/audio transmitters & receivers, wireless data modems	28245 Crocker Ave, Suite 200, Valencia CA 91355, USA	1 661 295 0300	1 661 295 0090	info@cocom.com www.cocom.com
Cohu	Cameras, housings, custom systems	5755 Kearny Villa Rd, San Diego CA 92123, USA	1 619 277 6700	1 619 277 0221	info@cohu.com www.cohu.com
Computar Chugai Boyeki UK	Lenses, cameras, multiplexers, switchers, VCR's, accessories	Computar House 6, Garrick Industrial Centre, Garrick Rd London, NW9 6AQ, UK	44 181 732 3328	44 181 202 3387	ota@cbcuk.com
CR Kennedy	Distributors of full range CCTV equipment of major CCTV manufacturer	663 Chapel Street, South Yarra, VIC 3141, AUSTRALIA	61 3 98231555	61 3 98277248	
Dallmeier	Digital video recorders	Wurzburg Strasse 5, D-93059 Regensburg, GERMANY	49 941 893158	49 941 893159	erwin.ullmann@dallmeier-electronic.com
Dedicated Micros	Digital multiplexers, digital transmission, coxial telemetry receivers	1 Hilton Square, Pendlebury, Swinton, Manchester M27 4DB, UK	44 161 7273200	44 161 7273603	www.dedicatedmicros.com
Dedicated Micros Australia	Distributors of digital multiplexers, digital transmission, coxial telemetry receivers	Unit 1/30 Leighton Place, Hornsby NSW 2077, AUSTRALIA	61 2 9482 1857	61 2 9482 1657	www.dedicatedmicros.com.au
Detection Systems Australia	Multiplexers, PTZ domes, VCR's, cameras	25 Huntingwood Drive, Huntingwood NSW 2148, AUSTRALIA	61 2 9672 1777	61 2 9672 1717	sattard@edm.com.au
Diamond Electronics	PTZ dome cameras, PTZ controllers	PO Box 200, Lancaster, Ohio 43130, USA	1 740 7569222	1 740 7564237	www.diamondelectronics.com
Dwight Cavendish Developments	Routers, switchers, distribution amps, auto VTR changeover units	Vincent House, Alington Rd Eynesbury, Cambridgeshire PE19 4YH. UK	44 1480 215 753	44 1480 474 525	www.dwightcav.com
Elbex Australia	Distributors of Elbex full range of CCTV equipment	Unit 15, 20-30 Stubbs Street, Silverwater, NSW 2128, AUSTRALIA	61 2 97486377	61 2 9748-6090	www.elbex-video.com
Elbex Video	Full range of CCTV equipment	25-5, Nishi Gotanda 7-Chome, Shinagawa-Ku, Tokyo 141, JAPAN	81 3 37795222	81 3 37795201	www.elbex-video.com
Elmo	CCTV cameras			81 528115243	www.elmo-corp.com
ERMES Electtronica S.r.l	Monochrome & color multiplexers, digital video recorders, analog switchers, VMDs	87/B Via Verri 31010 - Mareno Di Piave - TV, ITALY	39 0438 308470	39 0438 492340	www.nline.it/ermes
Ernitec A/S	Matrix systems, telemetry receivers, VMD's, lenses, cameras, multiplexers, tilt heads, housings	Hoerkaer 24, PO Box 720, DK-2730 Herlev, DENMARK	45 44 50 33 00	45 44 50 33 33	www.ernitec.dk
Euro Security	Magazine on security including CCTV	Peckhauser Strasse 29, D-40822, GERMANY	49 2104 958974	49 2104 5728	
Extreme CCTV	Explosion protected, bulletproof, waterproof, corrosion protected, infrared & total darkness systems	Suite 2, 6221, 202 St, Langley BC, V2Y 1N1, CANADA	1 604 533 6644	1 604 2995977	www.extremecctv.com
Fiber Options Inc.	Full range of fiber optic equipment	Suite 102, 80 Orville Dr, Bohemia NY 11716, USA	1 516 567 8322	1 516 567 8322	www.fiberoptions.com

Company Name	CCTV Products manufactured	Address	International Telephone	Fax	Web/E-mail
FM Systems Inc.	Alarm transmission systems, VDAs, video timing generators	3877 South Main St.- Santa Ana CA 92707, USA	1 714 979 3356		www.fmsystems-inc.com
Geutebruck	Matrix switchers, motion detectors, digital video recorders, telemetry controllers	Gewerbegebiet 53578 Windhagen, GERMANY	49 0 2645 1 37 0	49 0 2645 137 20	www.geutebruck.de
GIT Sicherheit + Management	Magazine on security including CCTV	Rösslerstrasse 90, D- 64293 Darmstadt, GERMANY	49 6151 80900	49 6151 8090144	www.gitwerlag.com
Gyyr	Time lapse VCRs, multiplexers, fast scan equipment, PTZ dome cameras	1515 S.Manchester Avenue, Anaheim, California 92802- 2907, USA	1 714 7711000	1 714 7807485	www.gyyr.com
Hanimex CCTV	Distributor of full range of CCTV products from major CCTV manufacturers	114 Old Pittwater Road, Brookvale NSW 2100, AUSTRALIA	61 2 94662600	61 2 94662694	www.hanimex.com.au
Hi-Sharp Electronics Co.	Monitors, cameras, housings, brackets, matrix switchers, quads	14- 1 Floor, 859 Ching Kuo Rd, Taoyua, TAIWAN	886 3 357 0000	886 3 357 0006	hisharp@msll.hinet.net
Hitachi	CCD Cameras				www.hdal.com
IDF	Manufacturer and distributor of a wide range of CCTV and security products	Hougang Central, PO Box 354, Singapore 915312, SINGAPORE	65 282 3187	65 285 5491	www.idfgroup.com
International Fire and Security Products News	Magazine on security including CCTV	Paramount House, 17- 21 Shenley Road, Borehamwood, Hertfordshire WD6 1RT, UK	44 181 2075599	44 181 2072598	
i Sight	Cameras	4 Keren Hayesad St, POB 290, 39101 Tirat HaCarmel, ISRAEL	972 4 857 0760	972 4 857 2488	www.i-sight.com
Ikegami Electronics	Cameras, monitors, accesories	37 Brook Ave, Maywood, NJ 07607, USA	1 201 368 9171	1 201 569 1626	www.ikegami.com
Impac Technologies	Multiplexers, matrix systems, digital recorders	3197 Airport Loop Dr, Costa Mesa, CA 92626, USA	1 714 755 1055	1 714 755 1070	jimm@impactechnologies.com
IPSS Inc.	Remote video monitoring	12555 W. Jefferson Blvd, East Tower Suite 225 - Los Angeles CA 90066, USA	1 310 574 3587	1 310 301 7635	www.instantview.net
IR-TEC International	CCTV cameras, quad & multiplexers, monitors, housing & brackets, lenses	8F, 14 Lane 530, Chung Cheng N. Rd. - Sanchung Tapei Hsein, TAIWAN	886 J 2982 6332	886 J 2983 3163	www.irtec.com
JAI	Specialized industrial and surveillance cameras	JAI A·S, Produktionsvej 1, 2600 Glostrup, Copenhagen, DENMARK	45 44918888		www.jai.com
Javelin USA	Multiplexers, housings & brackets, lenses, matrix switchers, VCR's	23456 Hawthorne Blvd. Bldg. 5, Torrance, CA 90505-4716, USA	1 310 3786823	1 310 3780283	javelin.com
JVC	Cameras, monitors, time lapse recorders	1700 Valley Road, Wayne, NJ 07470, USA	1 800 5825825		www.jvc.com/pro

Company Name	CCTV Products manufactured	Address	International Telephone	Fax	Web/E-mail
KERN electronic	Wireless video & audio transmission systems,	9 Finkengasse - 06295 Rothenschirmbach, GERMANY	49 34 776 20890	49 34 776 21870	www.kern-electronic.de
Kocom	Various CCTV products			82 32 6687651	www.kocom.co.kr
Kodak	CCD chips and CCD cameras				www.masdkodak.com
Loronix Information Systems Inc.	Digital video recording, video management equipment	820 Airport Rd, Durango CO 81301, USA	1 970 259 6161	1 970 385 4886	www.loronix.com
LTC Training Centre	Self directed courses and manuals, world-wide seminars	PO Box 3583, Davenport, Iowa 52808, USA	1 319 3226669	1 319 3368853	www.lrc-inc.com
Maxpro Systems	Maxpro matrix switchers, CCTV Management system	18-20 Ledgar Road, Balcatta, WA 6021, AUSTRALIA	61 8 92403888	61 8 92408040	www.maxpro.com.au
Molynx	Range of pan/tilt heads and auxilliary equipment	Albany Street, Newport, South Wales. NP9 5XW, UK	44 1633 821000	44 1633 850893	www.molynx.co.uk
NICE Systems	Digital video recording systems	8 Haphina Street, P.O.Box 690, Ra'anana 43107, ISRAEL	972 9 7753777	972 9 7434282	www.nice.com
OpiaVision	Digital recorders, face recognition, intelligent camera/recorders	Unit 5, 85 Pound Avenue, Davidson, NSW 2085, AUSTRALIA	61 2 94539343	61 2 94539900	www.opiavision.com
Optek	Distributor of miniature cameras, lenses	Unit B5, 164 Burwood Road, Concord, NSW 2137, AUSTRALIA	61 2 97157272	61 2 97157373	optek@netaus.net.au
Optical Systems Design	Fiber optic video, data, &audio transmission	7/1 Vuko Place, Warriewood NSW 2102, AUSTRALIA	61 2 9913 8540	61 2 9913 8735	osdsales@osd.com.au www.osd.com.au
Pacific Communications	Pacom matrix switcher, and distributor of full range of CCTV products of major manufacturers	Unit P2, 10-16 South Street, Rydalmere, NSW 2116, AUSTRALIA	61 2 96386400	61 2 96844264	www.pacom.com.au
Panasonic Video Imaging	Cameras, monitors, time lapse recorders, digital video recorders, multiplexers			1 201 3487372	www.panasonic.com/host/broadcast.html
Pecan Products	Covert & discreet cameras, domes, switchers, housings	6 Enterprise Centre, Cranborne Rd, Potters Bar, Herts EN6 3DQ, UK	44 1707 664 704	44 1707 662 060	
Pelco	Full range of CCTV products	300 W. Pontiac Way Clovis CA 93612, USA	1 559 292 1981	1 559 348 1120	www.pelco.com
Pettards International	Digital image transmission and storage			44-1932-788322	
Philips Australia	Full range of CCTV equipment	2 Greenhills Ave. - Moorebank NSW 2170, AUSTRALIA	61 2 9612 57744	61 2 9612 5740	www.philipscss.com
Philips Comms. & Security	Full range of CCTV equipment	1004 New Holland Avenue, Lancaster, PA 17601-5606, USA	1 717 2956865	1 717 2956071	www.philips.com
Plettac Electronics	Full range of CCTV equipment	Wurzburger Strasse 150, D-90766 Fuerth, GERMANY	49 911 75884425	49 911 7591271	www.plettac-electronics.com

Company Name	CCTV Products manufactured	Address	International Telephone	Fax	Web/E-mail
Practel	Matrix switchers, multiplexers, VDAs, VMDs, cable adaptors	446 South Rd, Marleston, SA 5056, AUSTRALIA	61 8 8351 2777	61 8 8351 1766	www.practel.com.au
Primary Image	Digital video recorders, outdoor video motion detectors	cb Millbank House 171-185 Ewell Road, Surbiton, Surrey KT6 6AP, UK	44 0 181 339 9669	44 181 339 9091	www.primary-image.com
Primary Image Inc	Digital video recorders, outdoor video motion detectors	PO Box 781207, Orlando FL 32878-1207, USA	1 407 382 7100	1 407 382 8004	www.primary-image.com
Pulnix America	CCTV cameras, industrial cameras, sensors, document scanner	1330 Oreleans Dr, Sunnyvale CA 94089, USA	1 408 747 0300	1 408 747 0660	www.pulnix.com
Rainbow CCTV/ISO	Lenses, cameras, monitors, power supplies, infrared illuminators	2495 DaVinci, Irvine CA 92614, USA	1 949 260 1599	1 949 260 1594	www.isorainbow.com
Ratech Electronics Limited	CCTV sewer & pipeline inspection systems	Unit 7, 260 Spinnaker Way, Vaughan, Ontario L4K 4P9, CANADA	1 905 6607072	1 905 6601519	www.ratech-electronics.com
Regard	Fast scan video transmission and storage			972 3 5776798	
Rexel Australia Video Systems	Panasonic cameras, muliplexers, matrix switchers, DVD storage	2 Giffnock Ave, Nth Ryde NSW 2113, AUSTRALIA	61 2 9887 6222	61 2 9888 3313	videoocctvvic@rexela.com.au
Richardson Pacific	Metal cabinets and 19" rack enclosures	58 Bath Road, Kirrawee, NSW 2232, AUSTRALIA	61 2 95423120	61 2 95421137	
Samsung	Cameras, monitors, time lapse recorders, multiplexers			82 27516089	www.samsung.com
Sanyo Australia	Dome cameras, cameras, multiplexers, VCR's, monitors, day/night camera, digital VCR	7 Figtree Drive, Homebush NSW 2140, AUSTRALIA	61 2 97353908	61 2 97461344	
Sanyo UK	Dome cameras, cameras, multiplexers, VCR's, monitors, day/night camera, digital VCR	Sanyo House, Otterspool Way - Watford Herts WD2 8JX, UK	44 1923 477 220	44 1923 477 225	www.sanyo.co.uk
Security Australia	Magazine on security including CCTV	Locked Bag 2999, Chatswood Delivery Centre, Chatswood NSW 2067, AUSTRALIA	61 2 94222909	61 2 94222877	adrian.dolahenty@reedbusiness.com.au
Security Electronics	Magazine on security including CCTV	P.O.Box 23, Leichhardt, NSW 2040, AUSTRALIA	61 2 95600749	61 2 95600849	bridge@hotlinks.net.au
Security Training and Marketing	Interactive CD-ROM on CCTV	9131 Taylor Court, Lawrenceville NJ 08648, USA	1 609 7509827	1 609 7501936	www.stamcctv.com
Sensormatic	Full range of CCTV products			49 210 2431341	www.sensormatic.com
Shawley	Pan/tilt heads, housings, brackets	Suflex Estate, Risca, Nr. Newport, NP1 6YD, UK	44 1633 619999	44 1633 619977	www.shawley.co.uk
Silent Witness Enterprises	Special camera systems, outdoor cameras, infrared cameras	6554 - 176 St - Surry, BC V3S 4G5, CANADA	1 604 574 1523	1 604 574 7736	www.silent-witness.com

Company Name	CCTV Products manufactured	Address	International Telephone	Fax	Web/E-mail
Sirrus Limited	Remote monitoring, digital recording, multiplexers, cameras	Sirrus House, 79 High St, Walton on Thames, Surrey KT12 10N, UK	44 7000 747 787	44 1932 230 299	www.sirrus.co.uk
Sony USA	CCD chips, cameras, monitors, video recorders (analog & digital)			1 201 3584943	www.sony.com
SyAC	Digital CCTV intergrated systems	via Ireneo della Croce 4 I-34126 - Trieste, ITALY	39 040 368881	39 040 368906	www.syac.com
Symagery Microsystems	CMOS cameras	3000 Solandt Road, Kanata, Ontario, K2K 2X2, CANADA	1-613-599-6500	1-613-599-6501	www.symagery.com
Taleus Systems Australia	Digital recorders, face recognition, intelligent camera/recorders	Unit 5, 85 Pound Avenue, Davidson, NSW 2085, AUSTRALIA	61 2 94539996	61 2 94539900	www.taleus.com.au
Tracam	Special cameras moving on tracks	P.O. Box 53, Alderley, QLD. 4051, AUSTRALIA	61 7 3356 6611	61 7 3356 6606	www.tracam.com.au
T. Satomi & Co.	VHF & UHF transmitters & receivers, surveillance equipment	29-3-506 Taito 1-chrome - Taito-ku Tokyo, JAPAN	81 3 3835 4925	81 3 3835 4920	plaza22.mbn.or.jp/~tstm/
Tecsec Europe Limited	Full range of CCTV equipment	7 Pavilion Industrial Estate, Poninewynydd - Pontypool Torfaen, NP4 6NF, UK	44 1495 752882	44 1495 751840	freespace.virgin.net/tecsec.europe
Tecton	Multiplexers	Fishers Court Fishers Pond Eastleigh Hampshire SO50 7HG, UK	44 1703 695858	44 1703 695702	tecton-cctv.com
The Dindima Group	Super-sleuth PC based VMD systems, distributor of JAI cameras	10 Argent Pl. - Ringwood VIC 3134, AUSTRALIA	61 3 9873 4455	61 3 9873 4749	www.dindima.com
The Imaging Source	Cameras, frame grabbers, software, lighting, lenses	Suite 103A, 900 Baxter St, Charlotte NC 28208, USA	1 704 370 0110	1 704 370 0906	www.theimagesource.com
Tiosys Co.	MPEG-1 & MPEG-2 video encoders, quads, multiplexers	Room 404, Nonhyun-dong, Namdong-gu, Inchon City 405-300, KOREA	82 32 818 0590	82 32 814 7708	www.tiosys.com
Tokina Co.	CCTV lenses	120-4 Nozuta, Machida-shi - Tokyo 195-0063, JAPAN	81 427 35 3612	81 427 35 1463	tokina@sepia.ocn.ne.jp
Ultrak	Full range of CCTV and Alarm products	1220 Champion Circle Suite 100, Carrollton, TX 75006, USA	1 214 2809675	1 214 2809357	www.ultrak.com
Vicon Industries	Full range of CCTV equipment				www.vicon-cctv.com
Vicon Industries P/L	Distributors of full range of CCTV equipment	1/49 Derby Street, Silverwater NSW 2128, AUSTRALIA	61 2 97379775	61 2 97379776	www.vicon.com.au
Videmech	Pan/tilt heads, infra red illuminators, PTZ drivers	Blackbushe Business Park, Saxony Way, Yateley, Hampshire GU46 6GB, UK	44 1252 864444	44 1252 864455	www.videmech.co.uk
Videolarm Inc.	Housings, cameras, controls, mounting accessories	2525 Park Central Blvd, Decatur GA 30035, USA	1 770 987 7550	1 770 987 9705	www.videolarm.com
Videoman Systems Co	Distributors of cameras, monitors, intercoms, car rearvision systems	Unit 13, 112 Benaroon Rd Belmore NSW, AUSTRALIA	61 2 9758 9509	61 2 9758 9510	www.ozemail.com.au/~eos
Videor Technical	Switchers, pan/tilt heads, drivers, lenses			49 607 4888100	www.videortechnical.com
Video Surveillance Warehouse	Distributors of a full range of CCTV products		1 888 8871375	1 604 6431789	www.video-surveillance.com

Company Name	CCTV Products manufactured	Address	International Telephone	Fax	Web/E-mail
Videotec	Range of housings, brackets, infrared illuminators	Via Lago Maggiore, 15 - 36015 Schio, ITALIA	39 0445697411	39 0445697414	www.videotec.com
Videotronic International	Full range of CCTV equipment	1 Lahnstrasse 24539 - Neumunster, GERMANY	49 4321 879 0	49 4321 879 97	www.videotronic.de
Vision Link UK	Distributors of branded CCTV products	March Way, Battlefield Enterprise Park, Shrewsbury, Shropshire SY133E, UK	44 1743 440500	44 1743 440700	
Vision Research Corporation	Digital multiplexers, VMDs, distibution amplifiers, fast-scan video transmission	8 Industrial Parkway, Ringwood NJ 07456, USA	1 973 962 9003	1 973 962 9005	www.visionresearch.com
Vision Systems - ADPRO	Fast-scan equipment, Outdoor VMDs, Multiplexers, integrated video alarm systems	2nd Ave, Technology Park - Mawson Lakes SA 5095, AUSTRALIA	61 8 8300 4400	6 18 8300 4422	www.vsl.com.au
Visions Televideo Technologies	Video adapters, transmission systems	8257 Elko Dr, Suite B, Ellicott City MD 21043-7228, USA	1 410 480 1600	1 410 465 6008	www.vtti.com
Visiontech	Cameras, lenses and related products	Suite B, 522 Thirteenth Street, Paso Robles, California 93446, USA	1 805 2377450	1 805 2377452	www.visiontechintl.com
VLS Video Communications Systems	Remote video surveillance products	4 Forchheimer St. - Nurnberg 90425, GERMANY	49 911 934 560	49 911 93456 66	www.videocom.de
VLSI Vision Limited	CMOS Cameras	Aviation House, 31 Pinkhill, Edinburgh EH12 7BF, UK	44 131 539 7111	44 131 539 7141	www.vvl.co.uk
Watec America	Various types miniature cameras			1 702 4343222	
Welding Engineering Limited	Camera towers, columns, brackets	Britannia House, Junction St Darwen, Lancashire, BB3 2RB, UK	44 125 4773 718	44 125 4873 637	welding@compuserve.com
Zone Communications	Digital PC-based video recorders, fast-scan video transmission	PO Box 6421, Baulkham Hills Business Centre, NSW 2154, AUSTRALIA	61 2 9894 7025	61 2 9899 2705	zoneaust@ozemail.com.au
Zylotech	Digital surveillance systems	The Australian Technology Park, Bay 16 - Suite G10, Cornwallis St, Eveleigh NSW 1430, AUSTRALIA	61 2 9209 4224	61 2 9209 4228	www.zylotech.com.au

Exhibition	Coverage	Contact	Internatioanl Telephone	Fax	Web/E-mail
Asial (Australia)	Security and CCTV exhibition			61 2 99064202	www.asial.com.au
Austrobau	Security and CCTV exhibition	Reed Exhibition Company, Heerdter Sandberg 32, D-40549 Düsseldorf, GERMANY	49 211 556281	49 211 556231	
Brand Amsterdam	Security and CCTV exhibition	Amsterdam RAI, Postfach 77777, 1070 MS Amsterdam, HOLLAND	31 20 5491212	31 20 5491839	security@jaarbeursutrecht.nl
CeBIT	General IT and multimedia exhibition	Deutsche Messe AG, Messegelände, D-30521, Hannover, GERMANY	49 511890	49 5118932626	
Elenex Thailand	Electronic end security exhibition	Overseas Exhibition Service, 11 Manchester Square, London W1M 5AB, UK	44 171 4861951	44 171 4138277	
ExpoSecurity Bucharest	Security and CCTV exhibition	Deutsche Messe AG, Messegelande, D-30521 Hannover, GERMANY	49 212 242140	49 212 2421444	
Ifsec	Security and CCTV exhibition	Miller Freeman Ltd. Blenheim House, Chiswick High Rd., Chiswick, London W45BG, UK	44 181 7422828	44 181 7473856	www.ifsec.co.uk
Internationale Eisenwarenmesse	Security and CCTV exhibition	Messe-u.AusstellungsGmbH, Messeplatz 1, D-50678 Köln, GERMANY		49 221 8212574	
ISC Expo Las Vegas	Security and CCTV exhibition	Convention Center, Las Vegas, Nevada, USA	1 203 840 5602		isc.reedexpo.com
ISC Expo Miami	Security and CCTV exhibition	Miami Beach Convention Centre, Miami Beach Florida, USA	1 203 840 5602		isc.reedexpo.com
ISC Expo New York	Security and CCTV exhibition	New York, USA	1 203 840 5602		isc.reedexpo.com
Police & Security Expo	Security and CCTV exhibition	Labelex Exhibitions Ltd. 131 Southlands Road, Bromley, Kent BR29QT, UK	44 181 3133535	44 181 4687472	
Securex Hungary	Security and CCTV exhibition	Reed Exhibition Company, Heerdter Sandberg 32, D-40549 Düsseldorf, GERMANY	49 211 556281	49 211 556231	
Securex Poland	Security and CCTV exhibition	Poznan International Fair, Glogowska 14, POL-60-734 Poznan, POLAND	48 61 692592	48 61 665827	www.mtp.pol.pl
Securex South Africa	Security and CCTV exhibition	Reed Exhibition Company, Heerdter Sandberg 32, D-40549 Düsseldorf, GERMANY	49 211 556281	49 211 556231	
Security Bulgaria	Security and CCTV exhibition	Bulgarian Chamber of Commerce, 42 Panchevich Street, 1000 Sofia, BULGARIA	359 2 9816626	359 2 9873209	fairs@bcci.bg
Security China	Security and CCTV exhibition	Adsale Exhibition Services Ltd, 4/F Stanhope House, 734 King's Road, North Point, HONG KONG	852 28 118897	852 25 165024	
Security Netherland	Security and CCTV exhibition	Jaarbeurs Exhibition Organizers, Postfach 8500, 3503 RM Utrecht, HOLLAND	31 30 2955524	31 30 2955869	security@jaarbeursutrecht.nl
Sicherheit Schweiz	Security and CCTV exhibition	Reed Exhibition Company, Heerdter Sandberg 32, D-40549 Düsseldorf, GERMANY	49 211 556281	49 211 556231	

Appendix D: Book Co-sponsors

This book has been made possible not only by Butterworth-Heinemann, but also by the CCTV manufacturers who have believed in me and co-sponsored this edition.

The following pages are dedicated to their high-quality CCTV products and they are listed in alphabetical order.

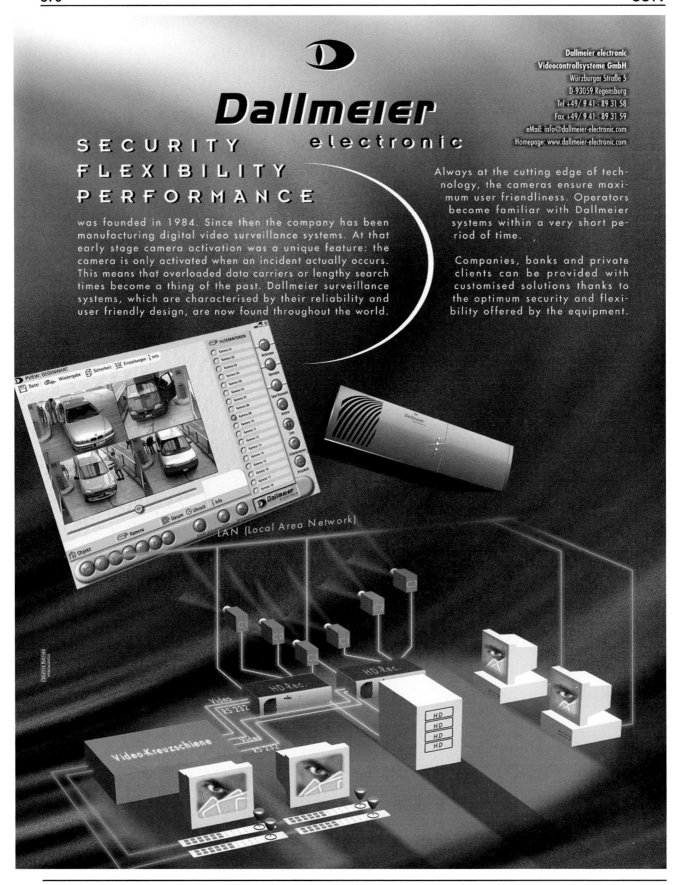

Dallmeier electronic

Dallmeier electronic
Videocontrollsysteme GmbH
Würzburger Straße 5
D-93059 Regensburg
Tel +49/ 9 41 - 89 31 58
Fax +49/ 9 41 - 89 31 59
eMail: info@dallmeier-electronic.com
Homepage: www.dallmeier-electronic.com

SECURITY FLEXIBILITY PERFORMANCE

was founded in 1984. Since then the company has been manufacturing digital video surveillance systems. At that early stage camera activation was a unique feature: the camera is only activated when an incident actually occurs. This means that overloaded data carriers or lengthy search times become a thing of the past. Dallmeier surveillance systems, which are characterised by their reliability and user friendly design, are now found throughout the world.

Always at the cutting edge of technology, the cameras ensure maximum user friendliness. Operators become familiar with Dallmeier systems within a very short period of time.

Companies, banks and private clients can be provided with customised solutions thanks to the optimum security and flexibility offered by the equipment.

ELBEX

THREE AXIS X-Y-Z MATRIX SWITCHING SYSTEM FOR VIDEO,
AND I-D-CODE® CONTROL SIGNAL, FOR CONTROLLING OF UP TO 504
FRAMELOCK® EXTERNALLY SYNCHRONIZED AND I-D-CODE® CAMERAS VIA
THE VIDEO COAX OR FIBER OPTIC FROM UP TO 96 INDIVIDUAL OUTPUTS

MATRIXYZ™

ELBEX LTD.	25-5, Nishi-Gotanda 7-Chome, Shinagawa-ku Tokyo 141-0031, Japan Tel:(03) 3779-5222 Fax:3779-5201
ELBEX AMERICA INC.	10761 Noel Street, Los Alamitos, CA 90720, U.S.A. Tel:(714) 761-8000/(800) FOR-CCTV, Fax:(714) 761-8400
	NORTHWEST OFFICE: 33430-13th Place South, Suite #214 Federal Way, WA98003 Tel:(206) 925-2111 Fax:(206) 925-2112
ELBEX AMERICA (N.Y.) INC.	300, Corporate Dr., Suite 5, Blauvelt, NY 10913, U.S.A. Tel:(914) 353-0600/(800) 343-5239 Fax:(914) 353-0657
ELBEX (DEUTSCHLAND) GMBH	Arzberger Str. 2, D-93057 Regensburg, Germany Tel:(0941) 69531-0 Fax:(0941) 68306
ELBEX (UK) PLC	ELBEX House, Phoenix Business Park, Avenue Road, Birmingham, B7 4NU, U.K. Tel:(121) 359-6611 Fax:(121) 359-8080
	LONDON OFFICE: The Pavillions, Kiln Lane, Epsom, Surrey KT17 1JG Tel:(0137) 274-7776 Fax:(0137) 274-7675
ELBEX BENELUX N.V.	Katwilgweg 11, 2050 Antwerpen, Belgium Tel:(03) 254-0954 Fax:(03) 254-0323
ELBEX NEDERLAND	De Maas 13, 5684 PL Best, Holland Tel:0499-372025 Fax:0499-372199
ELBEX FRANCE	17 rue Casimir Perier, 95875 Bezons Cedex, France Tel:(1) 34.23.59.00 Fax:(1) 30.76.16.13
ELBEX VIDEO LTD. (ISRAEL)	8, Kehilat Venezia St. Tel Aviv 69010, Israel Tel:972-3-6494149 Fax:972-3-6494561
ELBEX SCANDINAVIA A/S	Damhus Boulevard 98, DK-2610 Roedovre, Denmark Tel:(36) 730020 Fax:(36) 730029
ELBEX SWEDEN	Datavägen 6, S-436 32 Askim, Sweden Tel:(031) 748 07 95 Fax:(031) 748 07 99
ELBEX VIDEO (H.K.) LTD.	Unit 808, 8/F Metro Centre, Phase II, 21 Lam Hing Str., Kowloon Bay, Kowloon Tel:27987608 Fax:27987774
ELBEX AUSTRALIA PTY. LTD.	**SYDNEY:** Unit 15, 20-30 Stubbs Street, Silverwater, NSW 2128, Australia Tel:(02) 97486377 Fax:(02) 97486090
	MELBOURNE: Unit 2, 15, Shearson Crescent, Mentone, Vic. 3194, Australia Tel:(03) 95838122 Fax:(03) 95836447
	BRISBANE: Unit 1, 121 Newmarket Street, Windsor, Qld. 4030, Australia Tel:(07) 38576411 Fax:(07) 38576445
ELBEX SINGAPORE PTE. LTD.	Junjie Industrial Bldg., 153 Kampong Ampat #05-03, Singapore 368326 Tel:2856233 Fax:3823978

CE

Updated in March 1999!

COMPLETE CCTV TRAINING SOLUTIONS

FROM LTC TRAINING CENTER

SELF DIRECTED COURSES AND MANUALS

Learn CCTV with simple, organized, field proven methods that won't put you to sleep in the middle.

Presenting Charlie Pierce, one of the most sought after trainers in the CCTV industry. Charlie brings his unique flair and enthusiasm to two certification programs and three manuals. These are some of the most comprehensive self directed study courses and manuals available today. Join the thousands of others who have seen profits increase and installation problems disappear by using these courses.

WORLD WIDE SEMINARS

Self directed training courses not enough? LTC Training Center offers seminars for the *Application & Design of CCTV* and the *Installation/Field Service* of CCTV systems. These can be arranged for private organizations and they are also held yearly around the world. Contact us for a complete schedule of the available seminars in your area.

100% Satisfaction Guaranteed!

Two complete certification courses for the design, sales and installation of CCTV systems.

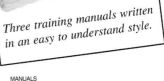

Three training manuals written in an easy to understand style.

MANUALS
PROFESSIONAL'S GUIDE TO CCTV	$145.00 US
APPLICATION & DESIGN	$ 75.00 US
INSTALLATION/FIELD SERVICE	$ 80.00 US

L.T.C. Training Center Inc
TOLL FREE USA
(800) 358-9393

CERTIFICATION PROGRAMS
APPLICATION & DESIGN PROGRAM	$375.00 US
INSTALLATION/FIELD SERVICE PROGRAM	$395.00 US

LTC TRAINING CENTER . PO BOX 3583 . DAVENPORT, IOWA 52808 USA . TEL (319) 322-6669 . FAX: (319) 336-8853

PACOM AND PELCO CCTV PRODUCTS

* COMPREHENSIVE RANGE
* IP66 RATED ENCLOSURES AND DOMES
* ULTRA HIGH/VARIABLE SPEED OUTDOOR INTEGRATED
  PAN AND TILT SYSTEMS
* EXPLOSION AND HARSH ENVIRONMENT ENCLOSURES
  AND PAN/TILT HEADS
* GENEX MULTIPLEXERS AND CONTROL SYSTEMS
* TRANSLATORS FOR COAXITRON AND INTERFACES
  TO MOST PROMINENT CARD ACCESS AND SECURITY
  SYSTEMS

FOR FURTHER INFORMATION CONTACT YOUR NEAREST
PACIFIC COMMUNICATIONS OFFICE

Pacific Communications

CLOSED CIRCUIT VIDEO SYSTEMS

A Division of Hills Industries Limited   A.C. N. 007 573 417

☐ **HEAD OFFICE:** 196 Turner Street, Port Melbourne VIC 3207   Ph: (03) 9646 2142   Fax: (03) 9646 2131
☐ **VICTORIA:** 196 Turner Street, Port Melbourne, VIC 3207   Ph: (03) 9646 2142   Fax: (03) 9646 2141
☐ **NEW SOUTH WALES:** Unit P2, 10-16 South Street, Rydalmere NSW 2116   Ph: (02) 9638 6400   Fax: (02) 9684 4264
☐ **QUEENSLAND:** Unit 1, 54 Caswell Street, East Brisbane QLD 4169   Ph: (07) 3391 2311   Fax: (07) 3391 4317
☐ **SOUTH AUSTRALIA:** 24 Raglan Avenue, Edwardstown SA 5039   Ph: (08) 8351 1422   Fax: (08) 8371 1685
☐ **WESTERN AUSTRALIA:** Unit 1/1 Natalie Way, Balcatta WA 6021   Ph: (08) 9349 9765   Fax: (08) 9349 9635

NEW ZEALAND   SINGAPORE   MALAYSIA

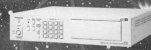

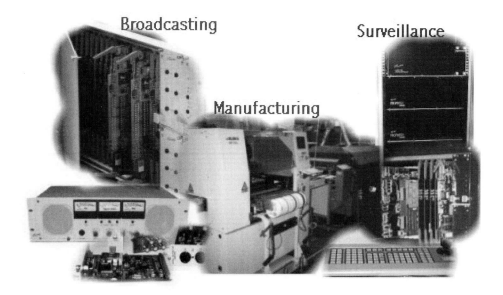

Broadcasting   Surveillance   Manufacturing

Practel is a specialist manufacturer of electronic surveillance and broadcast equipment.

Practel's surveillance section manufactures high bandwidth matrix switchers, 3-D video motion detection equipment, multiplexers, quads and a range of video distribution accessories including cat-5 (twisted pair) video distribution amplifiers, cable compensation amplifiers and isolation transformers.

Our broadcast equipment includes analogue and digital routers, audio monitor bridges, character generators, isolators and signal generators, text inserters and digital / analogue converters.

With engineering teams and surface mount production technology in-house, we can provide contract-manufacturing facilities for your next product development. From electronic circuit design to manufacture and assembly, our services are utilised by companies about the globe.

Practel International Ltd
446 South Road Marleston
South Australia 5033
AUSTRALIA
Telephone: 61-8-8351 2777   Facsimile: 61-8-8351 1766

enquiries@practel.com.au   www.practel.com.au

SuperSleuth

The Dindima Group offers an effective range of security surveillance products in place of conventional CCTV. These products have resulted from over 25 years of video expertise.

SuperSleuth

The Intelligent Video Surveillance System with video motion detection (VMD), Alarm Image Storage and transmission. All 16 cameras are programmable with auto switching to track activity.

An excellent surveillance and management system.

Application: Ideal for commercial sites, warehouses, schools and factories.

SuperSleuth Zip

A cost effective high performance video transmission system for 1 to 16 color and monochrome cameras. Features include battery backup, video motion detection on 2 cameras, modem reboot etc.

Application: Ideal for remote monitoring and alarm verification. Suitable sites include banks, chain stores, car washers, retail stores and homes.

SuperSleuth Wise

Based on the latest digital camera technology, this system is a compact unit comprising a single camera, storage and transmission. The unit can be battery powered.

Application: Ideal for all vending and ticket machines, portable surveillance and for front door home video security.

For more information on the above products contact:

The Dindima Group Pty Ltd

10 Argent Place, Ringwood, Victoria, Australia 3134

Telephone: 61 3 98734455 Facsimile: 61 3 98734749

Email: info@dindima.com Web: www.dindima.com

About the Author

I was born in Macedonia in 1956. I graduated with a degree in electronics and telecommunications from the University Sv.Kiril and Metodij in Skopje (Macedonia), and my thesis, in 1982, was on CCD cameras.

After my graduation, I started working as a CCTV design engineer in a company called Video Engineering in Ohrid (Macedonia), where I started putting together my theory of television and its challenging practice. I was involved in the design and manufacture of cameras, monitors, amplifiers, power supplies and other CCTV equipment. After a couple of years of working there, I joined the Republic's Radio and Television Company as the chief engineer on a local TV/FM station. I had a joyful two years of broadcasting television experience, and I participated in the first satellite TV reception experiment in Macedonia with experts from the European Broadcast Union (EBU) and engineers from Thomson LGT, in 1985. Later that year I was offered an R&D position in another electronics company in Ohrid where I designed a number of electronic products for commercial use. This job involved a complete design cycle including prototyping, mechanical assembly design, testing and defining production details.

In 1987, I moved with my family to Australia where my career started in TCN Channel 9 in Sydney as a maintenance engineer. I had a great time at Channel 9, especially with my involvement in the biggest television broadcasting event in Australia – the bicentennial global broadcast, in January 1988.

The very next year I was offered a service manager position in a company called Vamarc, where I started (again) my Australian CCTV career. I started as a service manager and went through a lot of systems, old and new, throughout the country with my technicians and learned a lot about where installers make mistakes and what makes a good design and installation. I soon started working on larger projects as a CCTV project engineer. After a couple of years, Vamarc closed down, and I started working for National Fire and Security as a CCTV product manager. NFS was a type of company where I had my say in regards to what kind of equipment should go on the shelves and what equipment is best to quote in larger systems. I designed a lot of important systems (at least in my developing career) while at NFS. Also, I conducted a lot of in-house CCTV seminars. Later, NFS's security division was purchased by a new owner and renamed to Security Warehouse. Basically, Security Warehouse continued the NFS concept, but it concentrated only on security products. I continued to work as a CCTV consultant and product manager and in 1990 I registered my own consulting company.

Apart from the independent design, consultancy and commissioning work, I have also conducted a lot of seminars all over the country. For over a year, having had a lot of people through my two-day seminars, I had a pleasurable experience talking to and listening to many CCTV technical people, and most of them have always asked where they can get a complete book on CCTV. This ultimately led to the idea of putting all my knowledge and experience in written form so it can be used by others, without their needing to go through all the odysseys I had to.

CCTV is an extremely rapidly growing and changing area and proves right the saying, "the more you know the more you realize how little you know." That's one of the reasons why I have put so much effort into preparing the book "CCTV" and the Web page on the Internet, hoping it will provide at least some answers for the knowledge-thirsty people.

One thing that distinguishes humans from animals is that their kids don't have to learn life from scratch, but rather they can build on the accumulated knowledge of their parents and grandparents.

I wish to think that I am one of the parents.

Index

2D-comb filter,205
3D-comb filter,205

A

A/V,206
aberration,33
absolute zero,2
activity motion detection,188
additive mixing,21, 157
AGC,137
Albert Einstein,7
ALC,54, 69
American Wire Gauge,150
anti-blooming,137
APD,264
apostilbs,16
aspect ratio,57
aspherical lens,41
ATWB,143
auto iris (AI),52, 68
automatic iris zoom lens,68
automatic tracking white balance (ATWB),143
automatic white balance (AWB),143
avalanche photo diode,264
AVSB-FDM,268
AWG,150

B

back light compensation (BLC),69
back-focus,49, 71, 73, 318
backscattering,276
balanced video transmission,242
bandwidth,91
basic units,1
BLC,69
blooming effect,137
BNC connector,235
brightness,159

C

C-mount,71
cable compensators,294
cable corrector,234
cable equalizer,234
cable markings,308
camera housings,286
camera resolution,131, 318
camera sensitivity,131
cameras,109

candela,14
CCD,113
CCD cameras,58
CCD chip,58, 77, 111
CCD-iris,123
CCIR,82, 96
CCTV System Design,299
characteristic impedance,231
charge-coupled device,113
chroma sub-carrier,92
chrominance,205
CIE,25
cladding,256
CMOS cameras,143
coaxial cable,229, 230
color difference,93
color filter array (CFA),141
color temperature,23
colors in television,21
comb filter,203
commissioning,310
compensator,66
composite sync,177
composite video signal,111
compression,216
concave,32
cones and rods,9
contrast,159
contrast transfer function,43
contrast/brightness,320
convex,32
correction factor,95
correlated double sampling,129
correlational color temperature,24
crush resistance,271
CS-mount,71
CTF,43
CVBS,92
CVS,177

D

D-VHS,225
D6500,25
dark current,111
dB,135
DC restoration,293
DC-driven AI lenses,54
DCT,219
DCT transformation,217

decibels,135, 259
degaussing coil,162
depth of field,47, 51
derived units,2.
diopter,11, 33
discrete cosine transformation,219
dual quad,184
duplex,190
duplex multiplexer,190
DV format,225
DVD,218
DVR,214
dynamic range,131, 137

E

efficiency,157
EIA,82, 96
electroluminescence,260
electromagnetic interference (EMI),230
electronic iris,123
EMI,231
extension rings,78
external ND filters,51, 74
external sync,177

F

F-number,21, 44
F-stop,44
farsightedness,11
fast Fourier transformation,220
fast scan,249
FED,172
FFT,220
fiber geometry,264
fiber optics,229, 252
fiber optics cables,269
fiber optics multiplexers,268
fiber optics windows,264
field emission,172
fire wire,213, 225
FIT,123
fixed focal length,65
FM-FDM,268
focal length,33
focus,33
foot-candelas,16
foot-lambert,16
Fourier spectral theory,90
fovea,10
frame interline transfer,123
frame lock device,194
frame switcher,185
frame transfer,121

framestore,193
fusion splicing,266

G

gamma,167
Gilbert Amelio,115
graded index,257
ground loop corrector,293
ground loops,293

H

H-V delay,163
halogen lamp illuminators,291
harmonics,90
HD,177
HDTV,105
heaters and fans,286
Heinrich Hertz,7
helical scanning,198
high impedance,296
high-definition television,105
horizontal hold,159
horizontal resolution,95, 133
horizontal sync,85, 177
hue,163
hum bug,293
hypermetropia,11

I

IEEE-1394,213, 226
illumination,14
imaging tube,57
impedance,164, 296
in-line amplifier,234, 294
index of refraction,31
infrared cut filters,119
infrared illuminator,290
Infrared link,229
infrared open air video transmission,247
installation,306
interline transfer,121
International Committee for Light,25
IR cut filter,119
IR light,291
ISDN,251
ISO,117

J

James Clerk Maxwell,7
Joseph Nicéphore Niépce,109
JPEG,217, 219

K

kilogram,2

L

lambert,16
LCD Monitors,168
LD,260, 262
LED,260, 261
level, in lenses,54
light intensifier,145
light units,13
lightning protection,293
line-locked,177
linearity,162, 319
LLL,145, 147
loose tube,270
low-light intensified cameras,145
low-pass optical (LPO) filtering,129
lumens,14
luminance,16, 93, 205
luminous flux,14
luminous intensity,14
lux,15

M

Manfred von Ardenne,81
manual iris (MI) lens,51
manual iris zoom lens,68
manual white balance (MWB),143
matrix switcher,179
Max Planck,8
mechanical splicing,267
metric prefixes,4
micro-bending,264
micromirror display (DMD),169
microwave,229
microwave links,244
Mini DV,226
minimum bending radius,241, 271
minimum illumination,131
modal distortion,257
modulation transfer function,43
Moiré pattern,129
monitors,155
motion JPEG,219
motorized iris,53
motorized iris lenses,70
MPEG-1,217
MPEG-2,107, 214, 217, 218
MTF,43
multi-fiber cables,269
multimode,257
multiplexer,185

MUX,185
myopia,11

N

NA,258
ND,49
ND filter,50
nearsightedness,11
neutral density,49
neutral density ND filters,50
newvicon,111
NTSC,29
numerical aperture,258
Nyquist frequency,129

O

objective,67, 75
optical axis,33, 38
optical high pass filter,291
optical plane,33
optical split-prism,139
optical time domain reflectometer,276
optical viewfinder,61
oscilloscope,97
OTDR,276

P

P-N photo diode,263
P/T head,281
P/T heads with PP pots,282
PAL,29, 82
pan and tilt domes,281
pan and tilt head,279, 280
PCM-TDM,268
peripheral vision area,10
permissible circles of confusion,48
persistency,27, 157
phase alternate line,82
phosphor,156
phosphor coatings,22
phot,15
photo diodes,263
photo-effect,8
photometric units,14
photometry,14
photopic vision,145
picture-roll,177
PIN photo diode,264
PINPD,264
pixel,115
plasma display,171
PNPD,264
polarizing filters,78

power supplies,149
preset potentiometers,282
preventative maintenance,312
primary color signals,93
primary colors,156
primary sources,13
principal planes,39
principal points,39
priority encoding,188
PSTN,250
PTZ camera,279
PTZ decoders,283
PTZ receiver drivers,283
PTZ site driver,182, 283

Q

quad,183
quad splitter,183
quadrature amplitude modulation,94

R

RAID,215
Rayleigh scattering,264
reflection,31
reflectivity,16
refraction,31
regulated power supply,151
resolution,95
RF,229, 246
RF video transmission,246
RG-58/U,237
RG-59/U,237
RG-59B/U,92
RS-170,82
RS170A,93

S

S-VHS,205
S/N ratio,131, 135
saturation,163
scotopic vision,145
SECAM,29, 82
secondary sources,13
sequential switcher,175
SI units of measurement,1
signal reflection,319
simplex,190
simplex multiplexer,190
single mode,257
slow-scan,248
solid-state infrared,292
source A,24
spark arresters,294

spectrum analyzer,97, 99
spectrum of an electrical signal,90
speed of light,7
spherical aberration,40
standard angle of vision,10
step index,256
subtractive mixing,22
super VHS,199, 202
synchronization,176

T

target,57
TBC,186
TDR,242
tele-converter,77
telephoto,11
test chart,315
TFT LCD,168
the second,2
Thomas Young,7
threshold current,263
time base correction,186
time division multiplexing,185
time domain reflectometer,242
TL VCR,197, 208
TL VHS VCR,208
total reflection,254
transmittance,17
transmittance factor,46
triplex multiplexer,190
TTL-AWB,143
tube cameras,111
TV field,84
TV frame,85
TV lines,135
TV Systems,81
twisted pair,229
twisted pair video transmission,242

U

UHF,159
unbalanced transmission,230
underscan,164

V

V groove,267
V-phase,151
vari-focal lenses,70
variable focal length,65
variator,66
VD,177
VDA,296
vectorscope,97, 99

vertical hold,159
vertical interval switcher,178
vertical resolution,95, 133
vertical sync,85, 177
VHF,159
VHS,199
video bandwidth,318
video distribution amplifier,296
video equalizers,294
video home system,199
video isolation transformer,293
video matrix switcher,179
video motion detector (VMD),190
video printer,194
video recorder,197
video-driven AI lenses,54
vidicon,111
viewfinder,75
viewfinder calculator,61
visible light,8
VITS,87, 137
Vladimir Zworykin,81
VLSI,145
VMD,190
VMS,179
voltage drop,149

W

wash and wipe assembly,287
wavelength division multiplexing,268
wavelet,217, 221
WDM,268
wide angle lenses,11

Y

Y/C,203

Z

zoom,65
zoom lens,65
zoom ratio,67